Study Guide

Business Law
Principles and Cases in the Legal Environment
Eighth Edition

Daniel V. Davidson

Radford University

Brenda E. Knowles

Indiana University South Bend

Lynn M. Forsythe

California State University, Fresno

Prepared by

Ronald L. Taylor

Metropolitan State College of Denver

THOMSON

SOUTH-WESTERN

WEST

Australia · Canada · Mexico · Singapore · Spain · United Kingdom · United States

THOMSON

SOUTH-WESTERN

WEST

Study Guide to accompany Business Law:
Principles and Cases in the Legal Environment, 8e
Daniel V. Davidson, Brenda E. Knowles, and Lynn M. Forsythe
Prepared by Ronald L. Taylor

VP/Editorial Director:
Jack W. Calhoun

VP/Editor-in-Chief:
Michael P. Roche

Publisher:
Rob Dewey

Developmental Editor:
Bob Sandman

Marketing Manager:
Steven Silverstein, Esq.

Production Editor:
Emily S. Gross

Manufacturing Coordinator:
Rhonda Utley

Design Project Manager:
Chris Miller

Cover Designer:
Beckmeyer Design

Cover Photograph:
Getty Images

Printer:
Victor Graphics, Inc.
Baltimore, Maryland

For permission to use material from this
text or product, contact us by
Tel (800) 730-2214
Fax (800) 730-2215
http://www.thomsonrights.com

For more information contact
West Legal Studies in Business,
5191 Natorp Boulevard,
Mason, Ohio, 45040.
Or you can visit our Internet site at:
http://www.westbuslaw.com

Dedication:

This work is dedicated to Chad Sophia Suiter, my love and constant support.

TABLE OF CONTENTS

PART SIX – DEBTOR-CREDITOR RELATIONS

PART SEVEN -- AGENCY

PART EIGHT – BUSINESS ORGANIZATIONS

PART NINE – GOVERNMENT REGULATION OF BUSINESS

PART TEN – PROPERTY PROTECTION

CHAPTER REVIEW

WHAT IS THE RELATIONSHIP AMONG LAW, ORDER, AND JUSTICE?: The law is a system composed of three elements: law, order, and justice. These three elements balance with one another, subject to limits arising due to practical considerations, such as cost.

- *Law*: Law consists of rules that, when broken, may lead to legal action and penalties, including fines or imprisonment.
- *Order*: Order is the absence of confusion and turmoil, and it usually results when the law is obeyed.
- *Justice*: The process by which the legal system achieves fairness. Sometimes justice is realized by treating everyone the same, called commutative justice, and sometimes it results by treating people individually, called distributive justice.

THE LAW AS AN ARTIFICIAL LANGUAGE SYSTEM: Legal terms must be learned in the context in which they are used. Words used in a legal context may mean something different than when they are used in ordinary conversation.

THE ORIGIN OF THE LAW OF BUSINESS: The law of business originated in the English law merchant, which was not part of the formal English court system. Now, the law of business is part of the common law, which is comprised of court decisions.

WHY STUDY THE LAW OF BUSINESS?: Having a basic understanding of law helps one to conduct business in a manner that avoids disputes and helps one to quickly resolve disputes that do arise.

WHAT ARE THE NEEDS OF A LEGAL SYSTEM?: There are several elements necessary for a legal system to appropriately balance law, order, justice, and practical concerns. The first element, the need to be reasonable, applies in two ways. First, laws must be enforced based on provable facts. Second, the law must be applied so that people have notice of legal actions that are brought against them.

Another requirement of a legal system is the need for laws to be clear so that people know what is expected so that they may comply with their legal obligations. Also, laws must be available to the public so people are aware of them. In addition, a legal system needs to accommodate the unique facts of each situation, and it must provide practical solutions to legal disputes, rather than mere theoretical possibilities. Finally, a legal system must provide a final solution to disputes.

WHAT ARE THE PURPOSES OF A LEGAL SYSTEM?: One purpose of a legal system is to achieve fairness. A legal system also provides for the creation and enforcement of laws, helps maintain order by resisting excessive change, and allows people to alter their behavior in order to conform to the law. Other purposes of a legal system may include protection of persons and their property, and the preservation of a free and open market, which is accomplished in part by allowing people to reach their own agreements.

JURISPRUDENCE: Jurisprudence is the study of the philosophy underlying the law. Different theories include natural law theory, legal positivism, sociological theory, historical theory, law and economic theory, feminist legal theory, and critical legal studies theory.

CHANGE IN THE LEGAL SYSTEM: Don't be misled by people's conduct; often they are violating the law.

LEGAL SYSTEMS IN OTHER COUNTRIES: The law often is quite different in other countries.

WHAT ARE THE SOURCES OF LAW IN THE AMERICAN LEGAL SYSTEM?: The American legal system derives its law from several sources, including federal and state constitutions. The federal and state governments also enact statutes, that is, laws passed by the legislature. Treaties with other nations and administrative rules adopted by governmental agencies are additional sources of laws. Finally, laws may arise as a result of court decisions rendered in individual cases. Lower courts in the same jurisdiction must generally follow these decisions, called precedents.

HOW IS THE LAW CLASSIFIED?: The legal system is organized into several classifications, some of which have authority over others.

■ *Federal versus State Law*: Each state has its own law, as does the federal government.
■ *Common versus Statutory Law*: In the American legal system, judges may make laws in those areas that are not governed by statutes. Judge-made law is called common law and is published in opinions issued by judges.
■ *Civil versus Criminal Law*: Criminal law consists of those laws that allow the government to punish people who do not follow the law. Civil law involves disputes between private parties rather than the government and a private party.
■ *Substantive versus Procedural Law*: Substantive law sets out the standards by which people must conduct themselves. Procedural law sets out the standards by which the substantive laws are enforced.

STUDY HINTS FOR NRW CASE STUDIES

The following study hints may be helpful when resolving the NRW case studies.

NRW 1.1	➤ When answering whether NRW should provide insurance, consider the concept of justice and whether or not justice is best served by providing insurance for the employees.
	➤ Focus in particular on the two theories of justice, commutative and distributive justice.
	➤ In the international context, recognize that foreign laws may differ from U.S. laws.
NRW 1.2	➤ Review the purposes of the American legal system, particularly the need to encourage commercial transactions.
	➤ Consider the nature of statutory law, whether citizens and businesses have access to legislators who enact laws, and the relation between federal and state law.
	➤ Recognize that foreign laws may differ on what one can do to influence legal decision-making.
NRW 1.3	➤ When responding, consider the need of the legal system to be flexible.
	➤ You should reflect upon the purposes of the legal system, especially providing police power, maintaining the peace, and the goal of protecting both the government and individuals.
	➤ In the international arena, consider laws of foreign countries and explore U.S. regulations relating to the exporting of American goods and technology.

MATCHING EXERCISE

Select the term or concept that best matches a definition or statement set forth below. Each term or concept is the best match for only one definition or statement.

Terms and Concepts

a. Amoral
b. Categorical imperative
c. *Caveat emptor*
d. Consequential principles

e. Egoism
f. Ethics
g. Game theory
h. Nonconsequential principles

i. Proactive
j. Reactive
k. Social contract theory
l. Utilitarianism

Definitions and Statements

___k___ 1. Theory suggesting that since society allows business to exist, business owes duties to society.

___i___ 2. Initiating steps to avoid potential problems before they arise.

___c___ 3. "Let the buyer beware."

___f___ 4. Principles of "right" and "wrong" determined according to society's values.

___g___ 5. Theory suggesting that the ultimate goal of business is to win.

___j___ 6. Initiating steps to deal with existing problems.

___e___ 7. Theory suggesting that one should act so as to produce the greatest good for oneself.

___h___ 8. Ethical principles that are determined by rules, not by consequences.

___l___ 9. Theory suggesting that one should act so as to produce the greatest good for the members of one's group.

___d___ 10. Ethical principles that are determined by the results of one's actions, not by fixed rules.

___a___ 11. Quality of not being moral or immoral.

___b___ 12. Theory suggesting that persons must follow certain universal rules.

COMPLETION EXERCISE

Fill in the blanks with the words that most accurately complete each statement.

1. _____ is society's values regarding what is right or wrong.

2. _____ are comprised of principles of right and wrong as measured by an individual's conscience.

3. Rawls' contract theory of justice is premised on the concept that the rules of society should be crafted behind a _____ ____ _____.

4. The game theory of business is based on the belief that businesses are _____.

5. When doing business internationally, businesspeople should bear in mind that the ethics of many societies may be _____ _____ the prevailing ethics followed in the United States.

TRUE-FALSE EXERCISE

Write **T** if the statement is true, write **F** if the statement is false.

_____ 1. There is no general code of ethics for businesses to follow.

_____ 2. *Caveat emptor* is universally followed in the American legal system.

_____ 3. Governmental regulation came about as a result of businesses' perceived abuses that occurred while the government followed a policy of laissez faire.

_____ 4. Ethical principles often form the basis for fundamental legal principles.

_____ 5. Utilitarians believe that a person should engage in conduct that produces the greatest good for the greatest number of members of a group.

_____ 6. Morals reflect what an individual believes is right or wrong.

_____ 7. According to Kant, each person should act in such a way that his or her action could become a universal law.

_F_ 8. There is one universal ethical theory that all persons should follow.

_____ 9. A person's values of right or wrong are not necessarily the same as society's values.

_F_ 10. Utilitarians and egoists generally believe that the consequences of an action are not relevant in determining whether the action is right or wrong.

APPLICATION OF CONCEPTS

MULTIPLE CHOICE QUESTIONS

_____ 1. Which of the following is an example of a nonconsequential ethical theory?
   a. If I drive carefully, I will be safe.
   b. If we all drive carefully, we will all be safe.
   c. If we all follow the speed limit, none of us will get hurt.
   d. Following the speed limit is the right thing to do.

_____ 2. Freddy owned a gasoline station. Other station owners who wanted Freddy to join them in fixing the price for gasoline in their town approached him. Freddy declined because, if all businesses fixed their prices, then this conduct would hurt the financial well being of most townspeople. Freddy is following the ethical theory of:
   a. Egoism.
   b. Act utilitarianism.
   c. Rule utilitarianism.
   d. The categorical imperative.

_____ 3. Fun Toys gave to a local children's charity because doing so is good for its business. Fun Toys is following the ethical theory of:
   a. Egoism.
   b. Act utilitarianism.
   c. Rule utilitarianism.
   d. The categorical imperative.

____ 4. In most states, adultery is neither a civil wrong nor a crime. However, society views adultery as being morally wrong. If Gina engages in an adulterous relationship, then Gina is acting:

    a. Legally.
    b. Illegally.
    c. Immorally.
    d. a and c.

SHORT ANSWER QUESTIONS

Answer the following questions, briefly explaining the reason for your answer.

1. A&A Used Cars sold a car to Fred after its salesman told Fred that the car "ran like a top." In fact, the car ran poorly. If Fred sues A&A, what legal doctrine might A&A raise as a defense?

_____

_____

_____

2. Mighty Machines Corp. determined that it would cost more to recall and repair its Ajax jackhammer that has a hidden defect, than it would cost to pay damages to persons who were injured due to the defect. Therefore, Mighty Machines decided against a recall of the jackhammer. What ethical theory supports this analysis?

_____

_____

_____

3. Pal's Publishing was committed to taking care of its employees. Therefore, it decided to make all of its employees undergo mandatory drug testing at least once a year. It undertook this action because drug use is illegal and a crime. What ethical theory supports this analysis?

_____

_____

_____

4. Wally's Shoe Warehouse has had trouble collecting accounts receivables from certain customers. Wally told his general manager to "do whatever is necessary to get paid." The general manager responded by hiring a collection agency that has a reputation for making threats and using physical force if necessary to convince customers to pay their debts. Evaluate the morality of the general manager's conduct.

_____

_____

_____

CASE PROBLEMS

Answer the following case problems, explaining your answers.

1. Gordon, president of Ace Cigarettes, believed that all people have the right to freedom of choice and action. Thus, he directed his marketing department to actively pursue sales to younger individuals, including minors. Society, on the other hand, has determined that it is both morally and legally wrong to sell cigarettes to minors.

   (a) Evaluate whether Gordon acted morally.
   (b) Evaluate whether Gordon acted ethically.
   (c) Evaluate whether Gordon acted legally.

   _____

   _____

   _____

   _____

2. For many years, U.S. companies manufactured, sold, and used asbestos. Hypothetically, assume that these companies engaged in this conduct even after they became aware of the potential health hazards posed by their conduct. Eventually, the government forbids the sale and use of asbestos in many situations, and thousands of people sued these companies for massive damages. Only then did some of these firms stop using asbestos.

   (a) Is the conduct of these firms representative of proactive or reactive conduct?
   (b) What could these firms have done differently to avoid this situation?
   (c) Did these firms act ethically or not in this case?

   _____

   _____

   _____

   _____

CHAPTER REVIEW

INTRODUCTION: When "going global," U.S. businesses can choose from several options. Agents can help businesses find foreign buyers, or distributors may resell businesses' goods to foreign customers. Alternatively, U.S. firms may use franchising whereby the firms, as franchisors, grant a license to a franchisee to conduct business under the name of the U.S. firms. Another option is a joint venture whereby a U.S. firm and a foreign firm form an association to carry out an enterprise. Finally, U.S. firms can create a new company (subsidiary) to engage in business in one or more foreign countries.

EXTRATERRITORIALITY: U.S. LAWS, INTERNATIONAL APPLICATIONS: In some cases, U.S. laws apply to business conduct that is in other countries.

- *Antitrust*: Under one test, the "direct and substantial effect" test, U.S. courts apply U.S. antitrust laws to business conducted outside of the United States if there is a significant effect on U.S. commerce. Congress passed the Foreign Trade Antitrust Improvement Act providing that the courts must examine the site of the injury to determine if U.S. antitrust laws apply. This protects U.S. markets from domestic antitrust harm while excluding pure U.S. export activities from antitrust coverage.
- *The Foreign Corrupt Practices Act (FCPA)*: The FCPA forbids U.S. companies from giving money or anything of value to high-level foreign government officials in order to influence their conduct. However, payments made to low-level officials to expedite routine services are allowed.
- *Employment*: U.S. nondiscrimination laws protect Americans working for U.S. companies abroad.

FREE TRADE ZONES

- *The European Union (EU)*: The EU is an organization of Western European countries, and it has four objectives: 1) eliminate duties among EU nations and set uniform tariffs for nations that trade with the EU; 2) allow citizens of EU nations to move to other member nations; 3) allow firms from EU nations to offer services anywhere in the EU; and 4) establish a common currency (the "euro," which has been adopted as the official currency in 11 of the 15 EU member nations).
  The EU has competition laws that are similar to U.S. antitrust law. Businesses can apply for an exemption from EU competition law by requesting issuance of a negative clearance from. Conduct anywhere in the world is subject to EU competition law if it affects the EU market.
- *The North American Free Trade Agreement (NAFTA)*: This agreement, between the U.S., Mexico, and Canada, seeks to eliminate all tariffs on goods traded between member nation by 1998. NAFTA also promotes greater movement of workers and investments between member nations.
- *Other Free Trade Zones*: There are other, less powerful, international trade associations.

THE GENERAL AGREEMENT ON TARIFFS AND TRADE (GATT): GATT was an international convention that reduced tariffs and quotas between member nations. GATT approved the WTO.

WORLD TRADE ORGANIZATION (WTO): The WTO is an organization comprised of 145 nations, including the United States. The WTO adopts rules relating to international transactions involving goods, services, and intellectual property, and its rules are binding on all member nations. The WTO can decide trade disputes between any member nations that relate to any recognized international trade agreement. The expanded coverage of the WTO now includes merchandise goods, some trade in services, and protection for intellectual property.

UNCITRAL The United Nations Commission for International Trade Law addresses issues involving private international trade. UNCITRAL is involved in the development and enactment of U.N.

Conventions dealing with international trade, such as the CISG, and it helps draft model laws, which serve as templates for nations that are addressing international trade issues.

THE INTERNATIONAL ORGANIZATION FOR STANDARDIZATION (ISO) The ISO, an international body comprised of 101 nations, develops standards for various areas of commerce and these standards are followed by all member nations. "Standards are documented agreements containing technical specifications or other precise criteria to be used consistently as rules, guidelines, or definitions of characteristics, to ensure that materials, products, processes and services are fit for their purposes." It also has developed two sets of quality standards for businesses. ISO 9000, deals with "quality management" in the production of goods and ISO 14000 deals with environmental management.

EXPORTS AND IMPORTS: All U.S. exports must be licensed. U.S. goods imported into a foreign country must pass customs, which usually requires payment of a tariff or duty. One increasing problem is "dumping" of goods into foreign markets, i.e., the sale of goods in foreign markets at a price below that charged in the domestic market.

LETTERS OF CREDIT: These documents help minimize some of the risk of international transactions. A letter of credit is a promise by a bank to pay the contract price, even if the goods turn out to be defective.

INFORMATION AND TECHNOLOGY: Although there are no global laws protecting intellectual property, there is increasing international protection of copyrights, patents, and copyrights.

NATIONALIZATION: Nationalization occurs when a foreign government converts a private business into a government-owned business. Nationalization is legal under international law only if the state had a proper public purpose and paid just compensation. This practice is common in developing countries.

ACT OF STATE DOCTRINE AND SOVEREIGN IMMUNITY: The act of state doctrine prohibits courts from judging the acts of a foreign government performed within its borders. Sovereign immunity prohibits individuals or countries from suing a foreign government based on its political activities. However, it is permissible to sue a foreign government based on its commercial activities. The U.S. Foreign Sovereign Immunities Act now permits American citizens to sue foreign nations officially classified as terrorist states for terrorist conduct that results in the death or injury of an American citizen.

DISPUTE RESOLUTION: All international contracts should provide for a way to settle disputes, and arbitration is the most common way to resolve international disputes.

STUDY HINTS FOR NRW CASE STUDIES

The following study hints may be helpful when resolving the NRW case studies.

NRW 3.1	➢ In support of Carlos' position, consider how new technological and communication advances have contributed to a great increase in international trade and competition. ➢ Consider various approaches that NRW may use in conducting international business.
NRW 3.2	➢ When preparing your response, explore the differences between the U.S. relationship with NAFTA member nations and EU member nations. ➢ Consider typical advantages accorded by membership in free trade zones.
NRW 3.3	➢ Consider the pros and cons of the various ways that CIT can do business internationally. ➢ Review Articles 85 and 86 of the Treaty of Rome, and U.S. licensing requirements.

REVIEW OF KEY TERMS AND CONCEPTS

MATCHING EXERCISE

Select the term or concept that best matches a definition or statement set forth below. Each term or concept is the best match for only one definition or statement.

Terms and Concepts

a. Act of state doctrine
b. Antitrust laws
c. Arbitration 试法
d. CISG
e. EU

f. Franchising
g. GATT
h. Letter of credit
i. NAFTA
j. Nationalization

k. Negative clearance
l. Remand 还回
m. Sovereign immunity
n. Uniform Commercial Code
o. World Trade Organization

Definitions and Statements

___j___ 1. Foreign government's act of converting a private business into a public enterprise.

___a___ 2. International doctrine that prohibits courts in one country from reviewing the legality of acts of a foreign government that are undertaken within the foreign country's borders.

___o___ 3. New international organization that can adopt binding rules for international transactions involving goods, services, and intellectual property.

___d___ 4. International convention that establishes uniform rules for the international sale of goods.

___e___ 5. Creates a free-trade zone among its member nations in Europe.

___b___ 6. U.S. laws that help protect competition.

___c___ 7. Nonjudicial resolution of a case by a third person.

___n___ 8. State statutory law that governs many types of commercial transactions in the United States.

___i___ 9. Trade agreement between the United States, Mexico, and Canada.

___m___ 10. Doctrine that holds that a nation is immune from liability for its actions.

___f___ 11. Permission by a company that allows another to do business under the company's name.

___l___ 12. Act of sending a case back to another court from which it came.

___g___ 13. International convention that promoted nondiscriminatory trade among its members and established the World Trade Organization.

___h___ 14. Bank's promise to pay a stated sum of money, such as the contract price for goods, upon presentment of required documents.

___k___ 15. Exemption from EU competition laws that is granted by the EU Commission.

COMPLETION EXERCISE

Fill in the blanks with the words that most accurately complete each statement.

1. Under the _____ _____ _____ _____, a U.S. company cannot give "anything of value" to foreign officials with the intent to corrupt.

2. The _____ _____ ____ _____ is an international court in which nations may sue one another.

3. _____ is the selling of goods in a foreign country at a price that is less than the price for which such goods are sold in the domestic market.

4. _____ is a United Nations commission that addresses many issues involving private international trade.

5. Identify three methods that a U.S. company can use in order to conduct international business.

a. _____.

b. _____.

c. _____.

TRUE-FALSE EXERCISE

Write **T** if the statement is true, write **F** if the statement is false.

F 1. U.S. law generally recognizes that sovereign immunity protects foreign nations from being sued for both their governmental and commercial activities.

T 2. U.S. antitrust law does not generally apply to conduct occurring outside of the United States if the conduct does not affect commerce within the United States.

F 3. Foreign countries are generally prohibited from imposing tariffs that may interfere with the sale of U.S. goods.

T 4. U.S. firms doing business in Europe are generally subject to the competition laws of the EU.

F 5. A private person can go to the International Court of Justice to resolve a grievance with a foreign company.

T 6. A popular method for conducting international business is franchising.

F 7. The FCPA prohibits a U.S. firm from paying low-level foreign officials to do their job.

T 8. U.S. law recently was amended to permit a person to sue a foreign state that is officially classified as terrorist states for terrorist conduct that results in the death or injury of an American citizen.

T 9. An international contract can typically state which country's law will govern the parties' rights.

F 10. Nationalization describes how much a foreign citizen identifies with his or her own nation.

APPLICATION OF CONCEPTS

MULTIPLE CHOICE QUESTIONS

_____ 1. Kirsten wishes to expedite a sale of household goods to a customer in a foreign country. Which of the following actions may Kirsten take without violating the Foreign Corrupt Practices Act?
   a. Kirsten may bribe a high government official in order to gain the official's approval.
   b. Kirsten may make valuable gifts to high government officials to gain their approval.
   c. Kirsten may pay low-level government officials to expedite routine paperwork.
   d. Kirsten may not make any kind of payment to any government official.

_____ 2.   Jensen Corp., a U.S. firm, wants to form a joint venture with a foreign company to engage in the coffee business in a third world country. However, Jensen fears that this country could at some point nationalize its business. What actions may be available to Jensen in order to reduce the financial risks associated with nationalization?
   a.   Purchase insurance to protect it against losses resulting from nationalization.
   b.   Require a short payback period for its investment in the joint venture.
   c.   There is nothing that Jensen Corp. can do to minimize the risk of loss from nationalization.
   d.   a and b.

_____ 3.   AllTech is a U.S. firm that has a plant in a foreign country staffed with U.S. employees. Jane, a U.S. citizen, works in AllTech's foreign plant. Jane was discriminated against by AllTech because she is a woman. This discrimination would violate U.S. law (Title VII of the Civil Rights Act), but not the law of the foreign country where Jane works. In this case, Jane can:
   a.   Sue AllTech in the foreign nation's court for discrimination.
   b.   Sue AllTech in U.S. court for violation of U.S. law.
   c.   Do nothing because U.S. law does not apply in foreign nations.
   d.   a and b.

_____ 4.   Vigneti Company, a foreign firm, sued GeoMap, a U.S. firm, in a foreign court. Following a full and fair trial before an impartial court during which GeoMap was allowed to present a defense, the foreign court issued a $50,000 judgment in favor of Vigneti Company. If Vigneti Company seeks to enforce this judgment against GeoMap in the United States, a U.S. court will likely:
   a.   Recognize and uphold the foreign judgment because foreign judgments are legally binding in the United States.
   b.   Recognize and uphold the foreign judgment based on the principal of comity.
   c.   Hold a new trial because U.S. firms cannot be sued in a foreign court.
   d.   Hold a new trial because foreign judgments are unenforceable in the United States.

SHORT ANSWER QUESTIONS

Answer the following questions, briefly explaining the reason for your answer.

1. Gill wants to do business with firms located in countries belonging to the EU. Gill plans to grant exclusive sales territories to each foreign firm, and he also plans to establish mandatory, uniform resale prices for his products. What foreign law should Gill be concerned with? What can Gill do, if necessary, to assure that his actions will not violate this foreign law?

_____

_____

2. Pedals-2-Go wants to sell its bicycles to a foreign firm, but it is worried that the foreign firm may not pay. Suggest several ways that Pedals-2-Go can assure that it will receive payment?

_____

_____

3. ArmorTech, a U.S. firm, produces a secret computer chip for the U.S. military. A foreign government has approached ArmorTech with an offer to purchase some of the chips. What must ArmorTech do in order to sell its computer chips to the foreign government? What problem may ArmorTech encounter?

_____

_____

4. Jacob has decided that his business should "go global" and sell its goods in North and South America. He is concerned, however, that there may be international laws that could affect his international dealings. Identify and briefly discuss two treaties or organizations that may be relevant to Jacob's plans.

_____

_____

CASE PROBLEMS

Answer the following case problems, explaining your answers.

1. Bill wants to do business with companies from the African country of Ruritania. Ruritania is a former British colony, and its businesspeople are generally quiet, reserved, individuals who prefer to proceed cautiously. Ruritanians emphasize honor, politeness, and personal relationships when negotiating. Bill is a forceful negotiator, who speaks quickly, roughly, and to the point. He also has a habit of gesturing, interrupting others, and yelling in order to get his point across. What matters should Bill think about when preparing to negotiate with his Ruritanian counterparts?

_____

_____

_____

_____

2. Coal companies from the nation of Abuk have gained an increasing share of the international coal market by fixing prices with one another and entering into uniform pricing agreements with their customers. These actions are legal under Abuk law, but would violate U.S. antitrust law. The Abuk coal companies have not yet sold coal in the United States, but they intend to do so in the near future. (a) Can U.S. coal producers presently sue the Abuk coal companies for violation of U.S. antitrust law? (b) Will the U.S. firms have the right to enforce U.S. antitrust law against the Abuk coal companies if they begin to sell their coal in the United States?

_____

_____

_____

_____

CHAPTER 4

CHAPTER REVIEW

THE FEDERAL CONSTITUTION:

- **Allocation of Power**: The federal Constitution allocates legislative, executive, and judicial power among the branches of the federal government. Congress enacts laws subject to the President's veto. The President is the commander in Chief, makes treaties and appoints major federal officials (subject to Senate ratification), and controls federal agencies that generally are created by Congress. Federal courts may hear only actual cases and controversies; they cannot issue advisory opinions, consider moot points, hear cases where the plaintiff lacks standing, or decide political questions.

- **Limitation of Power**: The federal Constitution limits governmental power by granting certain rights to individuals. These rights include:

  1) **Writ of *habeas corpus***: Order directing that a detained person be brought before a court and that the detaining party, such as a state, obey any order issued by the court relating to the detained person.

  2) **Bill of Attainder**: Congress cannot pass a bill of attainder, meaning Congress cannot convict a person of a felony or worse.

  3) ***Ex Post Facto* laws**: Congress cannot pass any ex post facto laws, meaning that Congress cannot pass a law that retroactively declare that a past act is a crime.

- **Amendments to the Constitution**: The first ten amendments to the Constitution, called the Bill of Rights, protect important individual rights such as the right to face one's accuser in a criminal case. A total of 27 amendments to the Constitution have been passed.

THE COURTS AND JURISDICTION

Jurisdiction is the power of a court to hear and decide a case. Different types of jurisdiction include:

- **Subject Matter Jurisdiction**: Subject matter jurisdiction determines the types of disputes that a court may review. For example, probate court has jurisdiction to decide cases involving decedents' estates.

- **Jurisdiction Over the Persons or Property**: To decide a case, a court must have authority (jurisdiction) over the persons or property involved. Also, the defendant must receive either actual notice or constructive notice of a lawsuit. Types of jurisdiction include:

  1) ***In personam* jurisdiction**: *In personam* jurisdiction means a court has authority to decide the rights of a specific person or business in a civil case. This jurisdiction is present when defendants consent to jurisdiction or they are served with process while present within the state in which they are sued. Service of process is delivery of a legal notice that informs a defendant that he or she is being sued and the nature of the proceeding. Long-arm statutes may be used to give a court *in personam* jurisdiction over persons who live in another state. Assuming proper service, a court may assert personal jurisdiction over a non-resident defendant if: (a) the defendant has sufficient "minimum contacts" with the forum state, (b) the claim asserted against the defendant arises out of those contacts, and (c) the exercise of jurisdiction is reasonable. In Internet-related cases, a defendant has sufficient contact with a jurisdiction if the defendant enters into contracts with residents of that jurisdiction and those contracts involve the knowing and repeated transmission of computer files over the Internet.

2) **In rem jurisdiction**: *In rem* jurisdiction occurs when property that is the subject of a lawsuit is located in the state where the court is located. This jurisdiction allows a court to decide everyone's rights in the property.

3) **Quasi in rem jurisdiction**: *Quasi in rem* jurisdiction allows a court to decide the rights of only certain persons in specific property that is under the control of the court.

- **Concurrent Versus Exclusive Jurisdiction**: When only one court has jurisdiction over a case, it has exclusive jurisdiction. If more than one court has authority, the courts have concurrent jurisdiction.
- **Venue**: Venue refers to the geographical area or district where a lawsuit may be filed.
- **Choice of Laws**: If parties from more than one state are involved in a lawsuit, choice of law rules determine which state's substantive law is used to resolve the dispute. However, the procedural law where the court is located is generally used in this situation.
- **Federal Courts**: Federal courts may hear: 1) cases involving a federal question, meaning the dispute primarily involves some sort of federal law, or 2) cases involving diversity of citizenship, meaning the plaintiffs and defendants reside in different states, if the lawsuit involves more than $75,000.
- **Specialized Courts**: Some federal courts, such as the tax court, hear only one type of case. There are 13 federal circuits, each with its own circuit court of appeals. Appeals from U.S. district courts are heard by the circuit courts of appeals. The U.S. Supreme Court hears appeals from the circuit courts of appeal.
- **State Courts**: Trial courts may have either general jurisdiction or limited jurisdiction. Appellate courts may review decisions of lower courts to determine if errors of law occurred.

HOW TO FIND THE LAW

- Federal court decisions are reported in a series of publications. Separate publications print the opinions rendered by: 1) U.S. district court cases (*Federal Supplement*); 2) circuit court of appeals (*Federal Reporter*); 3) U. S. Supreme Court cases (*United States Reports*, *Lawyers Edition, Second*, and *Supreme Court Reporter*); and 4) cases from specialized courts.
- Regional publications report state appellate court decisions.
- Two major sources for computerized legal research are Lexis and Westlaw.

STUDY HINTS FOR NRW CASE STUDIES

The following study hints may be helpful when resolving the NRW case studies.

NRW 4.1	➢ Review the power of the federal and state governments to regulate business in order to evaluate whether the states can regulate the NRW products. ➢ As a practical matter, consider ways that NRW can assure that its products comply with both existing and proposed regulations.
NRW 4.2	➢ Consider carefully the material dealing with allocation of power among the branches of government, particularly the limits on the power of the courts to hear and decide cases. ➢ Review the material relating to the WTO in Chapter 3.
NRW 4.3	➢ NRW should consider matters of jurisdiction, including diversity jurisdiction of the federal district court and long-arm jurisdiction of the Ohio state courts. ➢ For an example of this type of predicament and its affect on NRW's reputation, go online and look for articles dealing with the recent dispute between Ford Motor Company and Firestone Tires that arose in connection with Ford's Explorer automobiles.

MATCHING EXERCISE

Select the term or concept that best matches a definition or statement set forth below. Each term or concept is the best match for only one definition or statement.

Terms and Concepts

a. Advisory opinion
b. Appellant
c. Attachment
d. *Certiorari*
e. Defendant

f. *Ex post facto* law
g. Garnishment
h. *Habeas corpus*
i. *Mandamus*
j. Nonjusticiable issue

k. Plaintiff
l. Political question
m. Reverse
n. Standing
o. Subject matter jurisdiction

Definitions and Statements

___o___ 1. Authority of a court to hear and decide a certain type of case.
___m___ 2. Overturning of a lower court decision.
___h___ 3. Court order directing that a person be brought before a court or judge.
___l___ 4. Question that intrudes upon the power of the legislative or executive branch.
___k___ 5. Person who files a civil lawsuit.
___c___ 6. Seizure of property owned by a defendant.
___g___ 7. Process to take possession of defendant's money, which is held by another person.
___d___ 8. Writ issued by a higher court, agreeing to review a case.
___e___ 9. Person against whom a lawsuit is filed.
___i___ 10. Writ issued by a superior court, directing that a governmental officer do or not do something.
___a___ 11. Opinion rendered by a court relating to a question submitted by the legislature or executive that is not involved in an actual case.
___j___ 12. Question that cannot be properly decided by a court.
___b___ 13. Person appealing a court decision.
___n___ 14. Right to sue.
___f___ 15. Law that retroactively makes a past act a crime.

COMPLETION EXERCISE

Fill in the blanks with the words that most accurately complete each statement.

1. The federal courts can hear only cases that involve an actual _____ and _____.

2. The doctrine of _____ requires that only a person who has been injured can sue.

3. The power of a court to hear and decide a case is called _____.

4. A court's authority over a person is referred to as ____ _____ jurisdiction.

5. A _____-_____ statute allows a court to exercise jurisdiction over a person or corporation who is domiciled in another state.

TRUE-FALSE EXERCISE

Write **T** if the statement is true, write **F** if the statement is false.

_F_ 1. Federal courts can properly decide cases that involve only a political question.

_T_ 2. By filing a lawsuit, plaintiffs generally grant a court *in personam* jurisdiction over themselves.

_F_ 3. A court with *quasi in rem* jurisdiction can determine the rights of all persons in a particular item of property.

_T_ 4. A foreign corporation generally grants *in personam* jurisdiction to the courts of a state in which the corporation is doing business.

_F_ 5. Questions involving interpretation of a federal statute are not appropriate for a federal court.

_F_ 6. Cases involving diversity of citizenship can be heard by a federal court, regardless of the amount of money that is in controversy.

_F_ 7. The U.S. Supreme Court must hear all cases that are appealed to it from a lower court.

_F_ 8. A state juvenile court is an example of a court of general jurisdiction.

_F_ 9. In the federal government, the executive branch has the primary power to make laws.

_T_ 10. The power of judicial review allows the courts to review the validity of actions taken by the legislative or executive branch of government.

APPLICATION OF CONCEPTS

MULTIPLE CHOICE QUESTIONS

_____ 1. In which case is the defendant given *constructive* notice of the lawsuit?
   a. Karim sued Tonya and the summons and complaint was sent to Tonya by registered mail.
   b. Jack sued Ron and, when Ron could not be located, the summons and complaint were published in the local newspaper.
   c. Pat sued Rene and a licensed process server delivered the summons and complaint to Rene.
   d. a and b.

_____ 2. Jessica sued her employer, Enco Corp., for violation of federal nondiscrimination law. The U.S. district court ruled in favor of Enco and the circuit court of appeals upheld the trial court judgment. Jessica wants to appeal her case to the U.S. Supreme Court. Under these facts:
   a. Jessica has no right to request the U.S. Supreme Court to hear her appeal.
   b. Jessica has no right to request the U.S. Supreme Court to hear her appeal unless the circuit court of appeals admits that it made a mistake.
   c. Jessica may request the U.S. Supreme Court to hear her appeal, but the Court is not required to do so.
   d. Jessica may request the U.S. Supreme Court to hear her appeal, and the Court is required to do so.

_____ 3. Luke sued Rosa for breach of a contract, and Luke has requested that the court award him $5,000 in damages. What type of jurisdiction must the court have to grant this relief?
   a. *Quasi in rem* jurisdiction.
   b. *In rem* jurisdiction.
   c. *In personam* jurisdiction.
   d. No jurisdiction is required.

_____ 4. Peg works for a lawyer while attending college. Peg's employer asks her to locate several decisions rendered by various federal courts. Under these facts:
   a. Peg can locate U.S. district court cases in a regional reporter.
   b. Peg can locate circuit court of appeal cases in the *Federal Supplement.*
   c. Peg can locate U.S. Supreme Court decisions in the *United States Reports.*
   d. Peg can locate U.S. Supreme Court decisions in the *Federal Reporter.*

SHORT ANSWER QUESTIONS

Answer the following questions, briefly explaining the reason for your answer.

1. The state legislature recently passed a statute authorizing a tuition increase at the state's public university. Lisa graduated from this university 10 years previously and she is opposed to this increase in tuition because she thinks it will make a college education unavailable to poorer people. Although this tuition increase does not affect her, she wants to sue the state, challenging the validity of this statute. Does Lisa have standing to challenge this statute?

_____

_____

2. Jim is a political activist who believes that elected officials should have to disclose their personal financial statements. The state legislature considered, but rejected, a bill that would require this type of disclosure. Jim has now filed a lawsuit in order to obtain a court order requiring elected state officials to disclose their personal financial information. Will a court grant Jim's request?

_____

_____

3. Roger and Teresa owned competing grocery stores. Roger told a group of Teresa's customers that she had previously been convicted of selling spoiled meat. Teresa claimed this statement was false, and she sued Roger for $50,000 for defamation (i.e., the wrongful injury to the reputation of another). Roger asserted two defenses: (a) He did not commit this wrong because what he said was true; and (b) the court lacked jurisdiction over him because he had never been served with process. Are Roger's defenses based on substantive or procedural law?

_____

_____

4. The state legislature is concerned with health risks associated with domesticated lizards and other reptiles. Thus, the legislature passed a statute that makes it a crime for anyone to sell live lizards or other reptiles.

   The foregoing statute applies to any sales made within the past two years and any future sales. Is this statute valid to the extent that it applies to past sales? Is this statute valid to the extent that it applies to future sales?

_____

_____

CASE PROBLEMS

Answer the following case problems, explaining your answers.

1. Tortilla Wonders Corp. (TWC) and Ramon jointly own a chain of restaurants called "Chips Ahoy." TWC was incorporated under Arizona law and its principal offices are located in New Mexico. Ramon is a California resident. TWC and Ramon own and operate restaurants in 10 states, including Nebraska. Ginger, a customer, was injured in a Chips Ahoy restaurant located in Omaha Nebraska. Ginger wants to file suit against both TWC and Ramon in Nebraska state court.

   (a) Do TWC and Ramon have sufficient minimum contacts with Nebraska to enable its courts to hear and decide this lawsuit?
   (b) Can the Nebraska state court obtain *in personam* jurisdiction over TWC and Ramon?

_____

_____

_____

_____

2. Janet, a resident of Florida, plans to sue Carson, a resident of New York, for $100,000. Janet intends to sue for breach of contract, a claim that is based on Florida state law. Janet plans to file her lawsuit in U.S. district court. Would the U.S. district court have jurisdiction to hear and decide this case?

_____

_____

_____

_____

CHAPTER 5

Constitutional Regulation of Business

AN HISTORICAL PERSPECTIVE

Government regulation emerged after a time of abuse by big business. Businesses routinely mistreated workers, and the rule was "let the buyer beware."

SHOULD GOVERNMENT REGULATE BUSINESS?

Regulation takes two forms: social regulation concerns such issues as workplace safety and consumer protection; economic regulation concerns such issues as prices and industry conditions. A regulation's benefits should be weighed against its costs.

THE COMMERCE CLAUSE

The commerce clause allows the federal government broad regulatory power. This power includes:

- **Exclusive Federal Power**: The federal government has exclusive power to regulate commerce:
  1) with foreign nations;
  2) with Native American tribes; and
  3) between states (interstate commerce).

  The power to regulate interstate commerce also allows the federal government to regulate commerce originating in one state that has a national economic effect.
- **Concurrent State Power**: States may regulate commerce if the regulations:
  1) serve a state interest;
  2) do not impose an undue burden on interstate commerce;
  3) do not conflict with federal law; and
  4) do not discriminate against out-of-state businesses.
- **Exclusive State Power**: States have exclusive regulatory power over purely local activities that have remote effects on other states.

THE EQUAL PROTECTION CLAUSE

The equal protection clause protects individuals from invidious discrimination that arises from governmental (not private) action. Equal protection applies to federal and state governments. In some situations, the government may treat groups differently if the government has a sufficient justification for such disparate treatment. The classification that is used for treating groups differently determines what test is used to evaluate the constitutionality of the government's conduct. The three tests used are:

- **Level 1: The "Rational Basis" Test**: This test applies to most social and economic regulation; courts presume that such regulations are valid. This test allows the government to discriminate against similarly situated persons if the regulation is rationally related to a legitimate purpose.
- **Level 2: The "Compelling State Interest" Test**: This test applies to regulations based on suspect classifications (race or ethnic origin); courts presume that such regulations are invalid. A regulation based on a suspect classification is valid only if it furthers a compelling state interest, and there is no less burdensome way of accomplishing this interest. This test is used for affirmative action programs.

25

- *Intermediate Level: The "Substantially Important State Interest" Test*: This test applies to gender-based classifications; a regulation is valid if it furthers a substantially important state interest.

THE DUE PROCESS CLAUSE

The due process clause protects against deprivations of life, liberty, and property. Due process includes:

- *Procedural Due Process*: Before the state or federal government can deprive a person of life, liberty, or property, the government must provide some type of hearing. A fair hearing requires notice to the aggrieved party, an opportunity for the person to be heard, and an impartial decision maker.
- *Substantive Due Process*: A regulation is invalid under substantive due process if it fails to advance a legitimate government interest or is an unreasonable way of advancing a legitimate interest. Substantive due process applies to all persons, regardless of race, sex, or ethnicity. However, courts will defer to legislatures and uphold regulations unless they are clearly irrational.

THE "TAKINGS" CLAUSE

The takings clause prevents the government (federal or state) from taking property for public use without just compensation. A taking has occurred if the governmental action destroys the property's current use or unreasonably impairs the value of the property and the owner's reasonable expectations regarding it. In some cases, land use regulations may constitute a taking.

THE FIRST AMENDMENT/COMMERCIAL SPEECH

Laws regulating the content of speech (what you say) are valid only if they are narrowly written to advance a compelling state interest. Courts start with the presumption that laws regulating the content of speech are invalid. However, government may validly regulate the time, place, or manner of speech. Protection of commercial speech is more limited than protection of individual speech.

ADMINISTRATIVE AGENCIES

Administrative agencies have legislative and judicial powers. Congress can create and abolish agencies, and limit their power and authority by statute. Agencies are subject to substantive and procedural due process requirements. Courts have the power to review agency decisions.

STUDY HINTS FOR NRW CASE STUDIES

The following study hints may be helpful when resolving the NRW case studies.

NRW 5.1	➤ Review the material on The Equal Protection Clause and consider which test would be used to determine the constitutionality of the law.
	➤ When deciding whether to immediately comply with the law, carefully consider the economic and legal ramifications of not complying with this new regulation.
NRW 5.2	➤ You should consider the concept of substantive due process.
	➤ You should also consider the takings clause.
NRW 5.3	➤ Consider requesting a court with jurisdiction to review the constitutionality of the city's actions.
	➤ Consider requesting a court with jurisdiction to order the equitable remedy of restitution.

MATCHING EXERCISE

Select the term or concept that best matches a definition or statement set forth below. Each term or concept is the best match for only one definition or statement.

Terms and Concepts

a. Caveat emptor
b. Delegated
c. Disenfranchised
d. Due process clause
e. Eminent domain

f. Equal protection clause
g. Interstate
h. Intrastate
i. Invidious
j. Laissez-faire

k. Plenary
l. Quasi-judicial
m. Quasi-legislative
n. Taking
o. Transportation

Definitions and Statements

o 1. Carrying or conveying from one place to another; the removal of persons or goods from one place to another.

g 2. Between two or more states; between a point in one state and a point in another state.

h 3. Begun, carried on, and completed wholly within the boundaries of a single state.

l 4. Partly judicial; empowered to hold hearings but not trials.

j 5. A term meaning *hands-off*; the belief that business operates best when uninhibited by the government.

m 6. Partly legislative; empowered to enact rules and regulations but not statutes.

a 7. A term meaning *let the buyer beware*.

k 8. Full; complete; absolute.

n 9. Governmental action that destroys the property's current use or unreasonably impairs the value of the property and the owner's reasonable expectations regarding it.

d 10. Constitutional provision that generally prohibits unreasonable government actions.

e 11. Process by which the government can take private property for a governmental purpose.

i 12. Repugnant; discrimination stemming from bigotry or prejudice.

b 13. Assigned responsibility and/or authority by the person or group normally empowered to exercise the responsibility or authority.

f 14. Constitutional provision that guarantees all persons and classes the same protection of the law.

c 15. Restricted from enjoying certain constitutional or statutory rights; burdened by systemic prejudice or bigotry.

COMPLETION EXERCISE

Fill in the blanks with the words that most accurately complete each statement.

1. _____ _____ _____ have quasi-judicial and quasi-legislative functions.

2. Regulations are either _____ or _____.

3. The takings clause prohibits government from taking property without _____ _____.

4. The two types of due process are _____ and _____.

5. Identify the three tests used in an equal protection analysis.

    a. _____.

    b. _____.

    c. _____.

TRUE-FALSE EXERCISE

Write **T** if the statement is true, write **F** if the statement is false.

___T___ 1. The Constitution prohibits a state from adopting a law that directly discriminates against interstate commerce, such as imposing special restrictions on only interstate commerce.

___T___ 2. Subject to certain limits, both the federal government and a state may regulate a matter.

___F___ 3. A state that discriminates against nonresidents is violating the equal protection clause.

___F___ 4. Courts cannot review the actions of an administrative agency.

___F___ 5. The government may never regulate the content of speech.

___T___ 6. If a state government fires an employee, it has deprived the employee of a property right.

___T___ 7. Commercial speech receives less protection than individual speech.

___F___ 8. Interstate commerce is narrowly interpreted and includes only activities that directly involve the movement of goods or services across state boundaries.

___F___ 9. A state may regulate commerce with foreign nations if it directly affects state residents.

___T___ 10. Congress may regulate activity originating in a single state if the activity will affect the national economy.

APPLICATION OF CONCEPTS

MULTIPLE CHOICE QUESTIONS

_____ 1. Wood, Inc. manufactures and sells furniture in interstate commerce. Wood's manufacturing plant is located in Phoenix, Arizona. Under these facts:
    a. The federal government has the power to regulate Wood's business.
    b. Subject to limits, Arizona has the power to regulate Wood's business.
    c. Arizona does not have the power to regulate any aspect of Wood's business; states do not have the power to regulate any matters that the federal government regulates.
    d. Both a and b.

_____ 2. Federal law generally requires that certain private employers must pay time-and-a-half for hours worked in excess of 40 hours per week. Assume that a state law directly conflicts with this federal law by requiring payment of time-and-a-half for only those hours worked in excess of 50 hours per week. Under these facts:
   a. Federal law controls.
   b. State law controls.
   c. Neither federal nor state law controls; conflicting federal and state laws cancel each other.
   d. A court will decide which law to apply.

_____ 3. Which of the following actions may violate the constitutional guarantee of due process?
   a. Amy is fired by her private employer without a hearing.
   b. A government agency imposed a fine on Dill Corp. for violating federal law. Dill Corp. was not given a hearing to determine whether it actually violated the law.
   c. Congress adopts a law. Key Co., which is subject to this law, asserts that the law violates due process because the law is only of marginal value.
   d. The State of Michigan intends to criminally prosecute Paul for an alleged crime. Paul is notified of the charges and action, and he is given a chance to defend himself in court.

_____ 4. A state adopts a law forbidding the sale of products in plastic containers. This law does not prohibit the sale of products in glass containers. Assume that this law is rationally and reasonably related to accomplishing a legitimate environmental goal. The class of manufacturers that sell products in plastic containers asserts that this law violates equal protection. Does it?
   a. No, because equal protection only prohibits laws that discriminate on the basis of race, religion, or national origin.
   b. No, because equal protection does not prohibit laws that distinguish between classes of businesses if the classification is related to accomplishing a valid governmental interest.
   c. Yes, because equal protection prohibits the government from adopting a law that may treat any class of persons or businesses differently from other classes.
   d. Both a and b.

SHORT ANSWER QUESTIONS

Answer the following questions, briefly explaining the reason for your answer.

1. Roscoe owns a diner in a small southern town. He mostly serves local customers, but occasionally serves travelers from other states that stop for a meal. Is Roscoe engaged in interstate commerce?

_____

_____

2. Kathy has graduated from law school but has not yet passed the bar examination. She lives in a state that prohibits persons from placing the phrase "Attorney-at-Law" after their names unless they have passed the bar. This law is designed to protect the public from unqualified lawyers. Kathy feels she has worked hard in law school and deserves to have "Attorney-at-Law" after her name. She claims the state is violating her right to free speech. Is it?

_____

_____

3. The government has constructed a dam along a river. The dam caused the river to flood onto Sam's land. Because of the flood, he cannot use the land, and its value has substantially decreased. Is this a "taking?"

_____

_____

4. A state legislature passed a law prohibiting state residents from owning cars more than ten years old. The purpose of the law is to "improve the overall appearance of the state." The legislature believes it is a legitimate state interest to have a modern-looking state, and requiring state residents to own new cars is rationally related to that goal. Does this law violate substantive due process?

_____

_____

CASE PROBLEMS

Answer the following case problems, explaining your answers.

1. Amax Corp.'s manufacturing plant is located in Missouri. Amax Corp. sells its goods in several states, and it conducts a significant portion of its business in Colorado. (a) Is Amax Corp. engaging in interstate commerce? (b) Does the federal government have the right to regulate Amax Corp.'s business? (c) In general, does Colorado have the constitutional power to regulate business conducted by Amax Corp. in Colorado? (d) What restrictions will apply if Colorado regulates Amax Corp.'s business activities?

_____

_____

_____

_____

2. A state has just passed a law prohibiting Purple-Americans, a race of people, from serving on the police force. According to the state, Purple-Americans tend to be short and not very muscular. Because police officers may need to defend themselves in a fight with dangerous criminals, they need to be tall and muscular. The state claims that the law serves a compelling state interest because it promotes a physically strong police force, which is necessary to protect the public. Using an equal protection analysis, determine whether this law violates the equal protection clause.

_____

_____

_____

_____

The six basic steps in a civil lawsuit are 1) pleadings, 2) service, 3) discovery, 4) pretrial motions, 5) trial, and 6) enforcing the judgment.

COSTS OF LITIGATION: There are many obvious and hidden costs that may be incurred in litigation. Thus, a person should consider alternative dispute resolution (ADR) before filing a lawsuit.

CLIENT'S INTERVIEW WITH A LAWYER: During an initial interview with a potential client, an attorney will obtain the facts of the case and determine whether there is a conflict of interest in representing the potential client. Attorneys may charge a flat rate based on the nature of the work, an hourly fee, or a contingency fee, meaning the attorney receives a percentage of any damages awarded or settlement paid to the client. Attorneys are licensed by the state, not the country. Any attorney licensed in a state may appear before any court in that state.

A party may choose to represent himself or herself, appearing *pro se*. A non-lawyer's decision to represent oneself often is a mistake, however, because non-lawyers are not familiar with important substantive laws and the rules of procedure that govern the conduct of the trial.

INVESTIGATION OF THE FACTS: An attorney will investigate the facts of a case by obtaining any readily available documents and interviewing witnesses. The attorney will then develop a theory of the case to be used as a basis for settlement negotiations.

NEGOTIATION OF SETTLEMENT: Lawsuits should be filed only after attempts to settle have failed. A lawsuit must be filed within the statute of limitations, or deadline, for filing.

DISPUTE RESOLUTION ALTERNATIVES: Discussed later are a number of ADR choices.

ANATOMY OF A CIVIL SUIT: Important steps in a civil suit include the following:

- *Filing the suit*: Filing of the suit requires the filing of a complaint with the clerk of the civil court and service of the complaint, and in some states a summons, on the defendant. A defendant must be served with notice that a lawsuit has been filed before the lawsuit is considered to have commenced. The defendant must file an answer to the complaint or a default judgment will be entered against the defendant. A court may enter a default judgment, i.e., a judgment without a trial, if a defendant fails to properly answer or otherwise respond to the plaintiff's complaint.

- *Pretrial proceedings*: After the complaint and answer are filed, the discovery process begins. Discovery allows each party to learn facts about the case that will help both sides determine the issues that are disputed in the lawsuit. Many more facts can be discovered than can be admitted as evidence in a trial. Methods of discovery include:

  - **Depositions**: Depositions are the sworn testimony of witnesses that is taken outside of court. Depositions can be used to preserve testimony of witnesses who cannot appear at trial. They may also be used to show inconsistencies in trial testimony, called impeaching a witness.

> **Interrogatories**: Interrogatories are written questions that are served by one party on the other. The interrogatories are not as spontaneous as depositions but serve essentially the same purposes.

> **Production of Documents and Things**: A subpoena duces tecum requires witnesses to turn over specified documents and records that might be relevant to the case.

> **Physical or Mental Examination**: If the physical or mental condition of a party is an issue, the court may, upon request, order the party to submit to an examination by a physician or psychiatrist.

> **Request for Admission**: Parties may submit written questions asking the other side to admit to certain facts.

> **The Result of Discovery**: Evidence found out during discovery can help parties know how to proceed with a lawsuit. Evidence found out during discovery may not be admissible as evidence at a trial.

> **Pretrial Conferences**: Pretrial conferences are often required by the court to try to settle the case without an expensive and prolonged trial. The judge may take an active part in this phase of the case.

> **Demurrer, Motion to Dismiss, and Motion for Summary Judgment**: A demurrer challenges the legal sufficiency of a party's pleading. A motion to dismiss requests the court to dismiss a complaint because, even if the allegations in complaint are true, the plaintiff has failed to state a valid claim. Summary judgment may be awarded if there are no genuine, material, factual issues and one party is entitled to win as a matter of law.

- *The trial*: Unless both parties agree that the case should be heard by the judge, the selection of the jury is first. The jury in civil and criminal trials is called a *petit jury*. Prospective jurors are asked questions (voir dire) to determine whether they are fit to serve on the jury. Prospective jurors who are potentially biased are eliminated for cause. Prospective jurors may also be eliminated for no reason by either party's using of a peremptory challenge.

   After the jury is selected, each side gives an opening statement, outlining what they propose to prove. Beginning with the plaintiff, each side then calls witnesses and submits documentary evidence; direct and cross-examination is used to get to examine witnesses. Expert witnesses may be called to offer an opinion regarding a disputed issue.

   Closing statements summarize the facts that each side believes it has proved. The judge then informs the jury of the applicable law (jury instructions) and asks them to resolve the case by applying the facts to the law. The jury renders a verdict, general or special. In a civil case, many states do not require a unanimous decision although in federal court a civil case must be decided by a unanimous jury unless the parties agree otherwise. The judge then enters a judgment based on the verdict. The judge can enter a judgment that disagrees with the jury's verdict (judgment n.o.v.) only if the judge finds that there is no substantial evidence to support the jury's verdict.

- *Post-trial*: A party may appeal if it believes that an important issue of law was incorrectly decided. An appellate court can affirm (uphold) a decision, or reverse the decision, which indicates an error of law. Appellate courts sometimes affirm part of a decision and reverse the remainder. An appellate court also may reverse and remand a case because the lower court made a mistake of law and the case is returned to it to correct its judgment. The prevailing party in a civil case can attach or execute upon the losing party's property.

- *A comment on finality*: The doctrine of *res judicata* prohibits parties from suing a second time on a claim that has been decided by a final judgment.

THE NEED FOR ALTERNATIVES TO A CIVIL SUIT: Alternate dispute resolution (ADR) refers to a number of procedures that allow parties to settle legal disputes without going to court. ADR is generally a voluntary approach for settling disputes, although courts and legislatures are increasingly making it mandatory in some situations. Advantages of ADR include: 1) it lessens burden on the judicial system; 2) it is quicker and less expensive than litigation; and 3) it may help businesses avoid becoming adversaries, thereby allowing them to maintain a business relationship.

NEGOTIATION: Negotiation involves the discussion and resolution of a controversy by the parties who have a disagreement.

MEDIATION: Mediation is an out-of-court procedure whereby parties submit a dispute to a neutral third party that tries to help the parties find a solution. One mediation approach is caucusing, whereby the mediator meets with the parties separately. Another approach, shuttle mediation, involves the mediator's placing the parties in different rooms and then speaking privately with each party in an attempt to clarify the issues and explore possible options. The mediator then runs messages back and forth between the parties in an attempt to reach a mutually acceptable settlement.

The mediator does not make a decision that is not legally binding. Also, the matters discussed in mediation are generally confidential. It is best that the parties agree that any discussions during mediation should not be used at trial.

- *Standards of conduct*: The American Bar Association has drafted model standards of conduct for mediators.

- *Compensation*: There are no set rules on whether mediators should be compensated or the amount of compensation they should be paid.

ARBITRATION: Arbitration is an out-of-court procedure whereby parties submit a dispute to a one or more neutral third parties called an arbitrator. In a voluntary arbitration, the parties mutually select the arbitrator or agree upon the process for selecting the arbitrator.

Arbitration is most often a voluntary process to which the parties have freely consented. In most situations, voluntary arbitration is provided for in contracts, which identify the types of disputes that must be arbitrated. An agreement to arbitrate is legally enforceable (unless the agreement is unenforceable due to fraud or other defenses). If parties have a valid arbitration agreement, they must arbitrate the dispute, and they have given up their right to have this dispute decided by a trial court.

The arbitrator's decision is called an award. In most voluntary arbitrations, the award is legally binding on the parties. However, in nonbonding arbitration, the parties may consider the arbitrator's award but they do not have to follow it.

Broadly speaking, parties cannot appeal an award. If one party fails to perform in accordance with the award, the other party may file a petition with a court seeking its enforcement.

- *Controls on arbitration*: States have developed their own rules on arbitration, and some have laws that do not permit arbitration for certain types of disputes. Despite these laws, parties must still arbitrate a dispute if they have contractually agreed to do so. This is because a federal law provides that arbitration agreements must be enforced and state laws cannot make them unenforceable.

- *Statutory coverage*: Most states have adopted the Uniform Arbitration Act for the purpose of regulating arbitration. At the federal level, the Federal Arbitration Act provides limited regulation. At the international level, more than 80 countries follow the UN Convention on Recognition and Enforcement of Arbitral Awards.

- *Organizations*: There are many organizations that offer arbitration services including the American Arbitration Association (AAA). The AAA also offers other services such as mediation, minitrial, and fact-finding. In fact-finding, an arbitrator investigates a dispute and issues findings of fact and a nonbinding report.

MINITRIAL: Another procedure that may be used to settle disputes is a minitrial. This procedure is frequently used to decide a dispute between two companies.

A minitrial is an informal, out-of-court procedure that is conducted by a neutral advisor. A shortened form of the case is presented, with senior executives from both companies watching. After the presentation is completed, the executives try to resolve a dispute and reach a settlement.

RENT-A-JUDGE TRIAL: This procedure entails two parties to a dispute hiring a judge or retired judge to hear their case and render a judgment. It is quicker and less expensive than a normal trial. Typically, the decision in these proceedings can be appealed to public appellate courts.

SMALL CLAIMS COURT: Small claims courts are public courts and, therefore, their proceedings are actually trials. Nonetheless, these courts, which typically have limited subject matter jurisdiction, are a relatively quick, inexpensive method for resolving small legal disputes.

STUDY HINTS FOR NRW CASE STUDIES

The following study hints may be helpful when resolving the NRW case studies.

NRW 6.1	➤ You should refer the NRW executives to Exhibits 6.1 and 6.2. ➤ Emphasize to Anna and Dan that it is best not to hold anything back from their attorney. Information shared in confidence with one's attorney is generally privileged and cannot be disclosed by the attorney.
NRW 6.2	➤ Look at the reasons for dismissing a juror for cause, including the issue of juror bias. ➤ If cause cannot be established for dismissing the juror, then Mr. Jones may want to consider using a peremptory challenge to disqualify the potential juror.
NRW 6.3	➤ You should review the material dealing with mediation, especially those portions dealing with the selection, qualifications, and compensation of mediators. ➤ A confidentiality agreement entered into by the parties to mediation and the mediator can help legally assure the confidentiality of information disclosed during mediation.

MATCHING EXERCISE

Select the term or concept that best matches a definition or statement set forth below. Each term or concept is the best match for only one definition or statement.

Terms and Concepts

a. ADR
b. American Arbitration Association
c. Answer
d. Arbitration
e. Award
f. Caucusing
g. Complaint
h. Contingent fee

i. Deposition
j. General verdict
k. Group bias
l. Impeach
m. Interrogatories
n. Mediation
o. Mediator
p. Negotiation

q. Peremptory challenge
r. Petit jurors
s. Request for admission
t. *Res judicata*
u. Shuttle mediation
v. Subpoena duces tecum
w. Summons
x. Voir dire

Definitions and Statements

_j_ 1. Decision of a jury.

_f_ 2. Type of mediation whereby the mediator meets separately with the parties in hopes of finding a common ground for settlement of their dispute.

_w_ 3. Writ served upon a defendant, giving the defendant notice that he or she has been sued.

_b_ 4. Organization that provides experts to serve as arbitrators.

_n_ 5. Out-of-court proceeding whereby a third person tries to help parties reach a settlement of a dispute. The third person does not render a legally binding decision.

_l_ 6. To call into question the truthfulness of a witness.

_x_ 7. Examination of potential jurors to determine whether they are fit to serve on a jury.

_u_ 8. Type of mediation whereby the mediator separates the parties and goes back and forth between the parties, carrying messages and settlement proposals.

_p_ 9. Procedure whereby parties themselves try to reach a settlement of a dispute.

_h_ 10. Attorney's fee that is a percentage of any amount the attorney recovers on behalf of the client.

_a_ 11. Assortment of out-of-court procedures that help parties to settle disputes without going to court.

_g_ 12. Plaintiff's initial pleading that states the plaintiff's claim against the defendant.

_o_ 13. Person who conducts a mediation.

_i_ 14. Sworn testimony taken outside of court.

_s_ 15. Written request for a party to admit or deny facts that are relevant to the lawsuit.

_d_ 16. Out-of-court proceeding whereby a third person renders a legally binding decision regarding a dispute between two parties.

_r_ 17. Panel of citizens who decide issues of fact in civil and criminal trials.

_c_ 18. Defendant's response to the plaintiff's complaint.

_t_ 19. Doctrine holding that a final judgment bars the parties from filing a new lawsuit on a claim that has already been litigated.

_v_ 20. Court order directing a witness to produce specified evidence.

_e_ 21. Decision of an arbitrator.

_k_ 22. Presumption that jurors cannot be fair because they belong to a particular race or other group.

_q_ 23. Right of a party to exclude a potential juror without having to justify the person's rejection.

_m_ 24. Written questions that are served on the opposing party in a civil lawsuit to be answered under oath within a required time.

COMPLETION EXERCISE

Fill in the blanks with the words that most accurately complete each statement.

1. The _____ is the person who conducts a mediation.

2. The _____ _____ _____ is a uniform act that most states have adopted to regulate arbitration.

3. Some mediators believe that their role is only to help _____ the settlement of disputes while other others believe that their role is to _____ the parties' proposals.

4. _____ _____ is a type of arbitration in which the arbitrator's decision is not legally binding on the parties.

5. List three advantages of ADR.

   a. _____.

   b. _____.

   c. _____.

6. _____ is the process by which parties obtain evidence from one another.

7. Once the jury has issued its verdict, the court then generally issues a _____ based on the verdict.

8. _____-_____ occurs when a witness is questioned at trial by the lawyer who did not call the witness to the stand.

9. The losing party at a trial will often _____ a question of law to a higher court.

10. Identify five basic discovery devices:

   a. _____.

   b. _____.

   c. _____.

   d. _____.

   e. _____.

TRUE-FALSE EXERCISE

Write **T** if the statement is true, write **F** if the statement is false.

___F___ 1. A potential juror cannot be disqualified except for cause.
___F___ 2. A demurrer is a motion for a new trial that is made by a party who loses at trial.

_T_ 3. The plaintiff initiates a civil lawsuit by filing a complaint and having it served on the defendant.

_T_ 4. Voir dire is the process for examining witnesses to determine if they are fit to serve on a jury.

_F_ 5. People can keep filing new lawsuits on the same claim until they get a judgment they like.

_F_ 6. A party in a civil lawsuit cannot be required to undergo a physical or mental examination.

_T_ 7. Failure to respond to a request for admission will result in the matter being deemed admitted without need for further proof.

_T_ 8. The purpose of a jury is to decide questions of fact and render a verdict.

_T_ 9. In appropriate situations, expert witnesses may be called to testify as to their opinions.

_F_ 10. A pretrial conference is a proceeding in which the judge decides the case without having a trial.

_F_ 11. Businesses are increasingly opposed to arbitration and other forms of ADR as a means for resolving legal disputes.

_F_ 12. Small claims court is not a real court; rather it is a group of citizens who decide the legal rights of others.

_T_ 13. Increasingly, courts are requiring people to attempt ADR before allowing them to seek a judicial determination of their rights.

_F_ 14. Agreements to arbitrate a dispute are illegal and void.

_F_ 15. ADR is appropriate for resolving all disputes.

_F_ 16. States generally have the power to declare that arbitration agreements are null and void.

_T_ 17. An agreement to arbitrate cannot be enforced if the agreement was procured by fraud or other wrongdoing.

_T_ 18. Arbitration is a common method that is used for resolving disputes in international business.

_T_ 19. An arbitration may be heard by one arbitrator or a panel of arbitrators.

_T_ 20. A mediator should be a disinterested party.

APPLICATION OF CONCEPTS

MULTIPLE CHOICE QUESTIONS

_C_ 1. Jason and JoJo submitted a dispute to binding arbitration. The arbitrator issued a decision in Jason's favor and awarded him $5,000 to be paid within 60 days. JoJo has refused to pay the $5,000 or any portion of it. Under these facts:
   a. Jason can do nothing to enforce the award.
   b. Jason can have JoJo imprisoned for failing to comply with the award.
   c. Jason can file an action in court to obtain judicial confirmation of the award, thereby enabling him to legally enforce the award.
   d. b and c.

_a_ 2. Todd has a dispute with Carla and he wants to use some type of ADR or equivalent proceeding that will produce a legally binding decision. Which of the following would meet Todd's needs?
   a. Arbitration.
   b. Mediation.
   c. Minitrial.
   d. a and c.

_d_ 3. Advantage Corp. and Disadvantage Corp. had a trade name dispute. Advantage claimed that Disadvantage's name was deceptively similar to its name and confused consumers regarding their companies and their respective products. Advantage and Disadvantage agreed to retain an arbitrator to conduct a fact-finding regarding this dispute. Under these facts:
   a. The findings of fact determined by the arbitrator will be legally binding on the parties.
   b. The report issued by the arbitrator will be legally binding on the parties.
   c. The findings of fact determined by the arbitrator and the arbitrator's report will NOT be legally binding on the parties.
   d. a and b.

_a_ 4. Richard sued Quint in Small Claims Court for $500. Select the answer(s) that are probably correct regarding this lawsuit.
   a. The parties may represent themselves.
   b. The parties should not worry about being prepared when they go to trial.
   c. The court's judgment is not legally binding.
   d. All of the above.

_____ 5. Lawrence plans to sue Diane, his former partner, in order to recover partnership property that was wrongfully taken by Diane. Under these facts:
   a. Lawrence will commence the lawsuit by filing a judgment with the court.
   b. Lawrence will commence the lawsuit by filing a complaint with the court.
   c. Diane will respond by filing a request for deposition with the court.
   d. b and c.

_____ 6. Wendy sued her former tenant, Frank, for damaging the leased premises. Frank denies damaging the property. Wendy wants Frank to be personally questioned during the discovery process in order to obtain a spontaneous statement admitting that he damaged the premises. Which discovery technique would best serve Wendy's purpose?
   a. A subpoena duces tecum.
   b. Interrogatories.
   c. Demurrer.
   d. Deposition.

_____ 7. Jim sued Carol for breach of contract, and the case will be tried before a jury. Which of the following potential jurors is most likely to be dismissed for cause by the judge?
   a. A person who years ago was sued for breach of contract.
   b. All female prospective jurors.
   c. A business associate of Carol.
   d. All of the above.

_____ 8. Ellen sued SuCorp for breach of contract. Based on substantial evidence, the jury returned a general verdict in favor of Ellen for $10,000, and the judge entered judgment in favor of Ellen for this amount. If SuCorp appeals this judgment to an appellate court, the appellate court:
   a. May reverse the judgment if the lower court committed serious errors of law.
   b. Will not review the proceedings of the lower court.
   c. Will have the witnesses testify again.
   d. Will conduct a new trial.

SHORT ANSWER QUESTIONS

Answer the following questions, briefly explaining the reason for your answer.

1. Hin was involved in an automobile accident, and he suffered personal injuries and his vehicle was damaged. Hin is preparing for his first meeting with his attorney. What should Hin do to prepare for this meeting? What, if anything, should Hin bring to this meeting?

_____

_____

2. Chad needed a living will, which his attorney agreed to prepare for $120. Chad also was injured by a product and wanted to sue the manufacturer of the product for $10,000. Chad's attorney agreed to represent him in this suit and take 40 percent of the amount recovered as her fee. What type of fee arrangements have Chad and his attorney made? How much in fees will the attorney receive?

_____

_____

3. Joe's Diner bought all of its vegetables from Acme Farms. Joe's claims that one shipment of Acme vegetables was tainted, and Acme denies the allegations. Acme has now sued Joe's for breach of contract, and a jury trial is scheduled. In this case, what specific matters will the jury determine?

_____

_____

4. Sammy sued Franklin Corp. for injuries he suffered while using a tool manufactured by Franklin Corp. The trial court issued a judgment in favor of Franklin. At this point, is there a final judgment? If Sammy appeals the judgment and the appellate court upholds the judgment, can Sammy file a new lawsuit against Franklin for the same injuries?

_____

_____

5. Neuron Corp. agreed to arbitrate a trade secret dispute with Biomed, another nuclear physics company. The dispute involved a technical point of law and science. Explain who will select the arbitrator. Discuss who might be an appropriate person to arbitrate this type of dispute.

_____

_____

6. Two businesses owned adjoining property. When a flood destroyed a common roadway they shared, each insisted the other repair it. Unable to reach a solution, they submitted their dispute to mediation. Discuss two approaches the mediator may use to help the parties resolve their dispute.

_____

_____

7. Rigatoni Corp. had a dispute with a client regarding the client's unpaid bill. Both parties wanted to maintain their business relationship, but the client disputed the amount owed to Rigatoni. The parties are considering using a minitrial in order to help settle their dispute. Discuss what would occur in a minitrial of this dispute. Is the outcome of the minitrial legally binding on the parties?

_____

_____

8. Gina claims that her landlord has wrongfully failed to return $250 of her security deposit. The landlord refuses to negotiate this matter with Gina and refuses to agree to any type of ADR. Under these facts, what can Gina do in order to enforce her legal rights in a relatively quick, inexpensive manner?

_____

_____

CASE PROBLEMS

Answer the following case problems, explaining your answers.

1. West Fabricating installed a powerful grinder to use in its manufacturing operation. West operated its plant around the clock. Paul, who lives next door, is considering filing a suit against West because noise from the grinder disturbs his family at night. (a) Discuss the advantages that mediation may offer to West and Paul. (b) Analyze how the parties might settle this dispute without going to court.

_____

_____

_____

2. Randy was injured in a car accident. Randy claimed the other driver, Karen, negligently ran a red light causing the accident, but Karen insists that Randy ran the light. Randy sued Karen, the parties have filed all pleadings, and Randy has filed a motion for summary judgment. (a) Describe the purpose for a motion for summary judgment. (b) Under the facts stated, will the court grant summary judgment in favor of Randy? (c) If Karen admitted that she ran the red light, but defended that she is not liable because she didn't mean to collide with Randy, would the court grant summary judgment in favor of Randy?

_____

_____

_____

CHAPTER REVIEW

OBJECTIVES OF TORT LAW: Tort law provides a remedy for individuals and businesses that have been intentionally or unintentionally damaged by the wrongful acts or omissions (meaning, failures to act) of others. The remedy usually awarded under tort law is monetary damages.

THEORIES OF TORT LIABILITY: A tort is a civil wrong, which involves: 1) conduct that causes a harm or injury to a party, 2) thereby entitling the party to recover damages, and 3) the right to damages does not depend on the breach of a contract. There are three basic theories of tort liability: 1) intentional torts, 2) negligence, and 3) strict liability.

We all have a duty to protect other persons from harm. The question the courts must examine is what degree of duty exists under what specific circumstances. All theories of liability, however, require foreseeability.

INTENTIONAL TORTS: Intentional torts are wrongs that impose liability on persons who either wanted a wrongful act to occur or knew that it would occur. Intentional torts include:

- *Assault*: An assault is conduct that causes someone else to fear an immediate battery. Some movement toward the innocent person must accompany a verbal threat.
- *Battery*: A battery is the wrongful physical contact of another.
- *Defamation*: Defamation is conduct that wrongfully harms another person's reputation. Slander is spoken defamation, and libel is defamation made in a writing, photo, or similar manner.
- *Disparagement*: Disparagement (e.g., trade libel) arises when a business product is defamed.
- *False Imprisonment*: False imprisonment is the unlawful detention of a person against his or her will without just cause.
- *Emotional Distress*: Liability arises if a person intentionally causes another to suffer serious indignity (severe emotional harm) by engaging in outrageous conduct.
- *Invasion of Privacy*: Invasion of privacy is conduct that wrongfully invades another's privacy. This tort is committed when a person without permission: 1) uses someone else's name, likeness, or life story for its own commercial benefit, 2) invades someone else's physical privacy, or 3) discloses to the public private facts about someone else and the public has no legitimate interest in this information.
- *Trespass*: Trespass occurs when a person ventures onto another's land without permission.
- *Conversion*: A person is liable for conversion when he intentionally exercises exclusive control over another's personal property without permission.
- *Misappropriation of Trade Secrets*: This tort occurs when someone unlawfully acquires and uses trade secrets of another business. A trade secret is some exclusive knowledge of commercial value that has been generated by the labors of a specific person or group of people.
- *Fraud*: Fraud occurs when one party intentionally deceives a second party regarding a factual matter in order to benefit from the second party's reliance on the false information.
- *Civil RICO Violations*: Civil liability may be imposed under certain statutes if a person or business commits two or more racketeering acts within a 10-year period. Plaintiffs in a civil action may recover treble (triple) damages.

■ *Defenses to Intentional Torts*: Consent (express or implied), privilege (voluntary or involuntary), necessity (e.g., going onto another person's real property for your own protection), and truth (with regard to defamation) are potential defenses that defendants may use to avoid liability under tort law. Privileges recognized in many states include 1) self-defense; 2) merchants' right to detain persons who they reasonably believe have shoplifted; 3) a person's right to go onto another's property in order to recover the person's stolen property; and 4) a person's the right to speak in judicial and legislative proceedings without being subject to civil liability for slander even if the person defames another.

NEGLIGENCE: Liability for negligence may be imposed when people act in an unreasonably careless manner and, as a result, harm someone else. Negligence exists when the following four are established:

■ *Duty*: Everyone has a duty to act as a reasonable and prudent person would act under the same circumstances. Stated another way, everyone has a duty to act in a reasonable manner to prevent foreseeable harm to others. In some cases, a statute defines the standard by which a person's duty is measured. In most states, the breach of this statutory standard is called "negligence per se."

■ *Breach of Duty*: Breach of duty means to violate a legal obligation. One may breach a duty by acting carelessly or by failing to act (an omission) when action is required.

■ *Causation*: A person's act or omission must be both 1) the actual cause and 2) the proximate cause of the plaintiff's harm. Actual cause means that, as a factual matter, the breach substantially produced the harm. Proximate cause is a policy question, but generally means the breach is so closely related to the plaintiff's injuries that the law will hold the defendant responsible.

■ *Harm*: There generally is no liability for negligence unless harm is caused.

■ *Defenses to Negligence*: Defenses to negligence include: 1) assumption of risk (plaintiff knowingly and voluntarily undertook risk); 2) contributory negligence (plaintiff's negligence bars recovery); and 3) comparative negligence (plaintiff's negligence reduces recovery).

STRICT LIABILITY: Strict liability imposes liability on persons who engage in ultrahazardous activities and, as a result of these activities, harm others. Liability is imposed even if the person acts as carefully as possible and does not intend to harm anyone.

PRODUCT LIABILITY: Manufacturers may be held liable for harm caused by their defective products. Common theories for imposing liability include: 1) fraud; 2) breach of express or implied warranties; 3) negligence; and 4) strict liability.

TORT LIABILITY OF BUSINESS ENTITIES: Employers can be held liable for the torts of their employees that are committed while the employees are carrying out the business of the employers.

STUDY HINTS FOR NRW CASE STUDIES

The following study hints may be helpful when resolving the NRW case studies.

NRW 7.1	➤ Review the rules for disparagement when preparing your answer. While comparative advertising is allowed, tort law prohibits ads that falsely represent the truth.
NRW 7.2	➤ Review the elements required to prove the tort of invasion of privacy.
NRW 7.3	➤ Before advising Mai, review the defenses of privilege and truth.

MATCHING EXERCISE

Select the term or concept that best matches a definition or statement set forth below. Each term or concept is the best match for only one definition or statement.

Terms and Concepts

a. Assault
b. Bar
c. Conversion
d. False imprisonment

e. Foreseeable
f. Implied consent
g. Libel
h. Negligence per se

i. Privilege
j. Replevin
k. Slander
l. Trespass

Definitions and Statements

F 1. Permission that is inferred from one's words, actions, or other conduct.

K 2. Oral defamation.

b 3. Barrier; something that prevents one from suing on a claim.

A 4. Wrongfully causing another to fear an immediate, unlawful touching.

h 5. Presumption that a defendant was negligent.

e 6. Capable of being anticipated.

d 7. Wrongful detention of another.

l 8. Wrongful going upon or other interference with another person's land.

g 9. Written defamation.

c 10. Wrongful taking or other interference with another's personal property.

j 11. Action brought to recover possession of one's goods.

i 12. Legal right to do something.

COMPLETION EXERCISE

Fill in the blanks with the words that most accurately complete each statement.

1. A tort involves a _____ wrong whereas a crime involves a _____ wrong.

2. _____ torts are wrongs in which the defendant has acted in a willful manner and either wanted the act to occur which resulted in harm or knew that the act would probably result in harm.

3. Fraud requires proof that the defendant misrepresented a _____ _____.

4. A merchant who wrongfully detains a customer without having a sufficient legal basis for the detention may be liable for the tort of _____ _____.

5. Identify the four elements that must be established in order to establish liability for negligence:

a. _____.

b. _____.

c. _____.

d. _____.

TRUE-FALSE EXERCISE

Write **T** if the statement is true, write **F** if the statement is false.

___F___ 1. A tort is a crime against the public, which is punishable by fines and imprisonment.

___T___ 2. Remedies in a tort action are most often money damages.

___T___ 3. Under the doctrine of *res ipsa loquitur*, an inference of negligence arises if the instrument that caused the plaintiff's injury was under the exclusive control of the defendant and the injury suffered by the plaintiff ordinarily occurs only as a result of someone else's negligence.

___T___ 4. A person cannot be held liable for defamation for speaking only the truth about someone else.

___T___ 5. Libel and slander involve the same basic violation - wrongful injury to another's reputation.

___T___ 6. A person commits the tort of trespass by going upon another's land without permission, and proof of actual damage to the land is not required.

___T___ 7. A person who gives a resume to a prospective employer stating that he is a Harvard University graduate, when in fact he is not, is committing a fraudulent act.

___T___ 8. There is no trespass if someone goes upon another's land due to a necessity.

___T___ 9. The defense of contributory negligence is a complete bar to a lawsuit for negligence.

___F___ 10. An employer cannot be held liable for an employee's tort - only the employee is liable.

APPLICATION OF CONCEPTS

MULTIPLE CHOICE QUESTIONS

_____ 1. Joe was angry with a clerk and, standing a foot away from the clerk, Joe drew his arm back with a clenched fist and stated, "I am going to punch your lights out." What tort did Joe commit?
   a. Libel.
   b. False imprisonment.
   c. Battery.
   d. Assault.

_____ 2. One afternoon, Carrie slipped on grapes that had fallen on the floor in the produce department of Acme Groceries, injuring herself. Acme inspected the floor once in the morning and once at closing for spilled produce, even though it knew that produce was dropped on the floor more often. Is Acme liable for negligence?
   a. No, Acme owed no duty to Carrie.
   b. No, Acme did not breach its duty to Carrie.
   c. No, Acme's conduct was not the cause of Carrie's injuries.
   d. Yes, Acme was negligent and is liable to Carrie.

___ 3. John and Ken went to a baseball game at their college. They sat high up in the stands behind first base even though they knew that foul balls often landed in this area. In the third inning, a foul ball struck John in the head, causing him serious injuries. John sued the college for negligence. In all likelihood, is the college liable to John?

    a. Yes, the college was negligent in allowing spectators to watch the baseball game.

    b. Yes, the college is liable under strict liability because baseball is an ultrahazardous activity.

    c. No, John assumed the risk that foul balls would sometimes land in the stands.

    d. No, colleges owe no duty to protect students from unreasonable risks of harm.

___ 4. Which of the following is fraud?

    a. Nigel offered to sell his car to Jawan, explaining that the clutch was worn out.

    b. When negotiating to sell his car to Maureen, Jack stated that the car was "a beauty - worth every penny" of the asking price. Actually, the car was a worn-out junk heap.

    c. Sally offered to sell her car to Mark. She stated to Mark that all of the car lights worked, not knowing that one rear tail light had just burned out.

    d. Guillermo sold Kim a car that he claimed had two years left on the warranty even though he knew that the warranty had run out six months before.

SHORT ANSWER QUESTIONS

Answer the following questions, briefly explaining the reason for your answer.

1. Bob spread a false rumor at a party that Margo had a sexually transmitted disease. Identify the type of tort Bob has committed and list the elements that Margo must prove in order to recover.

_____

_____

2. Fran, a security guard for Northern Department Store, believed that she saw Ben shoplift a watch from a display cabinet. As Ben attempted to leave the store, Fran blocked Ben's exit and detained him for a few minutes to ask some questions in order to determine whether he was in fact guilty of the suspected theft. When Fran determined that Ben was innocent, he was released. Are Fran and Northern Department Store liable to Ben for the tort of false imprisonment?

_____

_____

3. Jessie and a group of other teenagers entered Dan's Candy Store. Dan decided that there were too many teenagers in his store, so he grabbed a purse that was slung over Jessie's shoulder and pulled her towards the door, telling her to leave. Jessie suffered a displaced shoulder as a result of this encounter. Is Dan liable for the tort of battery?

_____

_____

4. Patsy was fired as a waitress at the Blue Bull Cafe. To get back at the cafe owner, Patsy stood in front of the cafe and falsely told prospective customers that the cafe served spoiled food. As a result, a number of potential customers decided to eat elsewhere. Has Patsy committed a tort?

_____

_____

CASE PROBLEMS

Answer the following case problems, explaining your answers.

1. Will was hired to prepare a registration statement (disclosure document) for an offering of stock in "You're Connected," an Internet company. Will misstated important information in the statement regarding the risks that were associated with this company in return for a $50,000 bonus paid by "You're Connected" management. Management did not want Will to fully disclose the risks so that investors would not be scared away. Lilly bought stock in the company based on the information in the statement and, as a result, she suffered large financial losses.

    Analyze what tort claim, if any, Lilly may have against Will and "You're Connected."

    _____

    _____

    _____

    _____

2. For many years, Waste Disposal Corp. (WDC) intentionally dumped toxic wastes in porous soil near Megalopolis, a growing metropolitan area. WDC did not investigate the potential dangers associated with its dumping. Over time, the toxic wastes migrated towards Megalopolis. Five years later, a new residential subdivision was built in the Megalopolis suburbs, but many of the homes had to be abandoned because the toxic wastes previously dumped by WDC rendered them uninhabitable.

    (a) What tort duty, if any, did WDC have in connection with its dumping activities?
    (b) Analyze whether WDC has any tort liability in this case?

    _____

    _____

    _____

    _____

CHAPTER 8

Crimes and Business

CHAPTER REVIEW

WHY STUDY CRIMINAL LAW?: Businesses are constantly confronted with the effects of crime.

OBJECTIVES OF CRIMINAL LAW: Objectives of criminal law include:
- *Protection of Persons and Property*: Protection of the public from harm, which is accomplished under the criminal law by fines and imprisonment.
- *Deterrence of Criminal Behavior*: Criminal behavior is presumably deterred by punishment. Under the U.S. Constitution, however, punishment cannot be excessive.
- *Punishment of Criminal Activity*: Criminals are punished by fines and/or deprivation of their freedom. The use of criminal forfeiture (i.e., government confiscates property that is used in a crime or was acquired with illegal funds) as a punishment also is increasingly used.
- *Rehabilitation of the Criminal*: Criminals generally receive education and training in an attempt to reform them.

THE COMPONENTS OF CRIMINAL RESPONSIBILITIES: To convict a person of a crime, the government generally must prove beyond a reasonable doubt the two elements of all crimes: a criminal act and a criminal mental state.
- *The Act*: Conduct is criminal only if the law prohibits it and the actor voluntarily engages in such conduct. Criminal liability cannot be based solely on thoughts or involuntary acts. In some cases, the failure to perform a legally required act can be the basis of a crime.
- *Mental State*: Depending on the crime, a person can be held criminally liable only if they acted with:
  1) purpose, meaning, with a conscious objective to commit the act;
  2) knowledge, meaning, with awareness of what the person is doing;
  3) recklessness, meaning, with disregard for a substantial and unjustifiable risk of harm to others;
  4) negligence, meaning, the person should have known of a substantial, unreasonable risk of harm to others; or
  5) strict liability, meaning, the law imposes liability and requires no mental state.

SERIOUSNESS OF THE OFFENSE: There are three categories of crime:
- *Infractions or Violations*: Petty offenses that are generally punishable only by fines.
- *Misdemeanors*: Minor offenses punishable by fines or short jail sentences.
- *Felonies*: Major offenses punishable by long prison terms.
- *Treason*: Waging war against the state or giving aid and comfort to the enemy.

CRIMES VERSUS TORTS: One act can be both a crime and a tort.

SELECTED CRIMES: The following crimes may occur in connection with business activities:
- *Murder/Manslaughter*: Murder is the deliberate killing of another human being, whereas manslaughter is the involuntary killing of a human being.
- *Arson*: Intentional burning of real property (land and items permanently affixed to it) and many types of personal property (property other than real property).
- *Burglary*: Breaking and entering into a structure with the intent to commit a felony inside.

- **Embezzlement**: Taking of money or property by an employee.
- **Forgery**: Making or altering negotiable instruments, such as checks, or credit card invoices.
- **Credit Card and Check Legislation**: Bad check laws typically provide that a person commits a crime when: 1) the person issues a check that is not paid; 2) knowing there are insufficient funds to pay the check, and 3) (in some states) with the intent to defraud another.
- **Identity Theft**: Identity theft occurs when a thief steals a victim's personal information, such as name, address, Social Security number, and/or name of employer, and then uses this information to access the victim's credit.
- **Criminal Fraud**: Conviction for this crime typically requires proof that the speaker or author: 1) made a false statement of fact; 2) the statement was material; 3) the listener relied on the statement; and 4) the speaker intended to mislead the listener.
- **Larceny**: Wrongfully taking and carrying away another's personal property.
- **Robbery**: Larceny that is committed with violence or the threat of violence.
- **Espionage**: Economic Espionage Act makes it a crime to steal trade secrets in certain cases.
- **Computer Crime**: In many states the following acts may be a crime: 1) unauthorized use of computers or computer-related equipment; 2) destruction of a computer or its records; 3) alteration of legitimate records; and 4) accessing computer records to transfer funds, stocks, or other property.
- **Corporate Liability for Crimes**: Historically, corporations were not charged with crimes because courts held that corporations could not form the intent required to be guilty of a crime. Today, corporations may be held criminally liable for crimes that are committed by their employees when they are acting within the scope of their employment. This is especially true if a crime is *mala prohibita*.
- **RICO (crimes)**: RICO makes it a federal crime to obtain or maintain an interest in, use income from, or conduct or participate in the affairs of an enterprise through a pattern of racketeering activity.

SELECTED DEFENSES: Four classic defenses to criminal liability are:
- **Duress**: An accused is coerced into criminal conduct by the threat or use of force.
- **Insanity**: An accused did not know an act was wrong or could not stop himself or herself due to a mental disease or defect.
- **Intoxication**: Voluntary intoxication may be a defense only to crimes that require an accused to form a specific intent to commit the crime.
- **Justification**: When the act is necessary to prevent harm to the accused.

THE LAW OF CRIMINAL PROCEDURE: Criminal law is the area of law that assures an accused due process in connection with criminal prosecutions. Among other things, an accused must generally be afforded the following minimal protections: 1) notice of the criminal charges; 2) an opportunity to face his or her accusers and to present a defense, and 3) due process, including a requirement that there be probable cause to arrest and/or search an accused.

STUDY HINTS FOR NRW CASE STUDIES

The following study hints may be helpful when resolving the NRW case studies.

NRW 8.1	➢ The NRW principals should review the law relating to self-defense and other justifications. ➢ When devising security measures, do not forget the privacy rights of others.
NRW 8.2	➢ Explore arranging payment through a third party firm that will guarantee the validity of payments so NRW can avoid losses resulting from identity theft sales.
NRW 8.3	➢ NRW should focus on promptly responding to customer and vendor inquiries. Therefore, consider not using this message and arrange to pick up and respond to important e-mail.

REVIEW OF KEY TERMS AND CONCEPTS

MATCHING EXERCISE

Select the term or concept that best matches a definition or statement set forth below. Each term or concept is the best match for only one definition or statement.

Terms and Concepts

a. Arraignment
b. Bail
c. Beyond a reasonable doubt
d. Currency transaction report
e. Defraud

f. Deterrent
g. Due process
h. Equal protection
i. Grand jury
j. Indictment

k. *Mala prohibita*
l. *Nolo contendere*
m. Retainer
n. Sentence
o. U.S.C.

Definitions and Statements

_h_ 1. Concept that all persons are treated the same by the law.
_d_ 2. Report that banking authorities must file whenever a customer deposits $10,000 cash or more.
_o_ 3. Abbreviation for United States Code, the federal statutory code.
_n_ 4. Punishment of a criminal, as pronounced by the court.
_m_ 5. Attorney's fee paid in advance for legal services.
_k_ 6. Act that is considered wrong only because it is prohibited by law.
_g_ 7. Proper exercise of judicial authority.
_f_ 8. Something that prevents or discourages criminal conduct.
_j_ 9. Written accusation of criminal conduct issued to a court by a grand jury.
_c_ 10. Degree of proof required to find a person guilty of a crime.
_a_ 11. Accused's appearance in court for the purpose of entering a plea.
_b_ 12. Money paid to obtain the temporary release of a person charged with a crime.
_i_ 13. Jury that determines whether a crime has been committed and whether to indict an accused.
_l_ 14. Plea that has the effect of a guilty plea, without actually admitting one's guilt.
_e_ 15. Depriving another of his property by deceit.

COMPLETION EXERCISE

Fill in the blanks with the words that most accurately complete each statement.

1. One of the objectives of criminal law is to protect _____ and _____ .

2. In general, a crime cannot occur unless there is an _____ and a required
_____ _____ .

3. _____ is an acronym for federal and state laws that are intended to prevent and punish patterns of racketeering and criminal activities by organized crime.

4. In general, a person cannot be arrested unless there is _____ _____ to believe that the accused committed a crime.

5. Identify four classic defenses to criminal liability:

a. _____.

b. _____.

c. _____.

d. _____.

TRUE-FALSE EXERCISE

Write **T** if the statement is true, write **F** if the statement is false.

_T_ 1. One assumption of criminal law is that punishment for crimes will deter criminal behavior.

_T_ 2. In general, proof of both a criminal act and a criminal mental state are necessary in order to convict a person of a crime.

_F_ 3. Misdemeanors are the most serious category of crimes.

_T_ 4. Embezzlement includes the taking of money or property by an employee who has been entrusted with such money or property by his employer.

_T_ 5. Larceny is the wrongful taking of another's personal property with the intent to permanently deprive the owner of the property.

_F_ 6. Corporations cannot be held answerable for crimes committed by their officers.

_F_ 7. Insanity is no longer a valid defense to criminal acts.

_F_ 8. The purpose of the preliminary hearing is to decide the guilt or innocence of an accused.

_F_ 9. Once an accused is charged with a crime, the next immediate step is for the accused to be tried.

_T_ 10. The burden of proof for the prosecutor in a criminal case is to prove the accused's guilt beyond a reasonable doubt.

APPLICATION OF CONCEPTS

MULTIPLE CHOICE QUESTIONS

____ 1. Roger, an employee, systematically took tools from his employer whenever he was left to lock up his employer's store. Roger was arrested one night while taking more tools. What crime has Roger committed?
a. Larceny.
b. Burglary.
c. Embezzlement.
d. Criminal fraud.

____ 2. In which case does Janice commit the crime of forgery?
a. Without permission, Janice took a blank check belonging to Kim. Janice then filled the check out, signed Kim's name, and cashed the check.
b. Without permission, Janice took a credit card belonging to Sarah. Janice bought goods, charged the bill to Sarah's card, and Janice signed Sarah's name to the charge card slip.
c. Without permission, Janice printed and passed fake $20 bills.
d. a and b.

_____ 3. In which case did Kelly probably commit a crime?
   a. Kelly cashed a check for $50. Unknown to Kelly, she had insufficient funds in her account and the check was not paid. When informed that her bank refused payment, Kelly immediately paid the check.
   b. Kelly cashed a check for $1,000. She knew that she had inadequate funds to cover the check, but she planned to move soon and she figured the bank could write off her overdraft as a tax loss.
   c. Kelly took her roommate's credit card without permission and charged $200 merchandise.
   d. b and c.

_____ 4. Select the correct answer.
   a. Bob parked his bike outside a classroom while he attended class. Unknown to Bob, Lex stole the bike while Bob was in class. Lex has committed the crime of larceny.
   b. While drunk, Hal stole some beer. Hal knew what he was doing, but he wouldn't have done it if he was sober. Hal can assert the defense of intoxication to avoid criminal liability.
   c. Ted shoplifted a coat from J&J Department Store. Ted stole the coat because he was cold. Ted can assert the defense of justification to avoid criminal liability.
   d. All of the above.

SHORT ANSWER QUESTIONS

Answer the following questions, briefly explaining the reason for your answer.

1. Norma was fired as manager of the Java House, a small coffee shop. To get back at the owner of the coffee shop, Norma deliberately set fire to the premises. What crime has Norma committed? What elements must be established to prove Norma's guilt?

_____

_____

2. Sami forced open the door of a fur warehouse and entered it with the intent to take $10,000 worth of furs. What crime has Sami committed? What elements must be established to prove Sami's guilt?

_____

_____

3. Cal owns a cafe, and he unintentionally left raw fish at room temperature for several hours. Cal proceeded to serve the fish to customers who became quite ill as a result. Cal was charged with violating a strict liability health regulation that made it a misdemeanor to leave raw fish unrefrigerated for this long. What elements must be established to prove this crime? Can Cal be convicted of this crime?

_____

_____

4. Samuel offered to sell a plot of land to Roland. In order to induce Roland to buy, Samuel stated that there was an underground spring on the property with an attached irrigation system. Samuel knew that his statement was false. Since Roland was planning to grow corn on the land, the existence of adequate water and irrigation was important. Relying on Samuel's statement, Roland purchased the land for three times its actual value. What crime did Samuel commit? What must be established to prove Samuel's guilt?

_____

_____

CASE PROBLEMS

Answer the following case problems, explaining your answers.

1. Acme Electrical employees were repairing power lines when an Acme "cherry picker" came into contact with a power line, electrocuting a worker. Prior to this accident, the employees had complained to Acme supervisors that operation of this equipment so near to the power lines was unsafe and exposed the workers to a significant risk of injury or death. The supervisors responded: "We can always replace one of you if necessary, but we can't replace the client for whom we are doing this work."

   (a) What crimes, if any, have the Acme supervisors committed?
   (b) Can Acme be held criminally liable for its supervisors' conduct?

_____

_____

_____

_____

2. Over a period of four years, Allen knowingly and willfully engaged in numerous transactions that entailed the fraudulent sale of worthless swampland to elderly persons who lived in various parts of the United States. Mrs. Hinton unsuspectingly bought some of this worthless land from Allen, and she paid him $10,000 for the property.

   (a) What crimes did Allen commit?
   (b) What criminal penalties may be imposed against Allen?
   (c) What remedies does Mrs. Hinton have against Allen?

_____

_____

_____

_____

CHAPTER 9
Introduction to Contract Law and Contract Theory

THE IMPORTANCE OF CONTRACT LAW: Contracts occur in all aspects of daily life. Examples of common contracts include buying a car, leasing an apartment, purchasing insurance, making credit purchases, and writing a check.

- ***Commercial Law Contracts***: Contract law was once part of real property law. Separate rules developed to deal with commercial transactions, and mercantile courts developed apart from courts of law. The Uniform Sales Act and the Uniform Negotiable Instruments Act replaced the Law Merchant. Eventually these were replaced by the Uniform Commercial Code (UCC). Among other things, the UCC deals with sale of goods, commercial paper, and secured transactions.

    The Uniform Computer Information Transactions Act (UCITA) (adopted by only 2 states) sets out comprehensive rules for contracts related to computer information, including contracts involving the licensing or purchasing of software, computer games, and online access to databases. The Uniform Electronic Transactions Act (UETA) validates all electronic transactions in the business and governmental sectors, including, electronic contracts, electronic signatures, and the use of electronic agents for electronic contracting, but does not establish rules for such transactions. UETA, which has been enacted by more than 30 states, does not apply to transactions unless the parties agree to use electronic commerce in these dealings. The federal Electronic Signatures in Global and National Commerce Act (E-SIGN) states that no contract, record, or signature may be denied legal effect solely because it is in electronic form.

- ***Common Law Contracts***: Common law rules regarding contracts develop from court decisions. The common law supplements the UCC when the UCC is silent on certain matters.

- ***Definition of a Contract***: A contract is a legally enforceable promise made by two or more parties who are legally competent. Social promises or obligations are not legally enforceable.

- ***Elements of a Contract***: A valid contract requires:
    1) an agreement that is comprised of a valid offer and acceptance;
    2) consideration;
    3) legal capacity of the parties;
    4) genuine assent by the parties;
    5) legal subject matter; and
    6) certain formalities, such as a writing for certain types of contracts.

FROM STATUS TO FREEDOM OF CONTRACT AND BACK AGAIN: In feudal society contracts were relatively unimportant because individual rights were determined by status. As society grew increasingly dependent upon commercial activities, the freedom to contract became more important along with rights to enforce contracts. Today, there is once again growing interest in limiting contractual freedom in order to protect persons whose status places them at a disadvantage when making a contract.

CLASSIFICATIONS OF CONTRACTS: A contract may fall into several of the following categories:

■ *Formal versus Informal Contracts*: Formal contracts require the formality of being sealed with a wax insignia. Today, most contracts are informal (without a seal). Informal contracts may be oral or written, or they may by implied from the parties' conduct.

■ *Unilateral versus Bilateral Contracts*: A unilateral contract is an agreement pursuant to which the offeror promises to do something in exchange for the actual act or forbearance of the offeree. An offer for a unilateral contract can be accepted only by the offeree's actual performance of the act or forbearance requested by the offeror. A bilateral contract is an agreement in which the offeror and the offeree both promise to do, or not to do, something.

■ *Valid, Voidable, Void, and Unenforceable Contracts*: A valid contract is legally binding and enforceable, and it is not subject to any defenses. A voidable contract may be affirmed or rejected at the option of one or more of the parties. A void agreement cannot be enforced and it is not legally a contract. An unenforceable contract, although apparently valid, will not be enforced by a court because it violates certain requirements for the creation of a valid contract.

■ *Express versus Implied Contracts*: An express contract specifically sets out the parties' agreement and it may be either oral or written. An implied contract, on the other hand, is inferred, in whole or in part, from the parties' conduct. A contract is when, based on the facts, it is clear that the parties intended to enter into a contract even though they do not expressly create a contract.

■ *Executory versus Executed Contracts*: An executory contract is one that has not been fully performed by both parties. An executed contract has been fully completed.

■ *Quasi Contracts versus Contracts Implied in Fact*: A quasi contract is implied in law by a court in order to avoid one party being unjustly enriched at another's expense. Although no actual contract exists, in order to achieve justice a court imposes a quasi-contractual obligation to pay. On the other hand, a contract implied in fact is an actual contract and it is implied by a court because this is what the parties clearly intended.

STUDY HINTS FOR NRW CASE STUDIES

The following study hints may be helpful when resolving the NRW case studies.

NRW 9.1	➤ When a contract requires one party to both provide a service and sell goods, the parties' predominant purpose for making the contract determines which type of contract law will govern most contractual issues. However, you should also review the discussion relating to how the common law may supplement UCC rules.
NRW 9.2	➤ Carlos should consider whether he and his friend intended to form a binding contract. ➤ Review the section on quasi contract, paying particular attention to the discussion of volunteered services.
NRW 9.3	➤ Carlos and Mai should review the concepts relating to sales and goods. ➤ Regarding the restrictive covenants, Carlos and Mai should review the material on legality of contracts.

MATCHING EXERCISE

Select the term or concept that best matches a definition or statement set forth below. Each term or concept is the best match for only one definition or statement.

Terms and Concepts

a. Commercial paper

b. Counterclaim

c. Free enterprise

d. Goods

e. Mercantile

f. Public policy

g. Restitutionary

h. Secured transaction

i. Security interest

Definitions and Statements

_e_ _a_ 1. Dealing with business, commerce, or trade.

_g_ ___ 2. Equitable basis for restoring injured parties to their original position.

_b_ 3. Defendant's legal cause of action (claim) against the plaintiff.

_d_ _c_ 4. Items of identifiable and movable personal property.

_i_ 5. Interest that is held by a creditor in property of a debtor to assure payment of a debt or performance of an obligation.

_a_ _h_ 6. Negotiable instruments, such as checks, that are governed by UCC Article 3.

_h_ _e_ 7. Credit sale or loan transaction in which a creditor retains a security interest in the debtor's property to assure payment.

_f_ 8. Fundamental value of society.

_c_ _d_ 9. Carrying on free, legitimate businesses for profit.

COMPLETION EXERCISE

Fill in the blanks with the words that most accurately complete each statement.

1. A contract is a _legal_ _enforceable_ agreement between two or more parties.

2. In order to form a valid contract, an agreement must be supported by _consideration_

3. Parties must have the _legal_ _capacity_ to form a valid contract.

4. There must be _genuine_ _assent_ of the parties to the agreement; that is, they should not be influenced by fraud or duress.

5. The subject matter of a contract must be _legal_ and must not violate a statute or public policy.

TRUE-FALSE EXERCISE

Write **T** if the statement is true, write **F** if the statement is false.

____ 1. Historically, freedom of contract has been an important part of the American free enterprise economy.

____ 2. The UCC has completely replaced the common law of contracts.

____ 3. In feudal society, contractual rights were of little importance.

____ 4. Labor laws enacted by statute may restrict the freedom to contract.

____ 5. Formal contracts are commonly used in modern life.

____ 6. The agreement in a unilateral contract is formed by reciprocal promises made by the contracting parties.

____ 7. The absence of certain required formalities may render a contract unenforceable.

____ 8. A contractual offer that may be accepted by the offeree's promise to do a requested act is an offer for a bilateral contract.

____ 9. A quasi contract is a judicial remedy, not an actual contract.

____ 10. A voidable contract may be affirmed by the parties.

APPLICATION OF CONCEPTS

MULTIPLE CHOICE QUESTIONS

____ 1. A contract implied in fact is created in which of the following situations?

    a. John voluntarily fixed his sister's car.

    b. Kami and Tom entered into a complete, written contract to sell Kami's condominium to Tom.

    c. Luci and Mary orally agreed that Luci would make a suit for Mary for $100.

    d. Mark requested that Clay's Roofing repair his roof and Clay's did so. The parties did not expressly agree upon all of the terms of the transaction, but Clay's expected to be paid for its work and Mark knew this.

____ 2. Eddie agreed to sell stolen bicycles to Foster for $500 and Foster agreed to buy them. Which statement accurately describes their agreement?

    a. The agreement is a voidable contract, which the parties may later affirm.

    b. The agreement is void and unenforceable.

    c. The agreement is enforceable if it is stated in writing.

    d. The agreement is a valid contract.

d 3. In which of the following situations would a court recognize a quasi-contractual obligation to pay?

    a. Unknown to Grace, Todd's lawn service mistakenly mowed her lawn while she was at the store.

    b. Linda voluntarily cared for Sally's children for a week.

    c. Franklin and Lamar orally agreed that Franklin would paint Lamar's boat for $300.

    d. None of the above.

b 4. Roger promised to sell his car to Reggie and Reggie promised to pay Roger $3,000 for the car. The parties have not yet performed their respective promises. This contract may be classified as:

    a. An executed, bilateral contract.

    b. An executory, bilateral contract.

    c. An executed, unilateral contract.

    d. An executory, unilateral contract.

SHORT ANSWER QUESTIONS

Answer the following questions, briefly explaining the reason for your answer.

1. For years, Dave's Deli has supplied box lunches to Kelly's Construction Company. Each week, Dave called Kelly's ordering the required number of lunches. The lunches were then delivered in accordance with Dave's instructions and, at the end of month, Kelly's sent a check to Dave for the lunches delivered. This month, Kelly's refuses to pay Dave for the lunches delivered, arguing that the parties did not enter into a contract for the delivered lunches. Does a contract exist between the parties?

_____

_____

2. Martha accepted an invitation from Jeff to attend a charity ball. She purchased an expensive dress and spent the entire afternoon at the hairdresser. As she was preparing for her date, Jeff called to say that he had decided not to attend. Martha is furious and is considering legal action. Does Martha have a claim for breach of contract against Jeff?

_____

_____

3. Jason bought a car from Leo's Auto Sales. The sales contract described the car's engine as recently rebuilt. Soon afterwards, Jason took the car to his own mechanic and it was discovered that the engine had not been rebuilt. Is this contract valid, voidable, void, or unenforceable? What are Jason's options concerning this contract?

_____

_____

4. Merlin bought a new power saw from Brady's Hardware. Brady's offered to sell him the saw on credit if he signed a contract agreeing not to sue them for any accident that might result if the saw proved defective. Will a court uphold this contract?

_____

_____

CASE PROBLEMS

Answer the following case problems, explaining your answers.

1. Serena recently moved to town and she entered into the following transactions: (a) she granted Last Bank a security interest in her home to assure that she repaid the bank a loan; (b) she purchased a new TV; and (c) she hired Barb to paint her home.

   (a) What types of transaction did Serena enter into?
   (b) What law governs these transactions?

_____

_____

_____

_____

2. Ken took his car to Acme to get an estimate for painting one fender. Ken overheard an Acme employee tell others that he was preparing to completely paint Ken's car, but Ken did nothing to correct the employee's misunderstanding. Acme proceeded to paint Ken's car. Ken refuses to pay, arguing that he has no contractual obligation to pay.

   (a) Discuss whether the parties entered into a contract.
   (b) Does Ken have any legal obligation to pay for Acme's services?

_____

_____

_____

_____

CHAPTER 10

Contractual Agreement: Mutual Assent

```
┌─────────────────────────────┐
│       CHAPTER REVIEW        │
└─────────────────────────────┘
```

THE FIRST STEP IN CONTRACT FORMATION: The agreement is the basic element of a contract. An agreement is comprised of a valid offer by the offeror and a valid acceptance by the offeree.

MUTUAL ASSENT: An agreement cannot arise unless both parties agree to exactly the same terms. Without this mutual assent (agreement), a contract cannot be formed.

THE OBJECTIVE THEORY OF CONTRACTS: Formation of a contract requires that both parties intend to agree to a transaction. The law evaluates the parties' intent by an objective standard, that is, by what a reasonable person observing the parties' words and actions would believe was intended. Conversely, the parties' secret or subjective intentions do not generally control questions relating to intent.

OFFER: An offer is an expression to enter into a legally binding agreement upon the terms stated.

- *Clear Intention to Contract and Definiteness of the Offer*: An offer must be a clear and definite expression in order to give rise to a contract. However, the common law and the UCC differ regarding how definite an offer or agreement must be in order to form a contract.

   At common law, an offer must specifically state all important terms of the proposed contract. The UCC, however, applies a more relaxed standard and finds that a sales contract is sufficiently definite if: 1) the parties intend to contract and 2) there is a way to determine the essential terms of the agreement. The UCC also allows an output contract, which calls for a buyer to purchase all of a seller's production of a designated good, and a requirements contract, which requires a seller to supply and a buyer to purchase as much of a product or service as the buyer needs during the contract term.

   Courts generally enforce Internet-related "click-on" or "click-wrap" agreements or licenses (i.e., a buyer clicks on "I agree" box). The law is not settled regarding "shrink-wrap" agreements or licenses (i.e., contractual terms are enclosed with purchased goods). A contract typically is found if a buyer does not object to the terms and uses the product after having an opportunity to read the terms. Sometimes, though, courts will not enforce the terms if they are unconscionable (shockingly unfair).

- *Advertisements and Auctions*: In general, advertisements are not offers; they are instead viewed as invitations to do business. Similarly, unless an auction is stated to be "without reserve," the placement of goods for auction is not an offer; a person's bid is the offer.
- *Communication of the Offer to the Offeree*: An offer must be communicated to the offeree. An offer cannot be accepted by a person to whom it was not made.
- *Duration of the Offer*: An offer may terminate due to: 1) lapse; 2) revocation; 3) rejection; or 4) acceptance.

   ➤ An offer lapses (expires):
      1) at the time stated in the offer; or
      2) if no time is stated, upon expiration of a reasonable time.
   ➤ An offer terminates by operation of the law upon the death or insanity of either party, supervening illegality, or destruction of the offer's subject matter.
   ➤ The right to revoke an offer prior to acceptance may be limited by:

1) an option contract (promise to keep an offer open for a stated period of time in exchange for something of value);

2) UCC § 2-205 (an offer to buy or sell goods that is made by a merchant in a signed writing which promises that the offer will remain open for a stated time) (a merchant is a person who regularly deals in goods of the kind or has the knowledge or skill peculiar to the practices or goods involved in the transaction); or

3) the doctrine of promissory estoppel (a person makes a promise and should expect that another person will act in reliance on the promise, the other person relies on the promise, and injustice can be avoided only by enforcing the promise).

ACCEPTANCE: An acceptance is the offeree's agreement to all of the terms of the offer.

■ *Mirror-Image Rule*: The common law mirror-image rule provides that an acceptance is valid only if the acceptance and the offer are identical. The acceptance can neither delete nor change any term of the offer nor add any term not stated in the offer. Any deviation is a counteroffer, which effectively terminates the original offer and creates a new offer by the offeree. UCC § 2-207 establishes a different rule regarding contracts for the sale of goods.

■ *Manner and Time of Acceptance*: An offeree must accept in exactly the way stated in the offer. If the offer is silent, then an offeree may accept using any reasonable method of communication. Under the mailbox rule or implied agency rule that is followed in most states, a properly sent acceptance is effective when it is sent, even if it is never received by the offeror. If an acceptance is sent using an unauthorized method of communication, then the mailbox rule does not apply and the acceptance is effective only upon receipt by the offeror. Other communications, such as revocations or rejections, are effective only upon receipt.

■ *Silence*: As a general rule, an offeree's failure to respond to an offer, that is an offeree's silence, is not a valid acceptance.

■ *Bilateral versus Unilateral Contracts*: An offer for a bilateral contract may be accepted either by: 1) making a promise to the offeror to perform as requested or 2) by inferring a promise from surrounding circumstances or the offeror's conduct, such as the offeree's performance of the requested act. An offer for a unilateral contract can be accepted only by the offeree's actual performance of the requested act.

STUDY HINTS FOR NRW CASE STUDIES

The following study hints may be helpful when resolving the NRW case studies.

NRW 10.1	➤	When distinguishing sales talk from contractual statements, Chris should bear in mind the objective theory of contracts and the requirement that an offer be clear and definite.
	➤	Regarding the definiteness requirement for sales contracts, review UCC § 2-204.
NRW 10.2	➤	Carlos should review UCC § 2-205.
	➤	Evaluate whether Carlos has made a "firm offer."
NRW 10.3	➤	Mai should review the material dealing with acceptances of offers.
	➤	Do not overlook the requirement of contractual intent.

MATCHING EXERCISE

Select the term or concept that best matches a definition or statement set forth below. Each term or concept is the best match for only one definition or statement.

Terms and Concepts

a. Bona fide 真正的
b. Constructive acceptance
c. Declaratory judgment 審判力
d. Lapse 乙卦力
e. Objective standard
not thing inflenced by human emotions

f. Option contract
g. Output contract
h. Promissory estoppel 禁示发言
i. Rejection
j. Requirements contract

k. Revocation 廢除
l. Specific performance
m. Subjective standard
n. Supervening illegality
o. Vacate 撥連发出
主观 to go away from

Definitions and Statements

_k_   1. Offeror's termination of an offer.
_h_   2. Contract that requires the buyer to purchase all of the seller's production of a good.
_d_   3. Expiration of an offer due to the passage of time.
_e_   4. Contract in which the offeror promises to keep an offer open for a definite time.
_b_   5. Acceptance that is implied or inferred from the actions or words of an offeree.
_i_   6. Offeree's termination of an offer.
_o_   7. To nullify or make void, such as setting aside a judgment.
_c_   8. Court decision that determines the parties' rights in a particular transaction.
_m_   9. Standard that is used to evaluate a person's intent based on the party's words and conduct.
_h_   10. Doctrine that prohibits an offeror from revoking a promise if the offeree has reasonably relied upon the offer and justice requires enforcement of the promise.
_e_   11. Standard that is used to evaluate a person's intent based on the party's feelings and actual intent.
_n_   12. Unexpected event that makes it illegal to perform an act.
_l_   13. Equitable remedy by which a court orders the parties to perform the contract.
_a_   14. Honest and in good faith.
_j_   15. Contract that requires the seller to provide as much of a product as the buyer needs.

COMPLETION EXERCISE

Fill in the blanks with the words that most accurately complete each statement.

1. A contractual agreement cannot arise without the _mutual_ _assent_ of the parties to the same terms.

2. Advertisements are usually considered to be _invitations to deal_.

3. A contractual agreement is comprised of a valid _offer_ and a valid _acceptance_.

4. A _counteroffer_ is a statement by an offeree whereby the offeree rejects the original offer but indicates a willingness to enter into a contract upon newly stated terms.

5. Identify the four basic methods for terminating an offer.

a. _lapse of time_ .

b. _revocation_ .

c. _rejection_ .

d. _counteroffer ; acceptance_ .

TRUE-FALSE EXERCISE

Write **T** if the statement is true, write **F** if the statement is false.

_F_ 1. Under the mailbox rule, an acceptance that is sent in the proper manner is not effective until it is received by the offeror.

_t_ 2. If an offer states the exclusive method by which it can be accepted, any other method of acceptance will generally render the acceptance invalid.

_T_ 3. Silence by an offeree in response to an offer may be a valid acceptance if the parties' prior dealings with one another establish that they intended the offeree's silence to be an acceptance.

_F_ 4. A unilateral contract comes into existence the moment the offeree promises to perform the requested act.

_T_ _F_ 5. A merchant is a party who regularly deals in (e.g., buys and sells) goods that are the subject matter of an offer or contract.

_T_ 6. Under the UCC, merchants who make signed, written promises to buy or sell goods and promise not to revoke these offers give up their right to revoke their offers for the time stated.

_F_ _T_ 7. An offeree can accept an offer after it has been terminated.

_T_ 8. An offer must be communicated to the offeree in order to form a contract.

_T_ _F_ 9. At an ordinary auction (i.e., one that is not conducted "without reserve"), bids made by persons wanting to buy an item are only offers that the auctioneer may accept or reject.

_T_ 10. An option is not formed unless the offeree gives consideration (legal value) for the offeree's promise not to revoke the offer.

APPLICATION OF CONCEPTS

MULTIPLE CHOICE QUESTIONS

_b_ _C_ 1. In which case was Don legally entitled to revoke his offer?
   a. Don offered to sell his carpet business to Wilma. Don promised not to revoke the offer for 24 hours in consideration for $500 paid by Wilma. One hour later and before Wilma had accepted, Don revoked his offer and offered to return the $500 to Wilma.
   b. Don offered to build a home for the Burkes for $100,000. While they were considering this offer, Don revoked his offer.
   c. In a signed writing, Don (a merchant) offered to sell Pat a TV and Don promised not to revoke the offer for two days. The next day, Don revoked before Pat could accept.
   d. a and c.

d _____ 2. In which situation did the offer NOT terminate prior to its acceptance?
   a. Ty offered to sell a patent to Hal. Ty died, and Hal sent an acceptance two days later.
   b. ChemCo offered to sell chemicals to Wes. Congress then passed a new law making the sale of these chemicals illegal. Wes sent his acceptance after the new law was enacted.
   c. Ray offered to sell a parcel of land to Ely. The offer stated that it would lapse on May 1. On May 2, Ely sent an acceptance of the offer.
   d. Sissy offered to sell a stereo to Carl, and Carl accepted. Sissy then changed her mind and told Carl, "I revoke my offer."

C *a* 3. Sal offered to do certain accounting work for $5,000 for a new client, Louise. The offer stated that Louise's failure to expressly reject the offer within 24 hours would be an acceptance of the offer. Which of the following expressions or actions would be a valid acceptance?
   a. In writing Louise stated: "I accept your offer if your price is lowered to $4,000."
   b. Louise did not expressly reject or accept the offer.
   c. In writing Louise stated: "I accept your offer. Also, I would appreciate it if you did not smoke when you are working at my office."
   d. All of the above.

b 4. On May 1, Lilly mailed Patton an offer to buy his home. Patton received the offer on May 5. On May 6, Patton deposited a properly addressed, stamped acceptance in the mail. Lilly received the acceptance on May 10. On May 8, Lilly changed her mind, and she personally delivered a written revocation of the offer to Patton. In most states:
   a. A contract was formed on May 5.
   b. A contract was formed on May 6.
   c. A contract was formed on May 10.
   d. A contract was not formed.

SHORT ANSWER QUESTIONS

Answer the following questions, briefly explaining the reason for your answer.

1. Kelly drove off to the side of the road and yelled to her companion, Lorenz, "I'd take $10 for this car and be happy to get it!" Lorenz replied, "Here's $10, I'll take it." Did the parties form a contract?

_____

_____

2. Johnson Appliance Store placed an ad that read, "We will sell a new 24" Zenith® television sets for $10 to the first person in line when our doors open on Monday, June 21." Jake appeared two nights before, camped out, and was first in line when the store opened. However, the store refused to sell the TV to Jake for the advertised price. Was Johnson's ad an offer in this case?

_____

_____

3. Tricia offered to sell Jason her hang-glider for $3,000. Jason replied that he accepted, if Tricia would accept $2,500 instead. Tricia responded that she agreed to take $2,500. Was a contract formed?

_____

_____

4. Jerry's Van City offered to sell a new van to Susie's Caterers for $10,000. Susie's returned a signed, written "acceptance" of Jerry's offer, but the acceptance stated that Susie would take delivery of the van in 14 days, not 10 days as stated in the offer. Was Susie's acceptance valid?

_____

_____

CASE PROBLEMS

Answer the following case problems, explaining your answers.

1. Sally advertised a parcel of land for sale. Bryan delivered a signed, written purchase offer to Sally. The offer appeared to be sincere, and it stated all of the proposed contract terms. Unknown to Sally, Bryan did not intend to buy the land unless he first obtained financing. Sally accepted Bryan's offer.

   (a) Was Sally's advertisement an offer?
   (b) Did Bryan indicate a clear intention to contract?
   (c) Was a contract for the sale of the land created?

_____

_____

_____

_____

2. Fred offered to sell his gasoline station to Bess. Fred mailed the offer to Bess via first-class U.S. mail. The offer was silent regarding the required manner of acceptance or when it would lapse.

   (a) Can Bess accept the offer by remaining silent, or must she communicate an acceptance to Fred?
   (b) When will Fred's offer lapse?
   (c) How can Bess communicate an acceptance of the offer?
   (d) If Bess sends an acceptance via first-class U.S. mail, when will her acceptance be effective?

_____

_____

_____

_____

CHAPTER 11   Consideration (The Basis of the Bargain)

CHAPTER REVIEW

A valid contract requires consideration. One way for the courts to find that the parties have entered into a "mutual" agreement is by finding that the parties have made an exchange of value between themselves. This exchange of value, the quid pro quo of contract formation, is called consideration.

THE BARGAIN AS A CONTRACT THEORY: Consideration shows that parties intend to be legally bound.

DEFINITION OF CONSIDERATION: Consideration is what a party gives up in exchange for the other party's promise.

■ *Consideration as an Act or Forbearance to Act*: In a unilateral contract, the considerations are the offeror's promise and the offeree's actual performance of an act or forbearance (not doing) of an act.

Words that sound like a promise actually may be only an illusory promise and not consideration because the party really has no legal obligation to do or not to do anything (e.g., "I promise to rent your home next month if I still want to rent it at that time.")

■ *Consideration as a Promise to Act or to Forbear*: In a bilateral contract, the considerations are the promises made by the offeror and the offeree.

■ *Adequacy of Consideration*: As a general rule, the law does not examine the adequacy of the considerations that contracting parties give. In other words, the requirement that each party must give consideration is met even if the considerations exchanged are not of equal value.

As an exception to the foregoing general rule, courts may find that inadequate consideration is the result of fraud, duress, undue influence, mistake, or other similar situations at the time of contract formation, and allow one of the parties to rescind (terminate) the contract.

CONSIDERATION IN SPECIAL CONTEXTS: Special situations involving issues of consideration include:

■ *Contracts for the Sale of Goods*: Under the UCC "firm offer" rule, if a merchant states, in a signed writing, that an offer will not be revoked, then the offer must be held open for the stated time (up to three months) even if the promise was not supported by consideration.

■ *Suretyship Contracts*: A "surety" agrees to pay another's debt if the debtor fails to pay. The surety's promise to pay must be supported by separate consideration from the creditor unless the surety's promise to pay is made in exchange for the creditor's promise to extend credit to the debtor.

■ *Liquidated Debts*: Part payment of a liquidated (definite, undisputed) debt is not consideration for a discharge from the entire debt. In this situation, the debtor remains liable for the unpaid balance.

■ *Unliquidated Debts*: Part payment of an unliquidated (uncertain or disputed) debt that is paid and accepted by the creditor as payment in full is supported by consideration and does discharge (terminate) the entire debt.

■ *Composition Agreements*: A composition agreement is an agreement by a debtor to pay, and the debtor's creditors to accept, partial payment of their claims as payment in full. This agreement is valid.

ABSENCE OF CONSIDERATION: The below promises are NOT enforceable due to a lack of consideration:

■ *Illusory Promises*: Promisors are free to decide whether or not to do a promised act.

■ *Preexisting Duty*: A promise to do an act that the promisor is already legally obligated to perform or a promise to forebear from doing an act that the promisor already has a legal obligation not to do (e.g., promise not to wrongfully defame another person).

■ *Moral Consideration*: A person's promise to pay for a benefit already received is not legally enforceable even if the promisor feels a moral obligation to pay.

■ *Past Consideration*: A benefit already given is not consideration for a later promise to pay.

EXCEPTIONS TO THE BARGAINING THEORY OF CONSIDERATION: Consideration is not required in the circumstances discussed below:

■ *Promissory Estoppel*: A promise is enforceable if: 1) a promisor should expect a promisee to rely on the promise; 2) the promisee does rely on the promise; and 3) injustice can only be avoided by enforcing the promise.

■ *Charitable Subscriptions*: A promise to make a donation to a charity is enforceable.

■ *Promises Made After the Expiration of the Statute of Limitations*: A promise to pay a debt after the statute of limitations has run (i.e., a creditor has waited too long to sue on the debt) is enforceable.

■ *Promises to Pay Debts Covered by Bankruptcy Discharges*: A promise to pay a debt that may be discharged (terminated) in bankruptcy is enforceable if certain requirements are met.

STUDY HINTS FOR NRW CASE STUDIES

The following study hints may be helpful when resolving the NRW case studies.

NRW 11.1	➢ You should consider the concepts discussed in the "Suretyship Contracts" section. ➢ As a practical matter, you should also consider who the bank would accept as a surety.
NRW 11.2	➢ Determine whether other creditors are agreeing to similar revised payment terms and whether a composition agreement (or similar arrangement) may be appropriate. ➢ Think about what benefits, if any, CIT should request in exchange for the extended credit terms. Also, consider whether payment of the debt is secured by adequate collateral.
NRW 11.3	➢ Review the materials regarding illusory promises. ➢ Review the materials regarding discharge of contracts.

MATCHING EXERCISE

Select the term or concept that best matches a definition or statement set forth below. Each term or concept is the best match for only one definition or statement.

Terms and Concepts

a. Bankruptcy
b. Bona fide purchaser
c. Cancellation
d. Default
e. Firm offer

f. Guarantor
g. Guardian
h. Illusory promise
i. Promisee
j. Promisor

k. Promissory estoppel
l. Rescission
m. Stipend
n. Summary judgment
o. Waiver

Definitions and Statements

____k____ 1. Doctrine that may require performance of a promise if another has detrimentally relied upon it.

____o____ 2. Voluntary surrender of a legal right.

____h____ 3. Promise that allows the promisor to decide whether or not to do the promised act.

____j____ 4. Person who makes a promise.

____i____ 5. Person to whom a promise is made.

____n____ 6. Judgment that may be granted prior to trial if there are no genuine issues of fact.

____b____ 7. Person who purchases in good faith, for value, and without notice of any illegalities.

____c____ 8. Any action shown on the face of a contract that indicates an intent to destroy the obligation of the contract.

____l____ 9. To avoid, cancel, or terminate something.

____f____ 10. Person who promises to pay a debt if the principal debtor fails to do so.

____m____ 11. Sum of money paid for services or to defray costs.

____e____ 12. Irrevocable offer to buy or sell goods that is made by a merchant.

____g____ 13. A person legally responsible for taking care of another who lacks the legal capacity to do so.

____a____ 14. Area of law designed to give an honest debtor a "fresh start."

____d____ 15. Wrongful failure to perform a legal obligation.

COMPLETION EXERCISE

Fill in the blanks with the words that most accurately complete each statement.

1. A _composition_ _agreement_ is an agreement by a debtor to pay, and the debtor's creditors to accept, partial payment of their claims as payment in full.

2. _moral_ _consideration_ is a promise or act that is given because a party feels morally obligated to render such benefit to someone else.

3. A contract that is grossly unfair is _unconscionable_ and courts may examine the adequacy of consideration in such contracts.

4. A _preexisting_ _duty_ is an act that a person is already obligated to perform.

5. A _firm_ _offer_ is a merchant's offer to buy or sell goods that cannot be revoked for a stated period of time and consideration is not required to make this offer irrevocable.

TRUE-FALSE EXERCISE

Write **T** if the statement is true, write **F** if the statement is false.

_T_ 1. A party may give consideration by promising to do an act or forbearance, or by actually performing an act or forbearance.

_T_ 2. An agreement is not legally binding unless each party to the agreement gives consideration.

_T_ 3. A promise not to trespass on someone's land (a tort) is consideration if the promisor does in fact refrain from trespassing.

_T_ 4. Under a unilateral contract, the considerations are a promise for an act or forbearance.

_T_ 5. Consideration must be given to form a firm offer under the UCC.

_F_ 6. Charitable subscriptions are not legally enforceable unless consideration is given in exchange for the subscription or pledge.

_T_ 7. A promise to do something only if the promisor decides that he or she wants to do it is an illusory promise and is not consideration.

_F_ 8. Under promissory estoppel, a court will enforce any promise that is relied on by another person.

_F_ 9. A creditor cannot sue for the unpaid balance of a debt if the creditor received an agreed-upon partial payment pursuant to a composition of creditors.

_T_ 10. If a person agrees to pay more for something than it is worth, then the agreement is not a contract and it is not legally binding due to a failure of consideration.

APPLICATION OF CONCEPTS

MULTIPLE CHOICE QUESTIONS

_b_ 1. ABC Corp. hired Derrick for a fixed, three-year contract. One year after entering into the contract, ABC realized that Derrick's contract did not include an agreement not to compete. ABC drafted a separate agreement not to compete and Derrick signed it as requested by ABC. Under these facts, the agreement not to compete is:
   a. Enforceable because ABC signed the agreement.
   b. Enforceable because ABC gave consideration in exchange for signing the agreement.
   c. Unenforceable because ABC did not give Derrick consideration in exchange for signing the agreement.
   d. a and b.

d 2. _c_ Nina wanted to buy a VCR on credit from Seller. In exchange for Seller's agreement to sell the VCR to Nina, Sue agreed to guarantee Nina's obligation for the price. Under these facts:
   a. A suretyship contract is created.
   b. Sue has no obligation to pay if Nina defaults because the Seller did not give Sue any consideration in exchange for her promise to pay.
   c. Sue is obligated to pay if Nina defaults because the Seller gave Sue consideration in exchange for her promise to pay.
   d. a and c.

b 3. _c_ Lyle promised to write a book for Minda in exchange for her promise to pay him $10,000. When Lyle finished the book, he requested an extra $2,000 for his work. Minda initially agreed, but later she changed her mind and refused to pay the extra $2,000. Under these facts, Minda is obligated to pay Lyle:
   a. $0.
   b. $2,000.
   c. $10,000.
   d. $12,000.

4. _a_ Laura agreed to sell her ½ carat diamond ring to George for $150. The diamond is a good stone and is worth $800. Under these facts, the exchange of consideration:
   a. Is valid because the courts do not review the adequacy of the considerations exchanged.
   b. Is valid because it is an unliquidated debt.
   c. Is invalid due to the difference between the actual value of the ring and the amount that George agreed to pay.
   d. Is invalid based on the promissory estoppel doctrine.

SHORT ANSWER QUESTIONS

Answer the following questions, briefly explaining the reason for your answer.

1. Aries Inc. agreed to pay Randy a $5,000 bonus for extra services that Randy voluntarily performed the previous year. Is the agreement with Randy legally binding?

_____

_____

2. Aunt Millie wanted her nephew, Jim, to become a lawyer. She offered to pay Jim $10,000 if he graduated from law school. In response to this offer, Jim enrolled in and ultimately graduated from law school. After graduation Jim requested payment from Aunt Millie. However, she refuses to pay, arguing that the parties' agreement is not enforceable because Jim suffered no detriment by becoming a lawyer and she realized no benefit. Is the agreement between Aunt Millie and Jim enforceable?

_____

_____

3. Ina and Homeowner entered into a bilateral contract whereby Ina agreed to completely paint and prep Homeowner's home for $2,000. Due to higher than expected labor costs, Ina requested that Homeowner pay Ina an extra $500. Ina and Homeowner subsequently agreed that Homeowner would pay Ina an extra $500 in consideration for Ina's promise to completely paint and prep the house as originally agreed. Is the agreement regarding payment of the additional $500 enforceable?

_____

_____

4. Linda needed to print her Master's thesis, which was due the next day. Unfortunately, her printer did not work, and the computer center at her college was closed. At 3:00 a.m., she woke Fred, the only person with a printer that was compatible with her computer, and asked Fred if she could print her thesis. Annoyed at being awakened, Fred said she would need to pay five times the per-page rate charged by the computer center to print her document. Desperate, Linda agreed. Was this adequate consideration?

_____

_____

CASE PROBLEMS

Answer the following case problems, explaining your answers.

1. RDM, Inc. agreed to pay Ralph, a subcontractor, a $1,000 bonus in exchange for two promises:
    (a) his promise to complete an existing project by the date already required by a contract with RDM; and (b) his promise to perform some new work.
    Evaluate the enforceability of these agreements.

_____

_____

_____

2. Luis lived in Georgia. CompuTech, a Wyoming firm, called Luis and told him that they would be interested in hiring him if he moved to Wyoming. Luis and CompuTech never entered into a formal employment agreement. During their last conversation, CompuTech mentioned to Luis that although they were cutting back their staff, they were still interested in him. In response, Luis quit a well-paying job in Georgia, sold his house, and moved his family to Wyoming. When he arrived, CompuTech refused to hire him.

(a) Was it reasonable for Luis to rely on CompuTech's promise?
(b) Is CompuTech's promise enforceable under promissory estoppel?
(c) What would you have advised Luis to have done differently?

_____

_____

_____

CHAPTER 11 - CONSIDERATION (THE BASIS OF THE BARGAIN)

CHAPTER 12   Contractual Capacity and Reality of Consent

```
┌─────────────────────────────────────────┐
│                                         │
│            CHAPTER REVIEW               │
│                                         │
└─────────────────────────────────────────┘
```

LEGAL CAPACITY: Legal (contractual) capacity is the legal ability to enter into a contract. Both contracting parties must have contractual capacity in order to form a valid contract.

MINORS: In most states, a minor is a person (infant) under the age of 18. In some states, persons under the age of 18 are not treated as minors if they are married or emancipated (free from parental control).

- *Disaffirmance/Rescission*: Minors have the right to disaffirm (avoid) most contracts that they make prior to becoming an adult. To disaffirm, a minor must: 1) be a minor at the time of contracting; 2) give the other party notice of the minor's intent to disaffirm either prior to, or within a reasonable time after, becoming an adult; and 3) return all contract benefits received, at least to the extent that the minor still has such benefits. In most states, a minor may disaffirm even if the benefits received have declined in value, and the minor is not liable for paying for the decline in value.
- *Misrepresentation of Age*: Sometimes, minors lie about their age. Despite this deception, most states permit disaffirmance by the minor. But, courts in some of these states hold the minors liable for any actual losses suffered by the other party as a result of the minors' deception.
- *Ratification*: Ratification is a party's approval or confirmation of a contract. A minor cannot disaffirm a contract if the minor expressly or by implication ratifies the contract.
- *Necessaries, Special Statutes, Torts and Crimes*: A necessary is a good, service, and other thing that is required to maintain a minor's life or that is a basic necessity of life when the minor's personal circumstances are considered. Although minors may disaffirm contracts for a necessary, they must pay the reasonable value for any benefit received under the contract. Special statutes may forbid minors from disaffirming certain contracts. Minors cannot disaffirm liability for crimes or torts.

INSANE PERSONS, INTOXICATED PERSONS, ALIENS, CONVICTS ,AND MARRIED WOMEN: Insane persons may avoid a contract if they were actually insane when they made the contract, although they are liable for necessaries in quasi contract. However, the contract of a person whom a court has judicially determined to be insane is void, in other words a legal nullity. This is because only the incompetent's guardian, i.e., the person legally responsible for taking care of the incompetent individual, can enter into contracts on behalf of the incompetent.

    Legal aliens and married women have the capacity to contract, but the contractual capacity of convicts is limited in some states.

REQUIREMENT OF REALITY (OR GENUINENESS) OF CONSENT: A contract that looks valid may not be.

FRAUD: Fraud is an intentional misrepresentation of a material fact that is made with the intent to induce a person to enter into an unfair contract.

- *Elements of Fraud*: The elements of fraud are: 1) misrepresentation (misstatement) of a fact (does not generally include statements of value, future predictions, or mere opinions); 2) the fact is material (important); 3) the misrepresentation is made with scienter (the person knew or should have known the fact was false); 4) it was made with the intent to deceive; 5) the innocent party reasonably relied; and 6) the innocent party suffered injury or detriment as a result.

- *Silence*: In most states, a party must voluntarily disclose to the other party latent (hidden) defects relating to the subject of the contract. Fiduciaries also have a duty to disclose all material information.

MISREPRESENTATION: Misrepresentation (often called innocent misrepresentation) is a defense that includes the same elements as fraud except for the requirements of scienter and intent to deceive. While a plaintiff may recover punitive damages for fraud, such damages are not available for misrepresentation.

MISTAKE: Mistake is when the parties are wrong about a past or present material fact.

- *Unilateral Mistake*: If only one party is mistaken, the contract will generally be upheld.

- *Bilateral Mistake*: If both parties are mistaken about an essential element of the contract, then either party may elect to rescind the contract.

- *Reformation*: If a court can remedy a mistake, such as correcting a typographical error, then the court will in effect rewrite the contract to reflect the parties' actual intent and then enforce the contract.

DURESS: Duress is coercion that is so extreme that it prevents a party from freely assenting to a contract. Duress may be personal (e.g., threats against a person) or economic (e.g., threat to breach a contract). The party who claims economic duress must show 1) wrongful acts or threats by the defendant, 2) financial distress caused by the wrongful acts or threats, and 3) the absence of any reasonable alternative to the terms presented by the wrongdoer.

UNDUE INFLUENCE: Undue influence is the use of a relationship of trust or confidence to unfairly gain a a contractual advantage. It often involves elderly persons who are the victims of wrongful persuasion.

UNCONSCIONABILITY: A contract may be set aside if one of the parties' used their superior bargaining power to achieve a contract that it commercially shocking or unreasonably oppressive.

STUDY HINTS FOR NRW CASE STUDIES

The following study hints may be helpful when resolving the NRW case studies.

NRW 12.1	➤ You should consider the rules regarding the contractual capacity of a minor. ➤ When advising Lindsay, bear in mind that it is sometimes legal for a person to do ➤ something that is not necessarily ethical for one to do.
NRW 12.2	➤ Consider carefully the rules regarding fraud when advising the NRW principals. ➤ Sometimes it is best to pursue a business plan that represents a balance of both short-term and long-term goals.
NRW 12.3	➤ The answer relates to the rules and remedies pertaining to economic duress. ➤ Bear in mind that damages are the ordinary remedy that may be requested for breach of contract, not specific performance.

MATCHING EXERCISE

Select the term or concept that best matches a definition or statement set forth below. Each term or concept is the best match for only one definition or statement.

Terms and Concepts

a. Contract of adhesion

b. Fiduciary

c. Minor

d. Necessaries

e. Ratification

f. Reformation

g. Scienter *(the person knew the fact was false)*

h. Warranty

Definitions and Statements

__C__ 1. In most states, a person who is under the age of 18.

__d__ 2. Food, shelter, and clothing.

__g f__ 3. Knowledge that a misrepresentation is false.

__a f__ 4. Contract that is not open to negotiation, i.e., a take-it-or-leave-it contract.

__e b__ 5. Manifestation that a person agrees to be bound by a contract that was otherwise voidable.

__b h__ 6. Person who holds a position of trust or confidence, and is expected to act in good faith.

__f x__ 7. Contractual remedy whereby a court corrects an error in how a contract is stated in order to make the contract conform to the parties' original intent.

__h a__ 8. Contractual guarantee relating to the nature or quality of goods.

COMPLETION EXERCISE

Fill in the blanks with the words that most accurately complete each statement.

1. _legal (contractual) capacity_ is the legal ability to be bound by a contract.

2. A _testamentary devise_ is a transfer of property that is made by will.

3. An _ambiguity_ is a statement that is reasonably susceptible to two or meanings.

4. A _unilateral_ mistake occurs when only one party is mistaken about a fact.

5. A _bilateral_ mistake occurs when both parties are mistaken regarding the fact.

TRUE-FALSE EXERCISE

Write **T** if the statement is true, write **F** if the statement is false.

T ~~F~~ 1. An agreement may violate public policy even if the agreement does not require a party to commit a crime, tort, or require a party to violate a statute.

T ~~F~~ 2. Duress that renders a contract voidable may be personal or economic.

~~F~~ 3. A contract may be rescinded for fraud even if the fraud does not cause any injury or detriment to the defrauded party.

F **X** 4. If a single contract requires performance of two services, one legal and one illegal, then the entire contract is always illegal and void.

T 5. The legality of exculpatory clauses are evaluated on a case-by-case basis.

T ~~F~~ 6. The fact that a party agreed to pay more for an item than it is worth does not, standing alone, establish the defense of economic duress.

F **X** 7. Present-day courts still uniformly follow the traditional common law rule that a contracting party does not have a duty to voluntarily disclose facts to the other party.

F **X** 8. The defense of misrepresentation does not require proof of scienter or an intent to deceive.

F **X** 9. If a salesperson says "This is a great car" and the car turns out to be a lemon, then the salesperson has committed fraud.

T **X** 10. In an illegal agreement, courts may allow a less guilty party to recover.

```
APPLICATION OF CONCEPTS
```

MULTIPLE CHOICE QUESTIONS

a ~~b~~ 1. Which contract is voidable due to mistake?
   a. Earl contracted to sell a cabin to Phil. Unknown to either party, the cabin had burned down the previous week.
   b. Subcontractor submitted a bid to Contractor for $15,000. Contractor accepted the bid, not knowing that Subcontractor had made a mistake and the bid should have been $16,000.
   c. Andie purchased stock of ABC, Inc. from Paul. Both Andie and Paul expected the stock to increase in value, but it did not.
   d. a and c.

a *d* 2. Pete and Gail agreed to pay Jason, an employee of Rayon Corp., to steal valuable trade secrets belonging to Rayon. Pete gave Gail his share of the money, and Gail was to give the money to Jason. After Gail had paid Jason the money and received the stolen trade secrets, Pete reconsidered and told Gail that he did not want to participate in this undertaking. Under these facts:
   a. Pete cannot recover his money from Jason because the agreement is illegal and void.
   b. Pete cannot recover his money from Jason because he had a contractual obligation to pay the money to Jason.
   c. Pete can recover his money from Jason because the agreement is illegal, but not void.
   d. Pete can recover his money from Jason because he effectively repented.

CHAPTER 12 - CONTRACTUAL CAPACITY AND REALITY OF CONSENT

C   _a_ 3. Which contract is voidable due to fraud?
      a. During negotiations, Joe falsely stated to Susan that a car offered for sale was a 1965 Mustang when it was actually a 1967 Mustang. Susan bought the car, but she did not rely on Joe's false statement because she knew the car was a 1967 model.
      b. Kelly contracted to sell an antique desk to Pedro. Kelly told Pedro that she believed the desk was worth $3,000. The desk was actually worth $2,500.
      c. Al contracted to sell a vending machine to Maria. Al intentionally lied about the machine's prior earnings, showing Maria false income statements that inflated the machine's earnings for the past three years.
      d. All of the above.

_a_ 4. Nell was hired as president of a soft drink distributor located in Fizz City. When hired, Nell agreed not to compete in the soft drink industry after she quit. Under these facts, Nell's agreement not to compete would be:
      a. Valid if it prohibited Nell from competing in Fizz City for one year after she quit.
      b. Valid if it prohibited Nell from competing anywhere in the state in which Fizz City was located for ten years after she quit.
      c. Not valid, because all agreements not to compete are unenforceable.
      d. a and b.

SHORT ANSWER QUESTIONS

Answer the following questions, briefly explaining the reason for your answer.

1. Slick Larry has a reputation as a pushy car salesperson. Angela went to Larry and, after talking to him for two hours about a particular car, Angela bought the car just so Larry would "leave her alone." Angela has now decided that she doesn't want the car. Can Angela rescind the sales contract because of duress?

_____

_____

2. A state statute requires self-storage facilities to pay an annual fee and to obtain a license to operate. The statute does not protect the public, but is only intended to raise revenue for the government. U-Stor failed to obtain this license. Sally, who stored goods at a U-Stor facility for the past year, now refuses to pay the bill. Sally argues that her storage contract is unenforceable because U-Stor violated the statute in question. Is the contract between U-Stor and Sally void?

_____

_____

3. Ben is a financial planner and his client, Dee, completely relies on him to manage her financial affairs. Ben used his position of trust to convince Dee to buy stock in Star Corp., a speculative company that Ben owns an interest in. Ben knew that this investment was risky, but he wanted to earn the commission and obtain new capital for Star. If Dee loses money on her investment, can she rescind the purchase contract?

_____

_____

4. Bob and Earl are both sophisticated merchants who deal in antique automobiles. Bob contracted to purchase an antique car from Earl for $30,000. The day after the purchase, Earl took the car to an auto show, but the highest offer for the car was only $20,000. Is this contract unconscionable?

_____

_____

CASE PROBLEMS

Answer the following case problems, explaining your answers.

1. Luis agreed to employ Jim as an architect to design an addition to his house. Individuals are legally required to be licensed by the state to be architects, but Jim did not have this license. To assure the competency of architects and to protect the public from unqualified work, this license requires extensive education and successful completion of an exhaustive examination.
   (a) Is the required license a protective (regulatory) license or a revenue-raising license?
   (b) Is the agreement between Luis and Jim valid or void?
   (c) If Jim performs the work but Luis fails to pay him, can Jim collect his fee?

_____

_____

_____

_____

2. Laredo Ranch sold a parcel of land to Dynamic Developers. Prior to the sale, the parties retained Lawrence to do a survey and determine how many acres were in the parcel. Lawrence informed the parties that the parcel contained 100 acres. Unknown to the parties, the parcel actually contained only 75 acres. Laredo and Dynamic computed the contract price based on 100 acres.
   (a) Can Dynamic rescind this contract based on mistake?
   (b) What elements must Dynamic prove to establish this defense?

_____

_____

_____

_____

CHAPTER 13

Legality of Subject Matter and Proper Form of Contracts

CHAPTER REVIEW

THE REQUIREMENTS OF LEGALITY OF SUBJECT MATTER AND PROPER FORM: A valid contract requires that the subject matter of an agreement and its objectives be legal and not violate public policy. Certain types of contracts must also be evidenced by an appropriate writing in order to be enforceable in court.

MALA IN SE AND MALA PROHIBITA: In most states, a contract that violates a statute is void whether the prohibited act is evil in itself (*mala in se*), which includes all crimes and torts, or simply prohibited by a statute (*mala prohibita*). Some courts, however, do not invalidate a contract if it only violates a statute that does not further a strong public policy.

AGREEMENTS VIOLATIVE OF STATUTES: Important types of conduct prohibited by statute include:

- *Price Fixing Agreements*: Agreements between competitors to fix prices are illegal and void.

- *Performances of Services Without a License*: An agreement is unenforceable if it requires violation of a regulatory-license statute, but it is enforceable if it only violates a revenue-license statute.

- *Sunday Closing Laws*: These laws forbid the formation or performance of contracts on Sunday.

- *Wagering Statutes*: Wagering is paying consideration in the hope of winning a prize by chance.

- *Usury Statutes*: These statutes set a limit on interest rates. Interest that is charged in excess of the lawful limit cannot be collected in most states. Generally legal, however, are both acceleration clauses, i.e., contractual terms that advance the date for payment on the occurrence of certain events or a party breaches a contractual duty, and prepayment clauses, i.e., contractual terms that allow a debtor to pay a debt before it is due without penalty.

AGREEMENTS VIOLATIVE OF PUBLIC POLICY: A court may hold that a contract is void if it violates an important public interest, meaning a fundamental value or interest of society.

- *Covenants not to Compete*: A covenant not to compete is an individual's promise not to compete against another party. In general, a covenant not to compete is legal if: 1) it is made as part of or in connection with a contract for the sale of a business or an employment contract; and 2) it restricts competition for only a reasonable time and for only a reasonable geographic area.

- *Exculpatory Clauses*: An exculpatory clause is a contract term that eliminates a party's liability for certain wrongs that he or she may commit. The legality of these clauses are evaluated on a case-by-case basis.
    A contract of adhesion is a contract in which the terms are not open to negotiation, i.e., a "take-it-or-leave-it" contract. Courts may invalidate contracts of adhesion on the basis of illegality if the terms are unreasonably favorable to the dominant party.

EXCEPTIONS: UPHOLDING ILLEGAL AGREEMENTS: In some situations, a court may enforce an illegal agreement if the person suing has already performed his or her contractual obligations. This may occur in the following situations:

- *Parties not* **in Pari Delicto**: If one party is less guilty than the other, i.e., the party is not *in pari delicto*) then that party may recover under the contract if doing so will further the public interest.

- *Repentance*: If a party tries to undo or rescind an illegal agreement, then the law may allow that party to recover what has already been given under the agreement.

- *Partial Illegality*: If a contract involves both legal and illegal undertakings and these portions of the contract can be fairly separated, then a court may enforce the legal part and void the illegal part.

THE IMPORTANCE OF FORM: Because of the potential for fraud, the law places certain requirements on the form of contracts and certain limitations on their interpretation.

STATUTE OF FRAUDS: Every state has adopted the Statute of Frauds, which requires certain contracts to be evidenced by a signed writing in order to be enforced in court.

- *Types of Contracts Covered*: The Statute of Frauds requires the following categories of contracts to be evidenced by a sufficient writing in order to be enforceable:

  1) Contracts to Answer for the Debt of Another If the Person So Defaults: Includes contracts of guarantee or suretyship.

  2) Contracts for Interests in Land: Includes land sale contracts, mortgages, easements, and (most) real estate leases, sales contracts for standing timber or buildings attached to the land.

  3) Contracts Not to Be Performed Within One Year of the Date of Their Making: Measure the one-year period starting from the date the contract is made, not from the date the work is to actually begin.

  4) Promises of Executors and Administrators of Estates

  5) Contracts Made in Consideration of Marriage

  6) Contracts for the Sale of Goods priced at $500 or More, and Contracts for the Lease of Goods for $1,000 or More: Despite this rule, an oral sales contract for $500 or more is enforceable *to the extent* that: (a) the party who refuses to perform admits in judicial proceedings that the contract was made; (b) the goods are delivered by the seller and accepted by the buyer; or (c) the buyer pays the contract price and payment is accepted by the seller.

- *Writing*: The writing required to satisfy the Statute of Frauds need not be a complete contract, but under the common law it must identify: 1) the parties to the agreement; 2) the subject matter of the agreement; and 3) all material terms and conditions.

- *Signature*: The writing need not be signed by both parties, only by the party who opposes enforcement of the contract. A signature is anything intended to be a signature, including stamped signatures and letterheads.

PAROL EVIDENCE RULE: The parol evidence rule is a rule of substantive law that prohibits a party from using evidence of prior statements or writings to add to or change the terms of a final and complete written contract.

EXCEPTIONS TO THE PAROL EVIDENCE RULE: Exceptions to the parol evidence rule include the following

- ■ *Partially Integrated Contracts*: If a contract is partially integrated (i.e., it is the final statement of only part of the contract), evidence of prior statements or writings may be used to establish terms that are not stated in the writing.

- ■ *Mistake, Fraud, and Other "Reality-of-Consent" Situations*: Evidence that shows mistake, fraud, duress, and lack of consideration is permitted.

- ■ *Ambiguities and Conditions Precedent*: Parol evidence may be used to explain the meaning of ambiguous terms. Evidence is also admissible to show that a contract was not to become binding until a certain event occurred (i.e., obligations were subject to a condition precedent).

- ■ *Uniform Commercial Code*: UCC §§ 2-202 and 2-208 allow evidence a course of performance, course of dealing, or usage of trade in order to explain contract terms even if the contract is not ambiguous. Also, the UCC allows evidence of additional consistent terms unless a court finds that the parties to a contract intended the writing to be the final and exclusive statement of the agreement.

STUDY HINTS FOR NRW CASE STUDIES

The following study hints may be helpful when resolving the NRW case studies.

NRW 13.1	➤ You should review the state's usury statutes to determine if this interest rate is legal.
	➤ When preparing to answer this question, bear in mind that many states have different maximum rates of interest for different types of debtors, such as individuals versus corporations.
NRW 13.2	➤ The NRW principals should carefully review their state's laws regarding covenants not to compete.
	➤ Whether employees sign covenants not to compete is a matter to be negotiated between the company and the employees.
NRW 13.3	➤ The NRW principals should consider whether it is good business judgment to allow a company employee to read confidential business communications.
	➤ The NRW principals should explore the possibility of remotely accessing their own electronic mail.
	➤ An issue not to be overlooked are the possible privacy rights of other employees who may be violated by allowing another employee to have access to their e-mail.

MATCHING EXERCISE

Select the term or concept that best matches a definition or statement set forth below. Each term or concept is the best match for only one definition or statement.

Terms and Concepts

a. Acceleration clause
b. Administrator
c. Affirmative defense
d. Ambiguity
e. Chattel
f. Conditional sales contract
g. Condition precedent
h. Contract of adhesion
i. Easement

j. Exculpatory clause
k. Fiduciary
l. Merchant
m. Monopoly
n. Mortgage
o. Novation
p. Oligopoly
q. Parol evidence
r. Parol evidence rule

s. Partially-integrated contract
t. Prepayment clause
u. Reformation
v. Scienter
w. Statute of Frauds
x. Time-price differential sales contract
y. Tortious
z. Warranty

Definitions and Statements

___ 1. Economic condition when one firm controls an entire market.
___ 2. Economic condition when a small number of firms dominate a market.
___ 3. Relating to private wrongs or injuries.
___ 4. Contract with different prices, one price for immediate payment and another for later payment.
___ 5. Evidence of oral statements.
___ 6. Contractual clause that allows a creditor to advance the date that a debtor must pay.
___ 7. Contract that is not open to negotiation, i.e., a take-it-or-leave-it contract.
___ 8. Contractual remedy whereby a court corrects an error in how a contract is stated in order to make the contract conform to the parties' original intent.
___ 9. Type of personal property.
___ 10. Contract that is the final statement of only a portion of the parties' agreement.
___ 11. Uncertainty about the meaning of a contractual term.
___ 12. Sales contract in which the transfer of title is subject to a condition.
___ 13. Person who holds a position of trust or confidence, and is expected to act in good faith.
___ 14. Knowledge that a misrepresentation is false.
___ 15. Contractual guarantee relating to the nature or quality of goods.
___ 16. Defense to a cause of action that the defendant must assert.
___ 17. Law that requires certain contracts to be evidenced by a writing to be enforceable.
___ 18. Contractual clause that allows a debtor to pay a debt before it is due.
___ 19. Person who manages a decedent's estate.
___ 20. Law that prohibits prior evidence from being used to alter a final, complete written contract.
___ 21. Substitution of a new contract in place of a preexisting one.
___ 22. Contractual clause that limits the potential liability of a party.
___ 23. Limited right to use the land of another.
___ 24. Event or action that must occur before a party has a legal obligation to act.
___ 25. Conditional transfer of real property to secure payment of a debt.
___ 26. Person who regularly deals in certain kinds of goods.

COMPLETION EXERCISE

Fill in the blanks with the words that most accurately complete each statement.

1. A contract to steal the property of another is an example of a bargain that is _mala_ _in_ _se_ and, therefore, such a bargain is always illegal and void.

2. A _price_ - _fixing_ _agreement_ is an agreement between competitors to charge certain prices for their goods or services.

3. _usury_ is the lending of money for an interest rate that exceeds the legal rate of interest.

4. Parol evidence is admissible to show that certain contractual defenses may exist, such as _undue influence, fraud,_ and _others, mistake or lack of consideration_

5. The _general_ _usage_ standard gives words the meaning that would be given by a reasonable person who was acquainted with the circumstances surrounding the transaction in question.

6. Identify six types of contracts that must be in writing.

   a. _Contract to answer for the debt of another if the person so defaults_

   b. _Contract for interests in land_

   c. _contract not to be performed within one year of the date of their making_

   d. _promises of executors & administrators of estates_

   e. _contracts made in consideration of marriage_

   f. _Contract for the sale of good price at $500 or more & contract for the lease of good for $000 or more_

TRUE-FALSE EXERCISE

Write **T** if the statement is true, write **F** if the statement is false.

_T / F_ 1. An agreement may violate public policy even if the agreement does not require a party to commit a crime, tort, or require a party to violate a statute.

_F_ 2. All oral contracts are unenforceable.

_F_ 3. The parol evidence rule requires all contracts to be evidenced by a writing to be enforceable.

_F_ 4. If a single contract requires performance of two services, one legal and one illegal, then the entire contract is always illegal and void.

_T_ 5. An executor's promise to personally pay the debts of an estate must be evidenced by a writing to be legally enforceable even if the executor intended to be personally liable.

_F_ 6. The Statute of Frauds requires that writings be signed by all contracting parties.

_T_ 7. Mechanic agreed to install "ABS" brakes on Fred's car. In this case, Mechanic must install brakes that would comply with the technical meaning for "ABS" brakes. Installing brakes that would comply with the ordinary meaning for normal car brakes would not be sufficient.

_T_ 8. The Statute of Frauds (at common law) requires a writing to state all material contract terms.

_F_ 9. Only formal writings signed by all parties can satisfy the Statute of Frauds.

_T_ 10. In an illegal agreement, courts may allow a less guilty party to recover.

APPLICATION OF CONCEPTS

MULTIPLE CHOICE QUESTIONS

a 1. Pete and Gail agreed to pay Jason, an employee of Rayon Corp., to steal valuable trade secrets belonging to Rayon. Pete gave Gail his share of the money, and Gail was to give the money to Jason. After Gail paid Jason the money and received the stolen trade secrets, Pete reconsidered and told Gail that he did not want to participate in this undertaking. Under these facts:
   a. Pete cannot recover his money from Jason because the agreement is illegal and void.
   b. Pete cannot recover his money from Jason because he had a contractual duty to pay him.
   c. Pete can recover his money from Jason because the agreement is illegal, but not void.
   d. Pete can recover his money from Jason because he effectively repented.

a 2. Nell was hired as president of a soft drink distributor in Fizz City. When hired, Nell agreed not to compete in the soft drink industry after she quit. Nell's agreement not to compete would be:
   a. Valid if it prohibited Nell from competing in Fizz City for one year after she quit.
   b. Valid if it prohibited Nell from competing anywhere in the state in which Fizz City was located for ten years after she quit.
   c. Not valid, because all agreements not to compete are unenforceable.
   d. a and b.

d 3. Which of the following oral contracts is unenforceable?
   a. Bubba orally contracts with Madison to lease Madison's apartment for three years.
   b. Lewis orally contracts to grant High Finance, Inc. a mortgage on Lewis' home.
   c. Linda orally contracts to sell a parcel of land to Andy.
   d. All of the above.

b *c* 4. Paul orally contracts to sell land to Angela. Angela takes possession of the land, and Angela makes valuable improvements, the value of which is hard to determine. This contract is:
   a. Enforceable because the Statute of Frauds does not apply to land sale contracts.
   b. Enforceable due to Angela's part performance.
   c. Voidable and cannot be enforced because the contract violates the Statute of Frauds.
   d. Void and cannot be enforced because the contract violates the Statute of Frauds.

d 5. Which oral contract violates the Statute of Frauds?
   a. Frank and Joe make an oral contract whereby Frank promises to make Joe the general manager of a company in exchange for Joe's promise to marry Frank's daughter.
   b. Tim orally contracts to buy a TV for $400.
   c. Ursula orally contracts to buy a car for $10,000.
   d. a and c.

a *c* 6. On March 1, Julia orally contracted to work for Moose's Diner from April 1 through March 30 of the following year. Under these facts:
   a. The contract violates the Statute of Frauds because it cannot be performed within one year from the date the contract was made.
   b. The contract violates the Statute of Frauds because all service contracts must be written.
   c. The contract does not violate the Statute of Frauds because it can be performed within one year from when the work begins.
   d. The contract does not violate the Statute of Frauds because it may be terminated at any time due to a party's breach.

SHORT ANSWER QUESTIONS

Answer the following questions, briefly explaining the reason for your answer.

1. A state statute requires self-storage facilities to pay an annual fee and to obtain a license to operate. The statute does not protect the public, but is only intended to raise revenue for the government. U-Stor failed to obtain this license. Sally, who stored goods at a U-Stor facility for the past year, now refuses to pay the bill. Sally argues that her storage contract is unenforceable because U-Stor violated the statute in question. Is the contract between U-Stor and Sally void?

_____

_____

2. Ben is a financial planner and his client, Dee, completely relies on him to manage her financial affairs. Ben used his position of trust to convince Dee to buy stock in Star Corp., a speculative company that Ben owns an interest in. Ben knew that this investment was risky, but he wanted to earn the commission and obtain new capital for Star. If Dee loses money on her investment, can she rescind the purchase contract?

_____

_____

3. Bob orally told his good friend and employee, Steve, "You have a job at my company for the rest of your life." Steve is 26 years old. The next month, Bob fired Steve and hired someone more qualified. Does this contract violate the Statute of Frauds?

_____

_____

4. The Top Secret Research Center (TSRC) contracted to hire Ivan as a scientist. The contract stated that TSRC did not have a duty to hire Ivan unless he first passed a security check. Ivan failed the security check and was not hired by TSRC. Can Ivan sue TSRC for breach of contract?

_____

_____

5. Anna and Bob, both merchants, orally agreed that Anna would sell Bob's Vegetable Store 600 pounds of carrots per week. Anna sent Bob the following letter: "This confirms my sale to you of 600 lbs. of grade A carrots at $1.00/lb., delivery every Monday /s/ Anna." Ten days went by and Bob did not reply. Discuss whether this contract is enforceable or not?

_____

_____

CASE PROBLEMS

Answer the following case problems, explaining your answers.

1. Luis agreed to employ Jim as an architect to design an addition to his house. Individuals are legally required to be licensed by the state to be architects, but Jim did not have this license. To assure the competency of architects and to protect the public from unqualified work, this license requires extensive education and successful completion of an exhaustive examination. (a) Is the required license a protective (regulatory) license or a revenue-raising license? (b) Is the agreement between Luis and Jim valid or void? (c) If Jim performs the work but Luis fails to pay him, can Jim collect his fee?

_____

_____

_____

_____

2. Jim advertised a parcel of land for sale, and Edna orally made a generous cash purchase offer, which Jim orally accepted. Eager to seal the deal, Jim grabbed a piece of paper that had his letterhead on it and wrote down his name, Edna's name, a description of the land, and the cash purchase price. Edna took this paper with her as she left. After Edna left, Jim received a better offer, and he told Edna that he would not sell the land to her. (a) Does the contract between Jim and Edna come within the Statute of Frauds? (b) If so, does the piece of paper satisfy the requirements of the Statute of Frauds? (c) Does Edna have an enforceable contract against Jim?

_____

_____

_____

_____

3. Sally offered to sell Ralph her computer. When Ralph saw the computer, it had a color monitor. Sally and Ralph entered into a written contract that stated "Sally sells to Ralph her computer system for $1,000," with no other description of the computer. The contract also contained a merger clause and was signed by both parties. When the computer arrived, it did not come with the monitor. Sally says that she did not intend the "computer system" to include the monitor, whereas Ralph intended otherwise. (a) Identify the nature of this contract in terms of its completeness. (b) If a lawsuit arises regarding this transaction, could Ralph use parol evidence to prove the meaning of the term "computer system"? (c) What rules of interpretation may a court use to interpret this term?

_____

_____

_____

_____

CHAPTER 14

Contract Interpretation and the Rights of Third Persons

CHAPTER REVIEW

JUDICIAL INTERPRETATION: Courts use the objective or reasonable person approach when interpreting contracts. In other words, the courts interpret a contract from the perspective that a reasonable person would have in the same situation.

- *Standards*: Typically, courts use the "general usage" standard to decide the meaning of terms, that is, the courts ascribe the meaning that a reasonable person would give them. Sometimes, a court may use the standard of "limited usage," that is ascribing the meaning given to a word in a particular locale.

- *Rules of Interpretation*: Four of the most important rules of interpretation state that courts should: 1) attempt to give affect to the indicated intentions of the parties; 2) look at the contract as a whole to find the parties' intent; 3) give ordinary words their ordinary meaning and technical words their technical meaning unless the situation suggests otherwise; 4) give effect to handwritten words over typed words and typed words over printed ones when there is a conflict (printed words are words preprinted on a form contract; and 5) look at all of the circumstances of a transaction when interpreting it (subject, however, to the limits imposed by the parol evidence rule).

- *Conduct and Usage of Trade*: Courts will look at past dealings between the parties to help interpret an agreement. The UCC also allows evidence of usage of trade to aid in interpreting a contract.

PAROL EVIDENCE RULE: The parol evidence rule is a rule of substantive law that prohibits a party from using evidence of prior statements or writings to add to or change the terms of a final and complete written contract.

- *Total Integration*: Courts assume that a writing supersedes any terms discussed during negotiations.

- *Partial Integration*: If a writing is incomplete, courts will allow the parties to add terms as long as the additional terms do not contradict the written terms.

- *Rules of Integration*: If a writing looks formal and complete, courts will more likely find that the writing is totally integrated. If a writing is not integrated, some courts use the reasonable expectations standard to fill in missing terms. Some courts use the limited usage standard, which looks to local custom and trade usage, to fill in missing terms.

ADDITION OF THIRD PARTIES TO THE CONTRACT: As a general rule, a contract only affects the rights of the two (or more) parties who enter into the contract. One exception to this rule permits a third-party beneficiary to enforce a contract that others have made for his or her benefit.

THIRD-PARTY BENEFICIARY CONTRACTS: In a third-party beneficiary contract, the contracting parties typically agree to perform an act that will directly or indirectly benefit a third person, known as a beneficiary. The beneficiary may be an incidental or intended beneficiary. How the third party is classified determines what rights, if any, that he or she has to enforce the third-party beneficiary contract.

- *An Incidental Beneficiary*: An incidental beneficiary is one who may receive a benefit merely by accident or chance, not because one or both of the parties intended to directly benefit the beneficiary. An incidental beneficiary has no right to enforce a contract.

- *An Intended Beneficiary*: An intended beneficiary is a third party whom one or both of the contracting parties *clearly* intended to benefit. An intended beneficiary has the same (but no greater) right to enforce the contract as does the original contracting party who intended to benefit the beneficiary. A common example of an intended beneficiary is the beneficiary under a life insurance policy.

- *A Donee Beneficiary*: A donee beneficiary is an intended beneficiary whose benefit is intended as a gift from one of the contracting parties. In some states, the donee's rights are vested (cannot be terminated) once the contract is made; in other states the donee's rights vest only if the donee has accepted the contract, either expressly or by reliance.

- *A Creditor Beneficiary*: A creditor beneficiary is an intended beneficiary whose benefit is intended as payment of a debt that is owed by one of the contracting parties to the beneficiary.

- *Analysis of Third-Party Beneficiary Contracts*: When deciding whether a third party is an intended beneficiary of a contract between others, ask yourself three questions: 1) Did the contract benefit the third party from the beginning or was the benefit bestowed upon the third party later? 2) Was the benefit clearly intended by one or both contracting parties or was it merely accidental? 3) Was the benefit a gift from one of the contracting parties or did it satisfy an obligation owed to the third party?

DEFINING ASSIGNMENTS AND DELEGATIONS: If a third party is granted rights or duties under a contract after the contract was created, then the third party is not a beneficiary of the contract. Instead, there may have been either an assignment of rights to the third party or a delegation of duties to the third party.

ASSIGNMENTS: An assignment is the transfer of a contractual right to another. The person transferring the right is the assignor, and the party receiving the right is the assignee.

- *Formalities Required for Assignments*: An assignor must indicate a present intent to vest a right in another person. The assignment must be in writing if the contract in question was required to be in writing. Consideration is not required to make a valid assignment.

- *Notice of the Assignment*: Notice of assignment is not required. If the person obligated to perform the assigned right (the promisor) is given notice of the assignment but nonetheless delivers performance to the assignor, then the promisor remains obligated perform for the benefit of the assignee. If one right is assigned more than once to different assignees, courts may use one of two theories to determine the assignees' priority to the assigned right: 1) the American Rule, which generally gives priority to the first person to whom an assignment was made; and 2) the English Rule, which generally gives priority to the first assignee to give notice to the promisor. Two variations of the American Rule are the New York and Massachusetts rules.

- *Assignable Rights*: Courts generally favor and will enforce assignments. However, an assignment is not permitted if the assignment will significantly: 1) change the promisor's duty; 2) impair or reduce the value of a return performance; or 3) increase the burden or risk of performance.

    Certain types of assignments are limited by state law. Numerous states forbid or limit the assignment of wages. Some states are starting to question the validity of assignments of post-loss insurance payments, i.e., the obligations of insurance companies to pay after a covered loss has occurred.

■ ***Contract Clauses Restricting Assignments***: Courts interpret these clauses narrowly and many courts allow assignments despite these clauses. However, strong contractual language prohibiting assignments, such as "all assignments shall be null and void," are typically enforced, thereby barring any assignment of rights.

■ ***Warranties Implied by the Assignor***: An assignor warrants to the assignee that: 1) an assigned right is valid and actually exists; 2) the right is not subject to any defenses or limitations that are not stated or apparent; and 3) the assignor will not interfere with the assignee's rights.

■ ***Rights Created by the Assignment***: An assignee receives the same rights that the assignor possessed.

■ ***Waiver of Defenses Clause***: In a waiver of defense clause, the promisor agrees not to assert any defenses against an assignee that the promisor may have had against the assignor. The validity of these clauses depends on the nature of the transaction and the parties, and what law governs the transaction.

DELEGATIONS: In a delegation, the promisor (delegator) appoints a new party (delegatee) to perform one or more of the delegator's contractual obligations. A delegation is not valid unless the delegatee assumes the delegated obligations.

In general, the delegator remains liable for the proper performance of the delegated obligation. Whether the delegatee can be held liable generally depends on whether the delegatee contractually agreed to perform the obligation (delegatee may be liable) or agreed to perform the obligation as a favor or gift for the delegator (delegatee is not liable).

UNIFORM COMMERCIAL CODE PROVISIONS: UCC § 2-210 covers assignments and delegations for contracts involving sales of goods.

STUDY HINTS FOR NRW CASE STUDIES

The following study hints may be helpful when resolving the NRW case studies.

NRW 14.1	➤ First, ask yourself the three questions used for analyzing third-party beneficiary contracts.
	➤ You should then determine whether NRW is an intended beneficiary of the contract between Salma Systems and Vicente's Trucking, and what rights, if any, it may have to enforce the contract against Vicente's.
	➤ Also, review material in other parts of the textbook regarding a common carrier's (shipper's) obligations for the care of goods during shipment and the issue of when risk of loss passes from a seller to a buyer.
NRW 14.2	➤ When deciding how to advise NRW, you should consider all of the issues surrounding assignments, paying particular attention to the rights that NRW (as assignee) would have and the defenses that obligors could assert against NRW.
NRW 14.3	➤ You should review the discussion of delegations, especially the portions relating to the delegator's continuing liability and the duties of delegatees, if any.

REVIEW OF KEY TERMS AND CONCEPTS

MATCHING EXERCISE

Select the term or concept that best matches a definition or statement set forth below. Each term or concept is the best match for only one definition or statement.

Terms and Concepts

a. Assignee

b. Assignment

c. Assignor

d. Creditor beneficiary

e. Delegation

f. Donee beneficiary

g. Extinguish

h. Incidental beneficiary

i. Insured

j. Mortgage insurance

k. Post-loss duty

l. Vested interest

Definitions and Statements

___k___ 1. Obligation of an insurance company after a loss.

___c___ 2. Party who transfers a contractual right to another.

___l___ 3. Legal right that is fixed and cannot be arbitrarily taken away by another.

___i___ 4. Party who is covered under a policy of insurance.

___e___ 5. Transfer of a contractual obligation to a third party.

___d___ 6. Beneficiary who is intended to receive a contract benefit as satisfaction of an obligation owed by one of the contracting parties.

___h___ 7. Beneficiary who may by chance receive a benefit under a contract between others.

___g___ 8. To destroy or terminate something.

___f___ 9. Beneficiary who is intended to receive a contract benefit as a gift from one of the contracting parties.

___b___ 10. Transfer of a contractual right to another.

___j___ 11. Insurance that will pay a mortgage if the mortgagor dies.

___a___ 12. Party to whom a contractual right is transferred.

COMPLETION EXERCISE

Fill in the blanks with the words that most accurately complete each statement.

1. The presence or absence of an ___intent___ to directly benefit a third party under a contract is a primary factor in deciding whether the third party is an intended or incidental beneficiary under the contract.

2. Under the ___first___-___in___-___time___ approach, the first assignee to whom an assignment is made receives all assigned rights.

3. A ___Waive___ ___of___ ___defence___ clause attempts to shield an assignee from defenses that the promisor may assert in order to avoid performance of an obligation.

4. When assigning rights, an assignor creates three implied ___warranties___.

5. Identify three situations when an assignment may be prohibited:

   a. ___materially change the duty of promisor___.

   b. ___materially impair the change of return performance___

   c. ___materially budden increase the or risk to the other party___

6. An ___full___ ___integrated___ contract is one that represents the parties' entire, final agreement.

7. A ___partially___ ___integrated___ contract is one that represents only a portion of the parties' final agreement.

8. The ___general___ ___usage___ standard gives words the meaning that would be given by a reasonable person who was acquainted with the circumstances surrounding the transaction in question.

TRUE-FALSE EXERCISE

Write **T** if the statement is true, write **F** if the statement is false.

_F_ __T__ 1. Courts disfavor both assignments and delegations.

_F_ __T__ 2. An assignment of rights under a contract automatically terminates the assignor's duty to perform any duties under the contract.

__F__ 3. An incidental beneficiary may sue a contracting party in order to compel performance of the contract.

__T__ 4. An assignment must be in writing if the original contract was required to be in writing.

__F__ 5. An assignment is invalid unless the assignor notifies the promisor of the assignment.

__T__ 6. In general, a delegator remains liable for the proper performance of a delegated task.

__T__ 7. A third party beneficiary can enforce a contract only in accordance with the terms of the contract.

__T__ 8. If a party is legally entitled to assign a contract right, then the party may assign this right without first obtaining the consent of the other contracting party.

__T__ 9. A party cannot assign a right to be insured because the assignment may significantly increase the risk or burden to the insurer.

__F__ 10. An assignment is not valid unless consideration was paid by the assignee to the assignor.

agree & acceptance

MULTIPLE CHOICE QUESTIONS

a 1. Ace Imports sold a car to Trent on credit for $30,000. Ace assigned to C&C Credit all of Ace's right to payment under its contract with Trent. Trent was not informed about the assignment and he never consented to it. Trent later paid the entire $30,000 to Ace. Under these facts:
   a. Trent is obligated to pay nothing to C&C Credit because he was never informed about the assignment and he in good faith paid Ace.
   b. Trent is obligated to pay nothing to C&C Credit because he never consented to the assignment.
   c. Trent is obligated to pay $30,000 to C&C Credit.
   d. a and b.

b *a* 2. In which case is a third party entitled to enforce the contract in question?
   a. Jake lent Moe $2,000 to pay bills. The loan contract states that the parties do not intend for any of Moe's creditors to be third-party beneficiaries. Third party is one of Moe's creditors.
   b. Lewis contracted with West Life Insurance to pay Lewis' wife $20,000 on Lewis' death.
   c. Head Ache is a rock group that contracted to perform at City Coliseum. Ned's Hot Dog Stand, located near the coliseum, will benefit from sales to persons going to this concert.
   d. b and c.

a 3. Leo agreed to paint a portrait of Mona. Leo has a very talented student, Angelo, who wants to paint his first portrait. Will a court allow Leo to delegate the work to Angelo?
   a. No, because this is a personal service contract.
   b. No, because delegations are illegal.
   c. Yes, if Angelo is talented.
   d. Yes, because courts favor delegations.

d 4. Brett owed Fred $1,000. Fred orally told Brett and Alicia: "I transfer to Alicia my right to collect $1,000; Brett, pay Alicia the $1,000." Alicia did not give Brett anything in return. Assume no special statutes apply to this assignment. Under these facts, the assignment is:
   a. Invalid because Fred did not use the word assign.
   b. Invalid because the assignment is not in writing.
   c. Invalid because Alicia did not give consideration for the assignment.
   d. Valid.

SHORT ANSWER QUESTIONS

Answer the following questions, briefly explaining the reason for your answer.

1. Steve told a customer who owed him money to make all payments to Last Bank, a bank to whom Steve was indebted. Last Bank knew about this arrangement and verbally accepted it. If Steve changes his mind about this arrangement, does he have the legal right to unilaterally decide that payments should once again be paid to himself and not to Last Bank?

_____

_____

2. Brent Auto Trades (BAT) sold Laurie a personal car on credit. The contract contained a standard waiver of defense clause, whereby Laurie agreed not to assert any defenses against an assignee of the contract. BAT assigned its rights under the contract to Third Bank. As it turns out, the car is defective and Laurie does not want to pay. Was the assignment to Third Bank valid? Can Laurie assert her defense of breach of contract against Last Bank in order to avoid paying for the car?

_____

_____

3. Mike is a pilot for Air Freight, Inc. Air Freight assigned Mike's service contract to Thailand Air Freight. This assignment requires Mike and his family to move to Thailand. It also requires Mike to fly in unfamiliar regions, under somewhat risky flying conditions. Is this assignment valid?

_____

_____

4. Jasper contracted to build a storage shed for Juan. The contract price is $3,000. Jasper owes Rosa $3,000, and the contract states that Juan is to pay the $3,000 directly to Rosa in order to satisfy this debt. Jasper built the shed, but failed to install shelving worth $300. How much, if any, must Juan pay to Rosa?

_____

_____

5. Al's Butcher Shop has a long-term contract with Snortin' Pig Ranch to buy its "pork chops" from Snortin'. For the past year, Snortin' has always sent and Al has accepted center-cut pork chops. In the latest shipment under this contract, Snortin' sent loin-cut pork chops, an inferior type of pork chop. If Al sues Snortin' for breach of contract, what evidence can Al use to interpret the meaning of "pork chops"?

_____

_____

CASE PROBLEMS

Answer the following case problems, explaining your answers.

1. The City of Hope contracted with Virgil's Construction to build a parking garage on 23rd Street, a run-down area. Businesses on 23rd Street, including Harry's Cafe, may benefit from the construction of this garage. The city council approved the project in order to revitalize and stimulate economic growth in this part of town. (a) Is Harry's a beneficiary under this contract and, if so, what type of beneficiary is it? (b) If Virgil's Construction fails to properly build the garage, can Harry's sue to enforce the contract against Virgil's?

_____

_____

_____

_____

2. JobFinders helps recent college graduates find jobs. JobFinders contracted with Trina to help her locate a job. As part of its obligation, JobFinders was to design a resume and provide her with 50 copies of it. JobFinders subcontracted out the typing of all resumes, including Trina's resume. The subcontractor made numerous errors in typing Trina's resume. (a) The typing subcontract is what type of third-party transaction? (b) Was JobFinders legally entitled to subcontract the typing of Trina's resume without first obtaining her permission? (c) Is JobFinders liable to Trina for the improperly typed resumes?

_____

_____

_____

_____

CHAPTER 15

Contractual Discharge and Remedies

TERMINATION OF THE CONTRACT: A contract may be discharged (terminated) in four ways: 1) discharge by performance; 2) discharge by agreement of the parties; 3) discharge by operation of law; or 4) discharge by nonperformance.

DISCHARGE BY PERFORMANCE: A duty may be discharged by complete or substantial performance.

■ *Complete Performance*: A contract is discharged by the exact performance (or tender, meaning offer, of performance) of their contractual duties.

■ *Substantial Performance*: Substantial performance means that a party has in good faith fully performed a duty with the exception of minor, unintentional errors. In most cases, parties may discharge their contractual obligations by substantial performance so long as the errors were not material and were unintentional.

DISCHARGE BY AGREEMENT OF THE PARTIES: Parties may agree to discharge contractual obligations.

■ *Release*: A release discharges a legal claim that one party has against another. A release generally requires: 1) a writing; 2) consideration; and 3) an immediate relinquishment of the claim.

■ *Rescission*: A contract of rescission is a mutual termination of another contract.

■ *Accord and Satisfaction*: An accord is an agreement to accept a substituted performance as fulfillment of an existing duty. A satisfaction is performance of the accord. The original duty is not discharged until the satisfaction is completed.

■ *Novation*: In a novation, a new party is substituted for one of the original parties.

DISCHARGE BY OPERATION OF LAW: Bankruptcy law and statutes of limitations are examples of laws that may discharge contractual obligations.

DISCHARGE BY NONPERFORMANCE: Discharge by nonperformance may occur in the following situations:

■ *Impossibility*: The doctrine of impossibility excuses a party from a contractual duty if, after the contract is made, performance of the duty is made impossible because of an unforeseeable event. The event must be such that performance is objectively impossible, meaning no one can perform the contract. The fact that a particular contracting party cannot personally person is not sufficient.

■ *Commercial Frustration*: Commercial frustration discharges a party if an unforeseen event destroys the value of and purpose for a contract. However, the occurrence of foreseeable events and the fact that a contract is simply made less profitable than expected do not excuse performance.

■ *Actual Breach*: The complete (actual) breach of a contract by one party generally discharges the other party's obligation to perform.

■ *Anticipatory Breach*: An anticipatory breach of contract is: 1) a definite, unqualified refusal to perform contractual duties 2) that is made prior to the time that performance is required.

■ *Conditions*: A condition is an event that may create or discharge a contractual duty to perform. Conditions may be express or they may be implied from the nature of the contract or implied by law. Conditions are classified as conditions precedent, concurrent conditions, or conditions subsequent.

TYPES OF REMEDIES: The two types of contractual remedies are legal (damages) and equitable. The purpose of contractual remedies is to make a contracting party whole if the other party breaches.

DAMAGES: In a breach of contract, the injured parties are entitled to recover damages to compensate them for their foreseeable financial losses.

- *Compensatory Damages*: Compensatory damages place the injured party in the same economic position as if the contract had been performed.

- *Consequential Damages*: Losses that are suffered because of the parties' particular needs or circumstances are called consequential (special) damages. Consequential damages may be recovered only if they were reasonably foreseeable by the breaching party.

- *Duty to Mitigate*: An injured party has a duty to mitigate (minimize) its losses.

- *Punitive Damages*: Punitive damages cannot be recovered for a typical breach of contract. In extreme cases, an excessive punitive damages award may be unconstitutional. While uncommon, some statutes now permit the imposition of punitive damages in contractual situations, such as treble damages (i.e., three times the damages suffered as a result of the injury) under federal antitrust laws.

- *Liquidated Damages*: A contract may validly state the amount of liquidated damages to be paid if a party breaches if: 1) the amount is reasonable and 2) it is difficult to foresee the amount of damages.

- *Nominal Damages*: Nominal damages are a token amount given for a minor breach.

EQUITABLE REMEDIES: Equitable remedies may be awarded when money damages are inadequate. Equitable remedies include:

- *Rescission and Restitution*: Rescission means termination of a contract. Restitution means the return of goods, money, and property received under a contract (or their value if they cannot be returned).

- *Specific Performance*: Specific performance is a court order that requires contracting parties to perform their contract.

- *Quasi Contract/Reformation/Injunction*

LIMITATIONS ON REMEDIES: A contract may limit damages. Under UCC § 2-719, a contract may not provide for an exclusive remedy if such a remedy is inadequate. Also under UCC § 2-719, a contract may not limit remedies for consequential damages for personal injuries caused by defective consumer goods.

WAIVER OF BREACH: A contracting party may agree to accept less than complete performance by waiving a breach of contract that is committed by the other party.

STUDY HINTS FOR NRW CASE STUDIES

The following study hints may be helpful when resolving the NRW case studies.

NRW 15.1	➤ You should review the material dealing with complete and substantial performance, and make sure that the contract specifically requires exact, complete performance.
NRW 15.2	➤ Recall, that a party cannot assert these defenses if the events in question are foreseeable. Therefore, careful wording of the contract may help minimize this potential problem.
NRW 15.3	➤ Consider the purpose and requirements for a valid liquidated damages clause. Pay attention ➤ to the material discussing whether parties can use liquidated damages to penalize a party.

MATCHING EXERCISE

Select the term or concept that best matches a definition or statement set forth below. Each term or concept is the best match for only one definition or statement.

Terms and Concepts

a. Condition
b. Discretionary 任意な
c. Election of remedies
d. Forfeiture 丧失
e. Indemnify 赔偿

f. Insolvency 贷款无力偿还
g. Novation 势约更生
h. Prima facie 证据确凿
i. Remedy at law
j. Respondeat superior

k. Restitution 归还
l. Specific performance
m. Treble damages
n. Unconscionable 不公平な,不合理な
o. Waiver 弃权,放弃

Definitions and Statements

g 1. Substitution of a third party for one of the original parties to a contract.
k 2. Return property or money previously received from another.
e 3. Reimburse a person for expenses or liability already paid or incurred.
n 4. Blatantly unfair.
h 5. Something presumed to be true "on its face" unless disproved by contrary evidence.
i 6. Money damages.
o 7. Voluntary surrender of a legal right.
l 8. Equitable remedy that compels parties to perform a contract.
b 9. Freedom to make or not to make a decision.
a 10. Event or act that may create or destroy the obligation to perform a duty.
m 11. Damages multiplied three times; a remedy usually given by statute.
d 12. Loss of a right or privilege that is imposed as a penalty for certain conduct.
f 13. Inability to pay one's debts as they become due.
c 14. Doctrine that requires a plaintiff to choose between two inconsistent remedies in order to prevent the plaintiff from recovering twice.
j 15. Doctrine that holds employers liable for torts committed by employees while acting within the scope of their employment.

COMPLETION EXERCISE

Fill in the blanks with the words that most accurately complete each statement.

1. _discharge_ is the termination of a contract or contractual duty.

2. When one contracting party breaches a contract, the other party generally has a _due to mitigate_ its losses if it can reasonably do so.

3. _consequential_ (special) damages are indirect damages that may result from a breach of contract due to the particular circumstances of the parties.

4. ___punitive___ damages are awarded in order to punish a wrongdoer and to deter future wrongdoing.

5. ___specific___ ___performance___ compels a party to perform a contract and may be an appropriate remedy if the subject matter of the contract is unique and irreplaceable.

TRUE-FALSE EXERCISE

Write **T** if the statement is true, write **F** if the statement is false.

___F___ 1. A party cannot recover consequential damages unless that type of loss was foreseeable.

___T___ 2. Quasi contract is a remedy that is imposed by a court to prevent unjust enrichment.

___F___ 3. If performance is contingent on the occurrence of a condition and that condition does not occur, the duty to perform is discharged.

___F___ 4. Liquidated damage clauses are void and unenforceable.

___T___ 5. Subject to certain exceptions, contracting parties are generally free to impose limits on the remedies that may be sought if there is a breach of contract.

___F___ 6. A suggestion by one party that he or she might be unable to perform a future contractual obligation constitutes an anticipatory repudiation.

___F___ 7. Specific performance is typically available for enforcing land sale contracts.

___T___ 8. A court will discharge a contract under the doctrine of impossibility only if the event in question was unforeseeable.

___T___ 9. A contract may be discharged if both parties agree to cancel or rescind the contract.

___F___ 10. Courts commonly award punitive damages in breach of contract cases.

APPLICATION OF CONCEPTS

MULTIPLE CHOICE QUESTIONS

___C___ 1. William, a CPA, contracted to provide accounting services for Tyler. William promised to perform the work to Tyler's personal satisfaction. William rendered the required services. A reasonable person in Tyler's position would be satisfied with the services, but Tyler is not. Under these facts:

   a. Tyler's contractual duties are discharged because he is dissatisfied with William's services.

   b. Tyler's contractual duties are discharged because personal satisfaction contracts are illegal and void.

   c. Tyler's contractual duties are not discharged because a reasonable person would be satisfied with William's services.

   d. a and b.

___a___ 2. Which contract would be discharged under the doctrine of impossibility?

   a. Ventricle Corp. contracted to sell a heart medicine to Aorta. The contract was legal when made. Prior to performance, the FDA unforeseeably declared sale of the medicine illegal.

   b. Acme contracted to sell a standard Yomo stereo to Bob. Prior to performance, Acme's inventory of stereos was destroyed by a fire. Acme can obtain a replacement Yomo stereo elsewhere, but doing so will diminish Acme's profits on the contract.

   c. Larry contracted to buy a house. Prior to either party performing, Larry died.

   d. All of the above.

_a_/3. Juan contracted to sell coffee beans to the Wide-Eye Cafe each week. Delivery was required to be made every Friday. One week, Juan failed to deliver the beans until the following Monday, a breach of contract. The Wide-Eye Cafe waived Juan's breach. Under these facts:

    a. Wide-Eye Cafe cannot cancel the contract due to Juan's breach.
    b. Wide-Eye Cafe can cancel the contract due to Juan's breach.
    c. Wide-Eye Cafe has given up its right to insist that future deliveries be made on Friday in accordance with the contract.
    d. a and c.

_d_ _X_ 4. Pat contracted to buy a boat from Steve for $6,500. A dispute arose regarding the amount of the debt because the boat failed to satisfy certain warranties. Later, Pat and Steve entered into a second agreement whereby Pat agreed to pay, and Steve agreed to accept, $4,000 as payment in full for the disputed debt. Under these facts:

    a. The second agreement is an accord.
    b. Pat's $6,500 obligation was discharged when the parties entered into the second agreement.
    c. Pat's $6,500 obligation will not be discharged until the second agreement is performed.
    d. a and c.

SHORT ANSWER QUESTIONS

Answer the following questions, briefly explaining the reason for your answer.

1. Theo contracted to build storage shelving for Casey. The shelving is not unique, and any carpenter can perform the work. As Theo was working on the shelving, he severely cut his hand and he cannot complete the work. Is the contract discharged under the doctrine of impossibility?

_____

_____

2. Josh's Delivery Service contracted to buy a truck from Big Rig to use in its delivery business. Big Rig failed to deliver the truck on the required date, and it has informed Josh that delivery will be 5 days late. Discuss Josh's duty, if any, to mitigate his damages.

_____

_____

3. Leonardo, a sculptor, contracted with Albert, an eccentric millionaire, to cast a bronze sculpture of Albert. Albert told Leonardo how much the sculpture meant to him. The sculpture was a masterpiece; it received world acclaim. However, Albert is not pleased with the sculpture. Must Albert accept the sculpture and pay for it?

_____

_____

4. Craftsman Co. contracted with Todd to build him a pool for $20,000. Craftsman had barely begun, when it quit the job. As a result of Craftsman's default, Todd lost $500 in permit fees. Todd hired another company to complete the work. Todd had to pay this company $23,000 to complete the work. What type of breach has Craftsman committed? For how much can Todd sue Craftsman Co.?

_____

_____

CASE PROBLEMS

Answer the following case problems, explaining your answers.

1. Mark contracted to purchase a business that drills for natural gas. After the parties entered into this contract, the price for natural gas declined significantly, making it unprofitable to operate the business. It is well known in the natural gas industry that prices can rise and fall sharply and unpredictably, although prices had never before fallen this low.

   (a) When can a contract be discharged under the doctrine of impossibility?
   (b) When can a contract be discharged under the doctrine of commercial frustration?
   (c) Can Mark discharge the purchase contract under either of these doctrines?

_____

_____

_____

_____

2. Wainwright Construction contracted to build a house for the Johnsons for $100,000. Wainwright completed the house in accordance with the parties' contract, except it inadvertently painted the garage a different shade of white than the remainder of the house. It will cost the Johnsons $500 to hire someone else to repaint the garage the correct color.

   (a) Discuss the nature of Wainwright's contractual performance.
   (b) Can Wainwright enforce the contract or is the Johnsons' duty to pay discharged?
   (c) How much, if any, must the Johnsons pay?

_____

_____

_____

_____

CHAPTER 16   Formation of the Sales Contract: Contracts for Leasing Goods

INTRODUCTION: The Uniform Commercial Code (UCC) has been adopted in whole or in all part in all states. It has been adopted in order to modernize the law relating to a variety of commercial transactions, including sales, leasing of goods, banking, negotiable instruments (such as checks and negotiable promissory notes), secured transactions, and documents of title.

THE SCOPE OF ARTICLE 2: UCC Article 2 governs sale of goods.

A sale is a transaction in which a seller passes title (ownership) to a buyer for a price. The price may be any type of consideration, including payment of money or exchange of goods or services. Goods are movable personal property, but do not include most forms of intangible property, such as money, investment securities (stocks and bonds), promissory notes, accounts receivable, and trademarks. State statutes oftentimes exempt certain transaction (e.g., sale of blood) from sales coverage for reasons of public policy. Article 2 governs sales between merchants (e.g., persons who deal in the type of goods being sold) and nonmerchants, and it governs sales of new and used goods. All parties are required to act in good faith and to cooperate with each other. Merchants must also act in a commercially reasonable manner.

FORMING THE SALES CONTRACT: Sales contracts are basically formed in the same manner as other contracts except: 1) less formalities are required for sales contracts and 2) some special rules apply, especially if merchants are involved. For example, an acceptance may vary from the exact terms of the offer and yet still form a contract. Also, the courts may uphold a contract even if not all terms have been set forth as long as 1) the parties intended to contract and 2) there is a way to determine the essential terms. A seller may accept a purchase offer that requests prompt shipment by 1) promptly shipping the goods, 2) promptly shipping nonconforming goods, or 3) notifying the buyer that goods will be shipped.

■ *Standard Form Contracts*: UCC § 2-207 states that an acceptance may form a contract even if its terms are not exactly the same as the offer. In this case, these general rules apply in most situations: 1) an acceptance cannot add or change terms if nonmerchants are involved; and 2) if both parties are merchants, then the acceptance can add minor, standard (not important) terms if the buyer has not or does not object and the offer is not expressly stated to be limited to its terms.

■ *Firm Offers*: A firm offer is 1) an offer to buy or sell goods 2) made by a merchant 3) in a signed writing 4) which promises that the offer will not be revoked. A firm offer cannot be revoked for the time stated (not to exceed 3 months) and, if no time is stated, it cannot be revoked for a reasonable time. A firm offer is binding even if the offeree does not give consideration to keep the offer open.

■ *Statute of Frauds*: A contract for the sale of goods for $500 or more must be evidenced by a writing to be enforceable. The writing must: 1) be signed by the party who is using the Statute of Frauds as a defense; 2) indicate that a contract has been made; and 3) state the quantity of goods involved. If both parties are merchants and one merchant sends the other merchant a sufficient writing confirming the contract, then the confirmation is binding on the merchant receiving it if the merchant does not object to it in writing within 10 days from its receipt.

UCC § 2-201(3) provides that a writing is not required if the goods must be specially made and cannot be resold to another buyer and the seller has substantially started making the goods. Also, a sales contract is enforceable *to the extent*: 1) the defendant admits in legal proceedings that a contract existed, 2) the goods have been delivered and accepted, or 3) the price has been paid and accepted.

When interpreting a sales contract, terms are determined in the following order of preference: 1) express terms, 2) course of performance (repeated performances under the present contract),

3) course of dealing (repeated performances under past contracts between the same parties), and
4) usage of trade (trade customs).

The parol evidence rule prohibits *contradicting* the terms a *final, complete* written sales contract (i.e., totally integrated contract) by using evidence of prior oral statements or writings. But any contract can be *explained* or *supplemented* by additional evidence, such as parol evidence.

SPECIAL RULES UNDER ARTICLE 2: A contract is unconscionable if it is grossly unfair to one party. A court that finds a contract unconscionable may refuse to enforce the contract, refuse to enforce any unconscionable clauses, or limit the application of any unconscionable clause to avoid any unfair result.

- ■ *Open Terms*: If the parties do not state a term in a sales contract, then the court may supply the missing term by referring to certain "gap-filling" provisions of the UCC that supply most missing terms. See UCC §§ 2-305 to 2-309.
- ■ *Options*: Article 2 leaves some decisions, such as product mix and shipping arrangements, to the option of the buyer or seller.
- ■ *Cooperation*: Failure to cooperate or interference with a party's performance can be treated as a breach of contract or excuse for delayed performance.

THE SCOPE OF ARTICLE 2A: UCC Article 2A governs contracts for the lease of goods in nearly all states. Article 2A applies to "any transaction, regardless of form, that creates a lease."

CONTRACTS FOR LEASING GOODS: Many of the provisions of Article 2A are the same or similar to those stated in Article 2 relating to the sale of goods. Leases are generally classified as consumer leases or finance leases. It also recognizes an "installment lease" contract. A lease of goods for $1,000 or more must be evidenced by a writing to be enforceable.

CONTRACTS FOR THE SALE OF GOODS IN AN INTERNATIONAL SETTING

Roughly 60 countries have ratified the United Nations Convention on Contracts for the International Sale of Goods, the CISG, which is the controlling law for international sale-of-goods contracts when: 1) the contract is between firms from different countries that have ratified the CISG; or 2) the contract designates that it is governed by the law of a particular country that has ratified the CISG.

SCOPE OF THE CISG

While the CISG and UCC Article 2 are similar in numerous ways, important differences include: 1) the CISG generally does not apply to the sale of goods intended for personal or household use; 2) validity-of-the-contract issues, such as the requirement of consideration, are to be determined by applicable national law (not the CISG); 3) the CISG states that an acceptance is effective when it reaches the offeror; and 4) the CISG specifically states that oral contracts for the sale of goods are enforceable.

STUDY HINTS FOR NRW CASE STUDIES

The following study hints may be helpful when resolving the NRW case studies.

NRW 16.1	➢ Review the scope of both UCC Article 2. ➢ Do not overlook the fact that two or more areas of law may be crucial to NRW's business.
NRW 16.2	➢ Explore the advantages that NRW may gain in using a standard form contract. ➢ Consider UCC § 2-207 and the textbook materials dealing with the battle of the forms.
NRW 16.3	➢ Review the material on cooperation of parties. Remember that sometimes the best business decision is not to fully assert one's legal rights.

REVIEW OF KEY TERMS AND CONCEPTS

MATCHING EXERCISE

Select the term or concept that best matches a definition or statement set forth below. Each term or concept is the best match for only one definition or statement.

Terms and Concepts

a. Accommodation

b. Chose in action

c. Confirmation

d. Course of dealing

e. Course of performance

f. Firm offer

g. Investment security

h. Merchant

i. Open terms

j. Output contract

k. Parol evidence rule

l. Requirements contract

m. Seasonably

n. Unconscionable

o. Usage of trade

Definitions and Statements

____ 1. Repeated performances under a sales contract.

____ 2. Merchant's irrevocable offer to buy or sell goods.

____ 3. Contract that requires a seller to provide all of the goods that a buyer needs.

____ 4. Goods that are supplied for the convenience of a buyer.

____ 5. Rule that prohibits using prior oral or written statements to contradict the terms of a final, complete written contract.

____ 6. Occurring in a timely manner.

____ 7. Recognized and accepted practices in an industry.

____ 8. One who regularly deals in a particular type of goods.

____ 9. Intangible personal right, such as a claim for money under a contract.

____ 10. Grossly unfair.

____ 11. Written memorandum of an agreement.

____ 12. Terms that are omitted from a contract.

____ 13. Contract that requires a buyer to purchase all goods that a seller produces.

____ 14. Repeated performances by the parties under prior contracts.

____ 15. Investment that one expects to produce a profit primarily through the efforts of others.

COMPLETION EXERCISE

Fill in the blanks with the words that most accurately complete each statement.

1. Parties to a sales contract are required to act in _____ _____.

2. When a firm offer does not state a specific time for which an offer will be kept open, then the offer is irrevocable for a _____ _____.

3. The shipping of nonconforming goods to a buyer is not an acceptance of the buyer's purchase offer if the goods are sent as an _____.

4. An understanding in the lumber industry that a "2-by-4" piece of wood is not actually 2 inches by 4 inches is an example of a _____ ____ _____.

5. The _____ ____ _____ requires contracts for the sale of goods for $500 or more to be evidenced by a writing to be enforceable.

TRUE-FALSE EXERCISE

Write **T** if the statement is true, write **F** if the statement is false.

_____ 1. Merchants are required to cooperate in the performance of a sales contract.

_____ 2. The UCC permits a person to accept an offer by performance.

_____ 3. A sales agreement cannot be a legally binding contract if important terms are not stated in the parties' agreement.

_____ 4. The shipment of nonconforming goods as an accommodation is a breach of contract.

_____ 5. The UCC states that a contract between merchants always includes any new terms that are stated in the acceptance.

_____ 6. As a general rule, parties may, by their conduct, create an enforceable sales contract.

_____ 7. A firm offer may be oral or written.

_____ 8. Under Article 2, only a formal written contract will satisfy the Statute of Frauds.

_____ 9. If a contract includes an unconscionable term, then a court may choose to void the unfair clause and enforce the remainder of the contract.

_____ 10. If a sales contract does not specify the place of delivery, then Article 2 states that delivery shall be made at the buyer's place of business.

APPLICATION OF CONCEPTS

MULTIPLE CHOICE QUESTIONS

_____ 1. Jen offered to buy a truckload of Alberta peaches from Tom, requesting prompt shipment. Under the UCC, Tom can accept by:
   a. Promptly shipping the truckload of Alberta peaches to Jen.
   b. Notifying Jen that he will ship the Alberta peaches promptly.
   c. Promptly shipping a truckload of Hale Haven peaches to Jen.
   d. All of the above.

_____ 2. When a sales contract is made between two merchants, a new term that is stated in the acceptance will not be part of the contract:
   a. If the new term is objected to by the offeror within a reasonable time.
   b. If the new term may require the offeror to do or pay anything.
   c. If the new term would materially alter the contract.
   d. a and c.

____ 3. Rick orally offered to sell his personal auto to Basil for $10,000 and Basil accepted. Later, Basil recanted, stating that he refused to perform the contract. In which situation would this oral contract be enforceable?
a. Rick had delivered the auto to Basil who had accepted it.
b. When Rick sued Basil to enforce the contract, Basil admitted at trial that the parties made this contract, but defended that the contract was oral.
c. In a signed writing, Rick stated that he sold the auto to Basil. Basil did not sign the writing.
d. a and b.

____ 4. LaDonna agreed to purchase a case of CDs from Roger. The parties did not state the price. Under these facts:
a. There is a contract and the price to be paid is whatever price LaDonna wants to pay.
b. There is a contract and the price to be paid is whatever price Roger demands.
c. There is a contract and the price to be paid is a reasonable price at time of delivery.
d. There is no contract because the agreement does not state the price for the goods.

SHORT ANSWER QUESTIONS

Answer the following questions, briefly explaining the reason for your answer.

1. Jamal offered to sell his used personal computer for $400 to his friend, Betty. Betty replied, "Let me think about it until Tuesday." Before Betty accepted, Jamal called her and stated that he revoked his offer. What law governs this transaction? Was Jamal legally entitled to revoke his offer?

_____

_____

2. Centrex offered to sell a harvester to Carl for $50,000. The Centrex president made this offer in a signed writing. The offer stated that it would be held open for two days. Carl did not pay anything for Centrex's promise to keep its offer open. The next day, the Centrex president called Carl, stating that Centrex could not honor its offer and it was revoked. Was Centrex legally entitled to revoke its offer?

_____

_____

3. Geneva orally contracted to buy her bridal gown from Michelle's Bridal Shoppe for $2,000. The dress was custom designed for Geneva and made from special-order fabric. After the dress was partially done, Geneva called off the wedding and called Michelle's stating: "I don't need him, and I don't want the dress." Michelle's cannot resell the dress. Is the oral contract legally enforceable?

_____

_____

4. Shawna's Supply House orally agreed to sell Kim's Hair Salon 10 cases of shampoo for $500 per case. Shawna sent a signed, written letter to Kim, confirming the sale. Two weeks after receiving the letter, Kim wrote back, stating that she did not want the shampoo. Is the oral contract legally enforceable?

_____

_____

CASE PROBLEMS

Answer the following case problems, explaining your answers.

1. In a signed writing, Perrone's Farms agreed to supply all of the tomatoes that the Town Market needed for its two-week Harvest Festival sale. The agreement failed to state the time or place for delivery.

   (a) Did the parties' form a valid contract?
   (b) What type of agreement did the parties enter into?
   (c) Determine the terms of the agreement, including price, quantity, and time and place of delivery.

_____

_____

_____

_____

2. John, a consumer, sent a purchase order for new skis to Sport Manufacturers. The order was silent regarding how disputes between the parties would be settled. Sport sent back a definite, unconditional acceptance that contained a new term not addressed in John's order. The new term stated that any disputes regarding the skis must be submitted to arbitration. John received the acceptance, but he never agreed or objected to the new term.

   (a) Did Sport's acceptance form a sales contract between John and Sport?
   (b) If a sales contract was formed, was the new term in the acceptance part of the contract?
   (c) What would the outcome have been if John had agreed to the new term?

_____

_____

_____

_____

CHAPTER 17 Title and Risk of Loss

CHAPTER REVIEW

TITLE TO GOODS UNDER ARTICLE 2 OF THE UCC: Title includes ownership of a good and the legal right to control and dispose of it.

- *Modern Rule*: In a shipment contract, title passes at the time and place of shipment. In a destination contract, title passes when delivery is tendered at the destination. If the goods do not move, title passes on delivery of documents of title to the buyer; if no document exchange is required, title passes at the time and place the contract is made.

- *Fraudulent Retention*: If after a sale the seller retains possession, the retention will be fraudulent unless the retention was made in good faith and for a commercially reasonable time.

- *Voidable title*: A person with voidable title may pass valid title to goods to a buyer who is a good faith purchaser for value. A person has voidable title when he or she defrauds the original owner of the goods or pays for them with a bad check. A merchant who regularly buys and sells goods of a particular kind and to whom such goods are entrusted (entrustment) has voidable title to the goods.

INSURABLE INTEREST: A buyer has an insurable interest when existing goods are identified to the contract. A seller has an insurable interest in goods so long as the seller retains title to or a security interest in the goods. An insurance policy on goods cannot be enforced unless the seller or buyer who purchased the policy has an insurable interest in the goods.

RISK OF LOSS UNDER ARTICLE 2 OF THE UCC: Risk of loss is the financial responsibility for goods that are lost, damaged, or destroyed during performance of a sales contract. Risk of loss passes as follows:

- *Breach of Contract*: If the seller breaches, the risk of loss remains with the seller until the seller cures the defect or the buyer accepts the goods. If the buyer breaches, the risk of loss remains with the seller, but the buyer must compensate the seller for any loss that exceeds the seller's insurance coverage. If the buyer accepts the goods but later properly revokes acceptance of the goods, then the buyer bears the risk of loss, but the seller must compensate the buyer for any loss that exceeds the buyer's insurance coverage.

- *No Breach of Contract and Shipment of Goods*: Under a shipment contract, the risk passes to the buyer when the goods are delivered to the carrier. Under a destination contract, the risk passes to the buyer when the goods are tendered at the destination.

- *No Breach of Contract and Personal Delivery by the Seller*: Under these facts, title passes as follows: 1) if the seller is a merchant, then upon actual delivery of the goods to the buyer; or 2) if the seller is not a merchant, then upon tender of delivery of the goods to the buyer.

SPECIAL PROBLEMS: New sales techniques have created new problems including:

- *Sale on Approval*: Transaction allows a buyer to test goods for a stated time; a buyer may return the goods without obligation within this period. Title and risk of loss stay with a seller until acceptance.

- *Sale or Return*: In a sale or return contract, the buyer purchases the goods for resale; the buyer may return any unsold goods to the seller without obligation. Title and risk of loss stay with the buyer until the goods are returned.

- *Consignment*: This agreement allows a third person, the consignee, to sell goods for the owner.

- *Auctions*: An auctioneer sells goods for a third party; a sale is not complete until the auctioneer accepts a bid. In an auction "with reserve," the auctioneer may refuse to sell a good if the bids are not acceptable. In an auction "without reserve," the auctioneer must accept the highest bid.

LEASES UNDER ARTICLE 2A OF THE UCC: The concept of title is not important in determining the parties' rights under a lease of goods. Rules regarding the passing of risk of loss depend on whether the lease is a finance lease or other type of lease, whether or not the lessor is a merchant, and/or other factors.

TITLE TO GOODS UNDER THE CISG: While the CISG does not expressly discuss title, it appears to include warranty provisions that assure that a buyer will receive title to goods upon performance by a seller.

RISK OF LOSS UNDER THE CISG: In international sales contracts that call for shipment of goods, risk of loss rules under the CISG are basically the same as under the UCC. If the goods are not to be transported by carrier and are not in transit, then risk of loss passes to the buyer when the buyer either 1) takes possession of the goods or 2) fails to take possession of them within a reasonable time after the goods have been placed at the buyer's disposal if such failure to take possession is a breach of the contract.

STANDARD SHIPPING TERMS: The most commonly used shipping terms in domestic shipping contracts are the following:

- *FOB*: FOB place of shipment means the seller bears the expense and risk of loss for delivering the goods to a carrier. During shipment, the buyer bears the expense and risk of loss. FOB destination point means the seller bears the expense and risk of loss of shipping goods to the named destination.

- *FAS*: FAS means that a seller bears the expense and risk of loss for delivering goods alongside a named seagoing vessel. Title and risk of loss then pass to the buyer.

- *CIF and C & F*: CIF means the contract price includes the selling price and the cost of shipping and insurance to a named destination. C & F means that the contract price includes the price for the goods and the cost of shipping to a named destination.

- *COD*: COD requires the buyer to pay for the goods on delivery and before inspection.

In international transactions, there are four broad categories of incoterms, i.e., international shipping terms that are used to identify the buyers' and sellers' respective burdens and responsibilities. These categories are designated by letters: "E" terms, "F" terms, "C" terms, and "D" terms.

STUDY HINTS FOR NRW CASE STUDIES

The following study hints may be helpful when resolving the NRW case studies.

NRW 17.1	➤ Review the rules regarding the passing of risk of loss in destination contracts. ➤ Also review the textbook discussion on shipping terms in domestic shipment transactions.
NRW 17.2	➤ Review the material relating to sale or returns, especially the rules relating to risk of loss. ➤ Before advising the parties, review how the law treats most consignments.
NRW 17.3	➤ Suggest to Carlos that he use incoterms in connection with this transaction since it is an international shipment contract and the buyer will better understand such terms. ➤ Examine the textbook material regarding standard terms in international trade in order to help Carlos select the appropriate incoterm.

MATCHING EXERCISE

Select the term or concept that best matches a definition or statement set forth below. Each term or concept is the best match for only one definition or statement.

Terms and Concepts

a. Bailee
b. CIF
c. Common carrier
d. Conclusive presumption
e. Document of title

f. Entrustment
g. Insurable interest
h. Knocking down
i. Repudiation
j. Reservation of security interest

k. Revests
l. Risk of loss
m. Tender
n. Unsecured creditor
o. Warehouseman

Definitions and Statements

_____ 1. Interest in goods that a buyer acquires as soon as existing goods are identified to the contract.
_____ 2. Process of acceptance of a bid by an auctioneer.
_____ 3. Offer to perform a duty.
_____ 4. Seller's retention of a lien on goods until the buyer has fully performed the contract.
_____ 5. Creditor whose claim is not secured by collateral.
_____ 6. Person who is in the business of receiving and storing goods.
_____ 7. Legal responsibility for a financial loss that may result from a casualty to goods.
_____ 8. Vests again.
_____ 9. Contract price includes insurance and freight.
_____ 10. Person to whom goods are delivered with the understanding that they will be returned.
_____ 11. Delivery of goods to a merchant who regularly deals in goods of that kind.
_____ 12. Rejection of something.
_____ 13. Written evidence of ownership to goods being stored or shipped.
_____ 14. A binding inference of fact.
_____ 15. A company in the business of transporting goods or people for a fee and holding itself out as serving the general public.

COMPLETION EXERCISE

Fill in the blanks with the words that most accurately complete each statement.

1. Under a _____, the owner of a good transfers it to another person who will try to sell the good on behalf of the owner.

2. Under a _____ _____ _____ contract, the buyer purchases goods primarily for resale, enjoying the right to return any unsold goods.

3. A buyer who defrauds a seller in connection with the purchase of goods receives _____ title to the goods.

4. A _____ _____ _____ is a transaction whereby a buyer is allowed to test a product for a stated time, enjoying the right to return it without obligation to the seller within a stated time.

5. Identify four incoterms that may be used in international trade and state their respective meanings:

a. _____.

b. _____.

c. _____.

d. _____.

TRUE-FALSE EXERCISE

Write **T** if the statement is true, write **F** if the statement is false.

_____ 1. An entrustment occurs when a person delivers goods to a merchant who regularly buys and sells goods of that kind.

_____ 2. If a sales contract involves goods that are existing and identified at the time of contracting but a document of title is required to be delivered to the buyer, title and risk of loss do not generally pass to the buyer until the document of title is delivered to the buyer.

_____ 3. In a CIF contract, title and risk of loss do not pass until goods are delivered at the destination.

_____ 4. If a buyer purchases goods from a thief, then the buyer receives void (no) title, and the owner of the goods may recover the goods from the buyer.

_____ 5. Leases of goods are governed by Article 2 of the UCC.

_____ 6. In a FAS contract, a seller bears the expense of delivering goods alongside a named vessel.

_____ 7. Seller owns an existing inventory of shovels, and Seller contracts to sell one unspecified shovel from this inventory. In this situation, the shovel sold is an existing and identified good.

_____ 8. In a sale or return contract, the expense and risk of loss of returning goods is borne by the seller.

_____ 9. In a FAS contract, title and risk of loss pass to a buyer at the time the contract is made.

_____ 10. The fact that goods are shipped COD or that a seller retains a security interest in the goods does not affect when title or risk of loss will pass to a buyer.

APPLICATION OF CONCEPTS

MULTIPLE CHOICE QUESTIONS

_____ 1. If goods are to be delivered without movement and are represented by a document of title, title passes:
   a. at time and place of contract.
   b. upon delivery of document of title.
   c. upon tender of delivery.
   d. none of the above

_____ 2. On July 15, Seller contracted to sell a shipment of tools to Acme Co. The tools were not yet identified to the contract. As required by the contract, Seller duly delivered the tools to a carrier for shipment to Buyer on August 15. (Seller was NOT required to deliver the tools at the destination.) On September 15, the shipment was delivered to Acme at the destination. Under these facts, when did title and risk of loss pass to Acme?
   a. July 15
   b. August 15
   c. September 15
   d. Never.

_____ 3. Lisa operates a meat rendering plant in Seattle Washington. She sold 10,000 pounds of processed beef to the Buyer in Japan. The beef is sent "CFR Tokyo," but it never arrives in Japan. Which statement is true?
   a. Lisa bears the risk of loss.
   b. Buyer bears the risk of loss.
   c. Buyer must pay for the shipping cost.
   d. b and c.

_____ 4. On May 1, John contracted to buy an existing, identified filing cabinet from Seller, a merchant. Documents of title were not involved. Seller was required to deliver the cabinet to John's place of business, which was located in another city. On June 1, Seller delivered the cabinet to a carrier for shipment to John. On June 15, the cabinet was tendered to John at his place of business. Under these facts:
   a. Title passed to John on May 1.
   b. Title passed to John on June 1.
   c. Title passed to John on June 15.
   d. Title never passed to John.

SHORT ANSWER QUESTIONS

Answer the following questions, briefly explaining the reason for your answer.

1. Fran delivered her computer to Computer Traders, a merchant who regularly bought and sold used computers. Computer Traders was supposed to repair the computer. Instead, Computer Traders sold Fran's computer to Ted in the ordinary course of business. Did Ted receive title to the computer?

_____

_____

2. Jim, in Atlanta, contracted to sell peaches to Cindy in Chicago. The contract states that the peaches are sold "F.O.B. Atlanta." If the peaches are damaged during shipment, who bears the risk of loss?

_____

_____

3. Kathy received an exercise bike from Seller pursuant to a sale on approval agreement. The agreement allows Kathy to test the bike for 14 days, and Kathy may return the bike at any time during this period. Kathy received the bike on June 1. Kathy shipped the exercise bike back to Seller on June 9. During shipment, the exercise bike was damaged. Does Kathy bear the risk of loss for the exercise bike?

_____

_____

4. On May 1, Joan contracted to buy an existing, identified television from Seller, a merchant. Delivery was to be made at Seller's business. On June 1, Seller tendered delivery of the television to Joan, but Joan did not take the television. On July 1, Joan took physical possession of the television. When did Joan have an insurable interest in the television?

_____

_____

CASE PROBLEMS

Answer the following case problems, explaining your answers.

1. Jane delivered her car to Skweeky Kleen, a retail car wash that does not normally buy or sell cars. Without Jane's permission, Skweeky Kleen sold her car to Buyer for $12,000, a fair price. Buyer did not know that the car belonged to Jane or that the sale was improper. Does Buyer receive title to the car?

_____

_____

_____

_____

2. Sterling Seller delivers defective goods to Brenda Buyer. Brenda discovers a hidden, material defect in the goods and properly rejects them. If the goods are subsequently destroyed by an accidental fire while the goods are in Brenda's possession and Brenda has insured the goods for 80 percent of their fair market value of $10,000, who bears the risk of loss?

_____

_____

_____

_____

CHAPTER REVIEW

PERFORMANCE OF A SALES CONTRACT: The parties must act in good faith and cooperate.

SALES UNDER ARTICLE 2 OF THE UCC: General performance obligations under Article 2 are that the seller is to transfer and deliver conforming goods to the buyer is to accept and pay for the goods delivered. Conforming goods are goods that are within the description of the goods as set out in the contract.

SELLER'S DUTIES: The seller's basic duty, to tender delivery of conforming goods, can be accomplished in five ways: 1) the buyer takes the goods from the seller; 2) the seller takes the goods to the buyer; 3) the seller ships the goods to the buyer; 4) a third party (bailee) has the goods and no documents of title are involved; or 5) a bailee has the goods and the seller must provide a document of title in order to get the goods.

INTERVENING RIGHTS: UCC § 2-513 gives the buyer the right to inspect goods. The buyer must conduct a reasonable inspection; failure to do so may operate as a waiver, requiring the buyer to perform. If the buyer notices a nonconformity, then the buyer must promptly notify the seller of the condition. If the time for performance has not expired, the seller has a right to cure the nonconformity.

BUYER'S DUTIES: A buyer must accept conforming goods; failure to do so is a breach of contract. There are four ways by which a buyer can accept goods: 1) the buyer signifies that the goods conform to the contract; 2) the buyer signifies that the goods are nonconforming, but that they will be kept and accepted; 3) the buyer fails to properly reject the goods if they are nonconforming; or 4) the buyer does any act that is inconsistent with a rejection, in other words, that is inconsistent with the seller's ownership of the goods. The buyer is allowed to pay in any normal manner, such as using a check or draft. If the seller demands cash, the seller must give the buyer a reasonable time to obtain the cash.

LEASES UNDER ARTICLE 2A OF THE UCC: Performance of a lease contract under Article 2A is basically the same as performance of a sales contract under Article 2.

THE CISG: Under the CISG, the following general performance rules apply: 1) the seller is to tender delivery of goods to the buyer in accordance with the contract; 2) the buyer is to accept and pay for conforming goods; 3) the parties are to act in good faith; 4) the buyer may inspect the goods prior to acceptance; 5) the buyer is to notify the seller of any nonconformity in the goods within a reasonable time; and 6) the seller may have an opportunity to cure any nonconformity in order to avoid a breach.

- ■ *Obligations of the Seller*: In a carriage contract, the seller must deliver goods to the carrier. Otherwise, the seller must place goods at a location known to both parties. Goods are conforming if: 1) they are fit for their normal and intended purpose; 2) they are fit for a particular purpose about which the seller knew; and 3) they are properly packaged. A buyer has two years to detect a hidden defect and reject the goods.

- ■ *Obligations of the Buyer*: Unless the contract specifies otherwise, a buyer must pay the price generally charged for similar goods. If the price is based on weight, net weight is used. The buyer must pay the seller at the seller's place of business.

THE REASON FOR REMEDIES: Remedies are available because some contracts may not be performed as agreed. Remedies minimize the effects of a breach if it occurs.

SELLER'S REMEDIES: A seller's remedies may be broken down in terms of the remedies that are available if the buyer breaches before accepting the goods (preacceptance remedies) or the buyer breaches after accepting the goods (postacceptance remedies). In general, the seller may choose one or more of the remedies discussed below under each of these categories.

■ *Preacceptance Remedies of the Seller*: If the buyers breach before they accept the goods, then a seller may choose one or more of the following remedies (depending on the facts of the particular case):

1) withhold delivery of goods still in the seller's possession;

2) stop delivery of goods in transit to the buyers;

3) sue for incidental damages;

4) sue for the contract price (which includes the right to identify goods to the contract and the right to complete making goods);

5) resell goods the seller has in his or her possession (provided the sale is commercially reasonable and the buyer is given notice of the sale) and sue for the contract price minus the resale price; and

6) sue for damages due to the breach (lost profits for volume sellers or the difference between the contract price minus market price).

In situations 5) and 6) above, the seller may also cancel the contract and any future contractual duties that the seller may have under the contract.

■ *Postacceptance Remedies of the Seller*: If the buyers breach the contract after they have accepted the goods, then remedies available to the seller are:

1) sue for the unpaid contract price; and/or

2) sue to reclaim (recover) the goods if: (a) the buyers are insolvent and the seller asserts the claim within ten days of delivery or (b) the buyers misrepresented their solvency in writing.

BUYER'S REMEDIES: A buyer's remedies, in the event of a breach by the seller, may also be broken down into preacceptance and postacceptance remedies.

■ *Preacceptance Remedies of the Buyer*: If the seller breaches before the buyer accepts the goods, the buyer may:

1) sue for incidental damages;

2) claim identified goods still in the seller's possession if the seller became insolvent within ten days after receiving the buyer's payment;

3) cancel the contract and any future contractual duties of the buyer;

4) sue for damages equal to market price minus contract price;

5) cover (buy substantially similar replacement goods within a reasonable time and in a commercially reasonable manner) and sue for the difference between cover price minus contract price;

6) sue to recover the goods from the seller by suing for either specific performance (if goods are unique) or replevin (if goods are essential to the buyer's business); and

7) resell nonconforming goods that are in the buyer's possession (in certain situations).

■ *Postacceptance Remedies of the Buyer*: When the seller breaches the sales contract after the buyer has accepted the goods, then the buyer may:

1) revoke acceptance of the goods if the nonconformity substantially impairs the goods' value; and 2) either (a) sue for damages due to the nonconforming goods (in accordance with the rules stated above for preacceptance); or (b) deduct damages from the contract price (i.e., recoupment) to cover the buyer's loss.

MODIFICATIONS: In general, the parties may limit the remedies that are available if a party breaches the contract (e.g., a buyer's remedies may be limited to the seller's repairing or replacing a defective good).

The parties may also state in their contract a fixed amount of liquidated damages that are to be paid in the event of a breach. However, liquidated damages are appropriate only if: 1) they are reasonable and 2) the difficulty of setting the loss is substantial and establishing the actual loss would be inconvenient. A contract may limit consequential damages (except for personal injuries involving consumer goods).

SPECIAL PROBLEMS: Special problems associated with sales contracts include:

■ *(Anticipatory) Repudiation*: Parties repudiate a contract when they indicate that they will refuse to perform a contract when the time for performance arrives. If the repudiation will substantially reduce the value of the contract, the nonrepudiating party may: 1) postpone performance for a commercially reasonable period of time; 2) treat the repudiation as an immediate breach and seek remedies; or 3) suspend performance until the problem is resolved.

■ *Excused Performance*: A seller's performance may be excused if contract performance becomes impracticable. Performance is impracticable if an event has occurred which was not foreseen by either party and it renders performance unreasonably burdensome. Performance is also excused if a party must comply with a government order.

■ *Adequate Assurances*: An insecure party may demand, in writing, an assurance from the other parties that they intend to perform. The insecure party may suspend performance until assurance is given, and may treat the contract as repudiated by the other parties if an assurance is not given in 30 days.

■ *Duty to Particularize*: If a buyer rejects nonconforming goods, the buyer must state what the defect is. A failure to do so will preclude the use of that defect to prove breach if the seller could have cured.

STATUTE OF LIMITATIONS: A lawsuit for a breach of contract must begin within 4 years of the breach. The contract may specify a shorter period, but not less than 1 year.

REMEDIES UNDER LEASING CONTRACTS UNDER ARTICLE 2A: Article 2A specifies remedies in the event that the lessor or lessor breach the lease contract.

SELLER'S REMEDIES UNDER THE CISG: The seller may have the following remedies under the CISG:

1) require the buyer to pay the contract price, take delivery of the goods, or perform any other obligations under the contract unless the seller has chosen another remedy that is inconsistent with this remedy.

2) set an additional reasonable time during which the buyer can perform, provided that the buyer is notified of this extension. (The seller may not seek any other remedies during this extended time.

3) declare the contract avoided as to any unperformed parts of the contract.

4) if the contract calls for the buyer to specify any form, measurement, or other feature of the goods and the buyer fails to do so, then the seller may supply such specifications within a reasonable time.

BUYER'S REMEDIES UNDER THE CISG: The buyer may have the following remedies under the CISG:

1) require the seller to perform unless the buyer has chosen another remedy that is inconsistent with performance by the seller.

2) require the seller to deliver conforming substitute goods or to cure any nonconformity if the seller delivered nonconforming goods.

3) set an additional time for performance provided that the seller is notified of this extension. (The buyer may not seek any other remedies during this extended time.)

4) declare the contract avoided if the seller does not delivery the goods within the time permitted under the contract or before a time extension expires.

5) if the seller delivered nonconforming goods, then the buyer can reduce the price paid to the seller to reflect the value of the goods delivered.

6) if the seller tenders delivery prior to the agreed delivery date, then the buyer can accept or refuse to accept the goods.

7) if the seller tenders delivery of a larger shipment than called for in the contract, then the buyer may accept any or all of the excess amount, paying for any accepted goods at the contract rate.

DAMAGES: The CISG specifies damages that may be available to either party following a breach of the contract by the other party, and these damages are available even if other remedies are also sought.

The basic measure of damages under the CISG is "a sum equal to the loss, including loss of profit, suffered by the other party as a consequence of the breach. Such damages cannot exceed the loss which the party in breach foresaw or ought to have foreseen at the time of the conclusion of the contract."

If a contract is avoided and the buyer then purchases replacement goods, the buyer is entitled to the difference between the price of the replacement goods and the original contract price plus any other damages computed under the prior damage provisions.

If the contract is avoided and the seller then resells the goods, the seller may recover the difference between the resale price and the original contract price plus any other damages computed under the prior damage provisions.

The party seeking damages must take any and all reasonable steps to mitigate damages, or the other party can use the failure to mitigate as grounds for reducing the damages recovered to the amount that would have been suffered even with mitigation.

STUDY HINTS FOR NRW CASE STUDIES

The following study hints may be helpful when resolving the NRW case studies.

NRW 18.1	➢ Review the *limited* postacceptance rights of a seller to reclaim goods from a buyer.
NRW 18.2	➢ Review the concepts of anticipatory repudiation and requests for an adequate assurance.
NRW 18.3	➢ Before advising the parties, carefully review the material dealing with the seller's remedies under the CISG and the damages that may be recovered.

MATCHING EXERCISE

Select the term or concept that best matches a definition or statement set forth below. Each term or concept is the best match for only one definition or statement.

Terms and Concepts

a. Adequate assurance

b. Anticipatory repudiation

c. Consequential damages

d. Cover

e. Duty to particularize

f. Excused nonperformance

g. Liquidated damages

h. Reject

i. Remedies

j. Replevin

k. Specific performance

l. Substantially impair

Definitions and Statements

_____ 1. Promise or guarantee that a party will perform as promised.

_____ 2. Buyer's obligation to describe alleged defects so that the seller may cure.

_____ 3. Buying substitute goods from another source within a reasonable time of the breach.

_____ 4. Assortment of awards that may be granted to prevent or make up for harm resulting from a breach of contract.

_____ 5. Refusal to accept goods.

_____ 6. Definite and certain assertion that a party does not intend to perform the contract when performance becomes due.

_____ 7. Defense to performance of a contract because performance is impracticable or impossible.

_____ 8. Court order directing a seller to perform a contract relating to unique goods.

_____ 9. Court order directing a seller to deliver contract goods that are unavailable elsewhere.

_____ 10. Significant reduction in the value of goods.

_____ 11. Damages that arise due to the particular circumstances of the parties.

_____ 12. Amount of damages stipulated in the contract.

COMPLETION EXERCISE

Fill in the blanks with the words that most accurately complete each statement.

1. A party who is reasonably insecure regarding the intent or ability of the other party to perform a sales contract may make a written demand upon the other party for an _____ _____.

2. In general, a party has _____ _____ within which to file an action for breach of a sales contract.

3. A seller may reclaim goods from a buyer if the buyer is insolvent and the seller reclaims the goods within _____ _____ after delivery of the goods to the buyer.

4. A buyer may sue for _____ of the goods being sold pursuant to a sales contract if the goods are not readily available elsewhere.

5. A buyer may revoke his or her acceptance of nonconforming goods only if the nonconformity _____ · _____ the value of the goods.

TRUE-FALSE EXERCISE

Write **T** if the statement is true, write **F** if the statement is false.

_____ 1. If a seller refuses to deliver goods, a buyer is always entitled to specific performance.

_____ 2. A nonbreaching party's cancellation of a sales contract does not release the breaching party from his or her duty to perform the contract.

_____ 3. In certain situations, buyers may resell nonconforming goods that are in their possession.

_____ 4. In general, a sales contract may limit or exclude consequential damages.

_____ 5. A party who makes an anticipatory repudiation may, in some cases, retract the repudiation.

_____ 6. A seller may be excused from performance of a contract, if such performance is made illegal.

_____ 7. The UCC forbids liquidation of damage clauses in sales contracts.

_____ 8. A sales contract can limit the remedies that will be available if a party breaches the contract.

_____ 9. A buyer may revoke acceptance of goods on the basis on any minor or major nonconformity.

_____ 10. A buyer must cover whenever the seller breaches a sales contract.

APPLICATION OF CONCEPTS

MULTIPLE CHOICE QUESTIONS

_____ 1. Stan sold his personal motorcycle to Buyer for $5,000. Prior to delivery or payment, Buyer breached the contract and refused to take the cycle. After the breach, Stan properly held a public sale and sold the cycle for $4,500. Stan had to pay a $500 commission to the auctioneer who conducted the sale. Under these facts, Stan can recover how much in damages?
  a. $0.
  b. $500.
  c. $1,000.
  d. $5,000.

_____ 2. Acme Wares sold a stove to Kitty for $600. Kitty refused to accept the oven and breached the contract. Acme would have made a profit of $300 on the sale. At the time the oven was tendered to Kitty, the oven's market price was $500. Under these facts, Acme can recover how much in damages?
  a. $0.
  b. $100.
  c. $300.
  d. $500.

_____ 3. Henry bought a power drill from Seller for $500. *Prior to paying*, Henry properly rejected the drill due to Seller's breach. Henry purchased an identical drill elsewhere for $550. Under these facts, Henry can recover how much in damages?
   a. $0.
   b. $50.
   c. $550.
   d. Nothing, Henry's only remedy was to sue for specific performance.

_____ 4. Seller sold a set of encyclopedias to Betty for $1,000. Betty accepted the encyclopedias and loves reading them, but she refuses to pay any portion of the purchase price. The market price for the encyclopedias is $900. Under these facts, Seller may sue for:
   a. $0.
   b. $100.
   c. $900.
   d. $1,000.

SHORT ANSWER QUESTIONS

Answer the following questions, briefly explaining the reason for your answer.

1. A&A Orchards agreed to sell its apple crop to Royal Grocery next month. A few days later, the Financial News reported that Royal officials had stated that Royal may soon declare bankruptcy. Discuss what A&A should do in this case.

_____

_____

2. Jake purchased two ostriches that were warranted to be a "proven breeder pair." Jake accepted the ostriches. Jake accepted the birds not knowing that they were actually both males (it is quite difficult to determine the gender of ostriches). A few months later, Jake discovered that both birds were male. Briefly discuss Jake's rights in this case.

_____

_____

3. Jodi sold Vincent a car load of Italian figurines to be delivered by train and picked up by Vincent in New York. Jodi discovered that Vincent went insolvent just after she delivered the figurines to the carrier for shipment. Discuss Jodi's rights in this case.

_____

_____

4. Alta contracted with Farmer Fred to buy a specific crop of carrots. Fred had sprayed this crop with Alart, a powerful insecticide. After the parties made this contract, the EPA passed a regulation that made it illegal to sell vegetables sprayed with Alart. Discuss the parties' rights in this situation.

_____

_____

CASE PROBLEMS

Answer the following case problems, explaining your answers.

1. Hotshot Chile Dogs has a contract to buy Cardoza chiles from Chile's Inc. Chile's has lots of Cardoza chiles but wrongfully refuses to sell them to Hotshot. Cardoza chiles are in short supply this year and Hotshot cannot replace them. Hotshot has already lost $10,000 lost profits because of Cardoza's breach and, if Hotshot does not obtain these chiles soon, it may be forced out of business.

   Analyze Hotshot's remedies in this case.

_____

_____

_____

_____

2. Hilda purchased a Sturtz piano from Mistro Music Store. Mistro warranted that the piano was solid cherry. The piano was to be delivered on May 1. On April 20, Mistro delivered the piano to Hilda. The next day, Hilda discovered that the piano was actually pine, stained with a cherry finish. Under these facts:

   (a) What should Hilda do to protect her rights in this case?
   (b) Discuss Mistro's right to cure its error in this case.
   (c) If Mistro refuses to cure its error, briefly discuss Hilda's potential remedies.

_____

_____

_____

_____

CHAPTER 19

Warranties and Product Liability

INTRODUCTION: A warranty is a type of contractual promise that guarantees a degree of quality in the sale of goods. There are two types of warranties: express and implied.

EXPRESS WARRANTIES: An express warranty arises by virtue of the words or conduct of the seller. The promise or affirmation of fact made must also be part of the basis of the bargain. An express warranty may be created by: 1) an affirmation of a fact or promise about a product; 2) a description of the goods; or 3) a sample or model of the goods. The UCC does not require reliance by the buyer to create an express warranty. Express warranties focus on quantifiable (provable) facts, not opinions like "this is a good car."

IMPLIED WARRANTIES: Implied warranties are not given by the seller. They are implied by law into a sales contract in certain cases. There are four types of implied warranties: warranty of title, warranty against infringement, warranty of merchantability, and warranty of fitness for a particular purpose.

- ■ *Warranty of Title*: The UCC specifies that every seller of goods gives an implied warranty of title, unless this warranty is specifically excluded or the circumstances of the sale clearly indicate that the seller does not have clear title. The warranty of title assures the buyer that:
  1) the buyer will receive valid title to the goods being purchased;
  2) the seller has the legal right to transfer title to the buyer; and
  3) at the time of delivery of the goods to the buyer, the goods will not be subject to any liens that the buyer did not have actual knowledge of when entering into the contract.

- ■ *Warranty Against Infringement*: This warranty guarantees against a rightful claim of infringement by any third person. Patent infringement is the most common type of problem in this area.

- ■ *Warranty of Merchantability*: A merchant who regularly deals in goods of the kind being sold warrants that the goods are merchantable. The basic obligation imposed by the warranty of merchantability is that goods be "fit for the ordinary purposes for which such goods are used." This warranty assures buyers that the goods are suitable for normal and intended use.

- ■ *Warranty of Fitness for a Particular Purpose*: This warranty obligates a seller to furnish goods that are reasonably suitable for performing a particular task intended by the buyer. This warranty arises if:
  1) a seller knows that a buyer is planning a particular use for the goods;
  2) the seller knows the buyer is relying on the seller's skill in selecting the goods; and
  3) the buyer does, in fact, rely on the seller's judgment in selecting the goods.

WARRANTY EXCLUSIONS: The seller can modify or exclude express warranties. One method of excluding express warranties is simply not to give a warranty at all. Otherwise, a seller may disclaim express warranties orally, in writing, or by conduct. When it appears that there may be both an express warranty and an attempt to exclude it, the courts try to reconcile the differences and give effect to both. When this is not possible, the express warranty is given effect.

The seller may disclaim the warranty of merchantability by following these three rules: 1) the disclaimer may be oral or in writing; 2) the disclaimer must mention "merchantability;" and 3) a written disclaimer must be conspicuous. The seller can disclaim the warranty of fitness for a particular purpose if: 1) the disclaimer is in writing and 2) it is conspicuous. Both of these implied warranties may be excluded by general language like "AS IS."

STATUTORY WARRANTY PROVISIONS: The Magnuson-Moss Warranty Act, a federal statute, provides that manufacturers must provide buyers with all warranty information prior to the sale. The manufacturer need not give any express warranties, but if a warranty is given, it must be designated as full or limited.

SCOPE OF WARRANTY PROTECTION: The UCC has extended warranty protection to persons who are not part of the sales contract. States may choose among three alternative provisions.

PRODUCT LIABILITY: In addition to warranty law, negligence and strict liability may provide remedies for people who are injured by defective and unreasonably dangerous products.

- *Negligence*: To establish a negligence claim against a manufacturer or seller of a product, a plaintiff must prove the basic elements of a negligence claim, namely: 1) duty, 2) breach of duty, 3) proximate cause, and 4) harm. In general, privity of contract (i.e., a direct contractual relationship between the plaintiff and defendant) is not required to sue based on negligence.

- *Strict Liability in Tort*: Strict liability is based on widely followed court cases that have adopted Rule 402A of the Restatement of Torts (Second).

   In general, Rule 402A imposes liability for personal injuries that are caused by a defective product if the following elements are established:
   1) The defendant manufactured or sold a product;
   2) The product was expected to and did reach the buyer or user in the same condition as when sold;
   3) The product had not been substantially altered or modified; and
   4) The product was defective and unreasonably dangerous.

LEASES: When goods are leased, the lessee receives certain warranties. These warranties are similar to those made in connection with the sale of goods.

THE CISG: The CISG does not expressly provide for warranties. Warranty protection, however, may be implied from conduct of the parties, language of the contract, or trade usage. If a warranty exists and is breached, then the buyer will be entitled to remedies.

ISO 9000: ISO 9000 is a process to assure that a company's products comply with quality standards established for its industry.

STUDY HINTS FOR NRW CASE STUDIES

The following study hints may be helpful when resolving the NRW case studies.

NRW 19.1	➤ When advising the parties, remember the ways in which express warranties can be created. ➤ Also consider state and federal deceptive advertising laws.
NRW 19.2	➤ Review the warranty of title that is made in connection with the sale of goods. ➤ The NRW principals may wish to search the public patent records of the U.S. Patent and Trademark Office.
NRW 19.3	➤ To determine the extent to which and how warranties can be excluded, you should review the Warranty Exclusions material. ➤ As a practical matter, NRW should carefully monitor what competitors are doing with respect to warranties before it decides whether it wants to exclude warranties.

REVIEW OF KEY TERMS AND CONCEPTS

MATCHING EXERCISE

Select the term or concept that best matches a definition or statement set forth below. Each term or concept is the best match for only one definition or statement.

Terms and Concepts

a. Conspicuous

b. Express warranties

c. Fungible

d. Implied warranties

e. Innately dangerous

f. Privity of contract

g. Warranty of fitness

h. Warranty of merchantability

i. Warranty of title

Definitions and Statements

_e_ 1. Product that is inherently dangerous.

_c_ 2. Goods that are interchangeable.

_b_ 3. Category of guarantees that arise due to the words or conduct of the seller.

_d_ 4. Category of guarantees that are imposed by law.

_i_ 5. Warranty that assures buyers that they will own a good free and clear of others' claims.

_h_ 6. Warranty that goods are fit for their ordinary, intended purposes.

_a_ 7. Obvious; stands out.

_f_ 8. Direct contractual relationship between two parties.

_g_ 9. Warranty that goods will fulfill a special use that is intended by the buyer.

COMPLETION EXERCISE

Fill in the blanks with the words that most accurately complete each statement.

1. Historically, buyers were not protected regarding the quality of goods. Rather, the controlling doctrine was _____ _____.

2. In general, an express warranty is automatically considered to be _____ _____ _____ _____ _____, meaning part of the sales contract.

3. The _____ _____ _____ guarantees a buyer that goods being sold do not violate others' patents.

4. The term "_____ _____" will effectively exclude the implied warranties of merchantability and fitness for a particular purpose.

5. List two theories of tort law that may provide a remedy for persons who are injured by defective goods:

    a. _____.

    b. _____.

TRUE-FALSE EXERCISE

Write **T** if the statement is true, write **F** if the statement is false.

___T___ 1. A seller's advertisement about goods can create an express warranty.

___F___ 2. An express warranty does not arise unless the buyer actually relies upon it.

___F___ 3. It is unlawful to exclude all warranties in a sale of goods.

___T___ 4. In general, it is implied that both merchants and nonmerchants make the implied warranty of title unless the sales contract specifically excludes it.

___T___ 5. A nonmerchant who sells a good does not make the implied warranty of merchantability.

___F___ 6. Under the implied warranty of merchantability, the "reasonable expectations test" is automatically breached if any foreign object is found in food.

___T___ 7. An implied warranty of fitness for a particular purpose does not arise unless the buyer actually relies on the seller's judgment in selecting goods.

___F___ 8. Only persons who are a party to the sales contract are protected by implied warranties.

___F___ 9. Whenever a person is injured by a product, the law presumes that the manufacturer liable for negligence.

___T___ 10. Under Rule 402A of the Restatement (Second) of Torts, a manufacturer may be strictly liable for injuries caused by its product, even if the manufacturer exercised all possible care in designing, manufacturing, and selling its product.

APPLICATION OF CONCEPTS

MULTIPLE CHOICE QUESTIONS

_____ 1. In which case is an express warranty made?
    a. The salesman for PainBgone aspirin states that, in his opinion, PainBgone aspirin is the best painkiller on the market.
    b. The salesman for the Belchfire 500 automobile states: "This car will go from zero to 60 miles per hour in six seconds."
    c. The salesman in the jeweler's shop states: "This diamond is one karat."
    d. b and c.

2. The warranty of merchantability is breached in which case?

   a. Juanita (a nonmerchant) sold Buyer a new toaster that Juanita had received as a gift. The toaster cannot toast bread.

   b. Seller (a merchant) sold an ordinary private airplane to Buyer. The airplane operates safely and it is fit for ordinary private use. However, the plane cannot perform acrobatic stunts.

   c. Manufacturer, a merchant, sold a portable plastic pool to Buyer. The pool leaks badly, and it cannot be repaired. However, Manufacturer was not negligent in making the pool.

   d. All of the above.

3. In which situation does Seller make an express warranty?

   a. During negotiations, Seller gave Byron a brochure regarding a ring that Byron was considering purchasing. The brochure stated that the ring was sterling silver.

   b. During negotiations for the sale of a drill, Seller stated to Buyer: "This drill is the best little drill on the market today." Seller did not say or do anything else.

   c. During negotiations for the sale of a chair to be specially manufactured, Seller showed Buyer a model of what the chair would be like. Seller did not say or do anything else.

   d. a and c.

4. Amigos Cafe sold Joe a guacamole taco. The taco had a piece of avocado pit in it. Although guacamole is made from avocados which have pits, an ordinary person would not reasonably expect to find a piece of an avocado pit in a guacamole taco. Under these facts:

   a. Amigos did not breach the warranty of merchantability; the UCC does not apply to sales of food.

   b. Under the natural substance-foreign substance test, the taco is fit (merchantable).

   c. Under the reasonable expectations test, the taco is fit (merchantable).

   d. b and c.

SHORT ANSWER QUESTIONS

Answer the following questions, briefly explaining the reason for your answer.

1. ZydiCo. manufacturers accordions. It advertises in magazines that cater to accordionists. One of its advertisements states: "The ZydiCo. accordion cannot be topped." Is an express warranty created?

2. Brown Corp. manufactures bicycles for the national market. Brown manufactures the X-100, a mountain bike that retails for about $250, roughly the price charged for many mid-range mountain bikes. The X-100 functions fine on streets but it is unstable and unsafe to ride on unpaved terrain. Unaware of this problem, Gina bought an X-100. While riding her bike on a dirt trail, it unexpectedly flipped, throwing Gina to the ground and injuring her. Discuss Brown's potential warranty liability to Gina.

3. Len is an expert manufacturer of custom fly-fishing rods. Walt went to Len to purchase a rod. Walt explained his particular needs for a rod that would suit his unique fishing style, and he requested that Len make an appropriate rod. Len designed and manufactured a special rod for Walt. When Walt used the rod, he discovered that it was too stiff for his style of fishing. Has Len breached an implied warranty?

_____

_____

4. Bobbie needed a paint that could withstand unusual, prolonged heat. Bobbie developed a paint formula and furnished Acme Paints with specifications for the paint. Acme manufactured the paint in accordance with Bobbie's specifications, but the paint failed to accomplish its intended purpose. Is Acme liable for breach of the warranty of fitness for a particular purpose?

_____

_____

CASE PROBLEMS

Answer the following case problems, explaining your answers.

1. MicroView Inc., a maker of commercial microscopes, plans to sell a new microscope. MicroView is concerned about liability for implied warranties. MicroView asks you: (a) Can MicroView exclude the warranties of merchantability and fitness for a particular purpose, or are such exclusions unconscionable? (b) Can MicroView disclaim the warranty of merchantability by using a disclaimer in its contract that is the same size, type, and color of print as all other terms? (c) If MicroView's contracts conspicuously state that its microscopes are sold "AS IS," what effect would this term have on implied warranties?

_____

_____

_____

_____

2. Juan bought a new automobile. Juan drove the car for two years without any problems. However, Juan was recently rear-ended by a careless driver who was going 40 mph at the time of the impact. Juan's car burst into flames, severely injuring Juan. If Juan sues the car manufacturer for his injuries based on strict liability, what is the likely outcome of the suit? Explain.

_____

_____

_____

_____

CHAPTER 20

Introduction to Negotiables: UCC Article 3 and Article 7

CHAPTER REVIEW

HISTORIC OVERVIEW: Negotiable instruments historically included 1) negotiable instruments that are used to represent obligations to pay money and 2) negotiable documents that are issued in connection with the commercial shipping and storage of goods. Today, these important types of commercial documents are governed by the UCC.

THE SCOPE OF ARTICLE 3: A negotiable instrument (instrument) is an unconditional written promise or order to pay money that satisfies the requirements for negotiability stated in UCC § 3-104. UCC Article 3 governs negotiable instruments, but does not govern money, documents of title, or securities. A negotiable instrument must be payable "to bearer" or "to order" at the time it is issued or first comes into the possession of a holder unless the instrument qualifies as a check in which case it need not have these "words of negotiability." Any writing (except a check) that looks like an instrument is not negotiable if it contains a conspicuous statement that it is not negotiable.

USES OF NEGOTIABLE INSTRUMENTS: Generally, negotiable instruments are used as a substitute for money to pay bills and buy goods and services, and for credit transactions. Instruments include:

- *Checks*: Checks include: 1) a draft that is payable on demand and is drawn on a bank; 2) a cashier's check, which is a draft drawn by a bank on itself; 3) a teller's check, which is typically a draft drawn by a bank on another bank; 4) a negotiable money order; and 5) a traveler's check which is an instrument that is (a) payable on demand, (b) drawn on (or payable at or through) a bank, (c) is called a "traveler's check or similar name, and (d) requires, as a condition to payment, the countersignature by the person whose signature appears on the instrument.

- *Drafts*: Drafts are instruments whereby the party issuing the instrument orders another party to pay money. Drafts include sight drafts (payable on demand) and time drafts (payable at a future date).

- *Promissory Notes*: A promissory note is an instrument that states a party's promise to pay money.

- *Certificates of Deposit*: A certificate of deposit is a note issued by a bank that: 1) acknowledges receipt of money from a customer; and 2) states the bank's promise to repay the money.

FUNCTIONS AND FORMS: Commercial paper serves as a substitute for money and as a credit instrument.

PAPER CONTAINING AN ORDER ("THREE-PARTY PAPER"): Drafts and checks state an order to pay money and involve three parties: 1) the drawer who originally signs a draft or check, ordering 2) the drawee to pay the amount of the draft or check to 3) the payee, the person originally named on the face of the instrument.

- *Drafts*: The drawer issues a draft to the payee, who presents the draft to the drawee, requesting payment.

- *Checks*: A check is a special type of draft and it has two features that distinguish it from other drafts; 1) it is payable on demand and 2) the drawee must be a bank or it is payable at or through a bank.

- *The Order:* Drafts and checks must generally state an order (demand) that the drawee pay the payee.

- *The Drawer*: The person who issues an instrument is called the drawer.

- ***The Drawee***: The drawee does not have a legal obligation to pay a draft or check until the drawee "accepts" the instrument.
- ***The Payee***: The payee is the person to whom the instrument is originally issued, and the payee may direct the drawee regarding how and to whom to make payment.

PAPER CONTAINING A PROMISE ("TWO-PARTY PAPER"): Paper containing a promise to pay is an instrument that states a person's unconditional promise to pay money to another. There are two parties in a promise paper, the maker and the payee.

- ***(Promissory) Notes***: A note is a credit instrument in which the maker promises to pay the payee a sum of money on demand or at a later time. Payment may be made in installments or in a lump-sum.
- ***Certificates of Deposit***: A certificate of deposit is a special type of note that is issued by a bank acknowledging the receipt of money, and promising to pay it back at a future date with interest. Traditionally these were negotiable instruments commonly issued by banks, but they have largely been replaced by saver's certificates, which are not negotiable.
- ***The Promise***: The promise to pay must be unconditional.
- ***Maker***: The maker is the person who issues the promise paper and is the person who has the obligation to pay it.
- ***Payee***: The payee is the person to whom the note is originally issued.

THE SCOPE OF ARTICLE 7: Article 7 of the UCC governs documents of title. The two main types of documents of title are warehouse receipts and bills of lading.

FUNCTIONS AND FORMS: A document of title is used to define the rights of the owner when goods are turned over to someone else's custody. The documents also facilitate the transfer of title to such goods. When the owner negotiates a (negotiable) document of title to another person, the owner is transferring ownership of the goods covered by the document to the other person.

- ***Warehouse Receipts***: A warehouse receipt is a writing issued by a warehouseman (issuer) that 1) acknowledges receipt of goods for storage from a customer (depositor) and 2) states the terms of the parties' contract.
- ***Bills of Lading***: A bill of lading is issued by a carrier who is transporting goods. The consignor is the person who arranges the transportation, the consignee is the person who will receive the goods, and the issuer is the carrier.

STUDY HINTS FOR NRW CASE STUDIES

The following study hints may be helpful when resolving the NRW case studies.

NRW 20.1	➤ Before advising the NRW principals, review the permissible uses of negotiable instruments. ➤ Also, bear in mind the concept of "freedom of contract."
NRW 20.2	➤ To the extent that your advice may relate to the negotiable instruments, review the material dealing with checks and see how credit union checks are treated.
NRW 20.3	➤ Carefully review the material regarding uses of negotiable instruments. ➤ Note how revised Article 3 now treats credit union checks, formerly known as share drafts.

REVIEW OF KEY TERMS AND CONCEPTS

MATCHING EXERCISE

Select the term or concept that best matches a definition or statement set forth below. Each term or concept is the best match for only one definition or statement.

Terms and Concepts

a. Acceptance

b. Consignee

c. Consignor

d. Draft

e. Drawee

f. Drawer

g. Holder

h. Issuer

i. Maker

j. Note

k. Presentment

l. Warehouse receipt

Definitions and Statements

_____ 1. Written promise to pay a sum certain in money without conditions, on demand or at a future date, payable to order or bearer.

_____ 2. Written order directing a third person to pay a sum certain in money without conditions, on demand or at a future date, payable to order or bearer.

_____ 3. Person to whom an instrument is negotiated.

_____ 4. Demand for acceptance or payment of an instrument.

_____ 5. Agreement by a drawee to accept and/or pay an instrument.

_____ 6. Document of title acknowledging receipt of goods for storage.

_____ 7. Party who ships goods to another party.

_____ 8. Party to whom goods are shipped.

_____ 9. Person who, in general, creates and originally delivers any type of instrument.

_____ 10. Person who issues a note.

_____ 11. Person who issues a three-party instrument.

_____ 12. Person who is ordered to pay a three-party instrument.

COMPLETION EXERCISE

Fill in the blanks with the words that most accurately complete each statement.

1. The parties to a note are the _____ and the _____.

2. A _____ is a special form of draft which is payable on demand and is payable by, at, or through a bank.

3. When goods are turned over by the owner to another party's custody, a _____ _____ _____ is issued to define the parties' rights to the goods.

4. A carrier issues a _____ ____ _____ for goods that are received for shipment.

5. Four basic types of negotiable instruments are:

   a. _____.

   b. _____.

   c. _____.

   d. _____.

TRUE-FALSE EXERCISE

Write **T** if the statement is true, write **F** if the statement is false.

_____ 1. Cash is one form of negotiable instrument.

_____ 2. UCC Article 3 governs negotiable instruments and Article 7 governs documents of title.

_____ 3. Three-party paper includes drafts and checks.

_____ 4. A preaccepted check is one that the drawee has already agreed to pay.

_____ 5. Two-party paper states an unconditional promise to pay money.

_____ 6. A certificate of deposit is one type of three-party paper that is be issued by a bank and contains an unconditional order to pay on demand.

_____ 7. Notes are commonly used to evidence a debt obligation owed by the maker to the payee.

_____ 8. Credit union checks are one type of instrument that is governed by Article 3.

_____ 9. Traveler's checks are not instruments and, therefore, they are not governed by Article 3.

_____ 10. A party who stores goods belonging to another issues a warehouse receipt for the goods, a form of document of title governed by UCC Article 7.

APPLICATION OF CONCEPTS

MULTIPLE CHOICE QUESTIONS

_____ 1. Wilson sold goods to Brown for $1,000 on credit. Wilson issued a negotiable instrument that ordered Brown to pay the $1,000 on October 1. Brown signed the instrument, agreeing to pay as ordered. This instrument is a:
   a. promissory note.
   b. trade acceptance.
   c. check
   d. certificate of deposit

_____ 2. Myers issued a promissory note to Hays. In this case:
   a. Myers is the drawer.
   b. Myers is the maker.
   c. Hays is the payee.
   d. b and c.

_____ 3. Rankin issued a check that was drawn against his account at Last Bank. The check was issued to Douglas. In this case:
   a. Rankin is the maker.
   b. Last Bank is the drawer.
   c. Last Bank is the drawee.
   d. a and c.

_____ 4. Penny Ward issued an instrument that read: "August 1, 2003. John Haskins, you are hereby instructed to pay to the order of Steve Schwartz the sum of One Hundred Dollars ($100.00). /signed/ Penny Ward." This instrument is a:
   a. certificate of deposit.
   b. promissory note.
   c. draft.
   d. check.

SHORT ANSWER QUESTIONS

Answer the following questions, briefly explaining the reason for your answer.

1. Lites Abound Corp. sold 50 lamps to Jerry for $1,000 on credit. Lites Abound issued a document ordering Jerry to pay the $1,000 to Third Bank on July 1. What type of instrument is this document? Discuss Jerry's legal obligation, if any, to pay this document before he accepts it and after he accepts it.

_____

_____

2. Burton issued a check drawn on his account with First State Bank. The check ordered the bank to pay Roger $100. When Roger presented the check for payment, the bank refused to pay. Discuss the bank's legal obligation, if any, to pay this check.

_____

_____

3. Carla Imports, located in Los Angeles, delivered goods to Bonded Carriers for shipment. The goods were to be shipped to Ajax Distributors, located in Chicago. A negotiable bill of lading for the goods was issued to the order of Ajax. Carla then forwarded the bill of lading to Ajax. Discuss the rights of the parties to the goods.

_____

_____

4. Kendall Corp., located in Seattle, was sending a sales representative to Atlanta to make calls on customers. Kendall also owed $10,000 to a creditor who was located in Atlanta, and Kendall decided to have its sales representative deliver the payment personally. Kendall had just received a large cash payment from a customer. Kendall is trying to decide whether it should pay in cash or by check. What would you advise? Explain your answer.

CASE PROBLEMS

Answer the following case problems, explaining your answers.

1. Smithson issued an instrument that was drawn on his account with the Old Yorker Bank. The instrument was issued to the order of Molly, a creditor of Smithson, and it ordered the Old Yorker to pay $250 to Molly. While going to the Old Yorker Bank, Molly lost the instrument.

   (a) What type of instrument did Smithson issue?
   (b) Discuss the rights and duties of Old Yorker to pay this instrument.

---

2. Transatlantic Truckers accepted 300 crates of canned crab from Connecticut Crabbers for shipment to Supermarkets Galore in Montana. Transatlantic gave Connecticut Crabbers a document listing the contents and other relevant information regarding the shipment. The document stated 300 crates were received for shipment. Inexplicably, only 270 crates arrived in Montana.

   (a) What type of document did Transatlantic issue?
   (b) What is the purpose of this document?
   (c) Who is liable for the shortage?

CHAPTER REVIEW

INTRODUCTION: A person in possession of a negotiable instrument by means of a negotiation is called a "holder." The holder of a negotiable instrument has all of the rights of an assignee under contract law plus any rights granted by Article 3. A holder also may attain the status of "holder in due course."

One of the fundamental concepts of Article 3 and the law relating to negotiable instruments is the concept of holder in due course (HDC). This is because a HDC is entitled to enforce payment of an instrument without being subject to many defenses that would ordinarily allow others to escape their duty to pay. However, no one can be a HDC unless several requirements are met. The first requirement is that the paper in question (except for checks) must satisfy the six elements for negotiability stated in UCC § 3-104.

In general, paper is a negotiable instrument only if it meets the following six requirements:

1) the instrument is written;

2) it is signed by the drawer or maker;

3) it does not state any other undertaking or instruction by the person promising or ordering payment to do any act in addition to the payment of money;

4) a fixed sum of money;

5) it is payable on demand or at a definite time; and

6) it is payable to bearer or to the order of a party (i.e., words of negotiability).

If any element is missing, the paper is not a negotiable instrument and the person demanding payment cannot enjoy the rights of a HDC. The one exception to this general rule is that checks do not have to have the "words of negotiability" in order to be negotiable.

■ *Writing Requirement*: An instrument must be in writing to be negotiable, but it does not have to be a formal or preprinted form; any writing may satisfy this requirement.

■ *Signature Requirement*: To minimize forgery, the UCC requires an instrument to be signed by the maker or drawer, but any mark made with the intent to authenticate the writing suffices. A "telecheck" is created when a consumer agrees to pay for goods or services by allowing the vendor to prepare and issue a "pre-authorized check" drawn on the consumer's account at the consumer's designated financial institution containing the notation "verbally authorized by your depositor." Such a writing qualifies as a negotiable instrument and should be treated like any other check. The notation "verbally authorized by your depositor" takes the place of a written signature.

■ *The "Exclusive Obligation" Requirement*: Courts often use the "four-corner rule" to determine whether the promise or order in an instrument is unconditional. This means they look only to the instrument itself. If the instrument states that it is governed by or "subject to" terms of another writing, it is conditional and not negotiable. Also, if payment is conditioned upon some event occurring that is not absolutely certain to occur, then it is not negotiable. However, payment can be limited resort to a particular fund without rendering it nonnegotiable and a mere reference to another document does not affect negotiability.

- *Sum Certain Requirement*: As long as the amount to be paid is calculable from the information on the instrument, it satisfies the sum certain requirement and is negotiable.

- *Fixed Amount of Money Requirement*: The instrument must be payable in money which is defined to be the currency of any country. The interest to be paid may be stated as an amount, or as a fixed or variable interest rate. An instrument that does not expressly require payment of interest is presumed to be interest free.

- *Determinable Time Requirement: Payable On Demand or at a Fixed Time*: The payee or holder of an instrument must be able to tell from looking at the instrument when it is payable. The instrument must be either payable at a definite time or be payable "on demand." An instrument is payable on demand if it states that it is payable on sight, at presentment, or when no time for payment is stated. Language indicating that the instrument is payable after a future event of uncertain date renders the instrument nonnegotiable. A check must be payable on demand, but other drafts may be payable either on demand or at a definite time.

- *Words of Negotiability Requirement*: In general, an instrument must contain words of negotiability, meaning it must actually use the words either "pay to order" or "pay to bearer" or equivalent words, such as "pay to cash."

CONSTRUCTION AND INTERPRETATION: ARTICLE 3: Revised Article 3 attempts to foresee problems of interpretation that will arise frequently with negotiable instruments by setting out simple rules of interpretation. For instance UCC § 3-114 states: 1) handwritten terms control over typed or printed terms; 2) typewritten terms control over printed terms; and 3) words control over numbers.

REQUIREMENTS FOR NEGOTIABILITY: ARTICLE 7: Under Article 7, a document of title is negotiable if: 1) the document states that the goods are to be delivered to "bearer" or to "order" of a named person; and in international trade, it is negotiable if it runs to a named person or assigns. Whether a document is negotiable or not, the bailee still owes a duty of care to the bailor regarding the bailed goods.

STUDY HINTS FOR NRW CASE STUDIES

The following study hints may be helpful when resolving the NRW case studies.

NRW 21.1	➤ Review the formal requirements for negotiability, including the writing requirement and the signature requirement. ➤ As a practical matter, consider how NRW can maintain security over a mechanical or computerized system for executing company checks.
NRW 21.2	➤ Regarding the question of negotiability, consider the revisions to Article 3 relating to the requirement that a negotiable instrument state a fixed payment sum.
NRW 21.3	➤ Review the textbook material dealing with words of negotiability. ➤ Pay particular attention to the special rules relating to checks.

REVIEW OF KEY TERMS AND CONCEPTS

MATCHING EXERCISE

Select the term or concept that best matches a definition or statement set forth below. Each term or concept is the best match for only one definition or statement.

Terms and Concepts

a. Bearer

b. Fixed sum of money

c. Four-corner rule

d. Holder

e. Money

f. Order

g. Signature

h. Unconditional

i. Words of negotiability

Definitions and Statements

_____ 1. "Pay to order" or "pay to bearer."

_____ 2. Mark or symbol made with the intent to authenticate a writing.

_____ 3. Doctrine requiring that a document be interpreted solely by reference to its stated terms and without reference to outside events or other documents.

_____ 4. Absolute, without limitation.

_____ 5. Determinable amount of money that can be calculated from the terms of an instrument.

_____ 6. Person to whom an instrument has been negotiated.

_____ 7. Person who possesses an instrument that is payable to bearer or cash.

_____ 8. Written instruction to pay money signed by the person giving the instruction.

_____ 9. Currency of any recognized country.

COMPLETION EXERCISE

Fill in the blanks with the words that most accurately complete each statement.

1. A _____ instrument is one that fails to satisfy one or more of the requirements for negotiability.

2. A negotiable promissory note must be signed by the _____ , and a negotiable draft must be signed by _____.

3. In order to be a negotiable instrument, an instrument must state that it is payable in some form of _____.

4. Under the _____ - _____ rule, the negotiability of an instrument must be determined solely by reference to the terms of the instrument itself.

5. If the typed terms of an instrument conflict with preprinted terms, then the _____ terms will generally prevail.

TRUE-FALSE EXERCISE

Write **T** if the statement is true, write **F** if the statement is false.

_____ 1. An instrument that is issued in the United States, but payable in French francs, cannot be negotiable.

_____ 2. An instrument that promises to pay "six months after my college graduation" cannot be negotiable.

_____ 3. An instrument that promises to pay "$500 on delivery of the television" cannot be negotiable.

_____ 4. Negotiable instruments may be payable in money, goods, or services.

_____ 5. All negotiable drafts are payable on demand.

_____ 6. An instrument that is not payable to the order of a specific person or to bearer (or cash) cannot be negotiable.

_____ 7. If no time for payment is stated, an instrument is payable on demand.

_____ 8. An instrument that states that it is payable "with interest," without stating the amount of interest to be paid, cannot be negotiable.

_____ 9. An instrument that states that it is secured by collateral cannot be negotiable

_____ 10. A bill of lading stating "200 boxes of macaroni to be delivered to bearer" cannot be negotiable.

APPLICATION OF CONCEPTS

MULTIPLE CHOICE QUESTIONS

_____ 1. Jason issued a check, which promised to "pay to the order of Sam Turner Five Hundred Dollars ($50.00)." How much is Sam entitled to be paid?
   a. $0.
   b. $50.
   c. $500.
   d. Whatever amount Jason decides to pay.

___ 2. Ramsey Corp. wanted to borrow $5,000 from Kim. A promissory note was written out in longhand. The note stated that Ramsey Corp. promised to pay $5,000 on demand to the order of Kim. Ron Waters, President of Ramsey Corp., was authorized to sign the note and he signed it:

Ramsey Corp.
By _____
Ron Waters, President of Ramsey Corp.

    a. The note is nonnegotiable because it is handwritten.
    b. The note is nonnegotiable because it is only signed by an agent of Ramsey Corp.
    c. The note satisfies the writing and signature requirements and it may be negotiable.
    d. a and b.

___ 3. Which of the following terms in a promissory note would render the note nonnegotiable?
    a. Maria signed a note promising to pay $1,000 to the order of Jasmine. The duty to pay is subject to the terms of a separate loan contract made between Maria and Jasmine.
    b. Kyle signed a note promising to pay $1,000 and 100 bushels of wheat.
    c. Pete signed a note promising to pay $1,000, plus interest equal to the prime rate charged by Last Bank on January 1.
    d. a and b.

___ 4. Bill issued an instrument that stated: "August 1, 2005. I promise to pay to Jane Smith the sum of $500 with 10 percent interest from date. /signed/ Bill Adams." Is this instrument a negotiable instrument?
    a. No, because it does not state a time for payment.
    b. No, because it does not use words of negotiability.
    c. No, because it does not expressly state that the promise to pay is unconditional.
    d. Yes.

SHORT ANSWER QUESTIONS

Answer the following questions, briefly explaining the reason for your answer.

1. Martin purchased a gas station. Martin issued a $50,000 promissory note to the seller. The note stated that Martin's duty to pay was conditioned upon him obtaining a zoning change to expand the station. Is the promissory note negotiable?

_____

_____

2. Albert contracted to paint Johnson's house. Johnson issued and signed a promissory note to Albert that read in part, "I promise to pay to the order of Albert $2,000 on demand. This note arises out of a contract for painting services entered into by the parties on August 10, 2003." Is this a negotiable promissory note?

_____

_____

3. Harry contracted to repair Tina's car. Tina issued and signed a promissory note to Harry that read in part, "I promise to pay to the order of Harry Harrison the amount that is due pursuant to our contract dated July 1, 2004, together with 10% interest thereon until paid in full." Is this a negotiable promissory note?

_____

_____

4. Jennifer issued a check payable to the order of Acme Corp. for $100. Jennifer, however, stated on the check that it was nonnegotiable. Is the check a negotiable instrument?

_____

_____

CASE PROBLEMS

Answer the following case problems, explaining your answers.

1. Clarence Wellington III issued a promissory note to Alice stating: "I promise to pay to the order of Alice Haskins the sum of $500 on November 15, 2006 /signed/Clyde." Clarence used a pencil to write the promissory note on a piece of scratch paper. (a) Identify the six required elements of a negotiable instrument. (b) Is this promissory note negotiable?

_____

_____

_____

_____

2. Builders West, a contractor, hired Sparky, an electrician, to do the electrical work on an office project. According to their contract, Builders is obligated to pay Sparky $4,000 upon signing of the contract, with the balance payable upon completion of the project. The balance to be paid is undetermined and will be computed on an hourly rate after Sparky has completed his work. At Sparky's request, Builders issued a promissory note that stated, "Builders West promises to pay to the order of Sparky all sums due under its subcontract. Payment to be made 10 days after completion of the office project. /signed/Builders West." (a) Is the promissory note negotiable? (b) Does the promissory note represent a legal obligation to pay? (c) Does it matter whether the promissory note is negotiable or nonnegotiable?

_____

_____

_____

_____

CHAPTER 22 — Negotiation and Holders in Due Course/Holders by Due Negotiation

TRANSFER: Negotiable instruments are transferred by assignment or negotiation.

An assignment of an instrument is fraught with danger because the assignee (person who receives the instrument) takes it subject to any claims or defenses that the obligor (person required to pay the instrument) may assert against the assignor (the person who transferred the instrument). Negotiation, on the other hand, allows the transferee to become a holder and, perhaps, a holder in due course (HDC).

NEGOTIATION: Negotiation means the transfer of an instrument by one party (other than the maker or drawer) to a second party, in such a manner that the second party becomes a holder of the instrument.

What must be done to negotiate an instrument depends on the form of the instrument at the time it is transferred from one party to a second party. Negotiation may be accomplished in the following two ways: 1) If at the time of transfer the instrument is payable to bearer or cash ("bearer paper"), it may be negotiated by the authorized transfer of possession by the person who has possession of the instrument (an indorsement is NOT required); or 2) if at the time of transfer the instrument is payable to the order of a named person, then: (a) the named person must indorse (sign) the instrument and (b) the named person must authorize its transfer.

INDORSEMENTS: In general, an indorsement is any signature on an instrument, other than that of the maker, drawer or acceptor. Any of these indorsements by a holder is sufficient to negotiate the instrument. However, the different types of indorsements may affect how the instrument is subsequently negotiated and also affect the liability of the indorser. Types of indorsements include:

- *Special Indorsements*: A special indorsement is the signature of the indorser, together with words that specify an identified person to whom the instrument is next payable. A special indorsement: 1) passes ownership; 2) imposes liability on the indorser to pay the instrument if it is not properly paid by the maker or drawer; and 3) gives rise to certain implied warranties by the indorser. Following a special indorsement, negotiation of the instrument requires both indorsement and authorized transfer.

- *Blank Indorsements*: A blank indorsement is any indorsement that does not state an identified person to be paid. Typically, it is the indorser's signature without any other words. A blank indorsement generally has the same legal effect as a special indorsement EXCEPT that following a blank indorsement, an instrument is bearer paper and may be negotiated by transfer of possession alone.

- *Restrictive Indorsements*: A restrictive indorsement limits how the proceeds of an instrument may be applied. For instance, the restrictive indorsement "for deposit only" requires that the depository bank (first bank taking the instrument) to deposit the funds in a named account. Under revised Article 3, a restrictive indorsement that purports to restrict payment or negotiation may be disregarded by the indorsee with no affect on his or her rights or liabilities unless the restrictive indorsement restricts further negotiation of the instrument to banking channels.

- *Qualified Indorsements*: A qualified indorsement is an indorsement that includes the words "without recourse" or similar language indicating that the indorser denies liability to pay the instrument.

HOLDER: A holder is a party who 1) possess a negotiable instrument, 2) that is drawn, issued, or indorsed either to the party, to bearer, or in blank. The definition of "holder" is enlarged under revised Article 3. A person now can become a holder by gaining possession of an instrument through an involuntary transfer of possession. This means that if an instrument is payable to bearer or has been indorsed in blank and a person steals the instrument, then the thief becomes a holder.

HOLDER IN DUE COURSE: In order to be a HDC, a holder must take an instrument that appears to be regular, complete, and authenticate when he or she acquires the instrument, and the instrument must be taken 1) for value, 2) in good faith, and 3) with notice of defects or defenses affecting the instrument.

- *For Value*: Value includes: 1) actually performing a promise for which an instrument is issued; 2) taking an instrument as security for, or in payment of, an existing debt; 3) taking an instrument in exchange for another instrument; or 4) undertaking an irrevocable obligation of a third party in exchange. An unperformed promise is not value, even if it would be consideration for a contract.
- *In Good Faith*: Good faith is honesty in fact in the transaction and the observance of reasonable commercial standards of fair dealing. A holder lacks good faith if the holder 1) actually knew of a defect in the instrument, 2) ignored facts that would show such a defect or 3) fails to abide by reasonable commercial standards of doing business.
- *Without Notice of Defenses or Defects*: Notice is present if a reasonable person would know or have reason to know that there may be a defense, conflicting claim or ownership, or other defect.

EFFECT OF HOLDER IN DUE COURSE STATUS: A person who has liability to pay an instrument may assert a legal defense in order to avoid this liability. Any defense, whether personal or real, can be used to negate the right to be paid of a mere holder. A HDC, however, is subject only to real defenses.

- *Personal Defenses*: Personal defenses include right of recoupment, contract defenses that render an obligation voidable, fraud in the inducement, breach of contract, breach of warranty, and nondelivery.
- *Real Defenses*: Real defenses include: 1) the contractual defense of infancy (minority); 2) other contractual defenses, such as duress or illegality, that render a contractual obligation void under state law; 3) fraud in the execution; 4) discharge in insolvency (bankruptcy); 5) forgery of a person's signature; and 6) a subsequent material alteration of the instrument, *to the extent of the alteration*.

THE SHELTER PROVISION: With one exception, once a HDC has owned an instrument, then every subsequent holder can assert the rights of the HDC without having to prove his or her status as a HDC. The exception is that no one who engaged in any act of fraud or other illegality affecting the instrument can assert this right.

STATUTORY LIMITATIONS: Under FTC rules, if a transaction involves consumer credit, a holder or HDC is subject to *all* personal and real defenses that could be raised against the transferor.

HOLDER BY DUE NEGOTIATION: The holder of a duly negotiated document of title is a holder by due negotiation. A document of title has been duly negotiated if: 1) the holder purchased it in good faith and 2) without notice of any conflicting claims to the goods. Such a holder has the following rights: 1) title to the document; 2) title to the goods; 3) all rights under the laws of agency or estoppel; and 4) the right to have the goods held or delivered according to the terms of the document and free of any claims.

STUDY HINTS FOR NRW CASE STUDIES

The following study hints may be helpful when resolving the NRW case studies.

NRW 22.1	➤ Review the material relating to negotiation. ➤ It also may be valuable to look at Chapter 23 and the material relating to the liability of parties to pay an instrument.
NRW 22.2	➤ Review the material dealing with restrictive indorsements. ➤ Also consider the relevancy of the material relating to personal and real defenses.
NRW 22.3	➤ Carefully examine the negotiability requirements for an instrument. ➤ Evaluate what rights this document conferred upon NRW.

MATCHING EXERCISE

Select the term or concept that best matches a definition or statement set forth below. Each term or concept is the best match for only one definition or statement.

Terms and Concepts

a. Blank indorsement
b. Convert
c. Delivery (authorized)
d. Holder

e. Holder in due course
f. Indorsement
g. Negotiation
h. Personal defenses

i. Real defenses
j. Restrictive indorsement
k. Special indorsement
l. Qualified indorsement

Definitions and Statements

_____ 1. Person in possession of a negotiable instrument that is drawn, issued, or indorsed to the party, to bearer, or in blank.

_____ 2. Transfer of a negotiable instrument in such a manner that the transferee becomes a holder.

_____ 3. Defenses that may be asserted against a HDC.

_____ 4. Indorsement that does not specify the party to be paid.

_____ 5. Indorsement that limits how the proceeds shall be applied.

_____ 6. Holder that takes an instrument free of personal defenses.

_____ 7. Wrongfully take or hold.

_____ 8. Indorsement that does not impose signature (contractual) liability to pay.

_____ 9. Signature on a negotiable instrument that is made by someone other than the drawer or maker.

_____ 10. Indorsement that specifies the next party to be paid.

_____ 11. Defenses that cannot be asserted against a HDC.

_____ 12. Intentional transfer of a right or physical possession of a thing to another person.

COMPLETION EXERCISE

Fill in the blanks with the words that most accurately complete each statement.

1. A check that states "pay to the order of cash" is _____ paper.

2. A person to whom an instrument is negotiated is a _____.

3. _____ _____ means that a holder took an instrument with no actual knowledge or reason to suspect that something was wrong with the instrument or its transfer.

4. A _____ _____ is made when a person merely indorses his or her name to an instrument.

5. Identify the two requirements for negotiating an instrument that is payable to the order of a named person:

   a. _____.

   b. _____.

TRUE-FALSE EXERCISE

Write **T** if the statement is true, write **F** if the statement is false.

_____ 1. An ordinary holder does not have any right to demand or enforce payment of an instrument.

_____ 2. A person has notice of a fact only if the person has actual knowledge of the fact.

_____ 3. Under FTC rules, a HDC who has an instrument that arose out of a consumer credit transaction takes it subject to all defenses.

_____ 4. A forgery is a real defense that may be asserted against a HDC.

_____ 5. A holder who promises to do something has given value.

_____ 6. A personal defense cannot be asserted against a holder or a HDC.

_____ 7. Recoupment is a personal defense.

_____ 8. Illegality that would render a contractual obligation void under state law is a real defense and may be asserted against a HDC.

_____ 9. A person who takes an instrument after it has come due cannot be a HDC.

_____ 10. It is illegal to negotiate an instrument that is overdue.

APPLICATION OF CONCEPTS

MULTIPLE CHOICE QUESTIONS

_____ 1. In which case did Bill give value sufficient to be a holder in due course?
   a. Samantha issued a check to Paul. Paul indorsed the check, and delivered it to Bill as a gift.
   b. Tammy issued a check to Rod. Rod indorsed the check and delivered it to Bill in payment for services Bill promised to perform for Rod. Bill has not performed these services.
   c. Travis issued a negotiable note payable to Priscilla. Priscilla indorsed the note and negotiated it to Bill in payment of an existing debt that she owed Bill.
   d. b and c.

_____ 2.   Meg issued a negotiable note to Perry. Perry negotiated the note to Charles who paid value for the note. Which additional fact would prevent Charles from being a HDC?
   a.   The note was due May 1, and the note was negotiated to Charles on June 1.
   b.   When the note was negotiated to Charles, he knew that Meg had already refused to pay it.
   c.   One day after the note was negotiated to Charles, Meg told him that she refused to pay.
   d.   a and b.

_____ 3.   In which case does Marie have a personal defense?
   a.   Marie issued a check to Norm as payment for work that he improperly performed.
   b.   Marie issued a check to Rick due to his physical abuse. This abuse is duress and would render the obligation void under state law.
   c.   Marie's checkbook was stolen by a thief, and the thief forged her signature to a check.
   d.   All of the above.

_____ 4.   In which case does Monica have a real defense?
   a.   While mentally incompetent, Monica issued a check as payment for a car. Under state law, Monica's incompetency would render the obligation voidable.
   b.   Monica issued a check as payment for illegal drugs. Under state law, the illegal nature of the transaction would void Monica's obligation to pay.
   c.   Monica issued a check to Dean. Delivery of the check was conditioned on Dean's delivery of a stock certificate to Monica. Dean failed to deliver the certificate.
   d.   b and c.

SHORT ANSWER QUESTIONS

Answer the following questions, briefly explaining the reason for your answer.

1. Bob issued a check for $50 to Cathy as payment for cleaning services. Cathy raised the amount of the check to $500 and Steve cashed the check for Cathy. At the time Steve cashed the check, he noticed that the amount had been changed, but Cathy convinced him that it was nothing to worry about. Is Steve a HDC?

_____

_____

2. Dana bought a painting while intoxicated and she issued a check to the Art Studio as payment. Under state law, Dana's lack of capacity due to intoxication would render her obligation on the check voidable. The Art Studio negotiated the check to Last Bank, a HDC. Does Dana have to pay the amount of the check to Last Bank?

_____

_____

3. While Marie was a minor, she issued a negotiable promissory note to Todd as payment for a motorcycle. Todd negotiated the note to a HDC as payment of a debt that he owed the HDC. Marie is still a minor, but she no longer wants the cycle and she refuses to pay the note. Does Marie have to pay the HDC the unpaid balance of the note?

_____

_____

4. Anna, an attorney, rendered legal services for Bob. Anna was not licensed to practice law in the state where she represented Bob. Anna's failure to have the required license would void Bob's obligation to pay her. Nonetheless, Bob issued a check in the amount of $2,000 to Anna as payment for her services, and Anna negotiated the check to Harry, a HDC. Bob now refuses to pay the check to Harry. Can Bob assert his defense of illegality against Harry, thereby avoiding his obligation to pay?

_____

_____

CASE PROBLEMS

Answer the following case problems, explaining your answers.

1. Samantha issued a check payable to the order of Margaret Shelf. Subsequently, the following transactions occurred: (a) Margaret negotiated the check to Rob, indorsing it "Pay to Rob Akron /signed/ Margaret Shelf;" (b) Rob then negotiated the check to Chuck, indorsing it "/signed/ Rob Akron;" (c) Chuck negotiated the check to Jill, indorsing it "/signed/Chuck Ware, Without Recourse;" and (d) Jill negotiated the check to her bank, indorsing it "/signed/Jill Weaver, For Deposit Only."

What type of indorsement did each person make? Describe the legal effect of each indorsement.

_____

_____

_____

_____

2. Jacob issued a $50,000 negotiable note to Winston to pay for a parcel of land. Winston intentionally misrepresented to Jacob that the real estate had large oil reserves. Winston negotiated the note to Julia. Julia paid Winston $50,000 for the note, and she took it without notice of Winston's fraud. (a) Is Julia a HDC? (b) Is Jacob's defense of fraud a personal or real defense? (c) Does Jacob have to pay Julia the amount of the note?

_____

_____

_____

_____

CHAPTER 23

Negotiables: Liability and Discharge

CHAPTER REVIEW

BASIC CONCEPTS: Negotiable instruments are a substitute for money. When the holder of the a negotiable instrument wants to convert it to money, the holder must properly present it for payment to the maker or to the drawee. Proper presentment usually results in payment and cancellation of the instrument. Sometimes, though, the instrument is dishonored (payment is refused) which may create secondary liability to pay the instrument for prior holders and/or indorsers.

THE CHAINS OF LIABILITY: Liability refers to an obligation to pay an instrument.

■ *Primary liability*: A primary party is the party who is normally expected to pay an instrument. The primary liability of certain parties can be summarized as follows:

1) The maker of a note has primary liability to pay the holder of a note. As soon as the maker of a note signs it, the maker is primarily liable to the holder or any subsequent holders;

2) The issuer of a cashier's check or other draft drawn on the drawer has primary liability to pay; and

3) Upon acceptance, a drawee has primary liability to pay the accepted instrument. Prior to acceptance, however, the drawee is not liable to a payee or holder to pay.

■ *Secondary liability*: Except as stated below, secondary parties agree to pay an instrument if 1) presentment is properly made; 2) the primary party dishonors the instrument; and 3) notice of the dishonor is properly given to the secondary party. The drawer of a check or draft and every indorser (except for indorsers who sign "without recourse") have secondary liability to pay an instrument.

If a draft is accepted upon proper presentment and the acceptance is by a bank, the drawer is discharged. However, if the draft is accepted by a drawee that is not a bank, the drawer is not discharged.

An indorser is liable on an instrument if: 1) he or she made a qualified indorsement; 2) notice of any dishonor is required in order to hold the indorser liable and such notice is not given; 3) the instrument is accepted by a bank after the indorsement is made; or 4) the indorsed instrument is a check and it is not presented to the drawee bank or deposited within 30 days after the indorsement.

ESTABLISHING LIABILITY: The secondary (contractual) liability indorsers (and, in rare cases, also drawers) does not arise unless there is proper presentment, dishonor, and notice of dishonor of an instrument.

■ *Presentment*: Presentment is a proper and timely demand for payment that is made upon the maker, drawee, or acceptor of the instrument by the holder/presenter.

■ *Acceptance*: A drawee accepts a draft by writing its acceptance on the draft. However, UCC Article 4 makes a drawee bank liable for a draft if it does not pay or return the draft, or send notice of its dishonor, until after the drawee bank's midnight deadline (midnight of the next business day after the check is presented and dishonored). If a draft is accepted by a bank, the drawer and any indorsers who indorsed the draft prior to its acceptance are all discharged from secondary liability.

■ *Dishonor*: An instrument is dishonored when proper presentment is made and acceptance is refused.

■ *Notice*: Notice of dishonor may be given using any commercially reasonable means. Notice regarding an instrument taken for collection (such as a check) must be given: 1) by a bank by its midnight deadline or when it receives notice of dishonor; and 2) by anyone else within 30 days following the day on which the person receives notice of dishonor. Failure to give proper or timely notice will release all secondary parties except the drawer from liability.

TYPES OF LIABILITY: A negotiable instrument is a special type of contract. When a person signs an instrument (except "without recourse"), the person promises to pay it under certain circumstances.

■ *Indorsement liability*: An unqualified indorsement may give rise to secondary liability to pay. Two special types of indorsements relating to this rule are ones made as an accommodation or guarantee.

1) An accommodation party is one who signs an instrument in order to benefit another person to the instrument, and the accommodation party may sign as maker, acceptor, drawer, or indorser. The accommodation party's duty to pay corresponds to the capacity in which the party signs.

2) A person who signs an instrument guaranteeing collection (as opposed to payment) may have liability to pay if certain conditions are first met.

■ *Warranty liability*: A party who transfers an instrument or presents it for payment or acceptance makes warrants that certain matters are true regarding the instrument. One set of warranties are made when the instrument is transferred, and other warranties are made when it is presented for payment or acceptance. When a warranty is breached, the person making the warranty is liable for losses caused by the breach of warranty. A warrantor may have warranty liability even if the warrantor does not have a contractual obligation to pay the instrument.

SPECIAL PROBLEMS: In general, a forgery or illegal signature has no legal effect and does not impose liability on the person whose signature is forged, unless that person ratifies the unauthorized signature. However, two rules depart from this basic rule.

The "imposter rule" and the "fictitious payee rule" apply when a person is deceived into issuing an instrument to an imposter who pretends to be an intended payee, or a person is conned into issuing an instrument payable to a fictitious person. In these cases, the imposter or con artist usually forges the payee's indorsement or indorses the fictitious person's name and obtains payment of the instrument. In these cases, the issuer must pay anyone who, in good faith, subsequently pays or takes the instrument.

DISCHARGE: Discharge terminates the liability or potential liability of parties to pay an instrument. Discharge may result from the following actions:

■ *Payment*: Proper payment discharges everyone's liability; payment improperly made does not.

■ *Tender of payment*: A tender of payment that is wrongfully refused discharges secondary parties.

■ *Cancellation and renunciation*: Discharge occurs when the holder cancels the instrument or renounces his or her rights on the instrument in a signed writing.

■ *Impairment*: When a holder releases a prior party or collateral securing payment, the holder also generally discharges some or all of the secondary parties on the instrument.

■ *Other discharges*: Other acts may cause a complete or partial discharge of liability.

STUDY HINTS FOR NRW CASE STUDIES

The following study hints may be helpful when resolving the NRW case studies.

NRW 23.1	➢ Review the warranties made upon presentment of an instrument.
	➢ Analyze what type of liability a drawer has for his or her check.
NRW 23.2	➢ Determine what type of indorsement was made by NRW's customer, the nature of her liability, and the requirement that notice of dishonor be given.
	➢ Do not overlook the potential warranty liability that indorsers generally incur.
NRW 23.3	➢ Determine what type of defense is involved.
	➢ Determine whether NRW is a HDC or not.

REVIEW OF KEY TERMS AND CONCEPTS

MATCHING EXERCISE

Select the term or concept that best matches a definition or statement set forth below. Each term or concept is the best match for only one definition or statement.

Terms and Concepts

a. Accommodation

b. Discharge

c. Dishonor

d. Midnight deadline

e. Presentment

f. Presentment warranties

g. Primary liability

h. Secondary liability

i. Transfer warranties

Definitions and Statements

_____ 1.   Time by which a bank must generally give notice of a dishonored instrument.

_____ 2.   Liability to pay an instrument that is conditioned upon proper presentment, dishonor, and notice of dishonor.

_____ 3.   Request by a holder for payment or acceptance of an instrument.

_____ 4.   Guarantees that a party makes when negotiating or assigning an instrument.

_____ 5.   Refusal of a primary party to accept or pay an instrument that is properly presented.

_____ 6.   Guarantees that a party makes when demanding payment of an instrument.

_____ 7.   Termination of liability to pay an instrument

_____ 8.   Liability to pay an instrument that is NOT conditioned upon presentment, dishonor, and notice of dishonor.

_____ 9.   Act that is undertaken to benefit another.

COMPLETION EXERCISE

Fill in the blanks with the words that most accurately complete each statement.

1. The _____ of a note has primary liability to pay it.

2. A drawee does not have any liability to pay a draft or check until there is an express or implied _____ of the instrument by the drawee.

3. In general, a bank must give notice of dishonor of an instrument by its _____ _____ in order to hold an indorser contractually liable on the instrument.

4. Persons who transfer or present instruments may incur contractual liability to pay the instrument and also _____ _____ to pay damages if certain matters turn out to be false.

5. Identify four common ways by which a party can be discharged from liability or potential liability to pay an instrument:

a. _____.

b. _____.

c. _____.

d. _____.

TRUE-FALSE EXERCISE

Write **T** if the statement is true, write **F** if the statement is false.

_____ 1. A party who signs an instrument may incur primary or secondary liability to pay the instrument.

_____ 2. Presentment is a party's agreement to pay an instrument.

_____ 3. A drawee is not primarily liable to pay a check or draft until the drawee accepts the instrument.

_____ 4. A primary party is liable to pay an instrument even if a holder fails to present the instrument for payment when it is due.

_____ 5. If there are two or more unqualified indorsers of a draft and the drawee dishonors the instrument, the holder of the instrument can hold only the last indorser liable.

_____ 6. Parties (other than banks) must generally give notice of dishonor within 30 days following the day on which they receive notice of dishonor.

_____ 7. Parties are discharged from their liability to pay an instrument if the holder cancels the instrument.

_____ 8. A bank that issues a cashier's check has primary liability to pay it.

_____ 9. Payment, whether properly or improperly made, discharges everyone's liability on an instrument.

_____ 10. An indorser may be obligated to pay an instrument even if it is not presented for acceptance or payment when it is due.

APPLICATION OF CONCEPTS

MULTIPLE CHOICE QUESTIONS

_____ 1. In which case may Nick have secondary liability to pay if the instrument in question is subsequently dishonored?
   a. Nick issued a check to Clint.
   b. Nick issued a negotiable promissory note to Lonnie.
   c. Ed issued a check for cash to Nick. Nick negotiated the check to Kate without indorsing it.
   d. a and c.

_____ 2. In which case does Drake have primary liability to pay the instrument in question?
   a. Drake issued a check to Rhonda.
   b. Sally sold goods to Drake, and Sally issued a sales draft ordering Drake to pay the $500 purchase price to First Bank. Drake signed the draft, thereby accepting it.
   c. Dorothy issued a check to Drake. Drake indorsed the check "Drake Soren," and then negotiated the check to Frank.
   d. a and b.

_____ 3. Max issued Irene a $9,000 note. Irene sold the note to Fair Factors, indorsing it "without recourse." Max failed to pay the note because of a lack of funds. Under these facts:
   a. Irene has secondary liability to pay the note.
   b. Irene has warranty liability to pay the note.
   c. Irene has no liability to pay the note.
   d. a and b.

_____ 4. Abe issued a negotiable note to Kay. Payment of the note was secured by certain collateral. Kay indorsed the note "Kay Jones," and negotiated the note and security interest to Bart. In which situation is Kay discharged from liability on the note?
   a. Bart released Abe from liability on the note without Kay's consent.
   b. Bart accepted an early partial payment from Abe without Kay's consent.
   c. Bart terminated the security interest in the collateral without Kay's consent.
   d. a and c.

SHORT ANSWER QUESTIONS

Answer the following questions, briefly explaining the reason for your answer.

1. Pat issued a check to the order of Ken's Groceries. Ken properly indorsed the check and negotiated it to Last Bank. When Last Bank requested payment from Pat's bank, her bank refused due to insufficient funds in Pat's account. (Presentment, dishonor, and notice of dishonor were proper.) Under these facts, who has liability to pay the check to Last Bank?

_____

_____

2. Wally issued a check to Jake, and the check was drawn on Wally's bank, Peoria Bank. Jake presented the check to Peoria Bank and it accepted the check for payment. The next day, Peoria Bank discovered that Wally had no money in his account and it refused to disburse the funds to Jake. Must Peoria Bank pay the check to Jake?

_____

_____

3. Shirley issued a check payable to the order of John, and the check was drawn on Shirley's account at Third Bank. John indorsed the check in blank and negotiated it to Neil. Neil also indorsed the check in blank and presented it to Third Bank. Third Bank, however, refused to pay the check due to insufficient funds in Shirley's account. Third Bank immediately notified Neil of the dishonor, but Neil failed to inform John about the dishonor until several months later. Who has secondary liability to pay the check to Neil?

_____

_____

4. Ellen's checkbook was stolen by Lisa, and Lisa forged Ellen's signature on one of her checks and cashed it at Pizza To Go, who accepted the check in good faith and without notice that Lisa had forged Ellen's signature. Does Ellen have liability to pay this check?

_____

_____

CASE PROBLEMS

Answer the following case problems, explaining your answers.

1. Allison posed as James' landlord, Michelle. For two months, James wrote out his rent checks payable to Michelle, but gave them to Allison thinking she was Michelle. Allison indorsed and cashed these checks at Check-Rite Service. Discuss the rights of Michelle, James, and Check-Rite in this case.

_____

_____

_____

_____

2. On February 1, Mike issued a negotiable note to Patsy Bates. The note was due August 1. On June 1, Patsy indorsed the note "Patsy Bates," and negotiated the note to Noel. Noel did not present the note to Mike until November 1, and Mike refused payment due to cash flow problems. On that same day, Noel gave Patsy notice of Mike's nonpayment. (a) What is the nature of Mike's and Patsy's liability to pay the note? (b) Discuss whether the parties' respective liabilities are subject to any conditions? (c) Discuss whether Mike and/or Patsy are obligated to pay the note to Noel?

_____

_____

_____

_____

CHAPTER 24 — Bank-Customer Relations/Electronic Funds Transfers

---

> ## CHAPTER REVIEW

BASIC CONCEPTS: The bank-customer relationship is governed by Part 4 of Article 4 of the UCC. A checking account creates several relationships between the bank and the customer. First, a checking account a contract between the bank and customer. A checking account also makes the bank is an agent of the customer, and the bank must pay when a customer legally writes a check. Finally, the bank is a debtor of the customer as long as the customer's checking account is not overdrawn.

THE CUSTOMER: RIGHTS AND DUTIES: A bank customer has a duty to act with due care. UCC § 4-402 makes a bank liable to the customer for actual damages if the bank wrongfully dishonors a check. These damages include 1) damages due to arrest; 2) damages due to prosecution; 3) other consequential damages that can be proved. Under other theories of law, a customer may recover punitive damages if a bank acted recklessly or with malice. To collect damages, a customer must not have contributed to his or her loss.

A customer has the right to stop payment on a check. A valid stop-payment order can be oral or written, and must contain: 1) the check number; 2) payee's name; 3) amount of check; 4) date of check; and 5) reason for the stop payment. If a bank pays a check despite a valid stop-payment order, the customer may collect damages if the customer can prove a loss resulting from the bank's conduct. An oral stop-payment order expires after 14 days unless it is confirmed in writing within this time, in which case it is then good for 6 months.

A bank must send statements to its customers and a customer must exercise reasonable promptness to examine his or her bank statement, to reconcile his or her account with the statement provided by the bank, and to discover any unauthorized signatures or alterations on any items included in the statement. The customer must promptly report any such errors or wrongful actions to the bank. The bank can avoid liability to the customer for paying an unauthorized item if 1) the customer does not give the bank prompt notice and 2) the bank can prove that it suffered a loss due to the delay.

THE BANK: RIGHTS AND DUTIES: The primary duty of a bank is to exercise ordinary care. A bank cannot disclaim its responsibility for a lack of good faith or for a failure to exercise ordinary care, nor can it limit the measure of damages for lack of good faith or failure to exercise ordinary care. Basic rights of a bank include the following:

1) A bank has the right to charge the customers' accounts for their checks unless the bank has notice that a check was completed improperly or in bad faith.

2) A bank has the option of refusing to pay a stale check, which is a check more than six months old.

3) If a customer dies or becomes incompetent, the bank may pay on the customer's account until it learns of the death or incompetency.

4) If a bank learns of a customer's death or incompetency, the bank may honor checks for ten days after the date of death or incompetency, unless there has been a stop-payment order.

5) UCC § 4-407 gives the bank subrogation rights, which can give the bank the rights of: a) a holder in due course against the maker or drawer; b) a payee or any holder against the maker or drawer; or c) the drawer or maker against the payee or any holders.

6) A bank may pay an item or otherwise settle an item without liability to third parties so long as it exercises ordinary care in handling the item and follows its normal practices and procedures.

SPECIAL PROBLEMS: Certified checks and unauthorized signatures present special problems.

- *Certified Checks*: A certified check makes the bank primarily liable for the check. When requesting a certified check, a customer must typically pay the amount of the check in advance.
- *Unauthorized Signatures*: UCC § 1-201 provides that an unauthorized signature (for example, a forgery) cannot impose liability on the person whose name was signed without authority. However, UCC § 3-406 imposes liability on a person who, because of negligence, contributed to the unauthorized signing of the check.

FUNDS TRANSFERS: ARTICLE 4A: Technology, changes in banking laws, and growth of international banking have created the need for several new banking regulations. Article 4A governs wire transfers. Article 4A specifically excludes coverage of areas already governed by the EFTA.

FUND TRANSFERS: ELECTRONIC FUND TRANSFERS: There are four widely used methods of electronic funds transfers. The point of sale (POS) transfer uses a debit card, and the transaction looks like a credit card purchase. The automated teller machine (ATM) transaction allows customers to deposit into or to obtain money from a machine using a card and a personal identification number (PIN). Customers may authorize payments by phone if their bank is on a network. Finally, a customer may preauthorize payments or direct deposits. The Electronic Funds Transfer Act (EFTA) governs these types of transactions.

EFT consumers have the same type of rights and duties as checking account customers. If a consumer gives proper and timely notice of the loss or theft of a card, the consumer's damages are limited to $50. If notice is proper but not timely, the consumer may be liable for up to $500.

THE EXPEDITED FUNDS AVAILABILITY ACT: (1) If the customer makes a deposit of cash, a cashier's check, a certified check, a government check, a check drawn against the customer's bank, or by wire transfer, and the deposit is made with a teller, then the customer can write checks against the amount deposited on the next business day. (2) If a local check is deposited but it is not drawn against the customer's bank, the customer can write checks for the first $100 the next business day, checks for the balance of the amount deposited up to $5,000 on the second business day, and checks for the remainder on the ninth business day. (3) If the customer deposits a non-local check, the customer can write checks for the first $100 the next business day, checks up to $5,000 on the fifth business day, and checks for the remainder on the ninth business day.

CHECK TRUNCATION: Check truncation is the changing of a check into an electronic or digital image.

TRANSFERABLE RECORDS: A transferable record is the electronic equivalent of a promissory note.

STUDY HINTS FOR NRW CASE STUDIES

The following study hints may be helpful when resolving the NRW case studies.

NRW 24.1	➢ Review the material on the bank customer's rights and duties. As a practical matter, consider immediately talking to the stationer before resorting to a stop-payment order.
NRW 24.2	➢ Examine the material on the bank customer's rights and duties for time limits on reconciling bank statements.
	➢ Review the same material for the consequences of failing to give a bank prompt notice.
NRW 24.3	➢ Before advising the parties, review Article 4A regarding funds transfers.
	➢ When preparing your advice, remember that sometimes it is better not to be too demanding when establishing a relationship with a new customer.

REVIEW OF KEY TERMS AND CONCEPTS

MATCHING EXERCISE

Select the term or concept that best matches a definition or statement set forth below. Each term or concept is the best match for only one definition or statement.

Terms and Concepts

a. ATM

b. Certified check

c. EFT

d. Exemplary damages

e. Overdraft

f. Stale check

g. Stop payment

h. Subrogation

i. Unauthorized signature

Definitions and Statements

_____ 1. A check written for an amount over the amount on account, and accepted by the drawee.

_____ 2. A check over six months old, which a bank may dishonor.

_____ 3. An instrument that makes the drawee primarily liable.

_____ 4. An order for a bank to not pay on a check.

_____ 5. Punitive damages.

_____ 6. Given the rights of another.

_____ 7. Electronic funds transfers.

_____ 8. Signature made without express or implied authority.

_____ 9. Automated teller machine.

COMPLETION EXERCISE

Fill in the blanks with the words that most accurately complete each statement.

1. Wire transfer are governed by UCC _____ _____.

2. An _____ _____ is inoperative against the person whose name was signed.

3. A checking account creates the following three relationships between a bank and a customer:

   a. _____.

   b. _____.

   c. _____.

4. A bank customer generally has a duty to act with _____ _____.

5. If a bank wrongfully dishonors a customer's check, the customer may sue for the following damages:

a. _____.

b. _____.

c. _____.

TRUE-FALSE EXERCISE

Write **T** if the statement is true, write **F** if the statement is false.

_____ 1. A bank is legally required to dishonor stale checks.

_____ 2. A bank is always liable if it cashes a check with an unauthorized signature.

_____ 3. The EFTA governs consumers' funds transfers that are accomplished by issuance of checks.

_____ 4. A drawer may lose the right to assert against a drawee bank a claim that a check had been altered if the drawer's negligence substantially contributed to the alteration.

_____ 5. A drawer may be criminally liable for issuing a bad check if the drawer's account has insufficient funds to pay for the check.

_____ 6. If a bank wrongfully dishonors a check, a customer may sue the bank for damages only if the customer suffered actual damages, the customer did not contribute to the damages, and the bank's actions where the proximate cause of those damages.

_____ 7. A bank must dishonor a check if it will create an overdraft on a customer's account.

_____ 8. A bank may choose not to pay a check if the bank believes in good faith that the customer's funds will go to a dishonest person or be used in a shady business deal.

_____ 9. A reasonable time in which a customer must examine his or her bank statement is one year.

_____ 10. A bank must immediately stop paying on a customer's account once it is notified that the customer has died.

APPLICATION OF CONCEPTS

MULTIPLE CHOICE QUESTIONS

_____ 1. Dan's checkbook was stolen by Milton. Milton forged Dan's signature on a check and issued it to Penny, who was unaware of the forgery. Penny presented the check to Left Bank, the drawee bank. Left Bank paid the check and charged Dan's account for the amount of the check. Under these facts:
a. Left Bank was entitled to charge Dan's account for the check, and it has no obligation to recredit his account.
b. Left Bank must recredit Dan's account for the amount of the check.
c. Between Left Bank and Dan, Left Bank must bear any loss that may occur due to its payment of the check.
d. b and c.

____ 2. Consumer electronic fund transfers are governed by:
   a. Common law of contracts.
   b. The UCC.
   c. The Electronic Funds Transfer Act.
   d. All of the above.

____ 3. Cody has a checking account with State Bank. Cody has $10,000 in his checking account. Cody issued a check to Paul for $5,000. Paul properly presented the check for payment to State Bank, but the bank dishonored the check. As a result, Cody incurred $100 damages and Paul incurred $50 damages. Under these facts:
   a. State Bank is not liable to Cody or Paul.
   b. State Bank is liable to Paul for $50 damages, but it is not liable to Cody.
   c. State Bank is liable to Cody for $100 damages, but it is not liable o Paul.
   d. State Bank is liable to Cody for $100 damages, and it is liable to Paul for $50 damages.

____ 4. Bannock Company uses a rubber stamp with the company's name on it to sign its checks. Bannock keeps this rubber stamp, along with its company checks, securely locked in a safe. An employee broke into the safe and, using the company checks and the rubber stamp, wrote checks to himself for $10,000. Under these facts:
   a. Bannock may assert that the checks had an unauthorized signature and not be liable.
   b. Bannock will be liable for the checks because it failed to use proper measures to safeguard the checks and rubber stamp.
   c. Bannock will be liable for the checks because it is always negligent for a company to use a rubber stamp to sign its checks even if the rubber stamp is stored in a safe place.
   d. b and c.

SHORT ANSWER QUESTIONS

Answer the following questions, briefly explaining the reason for your answer.

1. Charlie had a checking account at West Bank. On May 1, Charlie wrote a check to Susan. On May 2, Charlie died in an auto accident, and West Bank was informed of his death. On May 13, Susan presented Charlie's check at West Bank for payment. May West Bank pay the check?

_____

_____

2. Maria wrote a check to Luis on April 15 from her account at Eagle Bank. On April 16, Maria gave Eagle Bank a written stop-payment order. On November 15, Luis presented the check at Eagle Bank, and the bank paid Luis. Did Eagle Bank act properly?

_____

_____

3. On June 1, Sandy wrote a check to Louis Lawyer for legal services. On June 2, Sandy realized that Louis had overcharged her, so she called her bank and requested a stop payment on her check to Louis. However, Louis had cashed the check on June 1. Can Sandy sue the bank for paying on the check?

_____

_____

4. Steve wrote a check to Robert for $500 and specifically told Robert to wait two days before depositing the check. Robert ignored Steve and deposited the check the same day in his account at North Bank. Also on the same day, Robert bought a new stereo from Al's Electronix for $520. At the time of deposit, Robert had $50 in his account. When Robert's check "bounced," Al assessed a $15 service charge against Robert and had him arrested for passing bad checks. Does Robert have any recourse against North Bank?

_____

_____

CASE PROBLEMS

Answer the following case problems, explaining your answers.

1. Jennifer, president of Jenco, hired Travis as her new secretary. Travis' responsibilities include "signing" employee paychecks twice a month by using a rubber stamp of Jennifer's signature. Jennifer always kept the rubber stamp with her signature in a locked drawer, and only she and Travis had the key. One day, Travis used the rubber stamp to sign a check, made out to himself, for $10,000. Travis left, never to be heard from again. Jennifer later learned that Travis was once convicted for embezzlement. However, she did not investigate Travis before hiring him. If the bank pays the check before Jennifer can place a stop-payment order, discuss whether Jennifer can recover her money.

_____

_____

_____

_____

2. Jeff duly issued a check to Ernie for $100. Ernie wrongfully raised the amount to $1,000, and he presented the check to Last Bank, the drawee. Last Bank paid Ernie $1,000, and it credited Jeff's account for this amount. Last Bank exercised reasonable care at all times. One week after receiving his bank statement, Jeff noticed the improper payment and informed Last Bank of the alteration. (a) Describe Jeff's duty to examine his bank statement and report alterations to Last Bank. (b) Did Jeff give timely notice of the alteration? (c) For how much, if any, can Last Bank charge Jeff's account?

_____

_____

_____

_____

CHAPTER 25   Secured Transactions: Attachment and Perfection

CHAPTER REVIEW

CREDIT FINANCING AND ARTICLE 9: Article 9 provides a means for selling goods on credit while allowing sellers to protect themselves in case the buyer defaults on payments. The seller in a secured transaction is called the secured party; the person whose property secures payment is the debtor; and the property, which secures the obligation, is the collateral. Collateral can include personal property as well as general intangibles, such as patents or goodwill.

SCOPE OF ARTICLE 9: Article 9 governs any transaction that is intended to create a security interest in personal property or fixtures. A security interest is "an interest in personal property or fixtures which secures payment or performance of an obligation." The UCC classifies collateral either according to its intended and actual use, or its nature. Types of collateral are:

1) **Consumer goods**: Goods are used or bought primarily for personal, family, or household purposes.

2) **Equipment**: Goods used or bought for use primarily in business (e.g., a company's fax)

3) **Farm products**: Crops, livestock, or supplies used or produced in farming operations. Also, products of crops or livestock in their unmanufactured states that are held by farmers.

4) **Inventory**: Goods held for sale or lease, and raw materials, work in process, and materials consumed in a business (e.g., an appliance shop's stock of TVs that are held for sale).

5) **Fixtures**: Goods that become a part of real estate (e.g., a furnace).

6) **Documents**: Negotiable documents of title to goods, such as bills of lading and warehouse receipts.

7) **Instruments**: Negotiable instruments, such as checks and negotiable promissory notes, and securities, such as stocks and bonds.

8) **Chattel paper**: Chattel paper is a writing or writings that represent: a) a promise to pay money; and b) either a security interest in, or a lease of, specific goods.

9) **Accounts**: Any right to payment for goods that have been sold or leased, or for services rendered, that is not represented by an instrument or chattel paper (e.g., accounts receivable).

10) **General intangibles**: Other personal property, such as goodwill of a business and trademarks.

ATTACHMENT: THE CREATION OF A SECURITY INTEREST: A security interest is not enforceable until it attaches to the collateral. Attachment creates a security interest in the collateral, and it establishes the rights of the creditor in the collateral. Following attachment, the creditor can assert rights superior to those of the debtor in the collateral if or when the debtor defaults on the agreement.

Attachment occurs when:

1) there is an oral agreement between the parties and the secured party physically holds the collateral (a pledge) or there is an authenticated record of the agreement with a sufficient description of the collateral ("authenticated" means a signed record or adoption and execution of a symbol or encryption of a record with the intent to identify the authenticating party and to accept the record, and "record" means information inscribed on a tangible medium or stored in an electronic, retrievable medium);

2) the debtor has legal rights in the collateral (ownership or a leasehold interest); and

3) the secured party gives value for the security interest (loan of money, sale on credit, or the collateral is given to secure a preexisting debt).

Property obtained by a debtor after signing a security agreement (after-acquired property) may serve as collateral (floating lien), and collateral may secure future credit extended to a debtor (future advance).

PERFECTION: In order to obtain priority over other creditors or buyers who may have an interest in the same collateral, a secured party must perfect its interest. Perfection may occur in one of four ways, depending on the type of collateral involved.

- ■ *Perfection by filing*: Filing a financing statement gives notice to other creditors and persons who are considering purchasing the collateral that the collateral is already subject to a security interest.

    In general, filing is done centrally in the state of the debtor's primary residence. Exceptions to this rule include: 1) a security interest in collateral related to real estate is filed locally; 2) many states require that a security interest in motor vehicles can be perfected only by having the security interest noted on the certificate of title; and 3) if the debtor is an individual who moves to another state after the secured party has perfected, then the secured party must refile in the new state within four months or the security interest will lapse.

    A filing is effective upon the due presentation of a financing statement together with the proper filing fees. It is effective for five years from the date of filing and may be continued for additional five-year periods if a continuation statement is timely filed. The financing statement must include the name of the debtor, the name of the secured party, and indicate the collateral that is covered.

- ■ *Perfection by possession of the collateral*: In most cases, a security interest in instruments, such stocks and bonds, can be perfected only by the secured party taking possession of the collateral. Otherwise, a secured party may choose to perfect a security interest in tangible collateral, such as equipment or inventory, and semi-tangible collateral, such as chattel paper, by taking physical possession of the collateral. Perfection begins at the time possession begins and ends when the secured party turns the collateral over to the debtor.

- ■ *Perfection by control of the collateral*: If a security interest is in investment property, deposit accounts, letter-of-credit rights, or electronic chattel paper, then the secured party may perfect by taking control of the collateral.

- ■ *Automatic Perfection*: In general, a purchase money security interest in consumer goods may be perfected automatically, meaning the secured party is not required to do anything to perfect it.

LEASE INTENDED AS SECURITY: Sometimes a lease may be a security interest that secures payment of a conditional sale. It is important to distinguish between a true lease and a lease used as a security interest. This is especially true in the event the lessee files for bankruptcy.

PROCEEDS: A secured party's security interest, once perfected, extends to identifiable money proceeds that are realized from the sale of the collateral.

STUDY HINTS FOR NRW CASE STUDIES

The following study hints may be helpful when resolving the NRW case studies.

NRW 25.1	➢ Itemize NRW's assets before responding to this question, and then compare this list to the types of property that may be used as collateral under Article 9. ➢ While Article 9 allows security interests in any kind of personal property, other state laws may not (e.g., no wage assignments). Thus, you may want to review other state laws.
NRW 25.2	➢ First determine the classification of the collateral. ➢ Now review the material dealing with perfection of a security interest by filing.
NRW 25.3	➢ NRW should first review its security agreement with the bank to determine whether it prohibits the removal of the collateral to another state.

REVIEW OF TERMS AND CONCEPTS

MATCHING EXERCISE

Select the term or concept that best matches a definition or statement set forth below. Each term or concept is the best match for only one definition or statement.

Terms and Concepts

a. Account

b. Chattel paper

c. Consumer good

d. Default

e. Equipment

f. Financing statement

g. Fixtures

h. General intangibles

i. Lien creditor

j. Mechanics lien

k. Pledge

l. Trustee in bankruptcy

Definitions and Statements

_____ 1. Notice of a security interest that is filed centrally or locally in order to perfect a security interest.

_____ 2. Security interest in which a secured creditor holds the collateral until the obligation is satisfied.

_____ 3. Failure to pay a debt or otherwise satisfy an obligation.

_____ 4. Type of collateral that is a monetary debt not evidenced by an instrument or chattel paper.

_____ 5. Type of collateral that includes various kinds of intangible property, except accounts.

_____ 6. Interest given by statute to secure payment to workers who repair property.

_____ 7. Court appointed administrator of a bankruptcy estate.

_____ 8. Creditor holding lien rights in property.

_____ 9. Writing that evidences both a monetary obligation and a security interest in goods.

_____ 10. Type of collateral that is primarily intended to be used to conduct a business.

_____ 11. Type of collateral that was originally personal property and has now become attached to the land or a permanent structure.

_____ 12. Type of collateral that is intended primarily for personal, family, or household purposes.

COMPLETION EXERCISE

Fill in the blanks with the words that most accurately complete each statement.

1. _____ is the process by which secured creditors protect their collateral from subsequent creditors or buyers who claim an interest in the same collateral.

2. The UCC requires a secured creditor to file a _____ _____ within ten days of written demand by a debtor who has satisfied the obligation.

3. Perfection by attachment is also known as _____ _____.

4. A security interest in stocks or bonds can be perfected only by _____.

5. List four ways that a security interest may be perfected under Article 9:

   a. _____.

   b. _____.

   c. _____.

   d. _____.

TRUE-FALSE EXERCISE

Write **T** if the statement is true, write **F** if the statement is false.

_____ 1. Chattel paper is a form of general intangible.

_____ 2. Article 9 governs secured transactions involving both tangible and intangible personal property.

_____ 3. A good may simultaneously be classified as being two different types of collateral, i.e., a good may be equipment and inventory at the same time.

_____ 4. Article 9 applies only to security interests created by the debtor's consent.

_____ 5. In general, a bona fide lease of goods is not governed by Article 9.

_____ 6. When a creditor's security interest attaches to the collateral, that creditor is assured of priority over other creditors.

_____ 7. Attachment of a security interest cannot occur unless the debtor has rights in the collateral.

_____ 8. A creditor may show evidence of an oral security agreement by possession of the collateral.

_____ 9. A valid security agreement may, but need not, recite the price of the goods.

_____ 10. Article 9 governs security interests in real property.

APPLICATION OF CONCEPTS

MULTIPLE CHOICE QUESTIONS

_____ 1. Barney sold a large screen TV to Raymond on credit and required Raymond to sign a security agreement. Which of the following items must be included to make the security agreement valid?
   a. The cost of the TV.
   b. Description of the TV.
   c. Requirement that Raymond carry insurance on the TV.
   d. The length of time for Raymond to complete payments.

_____ 2. Giuseppe bought a portable fan to help cool off his restaurant. How is the fan categorized under the UCC?

    a. Inventory.
    b. Consumer goods.
    c. Fixtures.
    d. Equipment.

_____ 3. Max sold Darla a new intercom system on credit and he permanently installed it into her house. What type of collateral is the intercom system?

    a. Inventory.
    b. Consumer goods.
    c. Fixtures.
    d. Equipment.

_____ 4. Ace Finance lent $500 to Dan. Dan agreed to repay the $500 in one year, and he signed a written security agreement. The agreement granted Ace a security interest in equipment owned by Dan. Ace did not perfect the security interest. In this case:

    a. The security interest is attached.
    b. The security interest is not attached because Ace does not have possession of the collateral.
    c. The security interest is not attached because Ace did not give value.
    d. The security interest is not attached because Ace failed to perfect the security interest.

SHORT ANSWER QUESTIONS

Answer the following questions, briefly explaining the reason for your answer.

1. Peg bought a microwave from Vanessa for $300, paying her $100, promising to pay the rest in two weeks, and validly granting Vanessa a security interest in the microwave to assure payment of the balance. Vanessa filed a financing statement, perfecting her security interest. A week later, Peg sold the microwave to Bob for $200 and placed the money in a separate account. Does Vanessa have any rights in the $200?

_____

_____

2. Carter's Feed and Seed sold seed corn to Kevin on credit and Kevin granted Carter's a security interest in existing corn to secure payment of this debt. What type of collateral is involved? How can Kevin perfect its security interest in the corn?

_____

_____

3. Owen leased a $5,000 copier to Rita's Record Bar. At the end of the lease, Rita can buy the copier for $50 or return it to Owen. Is the lease a security interest covered under Article 9? Why or why not?

_____

_____

4. Acme RV sold 15 RVs to Lomax Leasing on credit, and Lomax granted Acme a security interest in the RVs to secure the unpaid purchase price. The RVs will be located at Lomax's leasing outlets in three other states. What should Acme do to assure a perfected security interest in all of the RVs?

_____

_____

CASE PROBLEMS

Answer the following case problems, explaining your answers.

1. Alice purchased a stove for her restaurant from Reliable Appliances. Alice bought the stove on credit, and she granted Reliable a security interest in the stove. Reliable filed a financing statement with the secretary of state's office. Under these facts: (a) What type of collateral is the stove? (b) Did Reliable perfect its security interest? (c) Why is perfection of the security interest important to Reliable?

_____

_____

_____

_____

2. Thomas issued a $5,000 negotiable promissory note to Helen as payment for a trailer. On May 1, Helen borrowed $2,000 from Fourth Bank and orally granted the bank a security interest in the note to secure repayment of the $2,000. The bank took possession of the note on June 1 and returned it to Helen on August 1. (a) What type of collateral is the note? (b) Did the security interest attach? (c) If a security interest attached, was it perfected? (d) If the security interest was perfected, during what period was it perfected?

_____

_____

_____

_____

CHAPTER 26

Secured Transactions: Priorities And Enforcement

CHAPTER REVIEW

PRIORITIES: Generally, a perfected security interest in collateral takes priority over unsecured creditors and lien creditors who claim an interest in the same secured collateral. Only after the perfected claim is fully satisfied do other creditors receive any portion of the proceeds realized from a sale of collateral.

CONFLICTING SECURITY INTERESTS: UCC § 9-312 sets out the rules for priority to claims in the same collateral. The basic priority rules are as follows:

1) the first secured creditor to file a financing statement or perfect a security interest, whichever comes first, has priority over other creditors. (The date of filing, not the date of attachment, controls; therefore, a prudent creditor will file the financing statement as soon as possible.);

2) a perfected security interest has priority over a conflicting unperfected security interest; and

3) the first security interest to attach or become effective has priority if conflicting security interests are unperfected.

If a secured creditor has a perfected floating lien in after-acquired property, then the date of perfection relates back to the original date of filing, assuring the secured party priority to the after-acquired property (with one exception relating to perfected purchase money security interests - see Exceptions below).

EXCEPTIONS: Although the first creditor to file or perfect a security interest generally has priority over other creditors, there are several exceptions. Important exceptions include:

■ *Purchase Money Security Interests*: A purchase money security interest (PMSI) is a security interest that:

1) secures payment of the unpaid purchase price for the collateral; or

2) secures repayment of a loan that was both intended to be used and in fact used, to buy the collateral.

A creditor holding a perfected PMSI in inventory has priority to the inventory over a secured party who has previously perfected an interest in the inventory as after-acquired property (i.e., the previous security interest is a floating lien). In other words, a perfected floating lien in inventory loses to a later, properly perfected PMSI in the same inventory. This exception applies if: 1) the PMSI is perfected before the debtor gets the inventory; and 2) the secured creditor sends an authenticated notice to those who have previously filed financing statements covering the collateral.

A PMSI creditor in collateral other than inventory has priority over a previously perfected floating lien in the same collateral so long as the PMSI is perfected at the time the debtor gets the collateral or within 20 days afterwards.

If a seller and a lender each claim a PMSI in the same collateral, the seller of the goods has priority over a lender.

■ *Buyers in the Ordinary Course of Business*: UCC § 9-307(1) allows a buyer who purchases goods in the ordinary course of the seller's business to take priority over a previously perfected security interest provided that the buyer: 1) acts in good faith and 2) does not know that the sale violates the rights of a third party. *Warning:* In effect, this exception protects a good faith buyer for value who purchases an item of a merchant's *inventory*. It does not protect a buyer who purchases other types of collateral from a merchant, such as a piece of equipment or a fixture.

- **Bona Fide Purchasers of Consumer Goods**: UCC § 9-307(2) provides that a purchaser of consumer goods who (1) has no knowledge of the previously perfected security interest; (2) gives value for the goods; and (3) uses the goods for personal, family or household use, takes priority over an *automatically perfected* security interest in the same consumer goods. *Warning:* this exception does NOT apply if the prior security interest is perfected by the filing of a financing statement - in that event, the secured party and not the purchaser has priority to the consumer goods.

- **Other Exceptions**: Two other exceptions to the first to file/perfect priority rule are: 1) a purchaser of chattel paper has priority over a security interest in the chattel paper if the chattel paper is proceeds from the sale of the debtor's inventory and the purchaser gives new value for the paper, takes it in the ordinary course of his or her business, and the paper itself did not indicate that it had already been assigned to a third party; and 2) if a party purchases a negotiable instrument and qualifies as a holder in due course following this purchase, then the purchaser takes priority over any security interests filed against the negotiable instrument.

CONFLICTS BETWEEN SECURITY INTERESTS AND LIENS:

- **Judicial Liens**: A perfected security interest in property prevails over a conflicting lien creditor if the security interest is perfected before the creditor's lien attaches. A lien creditor includes a creditor that has acquired a lien on the collateral by attachment or levy, and a trustee in bankruptcy from the date of the filing of the petition

- **Common Law and Statutory Liens**: A possessory lien has priority over a properly perfected security interest, regardless of when either arose, unless the statute that creates the lien expressly makes the lien subordinate to a security interest.

- **Consensual Liens**: A creditor that finances the construction of a building and properly perfects a construction mortgage has priority over any conflicting security interests. In any other cases involving a fixture, if a secured party perfects a PMSI in a fixture by filing before the fixture is attached to the realty or within 20 days after it is attached, then the PMSI in the fixture has priority. If the security interest in the fixture in not a PMSI, however, the security interest in the fixture is subordinate to any interests in the real estate that are recorded prior to the fixture filing.

CONFLICTS BETWEEN SECURITY INTERESTS AND THE TRUSTEE IN BANKRUPTCY: A prior perfected security interest prevails over the judicial lien of a trustee in bankruptcy unless there are grounds to invalidate the security interest, such as it being a voidable preference.

ENFORCEMENT OF THE SECURITY INTEREST: The security agreement defines what a default is. Upon a debtor's default, a secured party has a variety of remedies including strict foreclosure (keeping collateral in satisfaction of the secured debt) or selling the collateral and suing for any deficiency (unpaid amounts).

NON-CODE REMEDIES: The secured party may have a variety of common law remedies in addition to those provided by the UCC.

- ***Right of Repossession***: Under the UCC, when a debtor defaults on a security agreement, the secured party may repossess the collateral without first obtaining a judgment or obtaining judicial permission, provided the action can be taken with breach of the peace. Breach of peace is not defined, but generally any action during repossession that results in physical violence is a breach of peace. The debtor may be required to assemble the collateral where the secured party can take possession.

  If procedures required by the UCC are not followed in connection with the repossession and sale of collateral, the secured party may be denied a deficiency judgment for the unpaid balance of the debt and may be liable for damages to the debtor.

- ***Strict Foreclosure***: Following repossession, a secured party generally has two choices: 1) the collateral may be sold and the proceeds applied to the debt, or 2) the collateral may be retained in full satisfaction of the debt.

  Keeping collateral in satisfaction of the secured debt is called "strict foreclosure." In most situations, this procedure requires a secured party to 1) send required authenticated notices to the debtor and certain creditors and 2) wait twenty-one days for the parties to respond with any written objections.

  Strict foreclosure is not permitted and the collateral must therefore be sold if: 1) any party entitled to notice objects, or 2) the debtor has paid at least 60% of the cash price for consumer goods or at least 60% of the amount of the loan. If a sale of collateral is required and the seller fails to sell it within 90 days, the secured party is liable for conversion or damages.

- ***Disposition by sale***: If a secured creditor sells the collateral, the sale must be conducted in a commercially reasonable manner. In most cases, a sale may be public or private.

DEBTORS' RIGHTS: The debtor may redeem (reclaim) the collateral prior to sale unless this right was waived after default. To redeem, the debtor must satisfy all obligations, including the cost of repossession, sale preparation, and legal expenses prior to sale or strict foreclosure.

SECURED PARTIES' DUTIES: A secured party must: 1) take reasonable care of the collateral; 2) keep the collateral identifiable (not commingle it with other property); and 3) turn any surplus proceeds over to the debtor. UCC § 9-507 identifies the liability that secured parties incur when their noncompliance results in a loss to the debtor or junior secured creditors.

STUDY HINTS FOR NRW CASE STUDIES

The following study hints may be helpful when resolving the NRW case studies.

NRW 26.1	➢ Review the priority rules and pay particular attention to the exceptions to the general priority rule.
NRW 26.2	➢ Analyze the textbook material relating to common law and statutory liens. ➢ Do not forget to look at non-code state laws relating to the priority of mechanic's liens.
NRW 26.3	➢ Review the materials on Debtor's Rights and Secured Parties' Duties. ➢ Revisit UCC §§ 9-501, 9-504, and 9-505.

MATCHING EXERCISE

Select the term or concept that best matches a definition or statement set forth below. Each term or concept is the best match for only one definition or statement.

Terms and Concepts

a. Accession
b. After-acquired property
c. Buyer in ordinary course
d. Conversion
e. Double financing
f. Encumbrancer
g. Fixture

h. Fixture filing
i. Floating lien
j. Foreclosure
k. Fungible goods
l. Garnishment
m. Junior secured parties
n. PMSI

o. Replevy
p. Repossession
q. Strict foreclosure
r. Writ of execution

Definitions and Statements

_____ 1.   Security interest that secures payment of the unpaid purchase price for the collateral or secures repayment of a loan that was used to buy the collateral.

_____ 2.   Security interest in fixtures that is perfected by filing a financing statement where the real property in question is located.

_____ 3.   Person who holds a lien on real property.

_____ 4.   Use of collateral to secure obligations with multiple creditors.

_____ 5.   Security interest in newly-acquired (after-acquired) collateral.

_____ 6.   Collateral that is acquired by a debtor after a security agreement is made.

_____ 7.   Personal property that becomes so closely associated with real property that it is treated as part of the real property.

_____ 8.   Person who, for value, buys goods from a merchant who regularly deals in goods of that kind, without knowledge that the sale may violate the rights of a third party.

_____ 9.   Addition or improvement to a good.

_____ 10. Court order allowing a party to recover personal property that is unlawfully held by another.

_____ 11. Court order allowing enforcement of a security interest in collateral.

_____ 12. Wrongful, unauthorized taking of another's personal property.

_____ 13. Court order directing a third party to pay to the court or a creditor money that the third party owes to a debtor.

_____ 14. Persons who hold security interests subordinate to those of a foreclosing party.

_____ 15. Repossession and retention of collateral as full satisfaction of a secured debt.

_____ 16. Goods that cannot be distinguished from others of the same kind; interchangeable goods.

_____ 17. Secured party's retaking of collateral upon a debtor's default.

_____ 18. Court order directing a sheriff to take and sell property belonging to a debtor in order to satisfy a judgment.

COMPLETION EXERCISE

Fill in the blanks with the words that most accurately complete each statement.

1. Property that secures payment of a debt or performance of an obligation is called _____.

2. Generally, the first creditor to _____ a security interest in specific collateral has priority over other creditors who subsequently acquire an interest in the same collateral.

3. If two or more creditors have conflicting, unperfected security interests in the same collateral, then the first interest to _____ has priority.

4. A PMSI in collateral other than inventory must file a financing statement within _____ _____ after the debtor receives the goods in order to have priority over a prior perfected security interest in the same collateral.

5. _____ is a general term that is used to describe who has a superior right to collateral.

6. Default is defined by the parties in their _____ _____.

7. Under the UCC, a secured party may repossess collateral through "self-help" so long as it can be accomplished without committing a _____ ____ ____ _____.

8. If repossession involves a breach of the peace, the secured party may lose the right to a _____ _____.

9. A secured party must wait _____-_____ days after giving notice before exercising the right of strict foreclosure.

10. A sale of collateral must always be conducted in a _____ _____ manner.

TRUE-FALSE EXERCISE

T if the statement is true, write F if the statement is false.

____ 1. The term "breach of the peace" is defined by the UCC.

____ 2. An ordinary foreclosure of a security interest generally requires the filing of a lawsuit.

____ 3. An improper repossession may subject a secured party to tort liability.

____ 4. A secured party's right to exercise self-help repossession terminates if it requires committing physical violence.

____ 5. There is no requirement that notice be given for a strict foreclosure.

____ 6. If a debtor has paid any portion of the cash price for consumer goods (the collateral), then strict foreclosure is not allowed.

____ 7. A secured party may purchase the collateral at a public sale.

_____ 8. The requirement for notice may be suspended if the collateral is perishable.

_____ 9. A sale price that is less than the market price for similar goods is not commercially reasonable.

_____ 10. A secured party may require the debtor to pay for the cost of protecting repossessed collateral.

_____ 11. A perfected security interest always takes priority over subsequent security interests in the same collateral.

_____ 12. A secured creditor's perfected claim against collateral must be fully satisfied before unsecured creditors can recover from the property.

_____ 13. The order in which financing statements are filed is the sole factor to determine the priority of conflicting perfected security interests.

_____ 14. Perfection by filing may occur without attachment.

_____ 15. Filing gives priority only if the security interest attaches before another interest is perfected.

_____ 16. A PMSI need not be perfected in order to have priority over a prior perfected security interest.

_____ 17. An unperfected security interest in collateral has priority over a conflicting statutory lien.

_____ 18. A person who buys a seller's equipment is not a buyer in the ordinary course of business.

_____ 19. Anyone who buys collateral from a merchant has priority over a prior perfected security interest in the collateral.

_____ 20. The holder of a statutory lien may have priority over a prior perfected security interest.

APPLICATION OF CONCEPTS

MULTIPLE CHOICE QUESTIONS

_____ 1. Campus Cycles (CC) sold a bike to Brenda on credit. Brenda intended to use the bike for her personal enjoyment. Brenda granted CC a security interest in the bike to secure payment of the unpaid purchase price. CC did not file a financing statement. Under these facts:
   a. CC's security interest is unperfected.
   b. If Brenda sells the bike to Don for his personal use, and Don pays for the bike and does not know about CC's lien, then Don has priority over CC's security interest.
   c. If Joe's Repair Shop obtains a common law lien on the bike for unpaid repair charges, then Joe's lien has priority over CC's security interest.
   d. b and c.

____ 2. Travis loaned $5,000 to John's Garage. John signed a security agreement granting Travis a security interest in John's existing inventory of mufflers. Travis did nothing to perfect this security interest and John kept possession of the inventory. Under these facts:
   a. Travis has a perfected security interest in the mufflers.
   b. Travis has an unperfected security interest in the mufflers
   c. Travis does not have a security interest in the mufflers.
   d. Travis has a common law lien on the mufflers.

____ 3. On December 1, First Bank perfected a security interest in ABC Garage's inventory of tires. On February 1, Jim bought a tire from ABC for cash. On April 15, Second Bank perfected an ordinary security interest in ABC's tire inventory. Under these facts:
   a. Jim bought the tire subject to First Bank's security interest.
   b. First Bank has a security interest in the proceeds received from the sale of the tire to Jim.
   c. First Bank's security interest has priority over Second Bank's security interest.
   d. b and c.

____ 4. J&J sold a new central air conditioning unit to Fred for his home on credit. Fred granted J&J a security interest in the unit to secure the unpaid purchase price and J&J properly executed a fixture filing prior to delivery and installation of the unit. Last Bank had a prior recorded mortgage that secured a loan that Fred used to purchase the residence. Later, Fred defaulted on his obligations to both J&J and Last Bank. Who has priority to the air conditioning unit?
   a. J&J
   b. Last Bank
   c. J&J and Last Bank each have priority to one-half of the unit.
   d. Fred.

____ 5. Sam loaned $1,000 to Larry, who granted Sam a security interest in equipment to secure the loan. Larry later defaulted, failing to repay the loan as agreed. Under these facts:
   a. Sam can repossess the equipment using self-help.
   b. Sam can repossess the equipment using self-help even if Larry objects to the repossession.
   c. Sam can repossess the equipment using self-help only if Sam first obtains a court order permitting the repossession.
   d. a and b.

____ 6. Gregg repossessed collateral from Dan and he properly sold the collateral for $6,000. The unpaid balance of the secured debt owing to Gregg was $5,000. The cost of the sale was $250. Jason, a junior secured creditor, had a $5,000 debt secured by the collateral. Under these facts:
   a. Gregg receives $6,000; Jason receives $0; and Dan receives $0.
   b. Gregg receives $5,250; Jason receives $750; and Dan receives $0.
   c. Gregg receives $5,000; Jason receives $1,000; and Dan receives $0.
   d. Gregg receives $2,000; Jason receives $2,000; and Dan receives $2,000.

____ 7. Tom lent $5,000 to Jill. The loan was secured by a lien in jewelry inventory. When Jill defaulted, Tom repossessed the jewelry and properly conducted a public sale. Tom spent $500 in repossessing and selling the collateral. The jewelry sold for $4,000. Under these facts:
   a. Tom receives $4,500; $500 for expenses and $4,000 as payment on the secured debt.
   b. Tom receives $4,000 as payment on the secured debt; he cannot recover his expenses.
   c. Tom can sue Jill for a deficiency.
   d. a and c.

____ 8. John bought a tractor on credit for $50,000, granting lien in it to secure the unpaid price. When John owed $30,000, he defaulted and the secured party repossessed the tractor, spending $750 in repossessing and storing the tractor. The tractor was sold at a properly conducted public sale for $25,000. The next day, John decided to redeem the tractor. Under these facts:

   a. John may redeem the tractor by paying the secured creditor $50,750.
   b. John may redeem the tractor by paying the secured creditor $30,750.
   c. John may redeem the tractor by paying the secured creditor $30,000.
   d. John cannot redeem the tractor.

SHORT ANSWER QUESTIONS

Answer the following questions, briefly explaining the reason for your answer.

1. Herb borrowed $1,000 from West Bank for his store. To secure the loan, Herb granted the bank a security interest in the store's inventory, and West Bank perfected the lien on June 1. The security agreement stated that the inventory secured payment of the $1,000 loan and any future loans made to Herb. On August 1, West Bank loaned an additional $3,000 to Herb. What loans are secured by the inventory?

_____

_____

2. On March 1, Doug borrowed $2,000 from Fran, and granted Fran a security interest in his inventory. Fran did not perfect her security interest. On August 1, Doug borrowed $3,000 from Tom and granted Tom a security interest in the same inventory. Tom perfected his security interest. Later, Doug defaulted on both loans. Who has priority to the inventory: Fran or Tom?

_____

_____

3. Ken bought equipment on credit from Acme. Ken granted Acme a security interest in the equipment which Acme perfected on June 1. In August, Ken borrowed money from Commerce Bank, granting the bank a security interest in the same equipment. The bank immediately perfected its security interest. Later, Ken defaulted on both obligations. Who has priority to the equipment: Acme or Commerce Bank?

_____

_____

4. Last Bank held a perfected security interest in the inventory of Shar's Wholesale Fish Market. In the ordinary course of business, Shar sold First Catch Cafe a shipment of fish that was subject to Last Bank's security interest. Shar then defaulted on its secured debt with Last Bank. Who has priority to the fish that First Catch Cafe bought from Shar: Last Bank or First Catch?

_____

_____

5. Wheels Inc. sold a motorcycle to Terry on credit and Wheels had a perfected security interest in the cycle to secure payment of the purchase price. Terry defaulted and Wheels decided to repossess the cycle. When a Wheels' employee started to drive the cycle away from Terry's house, Terry jumped in front of the cycle. The employee refused to stop, crushing Terry's foot in the process. Discuss the parties' rights in this case.

_____

_____

6. Sharlene loaned Iris $2,000 to purchase a Persian rug for her new apartment. Iris signed a security agreement granting Sharlene a security interest in the rug to secure the $2,000 debt. The agreement stated that Iris waived her right to a sale in the event of default. Later, Iris failed to pay the remaining $500 owed for the rug, and Sharlene repossessed it. Can Sharlene exercise strict foreclosure in this case?

_____

_____

7. Sheldon bought a vehicle from Expo Transportation on credit for $5,000. When Sheldon defaulted on this debt, he still owed $4,000. Expo repossessed the vehicle pursuant to valid security agreement. Expo spent $400 in attorneys' fees in connection with the repossession and $60 to advertise a sale of the vehicle which is scheduled in two days. Discuss Sheldon's right, if any, to redeem the vehicle.

_____

_____

8. Thorsen's Wholesale Jewelers sold 300 gold bracelets to Ricco's Ritzy Rocks. Following default, Thorsen's repossessed the bracelets and commingled them along with 200 other bracelets. Later, Thorsen's took 300 bracelets from this commingled group of bracelets and sold them. The proceeds failed to pay off Ricco's debt. Discuss the parties' rights in this case.

_____

_____

CASE PROBLEMS

Answer the following case problems, explaining your answers.

1. Logic Inc. Lent money to Hi-Tek, taking a perfected security interest in Hi-Tek's patent for a new computer chip. Hi-Tek defaulted and Logic properly repossessed the patent in accordance with the parties' security agreement.

    Logic is considering selling the patent to MicroPro in a private sale or conducting a public sale. Three other secured creditors have a recorded security interest in the patent; however, their interests were perfected after Logic's. (a) Must Logic notify Hi-Tek of the proposed sale? (b) What action must the junior secured creditors take to protect their rights in the collateral? (c) Discuss Logic's right to choose between a public and private sale of the patent. (d) If Logic conducts a public sale of the patent, can Logic buy the patent?

_____

_____

_____

2. Pursuant to a valid security agreement, A&A Appliances repossessed and sold a walk-in refrigerator unit that it had repossessed from Frank's Cafe. Prior to the sale, A&A contacted all restaurants and equipment dealers in town to notify them of the sale, and it ran ads in the newspaper for several weeks. The collateral sold for $8,000, although its market value was about $15,000.

    The unpaid balance of the secured debt owing to A&A was $10,000, and A&A incurred $500 costs in selling the collateral. Frank's argues that the sales price is not commercially reasonable. Under these facts: (a) Is the sales price commercially reasonable? (b) Assuming that the sale was properly conducted, how are the sale proceeds applied? (c) Can A&A sue for a deficiency?

_____

_____

_____

3. Stan owned a hardware store and he needed a line of credit. Merchant's Bank granted him credit, secured by a lien on his current and future hardware inventory. Two months later, Stan borrowed $5,000 from Trish so that he could replenish the store's inventory of saws that had been exhausted. Stan granted Trish a security interest in the new saws, and Trish perfected her security interest one week after Stan received the saws. Stan soon defaulted on both debts. (a) What type of security interest does Merchant's Bank have? (b) What type of a security interest does Trish have? (c) Who has priority to the new inventory of saws: Merchant's Bank or Trish?

_____

_____

_____

INTRODUCTION: Businesses and consumers both use credit in purchasing materials, goods, real estate, and other property and services. Many of these credit transactions fall outside UCC Article 9.

LETTERS OF CREDIT: A letter of credit is a document that provides for payment of a certain sum of money to a named party provided that the party strictly complies with certain stated conditions.

In a letter-of-credit transaction, an applicant (often a buyer) obtains a commitment from the issuer (the buyer's bank) that the issuer will honor the letter of credit upon the issuing bank's receipt of certain specified documents from the beneficiary (the seller).

UCC Article 5 authorizes the use of electronic technology in the creation, transmission, and presentment of a letter of credit. A letter of credit is deemed to be irrevocable unless the letter itself expressly provides for revocation. The UCC requires an issuer to dishonor any letter of credit that does not strictly conform, under standard customs and practices, to the terms and conditions contained in the letter.

UNSECURED CREDIT: In an unsecured credit transaction, a creditor grants credit to a debtor without taking a security interest in any collateral. In this type of transaction, the creditor relies on the debtor to repay the loan without the protection of security in the event the debtor defaults. Typically, a creditor will restrict such credit to those debtors who are better credit risks, or a creditor will charge a higher interest rate for such credit due to the additional risk. Unsecured credit sometimes is a signature loan, whereby a lender agrees to make a loan merely on the basis of the borrower's signature. Unsecured credit is found in most public utility accounts, bank credit cards, and travel and entertainment cards.

State law mainly regulates unsecured credit transactions. Federal rules mostly relate to assuring that information is given to debtors prior to incurring debt and to establishing acceptable ways of collection in the event of default. Title I of the Federal Consumer Credit Protection Act [Truth in Lending Act (TILA)] requires creditors to give credit applicants certain information regarding the cost of the credit.

If a debtor defaults on unsecured credit, the creditor cannot use "self-help" to take property of the debtor. Also, the federal Fair Debt Collection Practices Act, which only applies to persons who are attempting to collect debts owed to another person (e.g., collection agencies) and not to a creditor who is acting on his or her own behalf to recover payment, regulates conduct that may be used to obtain payment of a debt.

States regulate the terms of unsecured credit transactions. States typically limit the interest rates and other finance charges that may be charged on certain types of loans, and allow debtors to rescind certain types of transactions during a "cooling off" period. Each state establishes its own maximum permissible interest rates for various types of loans or credit transactions. A rate charged in excess of a state's maximum is usurious. Charging a usurious interest rate has different repercussions in different states.

INSTALLMENT LOANS: Installment loans are loans for a fixed time period with fixed periodic payments. Installment loans may be secured or unsecured, and some secured consumer installment loans fall within UCC Article 9. Installment loans are subject to many of the same rules as unsecured loans, such as TILA and the Fair Debt Collection Practices Act. At the state level, UCC Article 3 covers a transaction if a promissory note is involved, and the Uniform Consumer Credit Code applies to consumer credit transactions in 11 states. Mortgage loans involve loans that are secured by real estate. Mortgage loans are typically installment loans with long repayment terms, such as 30 years. TILA applies to these contracts, as well as the federal Real Estate Settlement Procedures Act (RESPA), which requires home mortgage lenders to provide loan applicants with a good faith estimate of loan settlement and closing costs.

CREDIT CARDS: There are three basic types of credit cards: bank cards such as MasterCard; travel and entertainment cards such as American Express; and store or merchant cards such as Sears. Credit cards involve open-ended credit and they are often treated differently from other types of loans under usury statutes. The debt is called "revolving credit" rather than a loan, and the methods for computing charges and fees are different than the methods used in other types of loans.

Federal regulation of credit cards is based on TILA. The provisions for credit card protection are found in Regulation Z, Subpart B, which deals with open-ended credit. The credit card issuer must provide full disclosure of the costs associated with the card, and Section 226.12 (a) forbids issuing unsolicited credit cards. However, there is no prohibition against solicitation of applications by a card issuer.

TILA limits the liability of cardholders in the event that their cards are used without authorization. If a credit card is lost or stolen, the cardholder faces a maximum liability of $50 for unauthorized use of the card, and liability is only for use of a card before the issuer is notified of the loss or theft. Once the card issuer is notified, the liability of the cardholder ends. This limit does not apply if a cardholder consents to the use of his or her card by someone else and the other person misuses the card.

Regulation Z forbids offsets by a card issuer. The Equal Credit Opportunity Act requires businesses that regularly extend credit as a part of their business to make credit available without discrimination. The Fair Credit Billing Act provides a method for cardholders to challenge alleged billing errors without liability until the alleged error is investigated. The Unsolicited Credit Card Act protects a person from liability for misuse of credit cards issued to that person without an application submitted by that person.

FTC CONSUMER CREDIT RULES: The Federal Trade Commission Holder in Due Course rule requires that consumer credit contracts include a statement that the debtor may assert against anyone any right, claim, or defense that the consumer could assert against the seller. (This rule does not apply to real estate transactions or credit card transactions.) Another rule makes it an unfair trade practice for a seller or creditor in a consumer credit transaction to take a contract containing a confession of judgment clause, a waiver of exemptions clause or wage assignment. A seller or creditor also cannot take a nonpossessory security interest in household goods or furnishings unless it is secure payment of the unpaid purchase price for such goods or furnishings or to secure repayment of a loan used to buy such items.

PAYDAY LOANS: In a "payday loan" a borrower goes to a lender to borrow funds until the borrower is paid his or her wages. Nineteen states prohibit this type of controversial loan, but federal banking regulations inadvertently permit payday lenders to operate even in these states.

STUDY HINTS FOR NRW CASE STUDIES

The following study hints may be helpful when resolving the NRW case studies.

NRW 27.1	➢ Review the material relating to unsecured credit. ➢ Also review the material relating to secured transactions in Chapters 25 and 26.
NRW 27.2	➢ Review the material relating to credit cards. ➢ Remember that usury statutes typically do not forbid teaser rates.
NRW 27.3	➢ Bear in mind that co-signing creates personal liability on the part of the co-signer.

MATCHING EXERCISE

Select the term or concept that best matches a definition or statement set forth below. Each term or concept is the best match for only one definition or statement.

Terms and Concepts

a. Collateral

b. Installment loan

c. Mortgage loan

d. Regulation Z

e. Signature loan

f. Solicitation

g. UCC Article 9

h. Unsecured credit

i. Usury

Definitions and Statements

_____ 1. Loan that is made for a fixed period of time with fixed periodic payments.

_____ 2. Promoting or advocating that a person do something, such as requesting a credit card.

_____ 3. Commercial law that regulates secured credit transactions that are secured by personal property.

_____ 4. Property that secures repayment of a debt.

_____ 5. Loan that is secured by real estate.

_____ 6. Credit that is extended without collateral securing its repayment.

_____ 7. Unlawful rate of interest.

_____ 8. Federal law that regulates open-ended credit.

_____ 9. Credit that is extended based solely on a person's promise to repay.

COMPLETION EXERCISE

Fill in the blanks with the words that most accurately complete each statement.

1. The _____ _____ _____ ____ forbids discrimination in extending credit by businesses that regularly extend credit to others.

2. The _____ _____ _____ ____ establishes procedures for consumers to question billing errors by credit card companies.

3. Identify three different types of credit cards:

    a. _____.

    b. _____.

    c. _____.

4. The _____ _____ _____ _____ ____
   requires home mortgage lenders to provide loan applicants with a good-faith estate of all charges
   relating to home mortgage loans.

5. List four types of credit that do not involve secured transactions that are governed by UCC Article 9:

   a. _____ .

   b. _____ .

   c. _____ .

   d. _____ .

TRUE-FALSE EXERCISE

Write **T** if the statement is true, write **F** if the statement is false.

____ 1. Only state law governs unsecured credit transactions.

____ 2. The Truth in Lending Act requires that credit applicants be supplied with certain information regarding the cost of the credit.

____ 3. UCC Article 9 does not apply to unsecured credit transactions.

____ 4. When a debtor defaults on an unsecured debt, the creditor may use "self-help" to repossess property from the debtor in order to obtain satisfaction of the debt.

____ 5. Signature loans are unlawful.

____ 6. In general, creditors can charge any rate of interest on loans so long as the debtors agree to pay such interest.

____ 7. TILA may apply to installment loans.

____ 8. A creditor may take a security interest in personal property to secure repayment of a debt, but a creditor cannot take a security interest in real estate to secure repayment.

____ 9. It is unlawful for lenders to send unsolicited credit cards to consumers.

____ 10. Teaser interest rates on credit cards are unlawful.

APPLICATION OF CONCEPTS

MULTIPLE CHOICE QUESTIONS

____ 1. Linda stole Pam's credit card. Linda forged Pam's signature on a $300 charge to Duke Hardware, who was unaware of the forgery. As soon as Pam learned of the theft of her credit card, she filed a report with A&A Credit, the credit card issuer. Later, Linda forged Pam's signature on another charge for $200. Under these facts, Pam is liable for how much of the charges made by Linda:
   a. $0.
   b. $50.
   c. $300.
   d. $500.

_____ 2. Credit card debt is best described as being:
   a. Mortgage loans.
   b. Revolving credit.
   c. Installment loans.
   d. All of the above.

_____ 3. The Fair Debt Collection Practices Act regulates which of the following types of conduct in connection with credit transactions:
   a. Conduct by collection agencies in trying to collect debts owed to other parties.
   b. Conduct by lenders in trying to collect debts owed to them by delinquent debtors.
   c. Disclosure by banks when offering to extend credit to consumers.
   d. a and b.

_____ 4. Which of the following requirements are established by the Truth in Lending Act?
   a. Creditors must provide credit applicants with certain information regarding the cost of the credit.
   b. Credit card companies cannot hold debtors liable for any unauthorized charges made on their cards.
   c. Credit card companies cannot offsets on debtor's accounts.
   d. a and c.

SHORT ANSWER QUESTIONS

Answer the following questions, briefly explaining the reason for your answer.

1. Discuss the primary purpose of the Truth in Lending Act.

_____

_____

2. Diane borrowed $5,000 from Ace Finance. Ace charged Diane 36 percent interest annually on the loan although state law limited the permissible rate of interest for personal loans to 18 percent annually. Discuss the legality of this loan transaction.

_____

_____

3. Sandy applied to Regent Department store for a credit card. Regent declined to issue her a credit card because she declared bankruptcy two years ago and because she is Hispanic. Identify what law controls in this case and whether Regent acted improperly in denying credit to Sandy.

_____

_____

4. Sherry gave her credit card to Tricia, her best friend, with instructions to use the credit card to buy Sherry a new blouse for an upcoming date. Tricia took the credit card, and she charge a new blouse for $50 as instructed by Sherry, Tricia, however, also used Sherry's credit card to buy $400 of clothing for herself. Under these facts, is Sherry liable for either or both of the charges made by Tricia?

_____

_____

CASE PROBLEMS

Answer the following case problems, explaining your answers.

1. Sam applied for a loan to purchase a used motorcycle. Sam will purchase the motorcycle for $2,500, paying $500 down and paying the balance in $250 monthly payments over the next two years. The seller took a security interest on the motorcycle to assure Sam's payment of all sums that would become due. Under these facts:

    (a) Is this a secured or unsecured credit transaction?
    (b) Explain whether this is an installment credit transaction?
    (c) Identify and explain what federal laws may apply to this transaction?

_____

_____

_____

_____

2. Manley issued a $20,000 negotiable promissory note to Preston to pay for a fishing boat. Preston misrepresented to Manley that the boat was new, when in fact it was several years old. Preston negotiated the promissory note to Carl who paid Preston $20,000 for the note. Carl took the note without notice of Preston's fraud and Carl qualified as a holder in due course. The note contained all notices required by FTC rules. When Manley discovered the fraud, he refused to pay Carl on the note. Under these facts, discuss Manley's obligation to pay Carl?

_____

_____

_____

_____

CHAPTER REVIEW

HISTORICAL BACKGROUND: The U.S. Constitution authorizes (but does not require) Congress to provide bankruptcy relief for honest debtors. There are three major type of bankruptcy proceedings: (1) Chapter 7 or liquidation; (2) Chapter 13 or personal debt reorganization; and (3) Chapter 11, generally viewed as a business or large personal debt reorganization. In addition, Chapter 12 provides relief for family farmers.

THE BANKRUPTCY REFORM ACT: The 1978 Bankruptcy Reform Act established a separate system of bankruptcy courts within in each U.S. district court. The U.S. Supreme Court declared the Act unconstitutional in a case arising from a contract dispute between two pipeline companies (one of which was in bankruptcy).

BANKRUPTCY AMENDMENTS AND FEDERAL JUDGESHIP ACT OF 1984: The Bankruptcy Amendments and Federal Judgeship Act generally corrected the constitutional problems identified by the Supreme Court, including: (1) change in appointment of bankruptcy judges; (2) providing original and exclusive jurisdiction for all bankruptcy matters to the federal District Court, giving them discretion to refer the cases to the Bankruptcy Court or to bring them back to the District Court upon showing of a good reason.

THE BANKRUPTCY REFORM ACT OF 1994: The 1994 Act created a National Bankruptcy Review Commission and increased the compensation for trustees and debt limits for Chapter 13 debtors. The Act provides for adjustments in dollar amounts based on the Consumer Price Index and also recognizes bankruptcy fraud as a crime.

CHAPTER 7: LIQUIDATION – A "STRAIGHT" BANKRUPTCY:

■ *Filing Fees*: A debtor must pay certain fees when filing for any type of bankruptcy.

■ *Voluntary Bankruptcy Petition*: Debtors filing under Chapter 7 must be informed of their right to file a Chapter 13 in order to encourage repayment where possible. Discharge in bankruptcy is no longer considered a "right"; however, most debtors are discharged unless a bankruptcy judge determines that the debtor has abused the system.

■ *Involuntary Bankruptcy Petition*: Creditors may force a debtor into bankruptcy proceeding if: (1) the debtor appointed a receiver or is not paying debts within 120 days before the filing;; (2) a prescribed number of creditors sign the filing; and (3) the aggregate unsecured, non-contingent debt among the creditors who sign the petition is $10,000 or more. If a debtor successfully contests the bankruptcy, the petitioning creditors are liable for damages.

THE BANKRUPTCY PROCEEDING: Upon filing of a bankruptcy petition, an order for relief is issued and a trustee is appointed to administer the case

■ *The Trustee*: The trustee represents the debtor's estate and the interests of the unsecured creditors.

■ *Automatic Stay Provision*: Once the bankruptcy petition is filed and order for relief granted, creditors must cease any action to collect debts.

- **The Creditors' Meeting**: Within a reasonable time after filing, the trustee holds a meeting with the debtor and creditors to ask questions regarding the debtor's financial affairs. A debtor must submit detailed financial schedules listing property and debts, which creditors may review.

- **The Debtor**: A debtor has certain duties to perform in his or her bankruptcy.

- **Secured Creditors**: Secured creditors may retain their security interest or proceed as an unsecured creditors.

- **Exemptions**: Federal bankruptcy law provides that certain assets may be retained by the debtor to begin a fresh financial start. Some states require a resident debtor to use only the state's exemptions, while other states allow a debtor to choose state or federal. Exemptions generally allow varying amounts of cash, equity in residence, clothing, tools of debtor's trade, insurance, and certain benefits.

- **Allowable Claims**: Creditors must file their claims within six months of the creditors' meeting. Two types of claims will be barred: (1) claims that would otherwise be unenforceable against the debtor, and (2) claims including interest extending beyond the petition date (the bankruptcy filing "freezes" accrual of debt). Two other types of claims may be partially allowed or limited: (1) claims for violation or termination of a lease; and (2) claims based on breach of employment contract.

- **Recovery of Property**: A bankruptcy trustee may avoid certain transfers made by the debtor, and recover that property for the benefit of unsecured creditors. These transfers include: (1) voidable preferences or preferential payments to some creditors at the expense of others; and (2) fraudulent conveyances or transfers of property made within one year of the bankruptcy to hinder creditors.

- **Distribution of Assets**: The debtor's non-exempt assets are sold and the proceeds distributed in the priority set forth in federal bankruptcy law. Following payment of priority claims, unsecured creditors receive a pro rata distribution of the balance of proceeds from the debtor's property, if any remain..

- **The Discharge Decision**: Federal bankruptcy law contains an extensive list of non-dischargeable debts, including court-ordered alimony and child support, taxes, and student loans (with certain exceptions). The discharged debtor remains liable for non-discharged debt. A creditor or the trustee may request a revocation of the discharge if a court determines the debtor has acted wrongfully in the bankruptcy. In some cases, a debtor may reaffirm a debt in spite of the discharge.

CHAPTER 11: REORGANIZATION PLANS: Both corporations and individuals may use reorganization plans under Chapter 11 to restructure debt without liquidation of assets. Creditors generally receive more than they would if liquidation occurred, and objecting creditors may be forced to accept the plan. The automatic stay applies in this type of proceeding.

Petitions may be voluntary or involuntary. A Chapter 11 debtor may fill the function as trustee ("debtor in possession"), or a trustee may be appointed upon request of an interested party. Committees of creditors, appointed by the court, meet with the trustee/debtor to discuss the restructuring. In some cases, the court may appoint an examiner to investigate the debtor's financial dealings. During the first 120 days after the petition, a debtor-in-possession retains the exclusive right to file a reorganization plan. If a trustee is appointed, or the debtor's plan is rejected within the first 180 days, other interested parties may file a plan. Small-business debtors using the "fast-track" reorganization allowed under the 1994 Act must file a plan within 100 days and plans by others must be filed within 160 days.

The court must approve: 1) sale of assets; 2) mergers, consolidations or divestitures; 3) satisfaction or modification or liens or claims; 4) issuance of new stock. More than half the creditors holding at least 2/3 of the dollar amount of claims for a given class of debt must vote for the plan in order for it to be accepted by that class. If at least one class of creditors accepts the plan, the court may confirm it despite the objection of one or more other classes (the "cram-down" exception). There are numerous requirements that must be satisfied in order for a court to confirm a plan unless the court approves the plan pursuant to the "cram-down" exception.

A confirmed reorganization plan binds the debtor and all creditors. A court may order conversion to a liquidation if it believes the plan cannot be successfully completed.

In recent years, numerous companies have used Chapter 11 Bankruptcy as a strategic tool to deal with various financial and business woes. In particular, companies have turned to Chapter 11 as a way to handle cash-flow difficulties and burdensome tort claims. In addition, some companies have used this route to rid themselves of unwanted collective bargaining agreements (union contracts). In order to reject a collective bargaining agreement, however, the following must occur: 1) the debtor must make a proposal to the union that sets out modifications necessary for that the reorganization and that treats all affected parties fairly; 2) the union rejects the proposal without good cause; and 3) the court believes that equity clearly favors rejection of the collective bargaining agreement.

CHAPTER 13: REPAYMENT PLANS: Individual debtors with regular income may propose a repayment plan if: 1) they have no more than $750,000 in secured debt, and 2) $250,000 in unsecured debt. Only voluntary petitions are permitted.

The repayment plan must: 1) extend for no more than three years, or five in special situations; 2) is fair to all parties; 3) is in the best interest of the creditors; 4) be feasible, that is, the debtor can carry it out; and 5) the debtor pays at least as much as under a liquidation. As in a Chapter 11, a confirmed plan is binding on all parties and results in the debtor's discharge once the plan is completed. Under certain circumstances, a court may grant a discharge during the plan, that is, before the plan is completed.

Several changes made during the 1984 Bankruptcy Amendments include: 1) beginning payments into the court before the plan has been confirmed; 2) permitting any unsecured creditor to block confirmation unless the creditor's claim is either fully satisfied or 100% of the debtor's disposable income is paid over the three year period. In addition, a plan may be modified during the period to increase, as well as decrease, payments.

THE [PROPOSED] BANKRUPTCY REFORM ACT: This proposed Act would make bankruptcy available for fewer people and would require more people to repay many debts that would be discharged under present law.

BANKRUPTCY IN THE INTERNATIONAL ENVIRONMENT: There now are numerous international statutes and treatments for bankruptcy, and as business becomes more global it is likely that other statutes and treatments will be enacted. UNCITRAL, the United Nations international trade law body, for instance, is developing a model law on insolvency.

STUDY HINTS FOR NRW CASE STUDIES

The following study hints may be helpful when resolving the NRW case studies.

NRW 28.1	➢ You should review the provisions of the Bankruptcy Code dealing with fraudulent conveyances. ➢ It also may be helpful to review state law relating to fraudulent conveyances.
NRW 28.2	➢ Remember that the rights of a secured party continue in bankruptcy. ➢ NRW should consider whether it is an impaired creditor under the plan and respond accordingly. Review the requirements for confirmation of a reorganization plan and do not overlook the "cram-down" exception.
NRW 28.3	➢ Discuss the criteria for approving a Chapter 13 plan. ➢ Evaluate NRW's rights under the 1984 bankruptcy amendments.

MATCHING EXERCISE

Select the term or concept that best matches a definition or statement set forth below. Each term or concept is the best match for only one definition or statement.

Terms and Concepts

a. Automatic stay

b. Exempt assets

c. Fraudulent conveyance

d. General assignment for benefit of creditors

e. Involuntary bankruptcy

f. National Bankruptcy Review Commission

g. Order for relief

h. Petition in bankruptcy

i. Reaffirmation agreement

j. Receiver

k. Schedules

l. Voidable preference

Definitions and Statements

_____ 1. Listings of assets and liabilities filed by a debtor in a bankruptcy case.

_____ 2. Nine-member group created by the Bankruptcy Reform Act of 1994.

_____ 3. Assets retained by debtors under the bankruptcy law to enable a "fresh start."

_____ 4. Effect of bankruptcy filing, which prohibits creditors from pursuing debtor's assets outside bankruptcy court.

_____ 5. Person appointed to manage debtor's property for benefit of a creditor outside of bankruptcy.

_____ 6. Order entered by bankruptcy court upon filing of petition.

_____ 7. Transfer of property by debtor to satisfy debts.

_____ 8. Agreement by debtor to pay a debt that would otherwise be discharged.

_____ 9. Transfer of property made by a debtor to hinder creditors' recovery of money owed.

_____ 10. Bankruptcy petition filed by creditors against a debtor against debtor's will.

_____ 11. Transfer of property or payment of debt that gives unfair advantage to some creditors.

_____ 12. Basic document that commences a bankruptcy proceeding.

COMPLETION EXERCISE

Fill in the blanks with the words that most accurately complete each statement.

1. The Bankruptcy Reform Act of 1978 was declared _____ by the U.S. Supreme Court.

2. Bankruptcy judges do not have _____ _____ jurisdiction under the Constitution.

3. Straight bankruptcy refers to a _____ of a debtor's non-exempt assets.

4. An involuntary bankruptcy requires _____ creditors out of twelve or more to sign the petition.

5. The accumulated debt limit for Chapter 13 debtors under the 1994 Bankruptcy Reform Act is _____ dollars.

6. A Chapter 13 repayment plan may also be referred to as a _____ _____ plan.

7. Within the first 120 days (or 100 days on the "fast-track") following a Chapter 11 petition, the _____ _____ _____ has the exclusive right to propose a reorganization plan.

8. A _____ must approve any plan to sell assets from the Chapter 11 bankruptcy estate.

9. Confirmed plans under Chapter 11 Chapter 13 repayment plan are _____ on all parties.

10. Identify the four criteria a court considers in approving a Chapter 13 repayment plan.

    a. _____.

    b. _____.

    c. _____.

    d. _____.

TRUE-FALSE EXERCISE

Write **T** if the statement is true, write **F** if the statement is false.

_____ 1. The constitutional challenge to the Bankruptcy Act raised issues of jurisdiction.

_____ 2. Under the 1994 Act, dollar amounts for involuntary petitions, priorities, and exemptions will be tied to the Consumer Price Index.

_____ 3. Savings and loan associations may lawfully commence a Chapter 7 bankruptcy.

_____ 4. Three creditors may file an involuntary bankruptcy against a farmer.

_____ 5. Charitable corporations may not be subjected to an involuntary bankruptcy.

_____ 6. A debtor need not be insolvent to file a voluntary petition in bankruptcy.

_____ 7. If a debtor made a general assignment of property for creditors' benefit within the previous 120 days, the creditors are barred from filing an involuntary bankruptcy against the debtor.

_____ 8. Creditors may under some circumstances be liable to the debtor for damages for filing an involuntary bankruptcy petition.

_____ 9. A trustee represents the secured creditors' interests.

_____ 10. Creditors may not repossess assets of a debtor after the petition is filed.

_____ 11. A Chapter 11 plan may be approved even if it is rejected by some creditors.

_____ 12. The proposed Bankruptcy Reform Act would make it easier for people to discharge their debts.

_____ 13. Small corporations may file Chapter 13 plans if they have a less than $1 million of debt.

_____ 14. Ordinarily, a Chapter 13 plan will not extend beyond one year.

_____ 15. A court cannot increase payments during the course of a Chapter 13 plan.

APPLICATION OF CONCEPTS

MULTIPLE CHOICE QUESTIONS

_____ 1. PetroMine Inc. filed a petition in bankruptcy on June 1. On June 3, OfficePro, a secured creditor, attempted to repossess a copier from PetroMine's office, resulting in shouting and general disruption. Which statement best describes OfficePro's legal rights?
   a. OfficePro legally exercised its right of self-help to recover the copier.
   b. OfficePro could not legally repossess the copier because it breached the peace.
   c. OfficePro could not legally repossess the copier because it violated the automatic stay.
   d. OfficePro could not hold a secured interest under the bankruptcy proceeding.

_____ 2. Marvin is considering whether to file a petition in bankruptcy. Which of the following actions may result in denial of a discharge?
   a. Marvin transfers his stock certificates to his brother's name so that he appears to have no assets.
   b. Marvin intentionally fails to disclose his substantial lottery winnings on the bankruptcy schedules.
   c. Marvin contracts for auto repairs for which he ultimately is unable to pay.
   d. a and b.

_____ 3. Paul files a voluntary petition in bankruptcy. Which of the following claims will not be allowed by the bankruptcy trustee?
   a. A claim by Paul's friend for a loan she made to Paul that is evidenced by a promissory note.
   b. A claim by Tom who fraudulently caused Paul to enter a contract to purchase stock.
   c. A claim by Sue for wages due during the past month while she worked as Paul's assistant.
   d. All of the above.

_____ 4. Which of the following transactions may be avoided by the bankruptcy trustee as a voidable preference?
   a. Brenda pays her $750 credit card charges in full 30 days before filing bankruptcy.
   b. Tim pays $400 to each of his creditors within 60 days of filing bankruptcy.
   c. Sean gives his piano to Ursula 10 days before filing bankruptcy as security for money he borrowed two years before.
   d. a and c.

SHORT ANSWER QUESTIONS

Answer the following questions, briefly explaining the reason for your answer.

1. Santos filed a voluntary petition in bankruptcy in order to get a fresh start. Santos owns a small life insurance policy, personal clothing, a motorboat, an extensive original art collection by world-famous sculptors, and an old car. Which of these assets will most likely be allowed under the federal bankruptcy exemptions?

_____

_____

2. Three weeks before filing bankruptcy, Al borrowed $500 from Foster and gave Foster a security interest in his rowboat. At the creditors' meeting George, an unsecured creditor, argues that Foster's security interest is a voidable preference and should be avoided by the trustee so that the row boat can be sold to benefit the many unsecured creditors. Is George correct?

_____

_____

3. Gordon was granted a discharge in bankruptcy on November 30. The following September one of his creditors learned that immediately prior to the bankruptcy, Gordon had transferred a large sum of money to a foreign bank account so that he would appear insolvent. What can the creditor do to correct the situation?

_____

_____

4. Martha owed Anna $5,000 for money she borrowed when her daughter was ill. Shortly before receiving her discharge in bankruptcy, Martha's conscience began to bother her and she agreed in writing to pay Anna the remainder of the debt. Is such an agreement valid and enforceable?

_____

_____

CASE PROBLEMS

Answer the following case problems, explaining your answers.

1. Sara filed a voluntary petition in bankruptcy under Chapter 7. At the time she filed, she owed money to the mortgage company, which had financed her house, and a credit card company for various clothing purchases. Sara also owed delinquent income taxes from the previous year. The auto dealer, which had financed her car, held a perfected security interest in the vehicle. Sara's total bankruptcy estate was determined to be $7,000. Expenses of administering the bankruptcy were $500. (a) How much money will be available to Sara's unsecured creditors? (b) Which, if any, of Sara's assets may be exempt under federal or state exemption laws? (c) If Sara wishes to keep her car, what action can she take? (d) Are there any debts from which Sara may not be discharged?

_____

_____

_____

_____

2. Downtown Office Products has several unpaid accounts with Tim, who has indicated that he may soon file bankruptcy under Chapter 7. Among the debts owed to the company by Tim are a fax machine, which is subject to a perfected security interest and miscellaneous office supplies. In addition, Tim has leased office space from the company and is liable for payment under a five-year lease. If Tim does file bankruptcy: (a) May Downtown Office Products repossess the fax machine? (b) What are the company's options regarding the fax machine? (c) Will the claim for payments under the lease be wholly allowed, partially allowed, or barred by the trustee? (d) In what general order of payment will Office Products recover on its claim for the office supply purchases?

_____

_____

_____

_____

3. Carla's Greenhouse filed a Chapter 11 bankruptcy. It has several classes of creditors, some of which would rather force the Greenhouse into a liquidation. The Greenhouse has operated as debtor-in-possession and filed a reorganization plan within the 120-day period. (a) May the secured creditors repossess their interests in property necessary for the reorganization? (b) May the Court approve the reorganization plan over the objections of disgruntled creditors? (c) Must the plan provide that all claims be paid in full? (d) May some creditors force the Greenhouse into a Chapter 7 absent some wrongful action on the debtor's part?

_____

_____

_____

_____

Chapter 29   Agency: Creation and Termination

CHAPTER REVIEW

AGENCY LAW AND AGENCY RELATIONSHIPS: Agency law concerns the duties and relationships that arise between employees and employers. In general, an agency is a fiduciary relationship.

RESTRICTIONS ON CREATING AN AGENCY RELATIONSHIP: Potential issues relating to the creation of an agency relationship include:

- *Capacity to be a principal*: Any person having the capacity to contract (not minors - in most states; or incompetents) can employ an agent.
- *Capacity to be an agent*: Anyone, even minors and incompetents, can be an agent.
- *Duties an agent can perform*: Agents can be authorized to do almost any legal task, unless the task involves a non-delegable duty.

TYPES OF AGENCY RELATIONSHIPS: Agents can be either general agents or special agents.

- *General and special agents*: General agents have more discretion in carrying out their employers' business than do special agents. Factors that help determine an agent's status include: 1) the number of acts an agent must complete in order to obtain an authorized result; 2) the number of people that must be dealt with; and 3) the length of time needed to obtain the desired outcome.
- *Gratuitous agents*: Agents who volunteer their services to a principal are gratuitous agents.

SERVANTS AND INDEPENDENT CONTRACTORS: The distinction between servants and independent contractors is important when determining the liability of an employer for an employee's conduct.

- *Servants*: A "servant" is a special types of agent/employee whose employer has the right to control how the employee will perform his or her duties. Importantly, employers are liable for the physical acts (torts) that are committed by their servants while acting within the scope of their employment.
- *Independent contractors*: An independent contractor is hired by employers to accomplish a task, but the employers do not have the right to control how the contractor will carry out this duty. Independent contractors who are agents of employers, (e.g., a lawyer), may owe fiduciary duties to the employers.
- *Responsibility for independent contractors*: Principals are liable for authorized contracts made on their behalf by agents, even if the agents are independent contractors. Employers are liable for damage caused by an independent contractor who was hired to perform an ultrahazardous (or, increasingly, hazardous) activity. The general rule, though, is that an employer is NOT liable for the *physical acts (or physical torts) or crimes* of their independent contractors. The trend, however, is to increase the circumstances when employers may be held liable for such wrongs. The Restatement (Second) of Torts indicates that an employer may be held liable for an independent contractor's in the following situations:
  1) the independent contractor is hired to engage in ultrahazardous activities;
  2) the independent contractor is hired to commit a crime;
  3) the hiring party reserves the right to supervise or control the work;
  4) the hiring party actually directs the independent contractor to do something careless or wrong;
  5) the hiring party sees the independent contractor do something wrong and does not stop it;
  6) the hiring party fails to adequately supervise the independent contractor; and
  7) the hiring party is negligent in selecting the independent contractor.

Either servants or independent contractors can also be agents. Agents have the authority to perform "legal acts." In other words, agents can represent their principals in contractual or other dealings with third parties.

DUTIES OF THE AGENT TO THE PRINCIPAL: To protect the interests of the principal the agent has the following duties: the duty of good faith (a fiduciary duty); the duty of loyalty; the duty to obey all lawful instructions (unless doing so places the agent at unreasonable risk of injury); the duty to act with reasonable care; the duty to segregate funds; the duty to account for funds; the duty to give notice of material facts to the principal; and the duty to perform the terms of any employment contract.

DUTIES OF THE PRINCIPAL TO THE AGENT: The principal has the duty to pay the agent according to their contract; the duty to provide a safe place to work; and the duty to provide safe equipment to use.

TERMINATION OF THE AGENCY RELATIONSHIP: An agency relationship may be terminated by:

- *Agreement of the parties*: An employment contract between the principal and agent may state when the agency relationship shall end.

- *Agency at will*: If the agency agreement does not state that the relationship shall last for a fixed time or until a specified event occurs, then it is terminable at any time by either party after notice. However, a principal cannot terminate for reasons that would violate an agent's legal rights.

- *Fulfillment of the agency purpose*: Fulfillment of the agency's purpose usually terminates the agency.

- *Revocation*: A principal has the absolute right to terminate an agency. If the termination violates the agent's legal rights, then the agent may sue the principal for wrongful discharge.

- *Renunciation*: When an agents notify a principal that they quit, this terminates the relationship.

- *Operation of law*: An agency can terminate by operation of law, without need for notice, if the following events occur: 1) the death of the agent; 2) either party becomes insane; 3) a bankruptcy affects the agency; 4) the agency cannot be performed; 5) unforeseen events destroy the agency's purpose; or 6) a change in the law makes the agency illegal.

- *Importance of notice*: Early termination of the agency by either party, except by operation of law, requires notice to the parties and to third parties who might be affected. Actual or constructive notice may be acceptable, depending on the facts of the case.

- *Breach of agency agreement*: If a principal wrongfully discharges an agent, the agent has a duty to mitigate his or her damages by seeking alternative employment.

STUDY HINTS FOR NRW CASE STUDIES

The following study hints may be helpful when resolving the NRW case studies.

NRW 29.1	➢ NRW should review the material relating to a principal's right to control the actions of agents.
	➢ To protect the company from competition by its agents, NRW should consider using confidentiality agreements and perhaps covenants not to compete.
NRW 29.2	➢ Developing a positive work environment may be a better way to deal with potential work place violence than having guns on the premises.
NRW 29.3	➢ Employee handbooks can be helpful in cultivating good employee relations.
	➢ NRW should carefully consider the possibility, however, that an employee handbook may become legally binding on the company.

REVIEW OF KEY TERMS AND CONCEPTS

MATCHING EXERCISE

Select the term or concept that best matches a definition or statement set forth below. Each term or concept is the best match for only one definition or statement.

Terms and Concepts

a. Agency at will

b. Agent

c. Common carrier

d Discretion

e. Fiduciary duty

f. Independent contractor

g. Principal

h. Renunciation

i. Trust

Definitions and Statements

_____ 1. Company that transports people or goods for a fee.

_____ 2. Person who is employed to accomplish a task. The person employed has the right to control how to accomplish the assigned work.

_____ 3. Using one's judgement to determine how to accomplish a task.

_____ 4. Legal duty to act in good faith and loyally for the benefit of another.

_____ 5. Legal relationship in which legal title is held separately from beneficial ownership.

_____ 6. Person who empowers another to negotiate contracts on his or her behalf.

_____ 7. Agency relationship that may be terminated by either party at any time.

_____ 8. Person who is empowered to negotiate contracts on behalf of another.

_____ 9. Act of an agent that terminates an agency relationship.

COMPLETION EXERCISE

Fill in the blanks with the words that most accurately complete each statement.

1. A _____ _____ is hired to conduct a series of transactions over time on behalf of a principal.

2. An agency is a _____ relationship between a principal and an agent, i.e., the law will not force the parties into this relationship.

3. In a _____ _____, an agent voluntarily agrees to perform a task for a principal.

4. The _____ of _____ requires the agent to look out for the principal's best interests.

5. Identify six general methods for terminating an agency.

a. _____.

b. _____.

c. _____.

d. _____.

e. _____.

f. _____.

TRUE-FALSE EXERCISE

Write T if the statement is true, write F if the statement is false.

_____ 1. Anyone can be an agent.

_____ 2. A contract is not essential in order to create an agency relationship.

_____ 3. A primary feature of the agency relationship is that all agents are paid for their services.

_____ 4. In general, a principal has the power to terminate an agency relationship even if the termination breaches a contract between the principal and agent.

_____ 5. Independent contractors who are agents can bind their principals to contracts.

_____ 6. An agent breaches the duty to obey the principal's instructions when the agent refuses to do an unreasonably dangerous task.

_____ 7. If the agency agreement does not specify a time limit, either party may generally terminate the relationship at any time.

_____ 8. *Traditionally*, when a principal dies, the agency immediately terminates.

_____ 9. If the principal wrongfully discharges an agent, the agent may have the right to recover damages from the principal.

_____ 10. In an agency coupled with an interest, a principal cannot unilaterally terminate the agency.

APPLICATION OF CONCEPTS

MULTIPLE CHOICE QUESTIONS

_____ 1. Jane appointed Ralph as her general agent. Nonetheless, Jane cannot:
   a. Authorize Ralph to buy and sell land on her behalf.
   b. Authorize Ralph to negotiate and execute contracts on her behalf.
   c. Delegate to Ralph the legal duty to provide safe working conditions for her employees.
   d. All of the above.

_____ 2. General Contractors Unlimited (GCU) hired Piper Plumbing, Inc. to install the plumbing for an apartment building. Piper is obligated to install the plumbing in accordance with certain building plans, but Piper may otherwise control its own workers, method of construction, tools, supplies, etc. In this case, Piper is an:
   a. Employee of GCU.
   b. Agent for GCU.
   c. Independent contractor for GCU.
   d. Servant for GCU.

_____ 3. Jenni owns a construction company that builds custom houses. She hired Steve as her agent to solicit new business. Steve was approached by a celebrity who wanted to have a $3 million custom house built. Steve did not disclose this information to Jenni so that he could take advantage of this opportunity himself. Steve has breached which of the following duties?
   a. Duty of loyalty.
   b. Duty of good faith.
   c. Duty to give notice.
   d. All of the above.

_____ 4. Zsa Zsa, a circus performer, employed Eddie as her agent to find her engagements for the next five years. Under these facts, the parties' agency relationship would terminate by operation of law after one year if:
   a. Eddie declared bankruptcy (his bankruptcy does not affect his ability to perform the agency).
   b. Zsa Zsa declared bankruptcy.
   c. Zsa Zsa decided that she no longer wanted Eddie to represent her.
   d. Zsa Zsa decided to limit the number of engagements she would accept each year.

SHORT ANSWER QUESTIONS

Answer the following questions, briefly explaining the reason for your answer.

1. Juan, owner of Juan's Antiques Unlimited, Inc. hired Mary to buy antiques for him in Europe. Mary bought antiques from many dealers and had them packed and shipped back to Juan's store. Mary has been buying for Juan for the past ten years. What type of agency exists between the parties?

_____

_____

2. Norton is an explosives expert. He was hired by Acme Construction to design, place, and set off the necessary explosive charges to blast a tunnel through a mountain. Acme dictated the dimensions for the tunnel, and Norton has the right to determine how the work is to be accomplished. What is the nature of the relationship between the parties? Would Acme be liable for harm that Norton may cause to others when carrying out the blasting?

_____

3. Jodi, an adult, wanted to sell her in-line skates. Jodi asked her 17-year-old friend, Ron, to find a buyer for the skates and to negotiate their sale on her behalf. Ron agreed, and contracted to sell the skates to a third party. What is the nature of the relationship between Jodi and Ron? Can Ron lawfully serve in this capacity? Is Jodi bound by the contract that Ron negotiated on her behalf?

_____

_____

4. Argie signed a contract to sell Cuttin'-To-The-Bone cutlery to retailers located in the Western United States for two years. When will this agency relationship terminate? Can the parties later agree not to terminate the agency?

_____

_____

CASE PROBLEMS

Answer the following case problems, explaining your answers.

1. Singh and Ratou are partners in a small turban manufacturing business. In their partnership agreement, the parties agreed that they may each act on behalf of the partnership in making partnership contracts. On behalf of the partnership, Ratou contracted with California Fabrics to buy muslin that was needed for making turbans. Ratou, however, agreed to a higher price than normal because California Fabrics promised to pay her a secret commission on the sale. Under these facts:

   (a) What relationship exists between the individual partners and the partnership?
   (b) What is the nature of this relationship?
   (c) Did Ratou breach any duty owed to the partnership?

_____

_____

_____

_____

2. Joe, general manager of Motorworks, Inc., an automobile service center, was fired in the morning and told not to return the next day. On the same day, Kathy paid money to Joe that she owed for work that Motorworks had performed on her car. Joe kept the money. The next day, Joe went to a Motorworks' supplier and bought a set of tires on behalf of Motorworks, a transaction that he had often done in the past. However, this time Joe kept the tires and absconded.

   (a) Discuss the rights of Motorworks, Kathy, and the supplier in this case.
   (b) What should Motorworks have done differently to avoid this situation?

_____

_____

_____

_____

```
┌─────────────────────────────────────┐
│            CHAPTER REVIEW             │
└─────────────────────────────────────┘
```

A FRAMEWORK FOR CONTRACTUAL LIABILITY: When agents make a contract for principals, a prime issue is whether the principal authorized the agent to enter into the contract. Principals may be disclosed, partially disclosed, or undisclosed. The status of a principal may affect the parties' legal rights and duties.

IMPOSING LIABILITY ON THE PRINCIPAL: Principals are liable on contracts made on their behalf by agents only when the agents had some type of authority to contract. In some situations, an agent may have more than one type of authority to act on behalf of a principal. Different types of authority include:

- *Actual authority*: Actual authority is authority that the principal in fact grants to the agent. This authority establishes the limits of what the agent should do in carrying out his or her duties for the principal. If the agent acts within the agent's actual authority, then the agent is not liable to the principal for actions undertaken.

  Actual authority may 1) be expressly stated by the principal, 2) be incidental to the agent's duties, 3) be implied from the context of the agency agreement, 4) arise as the result of the principal ratifying conduct of the agent, and 5) arise due to an emergency.

- *Express authority*: Agents have express authority when the principal tells them they can do an act.

- *Ratification authority*: When agents enter into an unauthorized contract, the agent is said to have ratification authority if the principal, knowing all of the terms of the contract, expressly or impliedly approves the entire contract.

- *Incidental authority*: Agents have the authority to do acts reasonable and necessary to complete an assigned task.

- *Implied authority*: Agents with a particular title have the authority that their position would normally suggest to third parties.

- *Emergency authority*: Agency relationships allow agents to respond to emergencies if the principal cannot be reached and the agents act reasonably under the circumstances.

- *Apparent authority*: Apparent authority exists when: 1) the principal creates an appearance that an agency exists or that an agent has broader powers than actually exist, and 2) a third party reasonably believes that the agent has such authority.

- *Authority by estoppel*: Principals who mislead third parties regarding an agent's authority cannot deny the authority of the agent after the contract is made.

- *Imputing the agent's knowledge to the principal*: Since an agent has a duty to inform the principal of important information relating to the agency, the principal is assumed to know what the agent knows and the courts will impute the agent's knowledge to the principal.

DISCLOSED PRINCIPAL: A principal whose existence is clearly disclosed is bound to the terms of a contract that is made by an agent who acted pursuant to any of the types of authority described above.

- *Liability of the agent*: Normally agents acting for a disclosed principal are not liable on the contract. However, an agent may be personally liable if: 1) the agent does not disclose that they are acting only as an agent or 2) if the agent agrees to be bound to the contract. The other contracting party may sue either the principal or agent, or both (the modern trend) in situation 1), but the other party must ultimately elect whether the principal or agent must perform the remedy.

- *Warranty of authority*: It is implied that agents warrant to the other contracting party that: 1) the disclosed principal exists; 2) the principal is competent to contract; and 3) the principal authorized the contract. If any of these warranties is false, the third party can sue the agent for any resulting losses.
- *Liability of the third party*: The third party is liable to the principal for breach of contract if the agent had any authority to act (rule does not apply to authority by estoppel). The third party is liable to the agent if the agent has a legal interest in the contract or is a party to the contract.

UNDISCLOSED PRINCIPAL: An undisclosed principal is one whose existence and/or identity are not known to the other contracting party.
- *Liability of the agent*: If a principal is completely undisclosed, the third party can sue the agent for any breach of the contract.
- *Liability of the principal*: If the other party later discovers the identity of the principal, the third party can sue the principal on the contract. The principal is liable on the contract if the agent had authority to enter into the contract.
- *Liability of the third party*: If the other contracting party breaches the contract, the other party can be sued for breach of contract.

PARTIALLY DISCLOSED PRINCIPAL: A principal is partially disclosed if the other contracting party knows that a principal exists, but does not know the principal's identity. A partially disclosed principal can be sued for breach if the agent was authorized to make the contract. However, the other contracting party must elect whether to the principal or the agent.

ANALYSIS OF AGENT'S CONTRACTS WITH THIRD PARTIES: Refer to six-step approach in textbook.

CONTRACT BETWEEN THE PRINCIPAL AND THE AGENT: Possible issues relating to an agency include:
- *The need for a writing*: The Statute of Frauds may require certain agency contracts to be evidenced by a writing. The equal dignities rule requires that an agency contract be written if an agent is to make a contract on behalf of the principal and that contract is required to be in writing.
- *Covenants not to compete*: Many agency contracts state that when an agent's employment is ended, the agent cannot compete against his principal. Such covenants (promises) are valid only if they are for a reasonable period of time and geographical area.

STUDY HINTS FOR NRW CASE STUDIES

The following study hints may be helpful when resolving the NRW case studies.

NRW 30.1	➤ Whether NRW is bound by the order depends on whether the salesperson had authority to enter the contract in question on behalf of NRW.
	➤ Review the different types of authority, particularly implied and apparent authority.
NRW 30.2	➤ The third party has the burden to prove the salesperson's authority to represent NRW.
	➤ Before advising the salesperson regarding his or her potential liability in this case, examine the concept of warranty of authority and evaluate whether it applies in this case.
NRW 30.3	➤ Review the material dealing with the fiduciary duties of agents, particularly the duty of loyalty.
	➤ Review the tort of unfair competition and rights associated with trade secrets.
	➤ Bear in mind that the fiduciary duties implied by law are minimum obligations; the NRW agency contract can enlarge upon these duties.

REVIEW OF KEY TERMS AND CONCEPTS

MATCHING EXERCISE

Select the term or concept that best matches a definition or statement set forth below. Each term or concept is the best match for only one definition or statement.

Terms and Concepts

a. Apparent authority
b. Assignable
c. Covenant

d. Express authority
e. Goodwill
f. Implied authority

g. Imputed knowledge
h. Partially disclosed principal
i. Undisclosed principal

Definitions and Terms

_____ 1. Knowledge of one person is attributed to another person as well.

_____ 2. Authority that is orally or in writing given by a principal to an agent.

_____ 3. Transferable.

_____ 4. Promise.

_____ 5. Good name and reputation of a business.

_____ 6. Principal whose existence, but not identity, is known to a third party.

_____ 7. Authority that arises because a principal falsely creates the impression that an agent has authority to act.

_____ 8. Principal whose existence and identity are not known to a third party.

_____ 9. Authority that arises because of an agent's position.

COMPLETION EXERCISE

Fill in the blanks with the words that most accurately complete each statement.

1. _____ by _____ arises when a principal has deliberately misled a third party regarding the authority of an agent.

2. When an agent represents a _____ principal, the agent does not ordinarily incur any personal liability on the contract in question.

3. When agents represent an _____ principal, the other contracting party actually believes that the agents are acting on their own behalf.

4. A covenant not to compete is unenforceable unless it is for only a reasonable _____ and a reasonable _____ _____.

5. Describe three guarantees that are encompassed by the warranty of authority:

a. _____ .

b. _____ .

c. _____ .

TRUE-FALSE EXERCISE

Write T if the statement is true, write F if the statement is false.

____ 1. If an agent makes an unauthorized contract on behalf of a principal, the principal may choose to ratify all or only a portion of the contract.

____ 2. A principal is liable for every contract that is made on the principal's behalf by an agent.

____ 3. If a principal ratifies a contract, the contract is treated as if it were valid from its inception.

____ 4. Builders Inc. hired Jim as supervisor for a building project. Jim hired, trained, supervised, and fired workmen as needed to complete the project. Jim is exercising incidental authority.

____ 5. Emergency authority may be implied in most agency relationships.

____ 6. When an agency relationship is terminated, a prudent principal will give third parties notice of such termination.

____ 7. Principals are not responsible for the actions of agents unless their authority is stated in writing.

____ 8. A principal cannot be held liable on a contract that is made by an agent who acted with only apparent authority.

____ 9. Principals can be held legally responsible for information that is known their agents only to the extent that the agents actually communicate the information to the principal.

____ 10. In general, agents are liable on contracts that they make on behalf of disclosed principals.

```
APPLICATION OF CONCEPTS
```

MULTIPLE CHOICE QUESTIONS

____ 1. Niles, as agent for an undisclosed principal, entered into a contract to buy and sell land with LandHo!, Inc. Which of the following is a true statement?
a. LandHo! can sue both Niles and the principal if the principal breaches.
b. LandHo! can sue Niles or the principal if the principal breaches.
c. LandHo! cannot sue Niles or the principal because the principal was undisclosed.
d. The principal can sue Niles for making the contract on its behalf.

____ 2. In which situation is Pat (the principal) liable on the contract in question?
a. Pat signed a written power of attorney, authorizing an agent to sell his house. On Pat's behalf, the agent contracted with a third party for the sale of the house.
b. An agent signed a contract to sell Pat's car, but Pat had not authorized this sale. Later Pat decided to accept the contract as written and signed it.
c. An agent purchased supplies from a third party on behalf of Pat, just as the agent had done many times before. Pat had never expressly authorized the agent to make these purchases, but Pat was aware that the agent had been making these acquisitions and never objected.
d. All of the above.

_____ 3. Sue applied for a job at Paul's Cafe. When Sue arrived for her job interview, Paul was busy with other business. To avoid having to interview Sue, Paul told her: "Go see Agnes, the head cashier. Agnes is responsible for all hiring decisions." Paul lied (Agnes was not supposed to hire anyone on her own), but Sue did not know this. After the interview, Agnes hired Sue to work at the cafe. What type of authority did Agnes have in this case?
     a. Express authority
     b. Implied authority
     c. Apparent authority
     d. No authority

_____ 4. Lynn is the purchasing agent for Patty, owner of a medical supply business. Lynn was expressly authorized to buy all necessary inventory on Patty's behalf. Acting pursuant to this authority, Lynn contracted to purchase some inventory from BandageCo. Patty breached this contract and failed to pay the purchase price. In this case, BandageCo. may hold Lynn personally liable on the contract if:
     a. Patty's existence and identity were disclosed to BandageCo. at the time of contracting.
     b. Pattys' existence, but not identity, was disclosed to BandageCo. at the time of contracting.
     c. Pattys' existence and identity were undisclosed to BandageCo. at the time of contracting.
     d. b and c.

SHORT ANSWER QUESTIONS

Answer the following questions, briefly explaining the reason for your answer.

1. Ali was sales manager for Adams Co., a crate manufacturer. Ali was orally told by Adams to sell 1,000 crates to Tri-State Groceries. On behalf of Adams, Ali contracted to sell the crates to Tri-State. Who are the parties to this contract? Who is liable to perform this contract?

_____

_____

2. Nolan was authorized by Ryan to purchase up to $500 of inventory for Ryan's business. When Nolan went to the supplier's warehouse, Nolan noticed that the supplier was having an unadvertised sale of inventory items that Ryan needed in his business. Nolan was unsuccessful in reaching Ryan, so he exercised his discretion and purchased $2,000 of merchandise for Ryan. Ryan was furious, but he decided to keep the merchandise after Nolan explained to him the terms of the contract. What type of authority, if any, did Nolan initially have to make this purchase? Is Ryan liable on the contract?

_____

_____

3. Elizabeth is the manager of a large clothing store. It is customary in Elizabeth's community and in the retail clothing industry that managers can hire necessary store clerks. Without consulting with the store owner, Elizabeth hired Rachel as a cosmetics sales clerk. What type of authority did Elizabeth have to hire Rachel? Could the store owner have limited or done away with this authority?

_____

_____

4. Roger was the general manager for the Stanley Farm. Stanley had instructed Roger never to contract for more than $1,000 without first obtaining Stanley's express authority. While Stanley was out of the country, a plague of locusts invaded the farm and threatened to wipe out the farm's entire crop. In order to save the crops, Roger hired Jenni's LocustBusters to exterminate the locusts at a cost of $500. Did Roger have authority to hire Jenni's extermination company?

_____

_____

CASE PROBLEMS

Answer the following case problems, explaining your answers.

1. Alton is a clerk at Preston's Mens Store. On behalf of Preston's, Alton contracted to buy 100 ties from All-Tied-Up, a tie supplier. Preston had never told Alton that he could make any purchases on behalf of the store. When Preston learned about the contract, Preston fired Alton and refused to perform the contract. (a) Discuss the nature of Alton's authority to make the purchase contract. (b) Who is liable to perform the contract? (c) Analyze whether Alton has any liability to Preston and/or All-Tied-Up.

_____

_____

_____

_____

2. Phyllis hired Jenkins to negotiate the purchase of a patent for her, but she asked Jenkins not to disclose her identity. Jenkins told the seller that he was acting on behalf of an anonymous third party. (a) What type of principal is Phyllis? (b) Discuss whether Phyllis and/or Jenkins can be held liable on the contract. (c) Can Phyllis hold the seller liable on the contract?

_____

_____

_____

_____

Chapter 31

Agency: Liability for Torts and Crimes

SERVANT'S LIABILITY: Servants who commit a tort are personally liable for their torts. The primary issue in this situation is whether the servant's master (employer) is also liable for the tort. This issue is addressed by the doctrine of *respondeat superior*.

MASTER'S LIABILITY: *RESPONDEAT SUPERIOR*:: Under the doctrine of *respondeat superior*, a master may have vicarious (i.e., derivative or imputed) liability for a tort that is committed by an employee (servant) who was acting within the scope of the agency relationship at the time that the tort was committed. The doctrine of *respondeat superior* is based on a theory of strict liability theory - since the master hired the servant, and the servant did something wrong - the master must be held accountable if the servant's actions were committed within the course and scope of the servant's employment. If respondeat superior applies, the victim will be allowed to recover from the master; if not, the victim may only seek recovery from the servant.

To establish vicarious liability of a master under the doctrine of *respondeat superior*, a third party must establish two elements: 1) a master-servant relationship existed between the master and servant; and 2) the servant was acting within the course and scope of employment at the time the tort was committed. These two elements are generally determined by the following inquiries:

1) A master-servant relationship exists if an employer has the right to control the details of an employee's work, whether or not the employer exercises this right. Conversely, an employer-independent contractor relationship exists (a master is generally NOT liable for torts of an independent contractor) if the employer has the right to control the end result, but not the method by which the agent accomplishes the task.

2) A servant is acting within the course and scope of employment when his or her conduct: (a) is the kind for which he or she was employed to perform; (b) occurs substantially within the time and territory authorized by the master; and (c) is performed in order to further the master's interests.

Common considerations and issues that arise when applying the doctrine of *respondeat superior* include the following:

- *Factors listed in the Restatement of Agency*: The key factors are whether the conduct of the servant was within the scope of the employee's employment or, if the conduct is not authorized, was it similar or incidental to the authorized conduct so as to be within the scope of employment. Whether the acts are within the course and scope of employment depends on the facts of the particular situation.
- *Time and place of occurrence*: Two of the most important factors analyzed in the Restatement is whether the tort occurred at the work place and during work hours.
- *Failure to follow instructions*: A master can be held liable for a servant's torts even though the master forbade the servant to commit torts.
- *Failure to act*: A master can be held liable if the servant fails to act as instructed.
- *Identifying the master*: Sometimes masters lend or borrow servants. In such cases, it is sometimes difficult to determine which master is liable for the torts of the borrowed servant.
- *Crimes and intentional torts*: The modern trend is to increasingly hold masters liable for the intentional torts of their servants, if the servants' actions furthered or were intended to further the master's interests (e.g., a battery committed by a nightclub bouncer, while evicting a patron). Since many criminal acts are also torts, the master may sometimes be held civilly liable for such acts.

DIRECT LIABILITY OF THE PRINCIPAL: In some cases, masters have direct liability in connection with their servants' torts because the masters themselves committed a wrong, either intentionally or negligently. Criminal law may also apply to a principal when an agent commits a crime.

Direct civil liability of masters may be based on any of the following types of conduct:

1) A master is directly liable to a third party if the master **tells a servant to commit a tort** against the third party and the servant does so.

2) A master is **negligent in** hiring a servant and placing the servant in a position where the servant agent can commit a tort against others.

3) A master is **negligent in supervising** a servant who has a known problem that may endanger others.

4) A master is **negligent in entrusting** a servant with equipment that the servant does not know how to operate and the servant then misuses the equipment, causing damage or injury to a third party.

NEGLIGENT HIRING: An employer can be held liable for negligent hiring if he or she is careless in the hiring process. In many states, negligent hiring also applies to the hiring of agents and independent contractors. Negligent hiring assumes that if an employer had investigated a job applicant's past it would have learned of prior misconduct and would not have hired the person, and the employer's negligent hiring allowed the employee to harm someone. Under this theory, an employer owes a duty to customers, to the public at large and, in some states, to other employees and agents. In many states, the employee's acts are not required to be in the course and scope of the employment in order to impose liability for negligent hiring.

INDEMNIFICATION: If the principal must pay a judgment because of an agent's tort, the principal has a right to repayment from the agent. Sometimes an agent has a right to indemnification from the principal if the agent pays the injured party for his or her tort. Also, the agent can obtain indemnification from the principal if the agent is directed to do a tortious act and does it believing that it is not tortious.

INJURY ON THE JOB : *At common law*, an employee injured on the job cannot recover from the employer if: 1) the employee assumed the risk; 2) the employee was negligent and the employee's contributory negligence caused the injury; or 3) the employee was injured by another employee of the same employer. The employer, however, may have a duty to warn if the danger is not commonly known, but the employer knows or should know of the risk inherent in the job.

In most states today, the foregoing issues are rendered moot by workers' compensation statutes. These statute typically allow an employee to recover workers' compensation benefits for work-related injuries and the foregoing defenses can NOT be used to deny an employee his or her benefits. On the other hand, when these laws apply, workers' compensation is the exclusive remedy for the worker and the employee cannot sue the employer based on common law tort law.

STUDY HINTS FOR NRW CASE STUDIES

The following study hints may be helpful when resolving the NRW case studies.

NRW 31.1	➤ Review the doctrine of *respondeat superior* and the material contrasting an employer's liability for torts committed by independent contractors versus those committed by servants.
NRW 31.2	➤ Consider the factors listed by the Restatement that define "scope of employment" ➤ Also, consider the issue of "time and place of occurrence" of the tort.
NRW 31.3	➤ For information dealing with NRW's potential criminal liability for such employee conduct, review the material dealing with direct Liability of a principal.

MATCHING EXERCISE

Select the term or concept that best matches a definition or statement set forth below. Each term or concept is the best match for only one definition or statement.

Terms and Concepts

a. Accessory to the crime
b. Assault
c. Battery

d. Conspiracy
e. Indemnification
f. Judgement proof

g. Personal representative
h. Vicarious liability
i. Workers' compensation laws

Definitions and Statements

____ 1. Person who handles a deceased person's financial affairs.
____ 2. Unable to pay a judgement, even if found liable for damages in a civil lawsuit.
____ 3. Statutory scheme by which workers receive benefits for work-related injuries.
____ 4. Unpermitted touching of one person by another.
____ 5. Liability imposed on one person for wrongs committed by another.
____ 6. Threat to imminently commit a battery against someone.
____ 7. Agreement by two or more persons to commit a crime.
____ 8. Person who assists another in the commission of a crime.
____ 9. Right to be repaid.

COMPLETION EXERCISE

Fill in the blanks with the words that most accurately complete each statement.

1. The doctrine of _____ _____ generally holds masters liable for torts that their servants commit while acting within the course and scope of their employment.

2. Employers have _____ liability under respondeat superior, meaning employers are liable because their servants did something wrong, not because the employers did anything wrong themselves.

3. Two factors that courts examine when deciding whether a servant's tort was committed within the scope of employment are the _____ and _____ that the tort occurred.

4. Masters who pay for damages caused by their servants are entitled to _____, meaning the masters are entitled to be reimbursement from the servants for the amount paid.

5. _____ _____ laws generally allow employees to recover statutory benefits for work-related injuries.

TRUE-FALSE EXERCISE

Write **T** if the statement is true, write **F** if the statement is false.

_____ 1. Employers are liable for every tort committed by their servants.

_____ 2. One justification for the doctrine of *respondeat superior* is that this doctrine makes masters more careful in supervising their servants.

_____ 3. An employer may be held vicariously liable for harm that is caused by an independent contractor while performing an inherently dangerous task for the employer.

_____ 4. Employees who commit torts within the course and scope of their employment are not personally liable for such torts - only their employers are liable.

_____ 5. A principal may be personally liable to a third party who is injured by an employee whom the principal was negligent in hiring.

_____ 6. Under the modern view, masters may be held liable for the intentional torts of their servants if the torts were committed in order to advance the masters' interests.

_____ 7. An employer is generally not liable for torts that are committed by an employee who is merely commuting to or from work.

_____ 8. Under the doctrine of *respondeat superior*, an employer is generally liable for torts that are committed by an independent contractor.

_____ 9. A principal who directs an agent to commit a crime is personally liable for the agent's criminal conduct.

_____ 10. An employer cannot be held liable for an employee's torts if the employer previously instructed the employee not to commit such wrongs.

APPLICATION OF CONCEPTS

MULTIPLE CHOICE QUESTIONS

_____ 1. In which scenario is Lupe, the owner of Lupe's Dress Shop, liable for her employee's tort?
   a. Ellen, an employee, struck her ex-husband, who had come into the store, because he told her that he was getting remarried.
   b. Ed, who was a janitor for the store and under Lupe's direction and control, failed to put away a ladder. Later, a customer was injured when the ladder fell on her.
   c. Edger, a salesperson, was driving his own car to a restaurant for lunch when he struck a pedestrian. At the time, Edger was not running any errands for Lupe.
   d. All of the above.

_____ 2. Todd was a delivery person for Kar World. While driving to deliver a part to a customer, Todd negligently damaged Kip's car. Todd was speeding at the time of the accident, a violation of a Kar World work regulation. Under these facts, who is liable to Kip?
   a. Only Todd.
   b. Only Kar World.
   c. Todd and Kar World.
   d. No one.

_____ 3. In which case would the principal be directly liable for the agent's tort?
   a. Norm, the principal, instructed Al, his agent, to assault Tim, a person who owed Norm's business a great deal of money.
   b. Zoe, owner of a lawn sprinkler firm, failed to supervise Del, foreman of the installation crew. As a result, Del incorrectly installed sprinklers, causing a customer's trees to die.
   c. Kevin, owner of Children Day Care Center, hired Carl as a staff worker. Kevin failed to do a background check on Carl, who had a string of child molestation convictions. Carl molested a child at the center.
   d. All of the above.

_____ 4. Tina slipped and fell on a piece of chalk while teaching at Elmer Elementary School. The chalk had been negligently left on the floor by a school janitor. Under these facts:
   a. At common law, Tina could not hold the school liable for her injuries.
   b. At common law, Tina could hold the school liable for her injuries.
   c. Under worker's compensation laws, Tina cannot recover benefits because her injury was caused by a fellow employee.
   d. a and c.

SHORT ANSWER QUESTIONS

Answer the following questions, briefly explaining the reason for your answer.

1. Orlando owned Orlando's Hideaway, a nightclub. Rose worked for him as a waitress. All wait staff were instructed by Orlando on how to pour hot coffee refills, so as to avoid injuring customers. Rose routinely ignored Orlando's instructions. One evening Rose, disregarding Orlando's instructions, spilled piping hot coffee on a customer, severely burning her. Who is liable for the customer's injury? Explain your answer.

_____

_____

2. Jessica is a driver for Reliable Concrete Company. After delivering a load of concrete to a customer, Jessica decided that she would visit a friend who was working at a job site about ten miles away. When she was nearing her friend's job site, Jessica negligently collided with Marilyn's car, injuring Marilyn. Under these facts, are Jessica and/or Reliable liable to Marilyn?

_____

_____

3. Orville was a temporary worker hired by LaborTemp, Inc. LaborTemp sent Orville on a two-week temporary assignment at Mann Warehouse. Mann's had the right to control what and how Orville did his work. While stacking boxes in the warehouse, Orville negligently dropped a box on a customer, injuring the customer. Who is liable for Orville's tort - LaborTemp and/or Mann Warehouse?

_____

_____

4. Bobby was driving a delivery truck for Tony's Meat Market when he negligently side-swiped Maria's car. At the time of the accident, Bobby was driving to a convenience store to get a cup of coffee. This diversion took him two blocks away from his authorized route. In this case, who is liable to Maria?

_____

_____

CASE PROBLEMS

Answer the following case problems, explaining your answers.

1. Carol hired Humboldt Remodeling Co. to remodel her house for $30,000. Humboldt was required to remodel the house in accordance with certain plans, and Humboldt was to complete the work by May 1. Humboldt had the exclusive right to control the manner and method for performing the work, including the right to select the workers and tools to be used. One day, a Humboldt employee was picking up a bathtub to be installed in Carol's house. While loading the tub into a truck, the employee negligently dropped the tub injuring Roger, a passer-by.

   (a) What is the relationship between Carol and Humboldt?
   (b) Is Carol vicariously liable for Roger's injury?
   (c) Is Humboldt vicariously liable for Roger's injury?

_____

_____

_____

_____

2. Sandra always spent her lunch hour out of the office, frequently driving to a nearby park to eat and nap. One day while Sandra was driving to the park to eat her lunch, she negligently ran a stop sign and struck Nora, a pedestrian.

   (a) Under these facts, is Sandra's employer liable for Nora's injuries?
   (b) Would Sandra's employer be liable for Nora's injuries if, at the time of the accident, Sandra was dropping off a package for her employer on her way to the park

_____

_____

_____

_____

CHAPTER REVIEW

SELECTING A BUSINESS FORM: There is not one correct form of business organization for every business. Each form of business organization has advantages and disadvantages. Franchises can operate in any form allowed by state law unless the franchise contract states otherwise.

HISTORIC OVERVIEW OF PARTNERSHIPS: Today, partnerships are governed by the UPA or RUPA.

PARTNERSHIPS DEFINED:
- *Uniform Partnership Act*: The UPA defines a partnership as: 1) an association; 2) of two or more persons; 3) to carry on a business; 4) as co-owners; 5) for profit. The Revised Uniform Partnership Act has been adopted in place of the UPA in some states.
- *Limited Partnership*: Must have 2 or more persons and at least one limited partner. A limited partner is not personally liable for partnership obligations, but cannot control the partnership's business.

PARTNERSHIP PROPERTY: UPA defines partnership property as: 1) property contributed as capital contributions; 2) property acquired on account; 3) property acquired with partnership funds; 4) interest in real property acquired in the partnership's name; and 5) any conveyance to the partnership in its name.

THE PARTNERSHIP AGREEMENT: A partnership is created by agreement, express or implied.
- *Imposed Rules*: Unless an agreement states otherwise, the law imposes the following rules: 1) partners are each entitled to one vote when deciding whether the partnership should take a particular action; 2) partners are entitled to share equally in partnership profits (regardless of the amount of their contributions); 3) partners share losses in the same proportion as they share profits; and 4) books must be kept at the central office. Regardless of what the partnership agreement states, partners: 1) are agents of the partnership; 2) partners have unlimited personal liability to partnership creditors for partnership obligations; and 3) each partner is a fiduciary of the partnership.
- *Express Terms*: At a minimum, the partnership agreement, if there is one, should state the purpose and duration of the partnership, how profits and losses are shared, and withdrawal procedures.

LIMITED LIABILITY PARTNERSHIPS: Many states recognize the limited liability partnership (LLP). With certain exceptions, a partner in an LLP is not personally liable for the malpractice, negligence, or other tort committed by a co-partner or partnership agent. But, partners remain personally liable for their own negligence and for contractual obligations of the partnership. The RUPA requires an election to become a LLP and requires the same percentage vote that is required to amend the partnership agreement.

TAXATION OF PARTNERSHIPS: A partnership is not taxed on its profits and losses. Instead, partners are personally taxed on their share of the partnership's profits and losses.

HISTORIC OVERVIEW OF CORPORATIONS: Corporations flourish because of their ability to raise capital.

CORPORATE NATURE: Corporations are artificial entities authorized by statute.
- *Advantages of the Corporate Form*: Advantages include: 1) shareholders are protected from personal liability; 2) centralized management; 3) continuity of existence; and 4) free transferability of shares.

FORMATION OF A CORPORATION: There are several types of corporations; choose wisely.

- ***Types of Corporations***: The types include: 1) public-issue private corporations; 2) close corporations; 3) professional corporations; and 4) municipal (also called public or quasi-public) corporations.
- ***Promoters***: Promoters help form the corporation by procuring subscribers for stock.
- ***Articles of Incorporation***: Articles create the corporation and must be filed with the secretary of state.
- ***Corporate Charter/Certificate of Incorporation***: This document begins a corporation's existence.
- ***Organizational Meeting***: In some states, a corporation exists only after its organization meeting.
- ***Bylaws***: Bylaws regulate the internal affairs of a corporation.

DE JURE VERSUS DE FACTO CORPORATIONS: A *de jure* corporation is valid by law. If a corporation fails to comply with incorporation laws, it may qualify as a *de facto* corporation if: 1) a law under which the corporation could have been incorporated exists; 2) there was a good faith effort to comply with the statute; and 3) there was some use or exercise of corporate powers.

CORPORATE POWERS: The articles set forth the corporation's express powers. Corporations also have the implied power to do anything reasonably necessary to conduct business.

ULTRA VIRES ACTS: An *ultra vires* transaction is a transaction that exceeds the purposes or powers of a corporation.

TAXATION OF CORPORATIONS: Profits and losses of a C corporation are taxed to the corporation. Profits and losses of an S corporation (Subchapter S corporation) are taxed to the shareholders. In order to elect Subchapter S status, a business must, among other things, have only one class of stock, have 75 or fewer shareholders, have no nonresident alien shareholders, have no partnerships, corporations, LLCs, LLPs, or other nonqualifying shareholders, and have the consent of all the shareholders.

DISREGARDING THE CORPORATE ENTITY: In certain cases, such as fraud, courts may ignore the corporate form and impose personal liability on shareholders. In the case of parent-subsidiary companies, there are two general theories for holding the parent liable for the acts of the subsidiary: alter ego (piercing the corporate veil) and agency principles (the amount of control the parent exercises over the subsidiary).

LIMITED LIABILITY COMPANIES: LLCs are now permitted in all states. Typical requirements include: 1) two or more members; 2) stated term of duration less than 30 years; 3) all members must have limited liability; 4) shares are not freely transferable; 5) central management is elected by the members; and 6) an indication in its name that it is an LLC. LLCs are taxed as partnerships. If properly formed, LLCs may elect to be taxed as partnerships. LLC laws vary from state to state.

OTHER TYPES OF BUSINESS ORGANIZATIONS: Partnership by estoppel; joint venture; mining partnership.

STUDY HINTS FOR NRW CASE STUDIES

The following study hints may be helpful when resolving the NRW case studies.

NRW 32.1	➤ Review the material regarding limited partnerships. ➤ For another option, suggest that the parties consider using an LLC form of business.
NRW 32.2	➤ Review the material "Formation of a Corporation." ➤ Consider using a shareholder agreement to address various issues among the shareholders.
NRW 32.3	➤ Suggest that the parties explore utilizing either an S corporation or an LLC.

REVIEW OF KEY TERMS AND CONCEPTS

MATCHING EXERCISE

Select the term or concept that best matches a definition or statement set forth below. Each term or concept is the best match for only one definition or statement.

Terms and Concepts

a. Corporation
b. Estoppel
c. General partner
d. Joint venture

e. Limited liability partnership
f. Limited partner
g. Mining partnership
h. Partnership

i. Proprietorship
j. Ratification
k. Rebuttable presumption
l. Registered agent

Definitions and Statements

_____ 1. Partner in a limited partnership whose liability is limited to his or her contribution.

_____ 2. Accepting or approving an unauthorized act.

_____ 3. Partnership wherein partners are generally not liable for torts of other partners or partnership agents.

_____ 4. Partner in a limited partnership who controls the business of the partnership.

_____ 5. Legal assumption that is followed unless stronger, contrary proof is presented.

_____ 6. Partnership formed to conduct mining operations; interests can be transferred by will.

_____ 7. Person designated by a corporation to receive service of process.

_____ 8. Association of two or more persons to carry on a single business enterprise for profit.

_____ 9. Artificial legal entity whose owners are stockholders or shareholders.

_____ 10. Business owned by one person.

_____ 11. Legal bar that prevents a person from claiming or denying certain facts.

_____ 12. Association of two or more persons to carry on an on-going business for profit.

COMPLETION EXERCISE

Fill in the blanks with the words that most accurately complete each statement.

1. A corporation that is formed in strict compliance with state law is a _____ _____ corporation.

2. A _____ ____ _____ is generally issued by a state to acknowledge the legal existence of the corporation.

3. _____ are the persons who conceive the idea for a business, organize the undertaking of this business, and take steps to form the corporation to engage in this business.

4. An _____ _____ transaction is a transaction that exceeds the purposes or powers of a corporation.

5. Identify four advantages of doing business as a corporation.

a. _____.

b. _____.

c. _____.

d. _____.

TRUE-FALSE EXERCISE

Write **T** if the statement is true, write **F** if the statement is false.

_____ 1. Property may be partnership property even if title is held in the name of an individual partner.

_____ 2. If a partnership does not have a definite duration or purpose, then any partner is legally entitled to withdraw at any time.

_____ 3. The fact that parties share net profits earned by a business is strong evidence that the parties' business relationship is a partnership.

_____ 4. LLCs are generally taxed as partnerships.

_____ 5. Limited partners may exercise limited participation in the management of the partnership without becoming personally liable for partnership obligations.

_____ 6. Shares of LLCs are freely transferable.

_____ 7. For federal income tax purposes, the profits and losses of a Subchapter S corporation are taxed to the shareholders.

_____ 8. A promoter is a fiduciary of the corporation and its shareholders.

_____ 9. A partnership cannot be created unless parties specifically call their relationship a partnership.

_____ 10. In general, partnership agreements are required to be in writing to be enforceable.

APPLICATION OF CONCEPTS

MULTIPLE CHOICE QUESTIONS

_____ 1. In which situation does a partnership probably exist between Felix and Art?
   a. Felix owed $10,000 to Art. Felix agreed to pay 10 percent of his company's profits to Art as partial payment of the $10,000 debt.
   b. Felix owns an insurance company. As compensation, Felix pays Art 5 percent of the gross premiums paid on insurance policies that are sold by Art.
   c. Felix and Art co-own a grocery store. Felix and Art jointly control the business and they share the net profits and losses derived from the store.
   d. Felix and Art own a rental house. Felix and Art share the rentals earned from the property.

_____ 2. Jim and Todd are the shareholders of J&T, Inc. In which situation would a court be justified in piercing the corporate veil and imposing liability on Jim and Todd for obligations of J&T?
   a. Jim and Todd form J&T in order to obtain substantial tax benefits.
   b. Jim and Todd form J&T in order to avoid personal liability for future corporate debts.
   c. Jim and Todd form J&T in order to engage in illegal stock sales that would otherwise cause them significant personal liability.
   d. All of the above.

_____ 3. Sylvia and Janet are forming a business to engage in the high-risk business of Internet advertising. The risk is that the business will undertake large contractual debts that it may not be able to repay if enough advertising is not sold. Sylvia and Janet are willing to risk their respective investments, but neither wants to lose all of their personal assets should the business fail. In this case, what type of business entity would fulfill the parties' desire to protect their personal assets?

    a. Partnership
    b. Limited liability partnership.
    c. Corporation.
    d. b and c.

_____ 4. Polly wishes to incorporate Polly's Pets Inc. When will the corporate existence for this proposed corporation begin?

    a. The corporation will exist as soon as Polly files corporate bylaws with the secretary of state.
    b. The corporation will exist as soon as Polly commences doing business as a corporation.
    c. The corporation will exist as soon as Polly officially declares that it exists.
    d. In most states, the corporation will not exist until Polly files an appropriate application (with articles of incorporation) and the state issues a certificate of incorporation.

SHORT ANSWER QUESTIONS

Answer the following questions, briefly explaining the reason for your answer.

1. Larry and Harry have started a new business that will prove to be very profitable. Several of Larry's and Harry's friends have offered to invest. However, these friends have indicated that they may eventually want to sell their interests in the business. Suggest several strategies that Larry and Harry might use to restrict the resale of the investors' business interests.

2. Sean was a promoter, organizing STR, Inc. Prior to incorporation of STR, Sean entered into a contract on behalf of the corporation to buy $25,000 worth of equipment. After STR was incorporated, Sean and STR entered into a contract whereby they agreed that STR will buy the equipment from Sean. Later, the corporation failed to pay for the equipment. Is Sean liable for the $25,000?

3. Bruce is a limited partner in B-MER Ltd. Bruce is also a licensed attorney. On occasion, Bruce gives legal advice to B-MER. Will Bruce's conduct be considered participation in management, thereby causing Bruce to forfeit his status as a limited partner?

4. Lee and Mindy are partners in L&M Partnership. Prior to formation of the partnership, Lee owned a truck. Lee now regularly allows Mindy and other L&M employees to use the truck to conduct partnership business. Also, the truck is usually parked at the offices of L&M, the keys are kept in the office, and the partnership typically pays for routine maintenance on the truck. The parties never stated whether the truck was to become partnership property, and title remains in Lee's name. Is the truck partnership property?

CASE PROBLEMS

Answer the following case problems, explaining your answers.

1. Ted and Alice intend to form a corporation and they are trying to determine what powers the corporation may have. Ted and Alice have asked you the following questions: (a) If the articles of incorporation are silent regarding corporate powers, most states will grant a corporation the right to exercise what powers? (b) Can the corporation be formed to have perpetual succession? (c) Can the corporation be empowered to buy, sell, and mortgage real and personal property?

2. Juan and Carol are engineers who have an idea for an invention that will increase the processing speed of older computers that cannot otherwise be upgraded. Some friends have offered Juan and Carol start-up capital. However, Juan and Carol want to maintain control over management of the business. Also, Juan and Carol anticipate losses during the business's first few years, and they want to assure that they can use their share of these losses to offset other personal income on their individual tax returns. Discuss the respective advantages and disadvantages of Juan and Carol doing business as a partnership, limited partnership, or corporation.

CHAPTER 33   Operation of a Business Organization

OPERATION OF A PARTNERSHIP: The partnership agreement controls the partners' rights; however, if there is no agreement, each partner is considered a manager, an agent, and a principal of the other partners. In a corporation, the officers and the directors are responsible for the corporation's operations and policies.

RIGHTS OF THE PARTNERS: Rights of partners vary depending on the partnership agreement and whether the UPA or RUPA governs. Unless otherwise agreed, the following rules usually apply:

- *Management*: Each partner has an equal voice in managing the partnership, but partners can define "equal." Majority votes control ordinary partnership decisions, and unanimous decisions are required to authorize extraordinary transactions. The RUPA allows a partnership to file a statement of partnership authority with the appropriate state office. This statement may limit a partner's authority and limit a partner's capacity to transfer partnership property. A partnership is not required to file such a statement and its existence is not dependent upon the filing of any statement. The statement does not affect a third party who does not know about the statement.
- *Reimbursement*: Partners are entitled to a return of their capital contribution when the partnership ends if there are sufficient funds to do so.
- *Profits and Losses*: Partners are entitled to an equal share of the profits unless they agree otherwise. Partners are not entitled to salaries unless the partnership agreement provides for them.
- *Books and Records*: Each partner is entitled to review the partnership's books and records.
- *Partnership Property*: Partners are co-owners with each other of any property owned by the partnership; this is called a tenancy in partnership. This means that a partner cannot possess partnership property for personal use without the unanimous agreement of the other partners.
- *Right to an Account*: A partner may demand an accounting of the partnership's business transactions.

DUTIES OF THE PARTNERS:
- *Agency's Duties*: Each partner is an agent of the partnership, meaning he or she can bind the partnership to ordinary business contracts. The RUPA makes each partner jointly and severally liable (personally liable) for partnership debts and is required to account for any profits. Generally, the RUPA requires a creditor to exhaust the partnerships assets before going against individual partners.
- *Fiduciary Duties*: As a fiduciary of a partnership, partners cannot gain secret profits from partnership business, compete with the partnership, or engage in actions that involve a conflict of interest.

RIGHTS OF THIRD PERSONS WHO DEAL WITH PARTNERSHIPS:
- *Contracts*: A third party is entitled to rely on a partner's apparent authority to enter into a contract, and if there is no such authority, the partner may be personally liable to the third party.
- *Borrowing in the Partnership Name*: Apparent authority is determined by influenced by whether the partnership is a trading or nontrading partnership, especially when borrowing money.
- *Torts and Crimes*: Trading partners have broader powers. If a third party is injured by a partner's tort, the partnership (and therefore the other partners) may be liable for the partner's tort under the doctrine of *respondeat superior*.

OPERATION OF A LIMITED PARTNERSHIP: While a limited partnership is an actual partnership, it typically operates differently than a general partnership. The general partners manage the partnership business and have personal liability for partnership debts. Limited partners, on the other hand, are more like investors than regular partners. They have a right to share in the partnership profits, but they do not manage the partnership business and they do not have personal liability for partnership obligations.

OPERATION OF A CORPORATION: Officers are generally responsible for the day-to-day business of a corporation and the board of directors is responsible for establishing the overall policies of the corporation.

OPERATION OF A LIMITED LIABILITY COMPANY: Nine states have adopted the Uniform Limited Liability Company Act and all other states have enacted their own LLC statutes. Many practical aspects of other forms of business are being used in connection with the operation of LLCs, such as managing partners. It is not uncommon for LLC agreements to impose additional duties and restrictions on members.

RIGHTS OF THE SHAREHOLDERS OF A CORPORATION:
- *Types of Stock Owned*: Common stock allows a shareholder to receive dividends, vote on corporate issues, and receive property upon liquidation; preferred stock confers priority as to dividends and liquidation rights - preferred stock does not vote on most matters that common stock may vote on.
- *Shareholders' Meetings*: There must be notice before a shareholder meeting, and a quorum of shareholders must be present. Shareholders vote on board members and amending bylaws. Shareholders can vote by proxy, giving their vote to someone else. Straight voting is one vote per share, and generally a majority vote is required to bind the corporation.
- *Dividends*: The board of directors has the power to decide whether to declare dividends. If dividends are declared, shareholders are entitled to them. Preferred stockholders are paid first. Preferred shareholders are protected from improper dividend declarations that may impair their rights.
- *Preemptive Stock Rights*: If a corporation issues new stock, it must make the new shares available to current stockholders first if the shareholders have preemptive stock rights
- *Inspection of Corporate Books and Records*: Shareholders are entitled to inspect a corporation's books and records, but only on a showing that it is for a "proper purpose."
- *Transfer of Shares*: Shareholders are free to transfer their shares, unless they are subject to limitations placed on the stock, such as giving current shareholders a right of first refusal to buy them.

LIABILITIES OF SHAREHOLDERS: In some instances, a shareholder can be liable for corporate obligations. These exceptional situations include the following:
- *Watered Stock*: If stock is issued as fully paid but it has in fact not been fully paid, then a shareholder owns watered stock and is liable for the difference.
- *Stock Subscriptions*: These are agreements by investors to purchase shares and the corporation can enforce them by requiring the subscriber to pay the subscription price.
- *Illegal Dividends*: If a dividend that impairs the original capital structure of the corporation is paid, it is illegal and the shareholder receiving it may be liable to repay it to the corporation.
- *Dissolution*: Controlling shareholders have a fiduciary duty to minority shareholders and may be liable for a dissolution arrangement that prejudices the minority shareholders.

RIGHTS AND DUTIES OF THE MANAGERS OF A CORPORATION: Directors are fiduciaries of a corporation and they may be held personally liable to the corporation if they breach these duties, causing harm to the corporation or shareholders. Officers are agents of the corporation and can bind the corporation to the extent that they have actual or apparent authority. Directors and officers owe fiduciary duties of obedience, diligence, and loyalty to the corporation.

STUDY HINTS FOR NRW CASE STUDIES

The following study hints may be helpful when resolving the NRW case studies.

NRW 33.1	➤ Analyze the rights and duties of partners before advising the parties. ➤ Review the agency material dealing with the authority of agents.
NRW 33.2	➤ To answer Helen, you should consider the rights and duties of officers and the business judgment rule.
NRW 33.3	➤ Contrast the rules regarding the operation of partnerships and corporations. ➤ Review the requirements for qualifying as a Subchapter S corporation.

REVIEW OF KEY TERMS AND CONCEPTS

MATCHING EXERCISE

Select the term or concept that best matches a definition or statement set forth below. Each term or concept is the best match for only one definition or statement.

Terms and Concepts

a. Alienation
b. Capital contribution
c. Common stock
d. Constructive trust

e. Goodwill
f. Liquidation preference
g. Outsider directors
h. Preferred stock

i. Proxy
j. Par value
k. Tenancy in partnership
l. Trustees

Definitions and Statements

_____ 1. Money or assets invested by people in a business as payment for their ownership interests.

_____ 2. Form of ownership in partnership property.

_____ 3. Good reputation of a business.

_____ 4. Voting stock of a corporation.

_____ 5. Face value of stock.

_____ 6. Directors who are not shareholders or officers.

_____ 7. Written authorization to vote someone's stock.

__l__ 8. Persons who are empowered to manage the business and affairs of others.

_____ 9. Priority granted to creditors or others when a business is terminated and assets are distributed.

_____ 10. Transfer of ownership to another.

_____ 11. Legal remedy imposed by law to preserve property that is wrongfully held by a party.

_____ 12. Stock that enjoys a preference to dividends and/or distributions upon dissolution of a corporation.

COMPLETION EXERCISE

Fill in the blanks with the words that most accurately complete each statement.

1. If a partner commits a tort while acting within the course and scope of partnership business, then all of the partners have _____ and _____ liability for the tort.

2. A _____ _____ is an agreement by an investor to purchase shares in a corporation.

3. When a dividend is declared, _____ _____ stock has the right to be paid dividends for prior years that dividends were not paid and a dividend for the current year, before a dividend is paid to common stockholders.

4. List three prerequisites regarding shareholder meetings generally found in corporate bylaws:

a._____.

b._____.

c._____.

5. Two lawful sources for declaring and paying dividends generally include:

a._____.

b._____.

TRUE-FALSE EXERCISE

Write **T** if the statement is true, write **F** if the statement is false.

____ 1. An extraordinary partnership transaction requires unanimous consent of all partners.

____ 2. A partner who pays a partnership obligation from personal funds is entitled to reimbursement from the partnership.

____ 3. Unless otherwise agreed, the UPA requires payment of reasonable compensation in the form of salary for a managing partner who devotes extra time to running the business.

____ 4. In general, a partner in a retail clothing store would not have apparent authority to sell the building in which the store is located.

____ 5. A shareholder is absolutely liable to repay an illegal dividend if the corporation was insolvent at the time the dividend was paid.

____ 6. Only the corporation, not shareholders, can transfer corporate property.

____ 7. A corporation may indemnify its directors for liabilities resulting from good faith actions that the directors took on behalf of the corporation.

____ 8. A quorum of shareholders ordinarily consists of shareholders who own at least a majority of the outstanding shares entitled to vote.

____ 9. Cumulative voting may enable minority shareholders to exercise greater influence in elections of directors than they could exercise under straight voting.

____ 10. Voting trusts and pooling arrangements are less frequently used in close corporations than in large publicly held corporations.

APPLICATION OF CONCEPTS

MULTIPLE CHOICE QUESTIONS

____ 1. Adams is a partner in a retail-clothing store. Without express authorization, Adams borrowed $5,000 on behalf of the partnership in order to purchase inventory for the store. Under these facts:
   a. The partnership is a trading partnership.
   b. The partnership is a nontrading partnership.
   c. Adams and the other partners are liable for this loan.
   d. a and c.

_____ 2. Cooper, Tex, and Chien are the partners in CTC Partnership. Cooper contributed $50,000 to the partnership, and Tex and Chien each contributed $25,000. The partnership agreement is silent regarding management rights and allocation of profits. Under these facts:
   a. Cooper has the exclusive right to manage the partnership.
   b. Cooper, Tex, and Chien are each entitled to an equal vote regarding partnership matters.
   c. Cooper is entitled to 100 percent of the partnership profits.
   d. Cooper is entitled to 50 percent of the partnership profits.

_____ 3. Pam was a partner in a partnership that sold office supplies. In which situation did Pam breach a duty that she owed to the partnership?
   a. Pam purchased supplies for the partnership. Pam had express authority to act and she used reasonable judgment, but the partnership lost money due to the purchase.
   b. Pam set up a new firm that purchased supplies from the partnership at discounted prices. Pam did not disclose her interest in the new firm, and she secretly profited from the firm's transactions with the partnership.
   c. After termination of the partnership, Pam opened an office supply company that competed with a new business that was created by her former partners.
   d. All of the above.

_____ 4. Don and Rene are the partners in a partnership that owns a retail paint store. Under these facts, Don does NOT have authority to make which contract on behalf of the partnership?
   a. Contract to purchase a case of paint.
   b. Contract to hire a salesclerk who is needed to run the store.
   c. Contract to sell the entire store.
   d. Contract to purchase fire insurance for the store.

SHORT ANSWER QUESTIONS

Answer the following questions, briefly explaining the reason for your answer.

1. A partnership agreement specifies that Adams, Baker, and Campbell are to receive $12,000 a year salary with profits to be allocated 20 percent to Adams, 45 percent to Baker, and 35 percent to Campbell. Is this agreement enforceable?

_____

_____

2. ABC Inc. issued common and preferred stock. Earl owns 60,000 shares of ABC common stock and Antonio owns the remaining 40,000 shares of common stock. Trisha owns 200,000 shares of ABC preferred stock, which has typical rights and preferences. At the annual meeting, the shareholders are to vote on a proposed pay raise for corporate officers. Who can vote on this matter? As a practical matter, who has the power to determine whether the pay-raise proposal is approved?

_____

_____

_____

3. Ed was a majority shareholder in MED Inc. In a shareholder agreement, Ed and the other shareholders agreed not to sell their stock to anyone else without first offering it to each other. This restriction was not stated on the stock certificates. In violation of this agreement, Ed sold and transferred his stock to Hank who bought it in good faith and without knowledge of the restriction. Is the stock transfer to Hank enforceable?

_____

_____

4. Roger is a minority shareholder in Neco Inc. Roger has demanded to inspect the corporation's financial records in order to compute the value of his stock. Is Roger entitled to inspect the corporation's records?

_____

_____

CASE PROBLEMS

Answer the following case problems, explaining your answers.

1. Glen and Tim were the partners in a partnership that owned a store. On behalf of the partnership, Glen bought inventory from Seller on credit for $5,000. Glen had authority to make this contract. The partnership failed to pay the contract price, and the partnership was later dissolved. The partnership agreement states that Glen and Tim shall each bear 50 percent of partnership losses. (a) Is the partnership liable on the contract made by Glen? (b) Does the partnership's dissolution terminate Glen's and Tim's liability for partnership obligations? (c) Does Tim have personal liability for the contract price owed to Seller? (d) If Tim pays the entire contract price, can Tim seek reimbursement from Glen?

_____

_____

_____

_____

2. Pat is a shareholder in EagleCo. Pat bought 10,000 shares of $10 par-value common stock from EagleCo for $10 per share. Pat paid the corporation $50,000 for the stock. EagleCo later paid Pat a $5,000 dividend out of capital at a time when it was insolvent. Discuss whether Pat has any personal liability to the corporation and/or corporate creditors in this case.

_____

_____

_____

_____

CHAPTER 34   Business Terminations and Other Extraordinary Events

CHAPTER REVIEW

TERMINATION OF A FRANCHISE: When a franchise is terminated, the franchisee must follow the rules below relating to termination of whatever form of business organization the franchise uses. The franchisee also must comply with the terms of the franchise contract.

TERMINATION OF A SOLE PROPRIETORSHIP: The owner pays the debts and keeps any remaining assets.

TERMINATION OF A PARTNERSHIP: A partnership terminates (ceases to exist) following dissolution and winding up of its business. Dissolution, winding up, and termination are three related, but separate, steps.

DISSOLUTION OF A PARTNERSHIP: A dissolution occurs any time a partner is admitted into an existing partnership or a partner leaves a partnership. A dissolution is a change in the partners' relationship among themselves and with the partnership. Following a dissolution, the partners must either: 1) wind up and terminate the partnership and its business or 2) elect to continue the partnership business. Actions or events that cause a partnership dissolution under the UPA include:

■ *Without Violation of the Agreement*: The partnership agreement may specify a time for dissolution or all the partners may agree to dissolve the partnership. Also, In a partnership at will, each partner has the legal power and right to withdraw from the partnership at any time, causing a dissolution.
■ *In Violation of the Agreement*: In any partnership, even a partnership for a definite term, each partner has the legal power to withdraw at any time. A partner's wrongful withdrawal causes a dissolution, although the remaining partners may unanimously agree to continue the business and not wind up.
■ *By Operation of Law*: A partnership is dissolved by law if: 1) it becomes unlawful to operate the business; 2) a partner dies; or 3) a partner or the partnership becomes bankrupt.
■ *By Court Order*: A court may order the dissolution of the partnership if: 1) a partner becomes insane; 2) a partner becomes incapacitated; 3) a partner commits serious misconduct; 4) a partner repeatedly breaches the agreement; 5) the business can no longer be operated profitably; or 6) any other circumstance the court believes will justify a dissolution.

TERMINATION UNDER RUPA: Under the RUPA, a partner is "dissociated" from (i.e., no longer an active member of) a partnership in several situations including: 1) the partner gives notice of withdrawal; 2) occurrence of an event specified in the agreement; 3) the partner is expelled pursuant to the partnership agreement; 4) the partner is expelled by court order; 5) the partner becomes a debtor in bankruptcy; and 6) if the partner is an individual, the partner dies. Section 701 of the RUPA provides that in most situations there is a buy out of the dissociating partner's interest rather than a winding up of the business.

A change in limited partners does not dissolve a limited partnership. Under most laws and agreements, new general or limited partners can be added only with the written consent of all limited partners.

CONTINUATION OF THE PARTNERSHIP BUSINESS: The remaining partners have a right to continue the partnership if: 1) the withdrawing partner withdrew in violation of the agreement; 2) the withdrawing partner consents to the continuation; or 3) the agreement permits a continuation after a dissolution.

■ *Withdrawing Partners*: Withdrawing partners must be indemnified and bought out. If the withdrawal was in violation of the agreement, the partnership may deduct damages.
■ *Entering Partners*: A new partner is liable for existing debts up to the partner's capital contribution.

WINDING UP THE PARTNERSHIP: In winding up, assets are liquidated and proceeds distributed.

- *General Partnerships*: Proceeds are distributed in the following order: 1) creditors; 2) partners, acting as creditors; 3) return of capital contribution to partners; and 4) distribution of profits.
- *Limited Partnerships*: Proceeds are distributed as follows: 1) nonpartner and partner creditors; 2) amounts owed to former partners prior to their withdrawal; 3) return of capital; and 4) profits.

CHANGES IN CORPORATE STRUCTURE: Changes in corporate structure include: dissolution, merger and consolidation, sale of substantially all of the corporate assets, and stock acquisition.
- *Liquidation of the corporation*: When a corporation liquidates, the corporation sells its assets, pays off in full its creditors, and any remaining proceeds are distributed to the shareholders in accordance with their rights and preferences. During liquidation, a corporation can sue and be sued.

DISSOLUTION OF THE CORPORATION: Dissolution terminates a corporation's existence as a legal entity.
- *Voluntary Dissolution*: Voluntary dissolution requires: 1) board authorization; 2) shareholder approval (usually two-thirds of the outstanding shares); and 3) notice to creditors.
- *Involuntary Dissolution*: The state, the shareholders, or creditors may seek an involuntary dissolution. Common reasons for involuntary dissolution include serious wrongdoing by the corporation's directors and/or officers that adversely affect the interests of shareholders and creditors.

CORPORATE MERGER AND CONSOLIDATION: A *merger* is a combination of two corporations by which only one of the corporations survives. The surviving corporation owns the assets of the original corporations and it is also liable for their combined debts. A *consolidation* is a combination of two corporations whereby a new corporation is formed, replacing the original corporations that cease to exist.
- *Rationales for Merger*: The most important rationales for merger include the attainment of economies of scale, acquisition of corporate "knowledge," diversification, and competition.
- *Procedure*: The board of directors must first adopt a merger plan, which must be approved by the shareholders, usually by two-third of the outstanding shares.
- *Effect of Merger*: When completed, the acquired company no longer exists whereas the acquiring company survives and has all of the assets and liabilities of the merged companies.
- *Appraisal Rights*: A shareholder who objects to a merger may be entitled to appraisal rights. To qualify, a shareholder must send a written notice of objection and make a written demand for the fair value of the shares. The corporation must then make a written offer to purchase the shares.

SALE OF SUBSTANTIALLY ALL THE ASSETS: Instead of a merger, a corporation may simply buy the assets of another corporation. However, such a sale may still require shareholder approval.

STOCK ACQUISITION: Instead of buying assets, a corporation may buy the shares of another corporation. The board of directors need not approve this transaction because a corporation may buy stock directly from individual shareholders. However, some courts consider stock acquisitions to be de facto mergers.

STUDY HINTS FOR NRW CASE STUDIES

The following study hints may be helpful when resolving the NRW case studies.

NRW 34.1	➤ You should consider whether the family is experienced in the fast-food industry. ➤ You should consider the effects and problems of a merger for the purpose of diversification.
NRW 34.2	➤ Consider options that would make the corporation less attractive to an unwanted suitor. ➤ Bear in mind, however, the fiduciary duties that directors owe to the corporation.
NRW 34.3	➤ Contrast the advantages of a merger versus a purchase of assets. ➤ Remember that if the firms merge, then NRW will be liable for the firms' combined debts.

REVIEW OF KEY TERMS AND CONCEPTS

MATCHING EXERCISE

Select the term or concept that best matches a definition or statement set forth below. Each term or concept is the best match for only one definition or statement.

Terms and Concepts

a. Appraisal right
b. At will
c. Charging order
d. Conglomerate merger

e. De facto merger
f. Economies of scale
g. Fair market value
h. Liquidate

i. Market value
j. Marshal
k. Receiver
l. Winding up

Definitions and Statements

_____ 1. Current price for which stock will sell on a national or regional stock exchange.

_____ 2. Current price that an asset will bring in a sale between two informed parties.

_____ 3. Unbiased person appointed by a court to take over, preserve, and manage the assets of another.

_____ 4. Sale of assets that, as a practical matter, effects a merger of two companies.

_____ 5. Reductions in per-unit costs resulting from a merger of companies.

_____ 6. Process for terminating a partnership that includes the marshaling and liquidation of assets.

_____ 7. Court order permitting a creditor to receive an owner's profits from the operation of a business; especially common in partnership situations.

_____ 8. Right that dissenting shareholders have to require a corporation to buy back their shares.

_____ 9. Duration of a relationship that is not expressly stated to be for a fixed period of time.

_____ 10. Mergers between noncompeting firms in different industries.

_____ 11. Settle with creditors and debtors and divide remaining assets among partners.

_____ 12. Arrangement of assets or claims in order to properly apply the assets to pay the claims.

COMPLETION EXERCISE

Fill in the blanks with the words that most accurately complete each statement.

1. In a _____, two or more existing companies combine to form a new corporate entity.

2. A _____-_____ _____ is a merger between a subsidiary and a parent company that owns 90 percent or more of the subsidiary's stock.

3. The dissolution of a corporation may be _____ or _____.

4. Identify three instances under the UPA when a partnership may be dissolved by operation of law:

   a. _____.

   b. _____.

   c. _____.

5. Identify three rationales for a merger.

a. _____.

b. _____.

c. _____.

TRUE-FALSE EXERCISE

Write **T** if the statement is true, write **F** if the statement is false. (Use the UPA to answer partnership questions).

_F_ 1. Misconduct by a partner automatically dissolves a partnership.

____ 2. Generally, shareholder approval is not required for a short-form merger.

____ 3. Bankruptcy of a partnership causes a dissolution, but bankruptcy of only one partner does not.

____ 4. If a partnership does not have a specified duration or purpose, then any partner is legally entitled to withdraw at any time.

____ 5. A partnership dissolution automatically terminates the partnership.

____ 6. A partner who withdraws in violation of an agreement has no right to demand that the partnership wind up if the remaining partners take certain steps required by the UPA.

____ 7. The sale of a sole proprietor's business terminates the sole proprietorship.

____ 8. Any time a partner leaves a partnership, the partnership dissolves.

____ 9. Two-thirds of the outstanding shares must generally approve a voluntary corporate dissolution.

____ 10. Shareholders may request a corporate dissolution if minority shareholders are oppressed.

APPLICATION OF CONCEPTS

MULTIPLE CHOICE QUESTIONS

____ 1. Jack, Audrey, and Zoe are partners in JAZ Partnership. The agreement states that the partnership will continue until January 1, 2005. Under the RUPA, which event causes a dissociation of Jack?
   a. On May 1, 2003, Jack dies.
   b. On May 1, 2003, Jack is declared bankrupt.
   c. On May 1, 2003, Jack withdraws in violation of the partnership agreement.
   d. All of the above.

____ 2. Sue and Rhonda are partners in L&M Partnership. The partnership agreement states that the partnership will continue until June 1, 2006. In which situation can Sue request a court to enter a decree dissolving the partnership prior to June 1, 2006?
   a. Rhonda made an ordinary contract on behalf of the partnership with authority to do so, but Sue now objects to the contract.
   b. Rhonda has embezzled partnership funds and she refuses to perform her partnership duties.
   c. The partnership is not as profitable as in the past.
   d. Sue cannot obtain a decree of dissolution; a court cannot dissolve a partnership.

_____ 3. The shareholders and board of directors of Acme, Inc. and Belco, Inc. have voted in favor of combining their respective corporations. Pursuant to this combination, Acme will terminate and Belco will continue to exist. This combination is a:
   a. Consolidation.
   b. Merger.
   c. Stock acquisition.
   d. Conglomerate.

_____ 4. Kendall was admitted into the Three Sons Accounting Firm, a general partnership. Kendall contributed $25,000 to the partnership. Which of the following statements is correct?
   a. Kendall has unlimited personal liability for all existing and future partnership debts.
   b. Kendall's liability to existing partnership creditors is limited to $25,000, the amount of his capital contribution, and he has unlimited liability for future partnership debts.
   c. Kendall's liability to existing and future partnership creditors is limited to $25,000, the amount of his capital contribution
   d. Kendall has no liability to existing or future partnership creditors.

SHORT ANSWER QUESTIONS

Answer the following questions, briefly explaining the reason for your answer.

1. Bob is a minority shareholder in Burgundy, Inc. Bob has been notified that Burgundy plans to merge with Chantilly, Inc., and he is opposed to this merger. What are Bob's rights in this case?

_____

_____

2. Earl, Rusk, and Aaron enter into a partnership. Ten months later, Aaron is declared insane by a court and enters a mental institution. Aaron's wife filed a petition to dissolve the partnership by court order. Earl and Roscoe object to the dissolution. Will the court dissolve the partnership?

_____

_____

3. Lightning Corp. has 20,000 shares of outstanding common stock. Pursuant to an agreement between Lightning Corp. and Blinder Corp., Lightning Corp. issued and sold 30,000 additional shares of its common stock to Blinder Corp. What type of extraordinary transaction did the parties accomplish? What is the legal effect of this transaction?

_____

_____

4. Chuck, Diane, and Bob are partners in a limited partnership, and they equally share partnership profits. The partners have agreed to dissolve the partnership. The partnership has $70,000 cash. The partnership owes $17,000 to Jim, an outside creditor, and it owes Diane $12,000 for an advance she made to the partnership. Chuck contributed $10,000 to the partnership, Diane contributed $15,000, and Bob contributed $5,000. Under the UPA, to whom and in what order will the partnership assets be distributed?

_____

_____

CASE PROBLEMS

Answer the following case problems, explaining your answers.

1. Clay, Bonnie, and Tess were partners in a partnership, and they equally shared partnership profits. The partnership has dissolved due to Clay's death. The partnership has $90,000 cash. The partnership owes $20,000 to Roscoe, an outside creditor, and it owes Tess $10,000 for an advance she made to the partnership. Clay contributed $15,000 to the partnership, Bonnie contributed $10,000, and Tess contributed $5,000. The partnership agreement is silent regarding the partners' rights upon the death of a partner. Under the UPA: (a) Can Bonnie and Tess indefinitely continue the partnership business or must they wind up the partnership's business? (b) In general, who is entitled to wind up the affairs of a partnership? (c) If the partnership is wound up, to whom and in what order will the partnership's assets be distributed?

_____

_____

_____

_____

2. MicroChem is a small chemical company that has just discovered a process that neutralizes some types of toxic waste. Unfortunately, MicroChem does not have the financial resources to fully develop the process, nor does it have a stable credit rating. MacroChem, a large chemical company, is looking for a new product to market. MacroChem has submitted an offer to acquire MicroChem. (a) What would be some reasons for MicroChem and MacroChem to merge? (b) What procedures must each company follow to complete the merger? (c) If the companies merge, what will be the legal effect on the two companies and their shareholders?

_____

_____

_____

_____

THE SIGNIFICANCE OF FRANCHISING AS A BUSINESS METHOD: Franchising has helped the United States become the world's largest market. Currently, over 2,000 U.S. companies use this business method.

DEFINITION: A franchise is an oral or written agreement, expressed or implied, in which the franchisor grants to the franchisee a license to use a trade name, service mark, trademark, logotype, or other symbol in which there is a community of interest in the business and in which the franchisee must pay a licensing fee.

There are two types of franchises. Distributorships allow the franchisee to sell a product in a designated area. Chain-style businesses, or business format franchises, allow the franchisee to operate under the franchisor's trade name, subject to the franchisor's operating methods.

BENEFITS OF FRANCHISING: There are many benefits of franchising for both the franchisee and the franchisor.

The benefits to the franchisee include:

1) the opportunity to start a business with limited capital;

2) goodwill;

3) the franchisor's business expertise; and

4) assured supply of materials.

The benefits to the franchisor include:

1) the franchisee's investment capital;

2) goodwill;

3) an assured distribution network; and

4) a larger asset base.

FRANCHISING COMPARED WITH OTHER BUSINESS RELATIONSHIPS: Generally, government agencies view the franchisor-franchisee relationship as an employment relationship. It is settled law that the following are not franchises: cooperatives, concessionaires, joint ventures, general partnerships, and sales agencies. Also, franchises are not securities.

SETTING UP THE FRANCHISING RELATIONSHIP: The franchisor typically plays a large role in the set-up stage. The franchisor will choose the franchise location, train the franchisee, advertise, and set stringent guidelines. The franchisee must follow the franchisor's operating procedures, obtain liability insurance, and meet workers' compensation requirements.

Legal problems frequently occur in the area of quality control and franchise termination. Typically, franchise agreements require franchisees to buy from only certain suppliers, provide factors that could cause a termination, and contain covenants not to compete. Because franchisees have limited bargaining power, case law and statutes have provided relief to franchisees from one-sided agreements.

DECISIONAL LAW AND STATUTES AFFECTING FRANCHISING: Several statutes and case law have attempted to protect franchisees against perceived abuses by franchisors. However, franchisors may still terminate the franchisee for misconduct, failure to meet sales quotas, failure to observe quality standards, and failure to maintain investment levels. Franchises are also subject to antitrust law and the UCC.

CHALLENGES TO FRANCHISING REGULATORY STATUTES: Because the laws that protect franchisees also limit the actions of franchisors, franchisors have challenged the laws on constitutional grounds. Franchisors have challenged state laws, claiming these laws: 1) impair contracts; 2) deny due process; 3) conflict with federal law; and 4) burden interstate commerce.

THE FRANCHISING ENVIRONMENT: The franchising field accounts for a large percentage of retail sales in the U.S. and elsewhere.

- *Industry Statistics*: Increasingly, franchisees are assuming ownership of the franchise units. In the past, franchisors tended to own the units. There is an oftentimes overlooked risk that franchises may and do fail.

- *International Markets*: Canada, Japan, and Australia are the three largest markets for U.S. franchisors, and U.S. franchisors continue to spread internationally. Increasingly, foreign franchisors are setting up in the United States.

STUDY HINTS FOR NRW CASE STUDIES

The following study hints may be helpful when resolving the NRW case studies.

NRW 35.1	➢ The parties should carefully consider the material dealing with the benefits for franchisors and franchisees.
NRW 35.2	➢ You should review the obligations of the franchisor in the section on "Setting Up the Franchising Relationship." ➢ You should also consider the material dealing with decisional law and statutes that may affect the franchise relationship.
NRW 35.3	➢ Carefully analyze the problems that NRW may experience with its franchisees, such as their providing inadequate customer service and failing to maintain sufficient capital in order to properly operate their respective franchises. Then carefully craft standards regarding these matters that franchisees must satisfy or lose their franchises.

REVIEW OF KEY TERMS AND CONCEPTS

MATCHING EXERCISE

Select the term or concept that best matches a definition or statement set forth below. Each term or concept is the best match for only one definition or statement.

Terms and Concepts

a. Chain-style
b. Concessionaires
c. Consignee
d. Cooperative

e. Distributorship
f. Franchisee
g. Franchisor
h. Logotypes

i. Royalty fee
j. Service marks
k. Stay
l. trademark

Definitions and Statements

_____ 1. Identifying symbols.

_____ 2. Distinctive marks or symbols used to identify a particular company as the source of its products.

_____ 3. Distinctive symbols designating services offered by a particular business or individual.

_____ 4. The person or firm that grants the franchise.

_____ 5. The person receiving the franchise.

_____ 6. This franchise method allows the franchisee to sell a product in a designated area.

_____ 7. Operators of refreshment centers.

_____ 8. Franchise method that allows the franchisee to operate under the franchisor's trade name, subject to the franchisor's operating methods.

_____ 9. Person to whom goods are shipped for sale and who may return unsold goods to the consignor.

_____ 10. Groups of individuals who unite in a common enterprise and share the profits proportionately.

_____ 11. Suspend.

_____ 12. Payment made in exchange for the granting of a right or a license.

COMPLETION EXERCISE

Fill in the blanks with the words that most accurately complete each statement.

1. The two most significant legal problems in a franchise agreement are _____ and _____ _____.

2. Identify four benefits of franchising to franchisors.

   a. _____.

   b. _____.

   c. _____.

   d. _____.

3. Identify four benefits of franchising to franchisees.

a. _____ .

b. _____ .

c. _____ .

d. _____ .

4. _____ _____ involves choosing the court or place of jurisdiction that will be most favorable to the litigant.

5. States require the franchisor to give the franchisee _____ before terminating the franchise.

TRUE-FALSE EXERCISE

Write T if the statement is true, write F if the statement is false.

_____ 1. Government agencies tend to view the relationship between a franchisor and franchisee as that of employer and employee.

_____ 2. A franchise contract cannot permit a franchisor to terminate a franchise if a franchisee fails to meet reasonable sales quotas.

_____ 3. Franchising was not a popular method of business until after World War II.

_____ 4. A franchising agreement may meet the definition of a security under the securities laws.

_____ 5. A partnership cannot operate a franchise.

_____ 6. Franchise agreements are subject to antitrust laws.

_____ 7. Generally, it is permissible for a franchisor to suggest, but not to require, certain resale prices for the franchisee.

_____ 8. Franchisors are not subject to the UCC.

_____ 9. A distributor of a product is *clearly* a franchisee.

_____ 10. Franchisees have wide discretion in how they run their franchise.

APPLICATION OF CONCEPTS

MULTIPLE CHOICE QUESTIONS

_____ 1. Beef 'N Beer, a franchisor, wants to assure quality in its products and uniformity in its sales prices. Beef 'N Beer would like all of its franchisors to buy from a single supplier that meets its standards for quality control. It would also like to set retail prices. Under these facts, Beef 'N Beer may:

a. Not require that franchisees buy from the supplier and set their sales prices according to its guidelines, because such action would violate antitrust law.

b. Require that franchisees buy from the supplier and set their sales prices according to its guidelines, without violating any laws.

c. Require that franchisees buy from the supplier and set their sales prices according to its guidelines, provided the requirements are reasonable.

d. Not *suggest* a supplier and sales prices for its franchisees.

_____ 2. Franchisors may be subject to which of the following laws?
   a. Constitutional law.
   b. The Federal Franchise Act.
   c. The UCC.
   d. Both a and c.

_____ 3. Which of the following elements are included in the typical definition of "franchise" found in most state statutes?
   a. An agreement, a license to use a trade name, trademark, or similar characteristic in which there is a community of interest in the business of offering, selling, or distributing goods, and a license fee.
   b. A written agreement, a license to use a trade name, trademark, or similar characteristic in which there is a community of interest in the business of offering, selling, or distributing goods, and a license fee.
   c. An agreement, a license to use a trade name, trademark, or similar characteristic in which there is a community of interest in the business of offering, selling, or distributing goods, a license fee, and an intensive training program that franchisees must complete.
   d. An agreement, a license to use a trade name, trademark, or similar characteristic in which there is a community of interest in the business of offering, selling, or distributing goods, a license fee, and an employer-employee relationship between franchisor and franchisee.

_____ 4. Which of the following is typically found in franchise agreements?
   a. A covenant not to compete.
   b. A notice period, usually ninety days, before the franchisor may terminate the agreement.
   c. A covenant not to sue the franchisor.
   d. Both a and b.

SHORT ANSWER QUESTIONS

Answer the following questions, briefly explaining the reason for your answer.

1. Big Burger entered into a franchise agreement with Rhonda and chose a location for Rhonda's store. The location of the store turned out to be terrible because there was insufficient foot traffic near the store. When Rhonda began to lose money she complained to Big Burger, which did nothing. May Rhonda sue Big Burger for breach of contract?

_____

_____

2. Jethro has always wanted to start his own business. However, he does not have much money to invest, and he is not a very sophisticated businessperson. Would a franchise be a good way for Jethro to start a business?

_____

_____

3. Durman, Inc. is a small company, known only in a local area. It does not have a recognizable logo or trademark, and has unstable relationships with its suppliers. Would Durman make a good franchisor? Hint: Would you want to be one of Durman's franchisees?

_____

_____

4. The Taco Hut, a franchisor, wants to assure quality in its products and uniformity in its sales prices. The Taco Hut would like all of its franchisees to buy from a single supplier that meets its standards for quality control. Can The Taco Hut force all of its franchisees to buy from a single supplier without violating any laws?

_____

_____

CASE PROBLEMS

Answer the following case problems, explaining your answers.

1. Davis, president of D&D, Inc., entered into a distributor's agreement naming Graham as the sales representative of D&D for a specified territory. Graham paid Davis $10,000. Davis gave Graham detailed instructions on how to market D&D's products. Davis also gave Graham a list of customers, promotional materials, cost sheets, and purchase orders. The advertising materials all contained D&D's distinctive logo. Did Graham and Davis enter into a franchise agreement? Explain.

_____

_____

_____

_____

2. Sally has a franchise agreement with Nevus Systems, a computer manufacturer. Nevus selected a location for Sally's store in the middle of a busy business district, and hers was the only computer store in the area. Nevus also provided Sally with several months of training, as well as detailed guidelines on how to sell Nevus computers. For several months, Sally could not meet Nevus's sales quotas, which were reasonable.

   (a) Can Nevus terminate Sally as a franchisee? Explain.
   (b) Before terminating Sally, what must Nevus do to comply with most state's laws on terminating franchisees?

_____

_____

_____

_____

CHAPTER 36 — Securities Regulation

CHAPTER REVIEW

FEDERAL LAWS: Securities regulation is the "federal corporate law."

■ *The Securities Act of 1933*: The Securities Act of 1933 (Securities Act) regulates the interstate sale of securities by an issuing company.

1) **Security defined**: A security is any note, stock, treasury stock, bond, debenture, participation in any profit-sharing agreement, or investment contract. Generally, when an instrument bears one of these titles, it is considered a security. One of the most common questions in this area is the definition of an investment contract. Courts will consider an investment contract a security when it involves an investment in a common enterprise in which the investor has no managerial functions, but expects to profit solely from the efforts of others. As a practical matter, a security is a: a) passive investment whereby b) one contributes capital and c) expects to make a profit from the efforts of others.

2) **Procedures**: Unless an exemption applies, a corporation issuing a security must: a) file a registration statement with the SEC, and b) provide a prospectus to all prospective investors.

3) **Exempt investments**: These classes of securities are exempt from registration: a) securities issued by federal and state governments; b) short-term commercial paper (9 months or less); c) issues by nonprofit organizations; d) issues by savings and loans; e) issues by common carriers; f) insurance policies and certain annuities subject to other government regulation; and g) intrastate offerings.

4) **Exempt transactions**: The following transactions are exempt from the registration and prospectus requirements: private offerings; transactions by persons other than issuers; certain broker and dealer transactions; and small public issues ($5 million cap to accredited investors).

5) **Antifraud provisions**: The Securities Act contains antifraud provisions. Section 12 forbids oral or written misstatements of material fact, or omissions of material facts that are necessary to keep statements from being misleading. Section 17 forbids the use of the mails or interstate commerce to further any form of fraud. Section 11 imposes civil liability for any registration statement containing misstatements of material fact, or omissions of material facts necessary to keep statements from being misleading. Due diligence is the only defense to Section 11 liability. The defense is generally available to any person who, after reasonable investigation, had reasonable grounds to believe, and did believe, that the registration statement was accurate and did not omit material facts.

6) **Liabilities and remedies**: Section 11 imposes civil liability for any registration statement that contains untrue statements of a material fact or omissions of material facts. A purchaser can receive damages up to the price paid for the securities. Under Section 12, a person who is fraudulently induced to buy securities through the mail or in interstate commerce can sue the person who actually sold the security and can rescind the purchase and recover the price paid.

■ *The Securities Exchange Act of 1934*: The Security Exchange Act of 1934 (Exchange Act) regulates the secondary securities market. These regulations include the following requirements:

1) **Registration and Reporting**. The 34 Act requires any issuer who trades securities on a national exchange to register with the SEC. Also, any company engaged in interstate commerce with assets over $5 million and at least 500 shareholders must comply with the registration provisions of §12.

2) **Information and proxies**: Publicly traded firms must make public detailed information. Also, their proxy solicitations are regulated. In a proxy solicitation, management must give shareholders a proxy statement and a proxy form. The proxy statement must disclose all pertinent information regarding the matters under consideration, including the participants and reasons for the proxy solicitation. The Exchange Act imposes absolute liability for misleading proxy statements or for the omission of a material fact necessary to make the statement true and not misleading.

3) **Tender Offers**: The Williams Act, included in §13 and §14, regulates tender offers and takeover bids, whether hostile or friendly, in which one publicly held corporation attempts to acquire control of another publicly held company.

4) **Insider trading**: The Exchange Act regulates insider trading. In transactions involving material nonpublic information, an insider must publicly disclose the information or abstain from trading in the security. The parties subject to this regulation are: insiders (directors, officers, etc.); temporary insiders (outside attorneys, accountants, etc.); tippees; and misappropriators.

Section 10(b) and 10(b)-5 impose liability for any manipulative or deceptive device used in connection with any purchase or sale of any security by any person. The elements for proving a 10(b) and 10(b)-5 violation are: a) an untrue statement of material fact or a failure to state a material fact that is needed to make a statement not misleading; b) reliance upon the statement; c) and an injury resulting from such reliance.

5) **Short-swing profits**: Insiders and persons owning more than 10 percent of a corporation's stock must file statements with the SEC disclosing the extent of their ownership and any changes that have taken place. Section 16(b) requires that insiders and persons with more than 10 percent of a company's stock pay to the corporation any short-swing profits, which is defined as any profit made by buying and selling securities in the company within a six-month period.

6) **Liabilities and Remedies**: Under 10(b) and 10(b)-5, a private action may be brought against any person who conducted a transaction in a fraudulent manner.

■ *Securities and Exchange Commission Actions*: The Exchange Act empowers the SEC to conduct investigations into security transactions. The SEC generally imposes administrative remedies (censures or fines); appropriate cases are referred to the Justice Department for criminal prosecution.

STATE REGULATION: In addition to federal laws, state securities laws called "blue sky laws," may regulate securities sales. Although state regulations vary from state to state, typical provisions include antifraud provisions, registration requirements for brokers and dealers, and/or registration prerequisites for the sale and purchase of securities. State exemptions are generally similar to the federal exemptions.

THE FOREIGN CORRUPT PRACTICES ACT: The purpose of the FCPA is to stop the bribery of foreign officials. The FCPA contains both antibribery provisions and accounting standards. Criminal penalties may be imposed if an officer, director, employee, agent or stockholder acting on behalf of the business offers or pays money to foreign officials to influence foreign officials to assist the firm in obtaining or retaining business. Payments or gifts to facilitate routine governmental action are permitted.

STUDY HINTS FOR NRW CASE STUDIES

The following study hints may be helpful when resolving the NRW case studies.

NRW 36.1	➤ Review the material dealing with exemptions, particularly exempt transactions. ➤ Review the procedures material relating to registration statements and prospectuses. Do not overlook the need also to comply with state blue sky laws.
NRW 36.2	➤ NRW principals should carefully consider the rules regarding insider trading set forth in SEC rule 10(b) and 10(b)-5.
NRW 36.3	➤ The material dealing with the Foreign Corrupt Practices Act is quite relevant.

REVIEW OF KEY TERMS AND CONCEPTS

MATCHING EXERCISE

Select the term or concept that best matches a definition or statement set forth below. Each term or concept is the best match for only one definition or statement.

Terms and Concepts

a. Censure
b. Disgorge
c. Due diligence
d. In *pari delicto*
e. Insider trading

f. Issuer
g. Post-effective period
h. Prefiling period
i. Prospectus
j. Securities exchanges

k. Security
l. Tender offer
m. Uncollateralized
n. Underwriters
o. Waiting period

Definitions and Statements

_____ 1. Document provided to potential investors disclosing material information relating to an offering of securities.

_____ 2. Buying or selling securities on the basis of nonpublic, material information.

_____ 3. Firms that ensure the sale of corporate securities by agreeing to sell the securities to the public.

_____ 4. Unsecured; performance is not secured by property.

_____ 5. Organized markets in which investors buy and sell securities at central locations.

_____ 6. Period when issuers may begin negotiations with underwriters.

_____ 7. Company that makes its own securities available for sale.

_____ 8. Note, stock, treasury stock, bond, debenture, evidence of indebtedness, or investment contract.

_____ 9. Period when an issuer may accept oral orders for its stock and place tombstone ads.

_____ 10. Equally at fault; equally wrong.

_____ 11. Period after a registration statement becomes effective.

_____ 12. Give up ill-gotten gains.

_____ 13. Takeover bid.

_____ 14. Defense that a party made reasonable investigation, and had reasonable grounds to believe that a registration statement was accurate and did not omit material facts.

_____ 15. Formal reprimand.

COMPLETION EXERCISE

Fill in the blanks with the words that most accurately complete each statement.

1. The _____ _____ _____ _____ is the primary federal law that regulates the initial offering of securities in interstate commerce.

2. The _____ _____ _____ _____ _____ is the primary federal law that regulates the securities industry, publicly-held companies, and the resale of securities in interstate commerce.

3. A preliminary prospectus is known as a _____ _____.

4. The only advertisements that are allowed during the waiting period are called _____ _____.

5. A _____ - _____ _____ is a profit that a controlling party of a company realizes from buying and selling the company's securities within any six-month period.

TRUE-FALSE EXERCISE

Write **T** if the statement is true, write **F** if the statement is false.

_____ 1. The FCPA prohibits the payment of any thing of value to any foreign official for any purpose.

_____ 2. Under Rule 10(b)-5, the only parties barred from insider trading are traditional insiders.

_____ 3. The Exchange Act imposes reporting requirements on all companies that issue securities.

_____ 4. In a tender offer, federal securities law requires the acquiring company to inform the target company's shareholders of the purpose for the takeover.

_____ 5. A sale of stock made solely to residents of the state in which the issuing company is incorporated and primarily does business may be exempt from the Securities Act registration requirements.

_____ 6. Under the Insider Trading Sanctions Act of 1984, a court may impose a penalty of up to three times the unlawful gain that a party made from insider trading.

_____ 7. The Securities Act may impose both civil and criminal penalties for its violation.

_____ 8. A proxy is an assignment by the shareholder of the right to vote his or her shares.

_____ 9. The fact that a company's securities are exempt from registration does not necessarily mean that they are exempt from the antifraud rules of federal securities laws.

_____ 10. In general, federal securities laws apply only if a transaction involves a security.

APPLICATION OF CONCEPTS

MULTIPLE CHOICE QUESTIONS

_____ 1. Mayfield Corp. is selling a variety of instruments and property in order to raise capital. Which instrument or property would not be a security within the meaning of the federal securities laws?
   a. A share of common stock in Mayfield Corp.
   b. A ten-year corporate bond issued by Mayfield Corp. that bears 15 percent annual interest.
   c. A 100-acre parcel of land.
   d. Investment interests in a shrimp farm operated by Mayfield Corp., with investors sharing in the profits made by the farming enterprise.

_____ 2. R&V Limited Partnership is planning to issue limited partner interests and to publicly offer these securities for sale in interstate commerce. What must R&V do to comply with the 1933 Act?
   a. R&V has no duties under the 1933 Act. R&V is only required to comply with blue sky laws in the states in which the securities are offered.
   b. R&V is only required to file a registration statement with the SEC.
   c. R&V is only required to provide a prospectus to prospective investors.
   d. R&V must file a registration statement and provide a prospectus to prospective investors.

_____ 3. Pepco Inc. has just received a conclusive, secret medical report that establishes that Pepco's only product causes cancer. As a result, the company may be liable to thousands of persons who may have contracted cancer by using this product. Under these facts, which party is engaging in insider trading in violation of Rule 10(b)-5?

    a. Tom, a Pepco director, sells his Pepco stock without disclosing the report.

    b. Bonnie, an outside financial analyst who was retained by Pepco to assess the financial impact of this report, sells all of her Pepco stock without disclosing the report.

    c. Faye, a receptionist, saw the report and sold her Pepco stock without disclosing the report.

    d. All of the above.

_____ 4. Frye Co. is subject to all provisions of the 1934 Act. Dick is a director of Frye Co. and he owns 5 percent of the company's common stock. Bonnie owns 15 percent of the company's common stock. Sally owns 4 percent of the company's common stock. Under Rule 16 of the 1934 Act:

    a. If Dick buys and sells stock in Frye Co. within a six-month period thereby earning a profit, Dick must pay the profit to the company even if he did not trade on inside information.

    b. Dick, Bonnie, and Sally must each file disclosure statements with the SEC.

    c. Dick, Bonnie, and Sally are each exempt from filing disclosure statements with the SEC.

    d. a and b.

SHORT ANSWER QUESTIONS

Answer the following questions, briefly explaining the reason for your answer.

1. Nassau Inc. plans to issue and sell $4 million worth of preferred stock. The stock will be sold to 45 banks, investment companies, and other accredited investors. There will be no general solicitation or public offering of the stock. Is this offering exempt from the registration requirements of the 1933 Act?

_____

_____

2. Kathy needed a visa to travel to the country of Ruritania on business. When she spoke with a low-level embassy employee, he told her it would take two months to get the visa. Kathy offered the employee $50 if he could speed up the process. Is Kathy's bribe prohibited under the FCPA?

_____

_____

3. Margaret is the president of Duffy Toys, a publicly held corporation, and she purchased 2,000 shares of its stock in September. Duffy came out with the Goober Doll, which proved extremely popular. After a huge Christmas season, Duffy's stock increased by $5 per share. Margaret sold her stock in January and realized a $10,000 profit. What duty, if any, does Margaret owe Duffy regarding the $10,000 profit?

_____

_____

4. Randolph is a janitor at GeoTech. While cleaning the CEO's office, Randolph notices a confidential corporate report on the CEO's desk marked "For Release to the Public Tomorrow." Randolph likes to dabble in the stock market, and he thinks the information will make him some money. If Randolph trades GeoTech securities based on this information before it is released to the public, is he guilty of insider trading?

_____

_____

CASE PROBLEMS

Answer the following case problems, explaining your answers.

1. Midas Inc. owns several gold mines. Unknown to the public, Midas engineers have just discovered a massive new gold deposit. After this discovery, the Midas board of directors made several public announcements denying that the company had made any new discoveries. Without knowledge of the secret discovery, Tom sold his Midas stock for $10 a share. One week later, Midas stock went to $20 per share when the Midas board announced the new discovery. (a) What federal securities act governs this case? (b) What must Tom prove in order to establish a securities violation by the Midas board of directors? (c) In all likelihood, did the board violate federal securities law?

_____

_____

_____

_____

2. CryoTech is in the waiting period after filing a registration statement with the SEC. CryoTech's underwriter, Penton & Thorton, sent the following notice to its best customers: "CryoTech produces an environmentally safe coolant for air conditioners that will not harm the ozone layer. CryoTech will offer 1 million shares of newly issued common stock to the public. Interested parties may contact Penton & Thorton, underwriter." (a) Does this notice violate the Securities Act? (b) When may CryoTech begin to sell the offered shares?

_____

_____

_____

_____

```
CHAPTER REVIEW
```

THE BASIS OF REGULATORY REFORM: Government regulation emerged because of business's irresponsible behavior during the 1800s.

THE SHERMAN ANTITRUST ACT: Passed in 1890, the purpose of the Sherman Act is to preserve competition. The Sherman Act prohibits 1) combinations that unreasonably restrain trade and 2) attempts to monopolize.

Whether conduct violates the Sherman Act is evaluated under one of three rules. Under the per se rule, certain conduct is so harmful to competition that it is an automatic antitrust violation. It is not necessary to prove that a firm intended to restrain competition or that competition was in fact restrained. Under the rule of reason, a court examines the 1) purpose and 2) effect of conduct to determine whether it is an unreasonable restraint of trade and, therefore, a violation of the Sherman Act. In other words, it is not the conduct itself, but its effect in a given industry that makes conduct legal or illegal. Recently, the courts have used a third approach for evaluating conduct under §1. This "quick look" analysis lets a defendant rebut the presumption that conduct is automatically anticompetitive, in which case the conduct is evaluated under the rule of reason. The Foreign Trade Antitrust Improvement Act, an amendment to the Sherman Act, helps U.S. companies that export domestic goods by exempting them from the Sherman Act so long as their export transactions do not injure affect the U.S economy.

- *Section 1*: Section 1 prohibits "contracts, combinations, or conspiracies" that unreasonably restrain interstate commerce. Section 1 also prohibits the following actions: 1) horizontal price fixing; 2) vertical price fixing; 3) horizontal market divisions; and 4) group boycotts. Courts infer violations from the actions of companies. Historically, the foregoing actions were *per se* violations

- *Section 2*: Under Section 2, monopolizing is illegal, that is, conduct whereby one or more persons attempt to gain a monopoly or maintain a monopoly if they already have one. Illegal monopolizing generally requires proof of two things: 1) possessing monopoly power in the relevant market or attempting to possess this power, and 2) intentionally acquiring or maintaining this power.

  Generally, if a firm controls 70 percent or more of a relevant market, the firm has monopoly power. The relevant market may include the market for the goods produced by the firm and substitute goods. The courts look at the elasticity of demand between the challenged product and the substitute. If the product controls 70 percent of this market, the company has monopoly power. Defenses to a charge of illegal monopolization include: 1) the company did not consciously try to retain this power; 2) the power was legally acquired; or 3) the company was thrust into this position.

- *Remedies*: The Sherman Act has both civil and criminal remedies. An individual may be fined up to $350,000 and be sentenced to three years in jail. A corporation can be fined up to $10 million. Injured parties may recover treble (triple) damages and attorneys' fees.

THE CLAYTON ACT: The Clayton Act is designed to *prevent* antitrust violations, not just remedy them.

- *Section 2: Price Discrimination*: Section 2, as amended by the Robinson-Patman Act, prohibits buyers from knowingly accepting a discriminatory price. Price discrimination may be either a 1) primary-line injury, which occurs at the seller's level when the seller prices its product lower in one market in order to hurt the seller's competitors in that market or 2) secondary-line injury, which occurs at the buyer's level when the seller sells the same product to some buyers at a lower price than for other buyers, thereby giving an advantage over to some buyers over their competitors who did not receive the same price.

Section 2 also prohibits dummy brokerage fees and promotional kickbacks. Section 2 is violated if a competitor is hurt. Defenses to a §2 violation are: 1) the price offered meets, but does not beat, a competitor's price; 2) a different price is being charge for goods because they are obsolete; 3) or the price difference is due to a bona fide cost savings, such as a quantity discount.

- ■ *Section 3: Exclusive Dealings and Tying Arrangements*: In an exclusive dealing contract, one party requires another party to do business only with them. In a tying arrangement, the seller refuses to sell one product unless the buyer also purchases another product. One defense to a charge of an illegal tying arrangement is that the tying arrangement is necessary to preserve the safety or performance of the product. Harm is not required to find a § 3 violation; the mere likelihood of harm is sufficient.
- ■ *Section 7: Antimerger Provisions*: Section 7, as amended by the Cellar-Kefauver Act, prohibits the acquisition of stock or assets of another firm that may tend to have a negative effect on any line of commerce. A violation typically involves showing that a "concentration trend" has been established. As a defense, a company might show that without the merger, one of the firms would have failed.
- ■ *Section 8: Interlocking Directorates*: In some situations, Section 8 prohibits a person from sitting on the board of directors of two or more competing companies.

THE FEDERAL TRADE COMMISSION ACT: The FTC Act created the Federal Trade Commission (FTC) to enforce antitrust laws. Section 5 of the Act prohibits unfair methods of competition and deceptive trade practices. Conduct need not actually deceive to be unfair and deceptive; it need only have a "fair possibility" of deception. A statement is considered deceptive if it is ambiguous, with one honest meaning and one deceptive meaning. Currently, the FTC primarily focuses on bait-and-switch and deceptive ads.

UNFAIR TRADE PRACTICES: Common law unfair trade practices include palming off goods and violating trade secrets. Palming offs goods means advertising, designing, or selling goods so they appear to be goods made by someone else. Trade secrets are special processes or formulas that are guarded by a holder of the trade secret. Employees who reveal trade secrets may be liable in tort. A person or firm who receives a trade secret is guilty of misappropriating the secret, and a court can prevent the person or company from using the information obtained. Illegal use of a trade secret may also subject the user to liability for damages. Other protections are found in patent, copyright, and trademark law. A utility patent grants an inventor the exclusive right to use the invention for 20 years. A copyright protects writers, artists, and composers. A copyright grants a creator the exclusive right to profit from a work for the creator's life plus 50 years. A trademark is a mark used to identify a product.

EXEMPTIONS: Labor unions are exempt from the Sherman and Clayton Acts. Farm cooperatives are also exempt from these laws as long as they are engaged in the sale of farm produce.

STUDY HINTS FOR NRW CASE STUDIES

The following study hints may be helpful when resolving the NRW case studies.

NRW 37.1	➢ Review the concept of relevant markets to determine whether NRW has monopoly power. ➢ Also, consider the three defenses to a § 2 action.
NRW 37.2	➢ You should consider § 3 of the Clayton Act and explore the concept of tying arrangements.
NRW 37.3	➢ You should consider the material relating to the Federal Trade Commission Act. ➢ Also, consider state unfair trade practices laws.

MATCHING EXERCISE

Select the term or concept that best matches a definition or statement set forth below. Each term or concept is the best match for only one definition or statement.

Terms and Concepts

a. Antimerger provision
b. Bait-and-switch
c. Clayton Act
d. Copyright

e. Exclusive dealing
f. Group boycott
g. Horizontal market division
h. Horizontal price fixing

i. Patent
j. Trademark
k. Sherman Act
l. Vertical price fixing

Definitions and Statements

_____ 1. Agreement on price among competitors.

_____ 2. Agreement on price between a supplier and customer.

_____ 3. Agreement among competitors dividing territories in which they will each sell.

_____ 4. Agreement among competitors not to sell to a particular buyer or not to buy from a particular seller.

_____ 5. Exclusive right to use, make, or sell an invention for 20 years.

_____ 6. Prohibits the acquisition of stock or assets in another firm that may tend to have a negative affect on any line of commerce.

_____ 7. Exclusive right to use, reproduce, or sell a creative work.

_____ 8. Advertising a product at an enticing price to get a customer into the store and then talking the customer into buying a more expensive item.

_____ 9. Arrangement that requires one party to deal only with one other party.

_____ 10. Federal antitrust law that prohibits combinations that restrain trade and prohibits attempts to monopolize an industry.

_____ 11. Mark or symbol that is used to identify the source of a product.

_____ 12. Federal antitrust law that is designed to prevent antitrust violations, not just remedy them.

COMPLETION EXERCISE

Fill in the blanks with the words that most accurately complete each statement.

1. _____ _____, which is prohibited by the Robinson-Patman Act, may result when a manufacturer charges different customers different prices for the same goods.

2. The Sherman authorizes injured private parties to recover _____ _____.

3. _____ _____ is indicated when a company captures 70 percent or more of a relevant market.

4. _____ _____ involves advertising, designing, or selling goods as if they were the goods of another.

5. Identify the two rules that are used to evaluate whether conduct violates the Sherman Act:

a. _____.

b. _____.

TRUE-FALSE EXERCISE

Write **T** if the statement is true, write **F** if the statement is false.

____ 1. It is a per se violation of the Sherman Act for a company to have a monopoly in any market.

____ 2. Section 1 of the Sherman Act requires an action by two or more people in order to find a violation, whereas one person, acting alone, may violate Section 2.

____ 3. Mergers between two large companies are not permitted.

____ 4. The FTC Act protects patents, trademarks, and copyrights.

____ 5. Trade secrets are protected for up to 50 years, after which time they become available for use by all persons and companies.

____ 6. Exclusive dealing arrangements are a per se violation of federal antitrust laws.

____ 7. Price fixing is a per se violation of the Sherman Act.

____ 8. The relevant market for purposes of antitrust law includes the goods in question and any substitute goods.

____ 9. Actual harm is required to show a violation of the Clayton Act.

____ 10. Traditionally, a tying arrangement is a per se violation of the Clayton Act.

APPLICATION OF CONCEPTS

MULTIPLE CHOICE QUESTIONS

____ 1. Which of the following actions violates the federal antitrust law?
   a. Oilco, Inc. is a large business that owns 50 percent of the oil refinery business in the United States.
   b. Manufacturer gives Ollie the exclusive right to sell Manufacturer's products in a certain area. This agreement does not substantially lessen competition in this case.
   c. Digger, Inc. manufactures earth-moving equipment. Digger and its distributors agree that the distributors will not resell Digger's equipment below certain minimum prices.
   d. San Francisco imposes certain residential rent limitations.

____ 2. Heffer, Inc. and other meat producers agree to fix prices that they charge for their competitive meat products that are sold in interstate commerce. Under these facts:
   a. Heffer may be liable for three times the actual damages caused by its price fixing.
   b. Heffer may be subject to fines up to $10 million.
   c. Individuals who are guilty of this price fixing may be fined, but they cannot be imprisoned.
   d. No one can be sued, fined, or imprisoned for their conduct because price fixing is generally legal under the Sherman Act.

_____ 3. Vectra and Spectra market their products in Georgia and Arkansas. Both agree that Vectra should market only in Georgia, and Spectra should market only in Arkansas. Under these facts Vectra and Spectra:
   a. Have violated the prohibition against horizontal market divisions, a per se violation of §1 of the Sherman Act.
   b. Have violated the prohibition against horizontal market divisions, but their agreement may be legal if it did not actually hurt competition.
   c. Have violated the prohibition against horizontal market divisions only if it can be shown that they had an actual agreement.
   d. Have violated the prohibition against horizontal market divisions, but their agreement may be legal if it did not actually hurt an individual or company.

_____ 4. Which of the following does not create a potential antitrust merger problem?
   a. ManCo, the sole manufacturer of gizmos, wants to merge with I&C, the sole user of gizmos.
   b. ManCo, the sole manufacturer of gizmos, wants to merge with I&C., one of four users of gizmos.
   c. ManCo, one of four manufacturers of gizmos, wants to merge with I&C, one of four users of gizmos.
   d. ManCo, one of 20 manufacturers of gizmos, wants to merge with I&C, one of 30 manufacturers of widgets, a product unrelated to gizmos.

SHORT ANSWER QUESTIONS

Answer the following questions, briefly explaining the reason for your answer.

1. LubeTech manufactures 1Lube, a universal lubricant that works on all engines and moving parts, in any temperature, and in all conditions. 1Lube is also cheaper than comparable lubricants. Because of 1Lube, LubeTech controls 80 percent of the lubricant market. Has LubeTech violated §2 of the Sherman Act?

_____

_____

2. CyberFun manufactures the Dude! portable video game. CyberFun has invented a portable virtual-reality video game that is comparable in price to current portable video games, and is sure to make regular portable video games obsolete. In an effort to clear its inventory of Dude!'s, CyberFun has offered to sell the games at a substantially reduced price to one of its distributors. Is CyberFun guilty of price discrimination?

_____

_____

3. Joe, Moe, and Doe manufacture widgets and are located in three different states. Recently, a fourth competitor, Shmoe, has dominated the widget market. Joe, Moe, and Doe agree that each would be better off if they sold only in their own state. Is this agreement a violation of §1 of the Sherman Act?

_____

_____

4. Big Muscle, which manufactures vitamins for body builders, is in severe financial difficulty. VitaHealth, a vitamin manufacturer that sells its products in all fifty states, offered to acquire Big Muscle when no other company offered to merge with Big Muscle. The merger may reduce competition somewhat in the muscle-building vitamin industry. Does this merger violate §7 of the Clayton Act?

_____

_____

CASE PROBLEMS

Answer the following case problems, explaining your answers.

1. LeatherTech has designed a process to make synthetic leather. It is virtually impossible to tell the difference between LeatherTech's product and real leather. LeatherTech's product is soft and pliable, it stretches, and it even smells like leather. LeatherTech uses this synthetic leather to manufacture coats, and it currently has a 90 percent share of the market for synthetic leather coats. However, it only has a 25 percent share of the winter coat market. (a) What is LeatherTech's relevant market? (b) Has LeatherTech violated the Sherman Act?

_____

_____

_____

_____

2. CompuTron makes the Micro Data Storage Unit (MiDSU) The MiDSU compresses data from a computer and transfers it to a 1.5 inch "minidisk." Currently, no other company manufactures a mini-disk that is compatible with the MiDSU. In fact, using any other mini-disk will destroy the MiDSU because only the CompuTron mini-disk has a secret patented processor that can protect the MiDSU from harm. Consequently, CompuTron will not sell its MiDSU to retailers unless they also buy its minidisk. (a) What type of arrangement is this? (b) Has CompuTron potentially violated any antitrust laws? (c) What defense is available to CompuTron?

_____

_____

_____

_____

Federal consumer protection laws have been adopted to provide uniformity and to correct abuses in commercial practices.

CONSUMER CREDIT: The large volume of credit transactions in the United States has led to a giant industry involving the sale of credit reports and has led to government regulation.

THE CONSUMER CREDIT PROTECTION ACT: The Truth in Lending Act (TILA), which is Title I of the Consumer Credit Protection Act of 1968, is a landmark consumer protection law. The TILA is primarily a disclosure statute, requiring creditors to inform consumers of the actual costs of credit. The statute carries civil, criminal, and statutory liabilities for a creditor's failure to comply. The TILA allows for a three-day period in which consumers who use their homes as collateral for loans can cancel those loans.

Lobbying efforts by lenders led to passage of the Truth in Lending Simplification and Reform Act in 1980. This Act relaxed the TILA's requirements for detailed disclosures by creditors.

In response to numerous class action lawsuits, the TILA was amended in 1995 to provide retroactive and prospective relief from liability for certain creditor finance charges.

The Federal Reserve Board enacted Regulation Z to cover persons who regularly offer credit to consumers for personal, family, or household use and the transactions have a finance charge or, by written agreement, are payable in four or more installments. This regulation requires detailed disclosures in a meaningful sequence in the initial statement, and it requires periodic statements containing specified disclosures. Regulation Z specifies procedures and time limits for consumers and creditors in dealing with billing errors. Regulation Z covers both open-ended credit (e.g., credit card purchases) and closed-end credit (e.g., credit purchases of cars).

THE FAIR CREDIT REPORTING ACT: The Fair Credit Reporting Act of 1970 (FCRA) regulates practices by companies that *regularly* engage in credit reporting. The FCRA requires consumer-reporting agencies to maintain reasonable procedures to avoid violations of the Act.

Agencies must report only accurate and up-to-date information, and must report the information only to those eligible to receive it. Consumers, however, have little recourse against agencies that report irrelevant information that arguably invades their privacy. Consumers have no right under the FCRA to see their files, but consumers do have the right to be notified if adverse actions have been taken based on a credit report. Consumers must be informed of the identity and address of the reporting agency that compiled a report that led to adverse action, and the consumer has a limited right to correct erroneous information contained in a report.

THE EQUAL CREDIT OPPORTUNITY ACT: The Equal Credit Opportunity Act prohibits discrimination based on sex, marital status, race, religion, national origin, age, receipt of public assistance, and exercise of consumer protection rights.

THE FAIR DEBT COLLECTION PRACTICES ACT: The Fair Debt Collection Practices Act (FDCPA) regulates the activities of those who collect bills owed to others. The FDCPA prohibits certain acts which harass or intimidate debtors or which coerce payment through false statements. The FDCPA provides for civil and criminal penalties.

THE UNIFORM CONSUMER CREDIT CODE: Few states have adopted the Uniform Consumer Credit Code (UCCC); most states rely on their own laws.

THE CONSUMER PRODUCT SAFETY ACT: The Consumer Product Safety Act of 1972 established the Consumer Product Safety Commission (CPSC). The Consumer Product Safety Commission may set safety standards for consumer products, collect information on consumer injuries, require corrective action for hazardous consumer products, and ban unsafe products.

STUDY HINTS FOR NRW CASE STUDIES

The following study hints may be helpful when resolving the NRW case studies.

NRW 38.1	➤ Review the discussion of the Fair Credit Reporting Act before answering this question. ➤ Consider what steps need to be followed to make sure any information provided is accurate and up-to-date.
NRW 38.2	➤ Review the section on The Equal Credit Opportunity Act.
NRW 38.3	➤ Review the section on the Fair Debt Collection Practices Act. ➤ Consider whether different restrictions would apply to a collection agency than to NRW itself.

REVIEW OF KEY TERMS AND CONCEPTS

MATCHING EXERCISE

Select the term or concept that best matches a definition or statement set forth below. Each term or concept is the best match for only one definition or statement.

Terms and Concepts

a. Closed-end credit
b. Cooling-off period
c. CPSC
d. Debt collector

e. ECOA
f. FCRA
g. FDCPA

h. Open-ended credit
i. Regulation Z
j. TILA

Definitions and Statements

_____ 1. Federal act that requires disclosure of actual costs of credit.

_____ 2. Credit transaction for a fixed term, such as a credit purchase of a refrigerator payable in 12 monthly installments.

_____ 3. Business that collects accounts or debts for someone else who has given credit.

_____ 4. Credit transactions available for an indefinite time period, such as credit card transactions.

_____ 5. Federal act that regulates the activities of those who collect bills owed to others.

_____ 6. Federal agency created to help protect the public from injuries from consumer products.

_____ 7. Federal Reserve Board's enactment summarizing the scope of the Truth in Lending Act.

_____ 8. Time allowed under the Truth in Lending Act for consumers to cancel loans which use their homes as collateral.

_____ 9. Federal act requiring consumer-reporting agencies to adopt reasonable procedures for collecting and disseminating consumer information.

_____ 10. Federal act prohibiting certain discriminatory practices in the extension of credit.

COMPLETION EXERCISE

Fill in the blanks with the words that most accurately complete each statement.

1. The _____ _____ _____ _____, Title I of which is known as the Truth in Lending Act, was a landmark consumer protection law passed in 1968.

2. Remedies available to individuals under the Truth in Lending Act include _____ _____, _____ _____ of twice the finance charges, and _____ _____ .

3. The Federal Reserve Board's _____ ____ implements the Equal Credit Opportunity Act.

4. The Truth in Lending Act requires _____ and _____ disclosure of credit terms.

5. Potentially hazardous consumer products are regulated by the _____ _____ _____ _____.

TRUE-FALSE EXERCISE

Write **T** if the statement is true, write **F** if the statement is false.

_____ 1. The Truth in Lending Act is part of the Equal Credit Opportunity Act.

_____ 2. Regulation B is the implementing regulation for the Truth in Lending Act.

_____ 3. Regulation Z is the implements the Equal Credit Opportunity Act.

_____ 4. A consumer must notify a creditor of a billing error within 60 days of the creditor's transmitting the bill to the consumer.

_____ 5. The Fair Debt Collection Practices Act does not apply to persons or businesses collecting their own bills.

_____ 6. The UCCC has brought uniformity to state laws governing consumer credit because of its adoption by all of the states.

_____ 7. The Truth in Lending Act regulates only credit disclosure.

_____ 8. The FCRA requires a credit bureau to allow consumers to see their files.

_____ 9. Lenders may not discriminate against recipients of public assistance.

_____ 10. The Consumer Product Safety Commission governs sales of tobacco and tobacco products.

APPLICATION OF CONCEPTS

MULTIPLE CHOICE QUESTIONS

_____ 1. Ms. Kim borrowed $20,000 from Lone Sharx Associates, using her house as collateral. Which of the following consumer protection statutes provides Ms. Kim with a three-day "cooling off" period to rescind the loan agreement?
   a. The Fair Credit Reporting Act
   b. The Uniform Consumer Credit Act
   c. The Truth in Lending Act
   d. The Equal Credit Opportunity Act

_____ 2. Burt believes that he did not incur a $200 charge reflected on his credit card. If Burt contacts the credit card company within the applicable time frame to dispute the charge, what action may the credit card company take against Burt?
   a. The credit card company may apply the disputed charge against Burt's credit limit.
   b. The credit card company may attempt to collect the disputed $200 from Burt.
   c. The credit card company may close Burt's account if Burt continues to dispute the charge.
   d. The credit card company may report Burt's failure to pay the $200 to a credit reporting agency.

_____ 3. Paula attempted to open a charge account at Marston's Department Store. The store denied her application based on an unsatisfactory credit report. What may Paula do to correct the situation?

    a. Paula may obtain a copy of the credit report by contacting the credit reporting agency.

    b. Paula may obtain information regarding the adverse information contained in the credit report.

    c. Paula may demand that the adverse information be removed from the credit report.

    d. All of the above.

_____ 4. Marty applied for a loan from First Bank. The Bank denied the loan, but failed to notify Marty regarding the reasons for its action. Under the ECOA, what are Marty's options regarding the Bank's failure to follow federal law?

    a. Marty may sue the Bank and seek attorney's fees and costs.

    b. Marty may sue the bank for actual and punitive damages.

    c. Marty may ask the U.S. Attorney General to impose civil penalties against the Bank.

    d. All of the above.

SHORT ANSWER QUESTIONS

Answer the following questions, briefly explaining the reason for your answer.

1. Terence reviews loan applications for The Friendly Loan Company. Karen has filed an application for a loan to buy a new car. Terence knows that Karen is planning to marry a college student and believes that Karen may have difficulty making the car payments. May Terence deny the loan based upon Karen's future wedding plans?

_____

_____

2. The Consumer Product Safety Commission has noted an unusually high incidence of injuries to children who use a certain brand of in-line skates. What actions may the CPSC take regarding the particular brand of skates?

_____

_____

3. Grace was denied credit for the purchase of a new home based upon erroneous information in her credit file. If Grace disputes the information and the credit agency's investigation fails to resolve the dispute, what action may Grace take to tell potential creditors her side of the dispute?

_____

_____

4. After several attempts between 8 a.m. and 7 p.m., the Moore Collection Agency was unable to reach Zach about his overdue account with Acme Rental. Moore then tried to call Zach at 7 a.m., hoping to reach him before he left for work. Did Moore's actions violate any laws?

_____

_____

CASE PROBLEMS

Answer the following case problems, explaining your answers.

1. On August 2, a representative of Vaughn Home Improvement came to Maurice's home to give him an estimate on replacement windows. While the representative was there, Maurice signed a contract to make a credit purchase of the windows for $12,000. Maurice's home was to be used as collateral. On August 3, Maurice decided he had made a bad choice by ordering the windows. (a) Does Maurice have any recourse? (b) What legislation covers Maurice's situation? (c) What factor triggers the application of this legislation? (d) How soon must Maurice take action?

_____

_____

_____

_____

2. Stuart owns the Quik-Serv Collection Agency. He instructs all employees to recover debts for their customers within thirty days. He also recommends that the employees aggressively pursue debtors by calling their employers and talking with their neighbors and thereby embarrass them into making quick payments. (a) Which consumer protection law regulates the collection agency? (b) May the agency contact debtors' employers and neighbors? (c) What kinds of penalties or other adverse actions might the agency face if it violates the law? (d) What additional action might Stuart face, if he includes the words "federal", "national", or "the United States" on written collection communications?

_____

_____

_____

_____

CHAPTER REVIEW

THE ENVIRONMENTAL PROTECTION AGENCY: The EPA, a federal administrative agency, enforces federal environmental laws, conducts research, and adopts regulations covering air, water, and waste products.

THE NATIONAL ENVIRONMENTAL POLICY ACT: NEPA requires all federal agencies to analyze the environmental impact of their policies and actions to avoid environmental degradation.

- *Environmental impact statement*: A federal agency must prepare an environmental impact statement (EIS) whenever the agency proposes legislation, recommends any actions, or undertakes any activity if the following three elements are present: 1) the activity involves a proposed federal action 2) that is "major" and 3) has a significant impact on the environment.

  An EIS examines the proposed action, possible alternatives including no action, long-term and short-term impacts, commitment of resources, and unavoidable adverse consequences.

- *Council on environmental quality*: NEPA established the Council on Environmental Quality to advise the president regarding developing and recommending federal environmental regulations.

Air Pollution: Particulates, carbon monoxide, nitrogen oxides, sulfur oxides, and hydrocarbons are five categories of air pollution that are regulated under the Clean Air Act.

- *The Clean Air Act*: This Act sets standards for air pollution emissions and establishes time tables for the reduction of air pollutants.

- *The 1970 amendments*: Amendments to the Act gave the EPA responsibility for establishing national ambient air standards (standards relating to mobile air emissions, such as automobile pollution). States must submit to the EPA a state implementation plan (SIP) setting out how the state plans to meet the federal standards.

- *The 1977 amendments*: These amendments delayed compliance with federal standards.

- *The 1990 amendments*: These amendments set new compliance dates. It also sets up a permit system aimed at controlling pollution at major stationary points. In addition, it increased the civil and criminal penalties for violating federal clean air laws. Penalties include administrative fines of up to $25,000 per day, and other fines up to $1 million for each violation and up to 15 years imprisonment.

Water Pollution: The Clean Water Act (CWA) establishes goals and timetables for cleaning up the nation's waterways.

- *The Clean Water Act*: Water pollution sources are classified as either point sources or nonpoint sources. A point source is: 1) any type of physical structure or device, such as pipes, tubes, ditches, or tunnels 2) that is regularly used to convey pollutants from an industrial source to waterways. Nonpoint sources are such things as farms, mining, and forestry operations.

  Point sources are regulated through a discharge permit system (NPDES). Nonpoint sources are exempt from having to comply with the CWA. Effluent limits are set for the amount and kinds of pollutants that may be discharged into streams or rivers through point sources. Individual states classify waters within their state and administer the permit program with EPA oversight.

  Companies are forbidden from discharging pollutants through a point source unless they have a discharge permit that allows such discharge. Discharge of pollutants through a point source is illegal if: 1) the discharging party does not have a discharge permit or 2) more pollutants are discharged than is allowed by a permit. A party who violates the CWA may suffer both civil and criminal liability.

- *Safe Drinking Water Act*: The Safe Drinking Water Act (SDWA) regulates water delivered through the public water supply systems, establishing maximum contaminant levels (MCL's) for various pollutants. States administer and enforce the federal law.

NOISE POLLUTION: Before passage of the Noise Control Act in 1972, nuisance laws provided the sole basis for protection from excessive noise. Federal law now preempts state laws in setting standards for major noise sources, such as construction equipment, transportation equipment, motors, and engines. Nonetheless, the states continue to bear the primary responsibility for enforcing noise pollution laws.

LAND CONSERVATION AND POLLUTION: Numerous laws prohibit pollution of public domain, meaning land owned or controlled by the federal government, and private land.
- *The Toxic Substances Control Act (TSCA)*: The TSCA screens (evaluates) chemicals before they are manufactured and marketed to the public in order to assess the risk that they may pose to humans and to the environment. The EPA is required to test and regulate only those chemicals that pose an "unreasonable risk."
- *The Federal Insecticide, Fungicide, and Rodenticide Act (FIFRA)*: FIFRA regulates the sale and use of pesticides and establishes civil and criminal penalties.
- *The Resource Conservation and Recovery Act (RCRA)*: This Act provides assistance to states for establishing programs for disposing of solid, nonhazardous waste programs. It also establishes a system for regulating the generation, transportation, storage and disposal of hazardous waste.
- *The Comprehensive Environmental Response, Compensation, and Liability Act (CERCLA)*: CERCLA, also known as the "Superfund," imposes strict liability on an owner or operator of a facility where emergency response actions must be taken to protect public health and environment. Sites may be cleaned up with federal funds with costs later recovered from potentially responsible parties (PRPs).

WILDLIFE CONSERVATION: The Endangered Species Act protects threatened or endangered species of wildlife both in the United States and abroad. Habitats are also protected.

ENFORCEMENT AND REMEDIES: Environmental laws are enforced by fines and/or imprisonment.

INTERNATIONAL ASPECTS: While many foreign countries are plagued by pollution, the European Union has adopted environmental protection measures.

STUDY HINTS FOR NRW CASE STUDIES

The following study hints may be helpful when resolving the NRW case studies.

NRW 39.1	➢ Review the discussion of environmental self-audits before answering this question.
	➢ Also, review the discussion of the Clean Air Act.
NRW 39.2	➢ NRW should explore obtaining an appropriate permit for its effluents.
	➢ Also, since penalties may depend on the good faith compliance efforts of a company, NRW should immediately undertake to bring its operations into compliance with the law.
NRW 39.3	➢ Carlos should review the material on CERCLA as well as the material on enforcement and remedies.

REVIEW OF KEY TERMS AND CONCEPTS

MATCHING EXERCISE

Select the term or concept that best matches a definition or statement set forth below. Each term or concept is the best match for only one definition or statement.

Terms and Concepts

a. Ambient air standards

b. Aquifer

c. CERCLA

d. Citizen suit

e. CWA

f. Effluent

g. EIS

h. Leachings

i. Manifest

j. NEPA

k. Nuisance

l. Public domain

Definitions and Statements

____ 1. Federal act that requires federal agencies to analyze environmental impact of their actions.

____ 2. Standards set for surrounding air in atmosphere.

____ 3. Legal action brought by private persons for others' violations of environmental laws.

____ 4. Liquid draining or percolating through substances.

____ 5. Report that analyzes an action's potential impact on the environment.

____ 6. Federal statute that provides for correcting serious hazardous waste pollution.

____ 7. Use of one's property that impairs use or enjoyment of property held by another person.

____ 8. Subsurface accumulations of water held in rock, gravel, or sand.

____ 9. Discharge of fluids.

____ 10. Lands held by the federal government for public use.

____ 11. Federal statute intended to preserve the water quality of navigable rivers and streams.

____ 12. A list, such as that required for the transportation of hazardous wastes.

COMPLETION EXERCISE

Fill in the blanks with the words that most accurately complete each statement.

1. The Environmental Protection Agency was created by _____ _____ in 1970.

2. The Safe Drinking Water Act sets _____ _____ _____ or MCLs for pollutants to drinking water supplies.

3. Most federal environmental laws provide both _____ and _____ penalties for violations.

4. NEPA requires federal agencies to prepare an environmental impact statement prior to undertaking any _____ federal action.

5. The Resource Conservation and Recovery Act (RCRA) generally regulates the disposal of

_____.

TRUE-FALSE EXERCISE

Write **T** if the statement is true, write **F** if the statement is false.

_____ 1. Federal environmental laws are often enforced by the states.

_____ 2. Violators of most environmental laws face only civil penalties.

_____ 3. Environmental laws often provide for the issuance of permits that allow companies to discharge certain amounts and kinds of pollutants into the air and water.

_____ 4. Under CERCLA, landowners are sometimes held liable for the cleanup of hazardous substances even if they did not personally dump these substances on their land.

_____ 5. The Endangered Species Act protects the habitat of a species as well as the species itself.

_____ 6. Environmental protection laws are unique to the United States.

_____ 7. In general, states can adopt water pollution laws that conflict with the Clean Water Act.

_____ 8. The federal Superfund is designed to aid in cleaning up inactive hazardous waste sites.

_____ 9. Under certain environmental laws, a private citizen can sue a polluter only if the citizen suffers a special harm, meaning harm that is different from the harm suffered by the general public.

_____ 10. The CWA regulates the discharge of pollutants from point sources, but not from nonpoint sources.

APPLICATION OF CONCEPTS

MULTIPLE CHOICE QUESTIONS

_____ 1. The government brought an action against Martin Co. for using pipes to illegally discharge residue wastes into the Roaring River in violation of the CWA. Martin had a permit that allowed it to discharge wastes, but the amount it discharged exceeded its allotted exemption. However, Martin did not intentionally violate its permit, and it did not discharge more wastes than other similar companies. Is Martin liable in this case?
   a. Yes.
   b. No, because it did not intend to violate the law.
   c. No, because it did not discharge more wastes that other similar companies.
   d. No, because the CWA does not apply to discharges from nonpoint sources, such as the discharge pipes in this case.

_____ 2. The U.S. Army Corps of Engineers (a federal agency) proposes building a large dam. The dam will affect the environment, and it will require abandonment of several towns. In this case:
    a. The U.S. Army Corps of Engineers must prepare an EIS before it builds the dam.
    b. An EIS must consider the impact that the dam may have on residents and businesses in the towns that must be abandoned if the dam is built.
    c. An EIS must consider feasible, practical alternatives to the dam.
    d. All of the above.

_____ 3. In the manufacturing of super-balls at its Pittsburgh plant, Orbit Inc. produces a toxic chemical waste that may cause lung cancer. Orbit plans to dispose of these wastes by burying them in a disposal area located in Nevada. Under these facts:
    a. RCRA regulates the production, transportation, and disposal of the waste in this case.
    b. RCRA forbids production of any toxic wastes, such as the waste in this case.
    c. RCRA forbids transporting any toxic wastes, such as the waste in this case.
    d. All of the above.

_____ 4. Olivia leased ten acres of her property to Brexus Corp. Brexus operated a hammer factory where hazardous chemicals are used in the manufacturing process. Some of these hazardous chemicals escaped from the Brexus factory, damaging the surrounding land. Who is liable in this case?
    a. Only Olivia.
    b. Only Brexus Corp.
    c. Olivia and Brexus Corp.
    d. No one.

SHORT ANSWER QUESTIONS

Answer the following questions, briefly explaining the reason for your answer.

1. Donald intends to build homes on property he recently purchased. When he purchased the property, Donald was aware that the prior owner had abandoned leaking tanks of hazardous waste on the property. As it turns out, the property is highly toxic, requiring massive clean-up. What federal law applies in this case? Who is liable for the cost of cleaning up this property?

_____

_____

2. Cows, Inc. owns a feedlot and meat processing plant. When it rains, water from the feedlot runs into a nearby river. Also, Cows Inc. discharges acid from its plant directly into the river, using pipes. Cows, Inc. does not have any permits that sanction its activities. Analyze whether Cows, Inc. is violating the CWA.

_____

_____

3. CleanOil has dumped hazardous waste into the Green River for five years, hurting its fish population. Fred has fished this river for ten years, but can no longer do so because of CleanOil's pollution. Does Fred have standing to bring a citizen suit against CleanOil for violating the CWA?

_____

_____

4. Acme Disposal Company transported a shipment of hazardous waste. Foster, Acme's employee, improperly disposed of this waste, contaminating the city's drinking water. What law applies in this case? Who violated the law in this case?

_____

_____

CASE PROBLEMS

Answer the following case problems, explaining your answers.

1. The Ski Corp. wants to build a new ski resort on Forest Service land and has filed for a permit allowing it to do so. The project will require clearing trees along numerous ski runs, and using large quantities of public river water for snowmaking and drinking purposes. (a) Does the proposed project involve a major federal action? (b) Must an EIS be prepared? (c) If an EIS is prepared, what matters must it address?

_____

_____

_____

_____

2. Tony wants to build a shopping mall next to an undeveloped expanse of land that is inhabited by the black-footed ferret. This type of ferret is an endangered species. (a) What federal environmental law may apply in this case? (b) What must Tony do in order to comply with this law?

_____

_____

_____

_____

CHAPTER 40

Labor and Fair Employment Practices

```
┌─────────────────────────────────────────┐
│              CHAPTER REVIEW               │
└─────────────────────────────────────────┘
```

LABOR: In the 1800s and the early 1900s federal courts saw union activities as criminal conspiracies.

■ *Federal Statutes*: A series of federal statutes establish, protect, and define the rights of employees to collectively bargain with their employers. These laws include:

1) **The Norris-LaGuardia Act (1932)**: The Norris-LaGuardia Act removed barriers that had hindered union organization, permitting unions to organize and collectively bargain. In addition, this Act: a) authorizes boycotts and picketing,, and b) outlaws yellow dog contracts, that is, agreements by which workers promise not to join a union.

2) **The Wagner Act (1935)**: Also called the National Labor Relations Act (NLRA), the Wagner Act encourages organizing activities and collective bargaining by allowing workers the freedom to: a) join unions, b) collectively bargain with an employer, and 3) engage in mutually beneficial activities. It also requires employers to bargain with unions in good faith. The Wagner Act established the National Labor Relations Board (NLRB), which is charged with administering and interpreting the unfair labor practice provisions of this law.

3) **The Taft-Hartley Act (1947)**: Also called the Labor Management Relations Act, the Taft-Hartley amended the Wagner Act to forbid certain union practices. Among other things, this Act: a) protects the employers' rights to express their opinions about unionization so long as they do not take reprisals against employees who are attempting to unionize; b) preserves the employees' rights to engage in informational picketing (picketing intended to inform the public that workers are receiving wages and benefits below what other employers in the area are providing); c) prohibits closed shops (workers cannot be hired unless they already have joined the union), while still permitting union shops (all workers in the bargaining unit must join the union after being hired, usually after a thirty-day grace period); d) mandates a "cooling-off" period in certain circumstances before employees can strike; and e) preserved the rights of states to enact right-to-work laws (right-to-work laws prohibit employers from requiring workers to join a union or to pay dues and initiation fees as conditions of employment, even if an employer's workers are represented by a union).

4) **The Landrum-Griffin Act (1959)**: Also called the Labor Management Reporting and Disclosure Act, this Act provides for civil and criminal penalties for union leaders who are corrupt. It also mandates democratic procedures in union affairs and a "bill of rights" for members.

5) **Further issues**: Some common issues include the following: (a) Decertification - Employers can contest the validity of a certification election by requesting the NLRB to decertify the union, i.e., determine that the union does not represent the employees; and (b) Soliciting - Employers can generally forbid soliciting unionization on the employers' premises and during working hours.

■ *State law*: State law regulating labor is preempted by federal law. Activities peripheral to federal law or of deep state concern are subject to state regulation.

EMPLOYMENT:

■ *Fair Employment Practices Laws*: Federal antidiscrimination laws include the following:
1) **Civil Rights Act of 1964**: Title VII of this Act applies to employers with 15 or more employees, unions with 15 or more member or who operate a hiring hall, and employment agencies.

This law forbids any form of employment discrimination on the basis an employee's race, color, religion, sex, or national origin.

Title VII forbids the following types of practices: a) disparate treatment (employer intentionally discriminates against a job applicant or employee because of the person's race, national origin, color, religion, or sex); b) disparate impact (employer adopts a neutral employment qualification that has a significantly different, unfavorable effect on a protected class and the qualification is not a business necessity); and c) harassment (verbal, nonverbal, written, and/or physical conduct in the workplace that causes an employee to suffer ridicule, humiliation, or physical injury due to the person's race, national origin, color, religion, or sex).

The Pregnancy Discrimination Act mandates that pregnancy be treated as any other disability protected by law, it expressly states that sex discrimination under Title VII includes discrimination on the basis of pregnancy, childbirth, or related medical conditions

2) **The Immigration Reform and Control Act**: This Act bans discrimination against persons because they are not U.S. citizens.

3) **The Equal Pay Act of 1963**: This Act prohibits discrimination in wages between men and women if they are both performing the same work under substantially the same working conditions.

4) **The Age Discrimination in Employment Act**: This Act prohibits discrimination against job applicants or employees because they are 40 years of age or older.

5) **The Rehabilitation Act of 1973**: This executive order directs federal contractors to reasonably accommodate "otherwise qualified" handicapped individuals in connection with employment.

6) **The Americans with Disabilities Act of 1990**: Among other things, this Act requires employers to make a reasonable accommodation in employment for qualified persons with disabilities. Recent Supreme Court decisions recognize the following principles regarding the ADA: 1) covered disabilities under the ADA do not include conditions that do not amount to "severe restrictions in the activities that are of central importance to most people's daily lives"; 2) it is a valid defense for an employer that a worker's disability on the job would pose a direct threat to his or her health; 3) an accommodation may not be reasonable if it amounts to a preference that would violate an established seniority system; and 4) employees who bring private actions under the Rehabilitation Act and the ADA cannot receive punitive damages – they can recover only compensatory damages; and 5) state employees cannot sue their employers for damages under the ADA.

7) **Other laws**: Other important employment laws include The Civil Rights Act of 1991; the Family and Medical Leave Act; the Occupational Safety and Health Act; the Social Security Act; and state workers' compensation statutes.

STUDY HINTS FOR NRW CASE STUDIES

The following study hints may be helpful when resolving the NRW case studies.

NRW 40.1	➤ Review the discussion regarding the Taft-Hartley Act.
NRW 1.2	➤ The NRW principals should understand "disparate impact" interpretations of employment requirements, but should also understand "business necessity" as justification for differential treatment.
W	➤ Review the material dealing with harassment under Title VII.

REVIEW OF KEY TERMS AND CONCEPTS

MATCHING EXERCISE

Select the term or concept that best matches a definition or statement set forth below. Each term or concept is the best match for only one definition or statement.

Terms and Concepts

a. Bona fide occupational qualification
b. Boycott
c. Family and Medical Leave Act

d. Informational picketing
e. Reverse discrimination
f. Secondary boycott

g. Severance pay
h. Unfair labor practice
i. Wildcat strike

Definitions and Statements

f _b_ 1. Refusal to do business with a supplier of an employer.

_i_ 2. Strike by a minority group of workers that is not authorized by the union.

_d_ 3. Picketing that is intended to inform the public that an employer does not employ union workers and/or does not pay the same as other employers.

_g_ 4. Wages paid when a worker is terminated from a job.

e _h_ 5. Discrimination against white employees that may result from affirmative action programs.

a _a_ 6. Characteristic or skill that is required because it is essential for the performance of a job.

h _e_ 7. Act by an employer or union that violates federal labor laws.

_c_ 8. Federal law that entitles some employees to take up to 12 weeks unpaid leave.

b _f_ 9. Refusal to do business with the employer.

COMPLETION EXERCISE

Fill in the blanks with the words that most accurately complete each statement.

1. _Picketing_ occurs when workers walk or stand in front of an employer's place of business.

2. A _collective_ _bargaining_ agreement is a contract between an employer and union that establishes the basic terms of employees who are represented by the union.

3. Title VII of the Civil Rights Act of 1964 prohibits discrimination against employees on the basis of _race_ , _national origin_ , _religion_ , _color_ , and _sex (gender)_.

4. The ___Occupational Safety___ and ___Health___ Act is a federal law that is intended to prevent accidents in the workplace and to provide a safe working environment.

5. The ___American With Disabilities___ Act prohibits employment discrimination against qualified persons with disabilities.

TRUE-FALSE EXERCISE

Write **T** if the statement is true, write **F** if the statement is false.

___T___ 1. Wildcat strikes are unlawful.

___F___ 2. The National Labor Relations Board has the power to punish employers and unions who engage in unfair labor practices.

___F___ 3. Good faith bargaining that is required under federal labor law means that each side must continue to make concessions during negotiations until an agreement is reached.

___T___ 4. The EEOC enforces most federal antidiscrimination laws, including Title VII.

___T___ 5. An employer who intentionally pays Hispanic employees less than other employees has committed a disparate treatment violation of Title VII.

___F___ 6. An employer must take any steps needed in order to accommodate employees' religious beliefs.

___F___ 7. The Age Discrimination in Employment Act forbids employers from firing anyone who is 40 or older.

___F___ 8. An employee generally has 2 years within which to file a discrimination complaint under Title VII.

___T___ 9. The Family and Medical Leave Act only applies to certain employers who have 50 or more employees.

___T___ 10. When employees are involuntarily laid off due to a lack of work, the employees may be entitled to receive unemployment benefits.

APPLICATION OF CONCEPTS

MULTIPLE CHOICE QUESTIONS

___d___ 1. Niles was concerned about the unsafe working conditions in his employer's factory and he contacted OSHA. OSHA inspectors came to the factory and asked to inspect the plant. Under these facts, the Occupational Safety and Health Act provides for which of the following:
   a. OSHA inspectors may inspect the plant without first obtaining a warrant.
   b. OSHA can issue a citation and fine the employer if it is in violation of OSHA regulations.
   c. Niles can be discharged for filing the complaint with OSHA.
   d. All of the above.

___a___ 2. In most states, which individual would be eligible for unemployment benefits?
   a. Niya was laid off of her job as a computer programmer because of a recession in the industry.
   b. Jay is a full-time student and not available for work.
   c. Steve was fired because he was drunk on the job and pilfered tools from his employer.
   d. a and b.

a d 3. Shari was injured in an accident at work. Both Shari and employer were negligent. Under these facts, in a state with a typical Workers' Compensation statute:
   a. Shari can recover workers' compensation benefits.
   b. Shari cannot recover workers' compensation benefits because she was negligent.
   c. Shari can sue her employer under tort law because her employer was negligent.
   d. a and c.

C 4. Marlene has been a full-time employee of Garland Corp. for two years. Marlene recently became pregnant and gave birth to a son. Garland Corp. is subject to the Family and Medical Leave Act of 1993. Under these facts:
   a. Marlene is entitled to receive one year of paid leave so she can care for her son.
   b. Marlene is entitled to receive twelve weeks of paid leave so she can care for her son.
   c. Marlene is entitled to receive twelve weeks of unpaid leave so she can care for her son.
   d. Marlene is not entitled to receive any paid or unpaid leave so she can care for her son.

SHORT ANSWER QUESTIONS

Answer the following questions, briefly explaining the reason for your answer.

1. Dr. Kathy Payne advertised for an "experienced receptionist, females preferred." Payne is a gynecologist and she believes that her patients feel more comfortable when greeted by a female receptionist than when greeted by a male receptionist. Bill, a highly qualified job applicant applied for the advertised job, but was rejected because of his gender. Has Payne violated Title VII in this case?

_____

_____

2. Julio was born in Mexico and currently lives in the United States. Julio is not yet a U.S. citizen. He applied for an analyst position at the Intelligence Research Center (IRC), a private company that provides intelligence analysis for the government. Analysts must have a top secret security clearance, which is impossible to obtain without U.S. citizenship. IRC refused to hire Julio because he did not have the required clearance. Has IRC violated any federal antidiscrimination law in this case?

_____

_____

3. Ames Fire Department requires its firefighters to be able to lift 250 pounds because, on rare occasion, a firefighter may have to lift this amount of weight. Chris applied for a job as fire fighter and she was qualified to perform the duties of the job. Chris and all other female applicants were rejected, however, because they could not lift this weight. Fifty percent of the qualified applicants were women. Has the Ames Fire Department violated Title VII?

_____

_____

4. St. Leo University, a Catholic college, refused to hire Mohammed as a professor because he is a Muslim. Instead it hired Paul, who is Catholic, even though he was less qualified. Has St. Leo violated Title VII?

_____

_____

CASE PROBLEMS

Answer the following case problems, explaining your answers.

1. Joe Wiper, the head custodian at Blinker High School, often makes crude sexual remarks in the presence of Maria and other male custodians. Maria complained to the assistant principal in charge of custodians, Dave Dingle. Dingle told her to "lighten up"and refused to do anything about Joe's constant comments and sexual innuendo. Joe recently told Maria that her job may be in jeopardy because of cutbacks in the janitorial force, but that he can protect her if she agrees to have sex with him. Has Joe and/or Blinker High School violated Title VII?

_____

_____

_____

_____

2. Kim Pak was born in Korea and she recently became a U.S. citizen. Kim speaks fluent English, but she has a mild Korean accent. Her accent does not interfere with her ability to communicate with others. Kim applied for the job of manager at the Jasper Hotel, for which she was qualified. However, Kim was not hired for this position because: (a) Kim speaks with a Korean accent; (b) Kim is fifty years old and she may not work for as many years as someone younger; and (c) Kim has a hearing disorder and the hotel would have to spend $300 to purchase a special telephone for her. Separately discuss the validity of each of these reasons for not hiring Kim.

_____

_____

_____

_____

CHAPTER 41 — Real Property and Joint Ownership

CHAPTER REVIEW

PROPERTY RIGHTS: Property is both an object subject to ownership and a group of rights and interests.

CLASSIFICATION OF PROPERTY: Property is real property (land and things that are growing on, attached to, or erected on the land) and personal property (all other property). Property also is either tangible property (property has physical existence) and intangible property (property without a physical existence).

REAL PROPERTY DEFINED: You should understand the difference between fixtures and nonfixtures.
- ■ *Definition of Real Property*: Land and things permanently attached to land, like structures and roads.
- ■ *Definition of a Fixture*: Property that at one time was movable and independent of real estate but became attached to it. Common examples include water heaters and built-in ovens.
- ■ *The Nature of Plants*: Plants typically are real property. The UCC classifies plants based on who removes them. If a seller removes plants, then they are goods; if a buyer removes, then real estate.
- ■ *State Governance*: The laws of the state where the property is located govern the land.
- ■ *Federal Regulation*: The federal government, through the Americans with Disabilities Act (ADA), regulates property open to the public so that it can accommodate handicapped persons. Under the Act, newly constructed public accommodations must be designed to accommodate handicapped individuals. In general, new buildings must be designed and built to be readily accessible to and usable by persons with disabilities unless this is impossible.

ACQUISITION OF REAL PROPERTY: Land ownership is a society-based concept.
- ■ *Original Occupancy*: Occurs when the government allows private occupancy of land that was previously government owned.
- ■ *Voluntary Transfer by the Owner*: Transfer is accomplished by a written deed, which contains key information. The three type of deeds are 1) warranty, 2) grant, and 3) quitclaim. It is prudent, but not necessary, to record a deed.
- ■ *Transfer by Will or Intestate Succession*: A valid will can pass property to a named beneficiary.

PROTECTION OF REAL PROPERTY: Real property can be lost by operation of law or government action.
- ■ *Involuntary Transfers by Operation of Law*: A lender may foreclose if a person is in default on a mortgage. Property may be attached to satisfy a legal judgment. Failure to pay for labor or materials for the premises will create a mechanic's lien.
- ■ *Involuntary Transfers by Government Action*: Under the doctrine of eminent domain, the government may take land for public use, but it must provide compensation. The government may also enact zoning ordinances.
- ■ *Private Restrictions on Land Use*: Restrictive covenants, which are private agreements between landowners, may limit how land can be used.
- ■ *Adverse Possession*: A person who has open, notorious, continuous, and actual possession of property will acquire title to it after the expiration of a holding period (ranging from five to thirty years).
- ■ *Easements*: An easement is the right to use land in a particular manner. An express easement is stated. An easement by prescription arises when a person starts to use land openly. After a period of time, the person will gain an easement. An easement by necessity arises when there is no means of access to the servient estate. An easement by implication arises when someone needs to use land, but the need is not as great as in an easement by necessity. An easement may also be created by contract.

RENTAL OF REAL PROPERTY: Understand the types of tenancies and the duties of landlord and tenant.

- *Types of Tenancies*: A tenancy for a fixed term automatically expires after a set period of time. A periodic tenancy continues for successive periods (such as a month) until terminated. Notice must be given before termination. A tenancy at will can be terminated at any time by the landlord or tenant. A tenancy at sufferance arises when a tenant wrongfully remains on the property.
- *Rights and Duties of Tenants*: A tenant has the right of quiet enjoyment, and some courts recognize the warranty of habitability. Assignments and subleases are allowed unless prohibited by the lease.
- *Rights and Duties of Landlords*: A landlord has the right to rent and to collect for damage. A landlord does not warrant that premises are safe, but must warn tenants of latent defects.
- *Legislative Trends*: The Fair Housing Act prohibits discrimination by landlords.

LEGISLATIVE TRENDS: The federal Fair Housing Act, which is contained in the Civil Rights Act of 1968 forbids discrimination in housing based upon a person's race, color, religion, national origin, sex, or familial status.

JOINT OWNERSHIP OF PROPERTY: Exists when two or more people have concurrent title.

- *Tenancy in Common*: Exists when two or more people have an undivided interest in property.
- *Joint Tenancy with Rights of Survivorship*: Each tenant has an undivided interest, and the property passes to the other tenants upon the death of a tenant. A will has no effect on this type of tenancy.
- *Tenancy by the Entireties*: The tenants must be husband and wife, and each has an undivided interest with right of survivorship.
- *Community Property*: This law, recognized in eight states, provides that each spouse owns one-half of most property accumulated *during* marriage. Property acquired before marriage, inherited, received by gift, or purchased with separate funds remains separate property.
- *Distinguishing Among the Forms of Joint Ownership*: The words used on a deed are controlling. If the deed does not specify the form of joint ownership, then: 1) If the tenants are married, most states presume community property or tenancy by the entireties. If the state does not recognize these forms, then the law presumes joint tenancy with right of survivorship. 2) If the tenants are not married, most states presume a tenancy in common.
- *Transfer on Death Ownership*: Transfer on death or pay on death ownership should be distinguished from forms of joint ownership. When an owner opens a bank account, buys securities, or acquires other assets, he or she may designate the form of ownership as transfer or pay on death. For example, pay on death (POD) is generally used for bank accounts. In most states, the recipient does not have an interest in the asset during the owner's life and the recipient cannot withdraw the assets or mortgage them. The recipient only is entitled to the assets at the owner's death, if the owner has not changed the title.

STUDY HINTS FOR NRW CASE STUDIES

The following study hints may be helpful when resolving the NRW case studies.

NRW 41.1	➤ The NRW principals should explore the concept of mechanic's liens.
NRW 41.2	➤ Review the zoning laws where the barn is located.
NRW 41.3	➤ You should consider notice provisions required in periodic tenancies. ➤ Also consider tenants' rights with regard to installed fixtures and renovations.

MATCHING EXERCISE

Select the term or concept that best matches a definition or statement set forth below. Each term or concept is the best match for only one definition or statement.

Terms and Concepts

a. Community property
b. Constructive eviction
c. Decedent
d. Easement

e. Escrow
f. Fixture
g. Nuisance
h. Periodic tenancy

i. Separate property
j. Tenancy at will
k. Tenancy for a fixed term
l. Title

Definitions and Statements

____ 1. Rights to the access and use of someone else's real estate.

____ 2. Unlawful interference with the use of public or private property.

____ 3. Starts at a fixed time and continues for successive periods until terminated.

____ 4. Normally includes property: a) owned by either spouse before marriage; b) given to a spouse by gift or will; and c) acquired with separate funds.

____ 5. Property that at one time was movable and independent of real estate but became attached to it.

____ 6. Legal doctrine providing that one-half of property that is acquired during marriage belongs to each spouse.

____ 7. Tenancy for a set period of time.

____ 8. A person who has died.

____ 9. Legal ownership of property.

____ 10. Tenancy that can be terminated any time at the desire of either the landlord or the tenant.

____ 11. Process of preparing for the exchange of real estate.

____ 12. Occurs when a landlord materially interferes with a tenant's right to quiet enjoyment.

COMPLETION EXERCISE

Fill in the blanks with the words that most accurately complete each statement.

1. _____ _____ includes land, buildings, fixtures, and rights in land.

2. In some states, the law provides to tenants an implied _____ _____ _____, which states that a landlord impliedly warrants that the premises will be fit for living.

3. A _____ _____ contains a number of implied promises by the grantor to the effect that a good and marketable title is being conveyed.

4. A party may acquire title to property by _____ _____ if the party takes possession of the property, and such possession is actual, visible, notorious, exclusive, hostile, and continuous for the legally required period of time.

5. _____ proceedings are the means by which a lender can take possession of property in the event of _____.

TRUE-FALSE EXERCISE

Write **T** if the statement is true, write **F** if the statement is false.

_____ 1. An easement by prescription can be considered to be an "easement by adverse possession."

_____ 2. A landlord has a duty to inform the tenant of all latent defects on the premises.

_____ 3. In determining whether property is a fixture, courts will look at the reasonable expectations and understandings of most people.

_____ 4. In general, movable machinery and equipment are fixtures.

_____ 5. A deed is not valid unless consideration is given for the deed.

_____ 6. In general, a deed is not effective and does not transfer title unless the grantor effectively delivers the deed to the grantee.

_____ 7. In general, a deed must be recorded to be effective.

_____ 8. Statutes commonly hold that a grantor who conveys land by a quitclaim deed warrants that the grantor owns the land and that the land is not subject to any liens.

_____ 9. In some instances, government regulation may constitute a taking of property.

_____ 10. The Fair Housing Act requires landlords to act in good faith when leasing property.

APPLICATION OF CONCEPTS

MULTIPLE CHOICE QUESTIONS

_____ 1. Joseph owns a farm. In a signed writing, Joseph granted Fran the irrevocable right to use a road on his farm so that Fran could more easily reach her own property. What kind of interest in land did Joseph grant to Fran?
   a. Express easement.
   b. Easement by implication.
   c. Easement by prescription.
   d. Lease for a fixed term.

_____ 2. Shanti leased a building. Shanti installed a stove and a boiler in the building. Upon expiration of the lease, Shanti intends to remove the stove, but not the boiler. The stove can be easily removed without harming anything. Removal of the boiler, however, will seriously damage both the building and the boiler. Are the stove and boiler fixtures?
   a. The stove and boiler are both fixtures.
   b. The stove is not a fixture, but the boiler is a fixture.
   c. The stove is a fixture, but the boiler is not a fixture.
   d. Neither the stove nor the boiler is a fixture.

_____ 3. Margaret contracted to sell a seaside cottage to Lex. Margaret executed a deed to convey title to Lex, three witnesses signed the deed, and the deed was acknowledged. Pursuant to the contract, Margaret delivered the deed to an escrow company, with instructions to deliver the deed to Lex when he delivered the purchase price to the escrow company. Under these facts:
   a. Title passed to Lex when Margaret signed the deed.
   b. Title passed to Lex when Margaret delivered the deed to the escrow company.
   c. Title will pass to Lex when he pays and the escrow company delivers the deed to him.
   d. Title will not pass to Lex until he makes the required payment, the escrow company delivers the deed to Lex, and Lex records the deed.

_____ 4. Select the correct answer.
   a. A person who owns an interest in property by joint tenancy can generally transfer the interest by a will.
   b. In states recognizing community property, any property received by an inheritance becomes community property if the property was received during the marriage.
   c. Persons who own property as tenants in common may not transfer their interest by a will.
   d. Persons owning property as tenants in common do not need to have equal interests.

SHORT ANSWER QUESTIONS

Answer the following questions, briefly explaining the reason for your answer.

1. Landlord inspected an apartment and noticed a rotted staircase. The defect would have been noticed only by persons who had experience in inspecting wood. Tenant moved into the apartment, fell through the rotted staircase, and was injured. Landlord never told Tenant about the rotted staircase. Is Landlord liable for Tenant's injuries?

_____

_____

2. Samantha purchased land adjacent to Stan's. One way for Samantha to get to a road is to cross Stan's driveway. The other way is to cross through a trail, which is rocky and usually muddy. Samantha could use the trail if she purchased a four-wheel drive vehicle. Can Samantha claim an easement over Stan's driveway?

_____

_____

3. Murray leased office space for three years. After three years, he remained in the office. Murray's landlord then told him to leave immediately, without giving Murray any notice. Was the landlord required to give Murray notice before evicting him?

_____

_____

4. Anna gave Bob a quitclaim deed to some property. Bob later discovered that the property had a lien on it. Can Bob sue Anna for breach of implied covenants?

_____

_____

CASE PROBLEMS

Answer the following case problems, explaining your answers.

1. Humphrey granted Karen an easement to use his driveway to get to her house. The easement stated that Karen was the only person who could use the easement. After several months, Karen opened a day care in her home. Every morning and afternoon, several cars drove on Humphrey's driveway. Humphrey was greatly annoyed by the increased number of cars using his driveway. (a) What type of easement did Humphrey grant to Karen? (b) Is Karen properly using the easement?

_____

_____

_____

_____

2. Steve had a one-year lease for an apartment in Sleepy Hollow. The lease provided that a tenant must give one month's notice before termination. Steve's neighbor liked to play his stereo late into the night, which interferes with Steve's sleep. Steve complained to the building manager several times, but the neighbor continued to play his stereo. With six months remaining on his lease, Steve moved out. (a) What type of tenancy was this? (b) Was it proper for Sleepy Hollow to require a tenant to give notice before termination? (c) Under the laws of most states, what doctrine can Steve use to justify his leaving without notice? (d) Is Steve required to pay Sleepy Hollow for the remainder of his lease?

_____

_____

_____

_____

CHAPTER 42   Personal Property and Bailments

CHAPTER REVIEW

OWNERSHIP OF PROPERTY: Personal property is anything that can be owned or possessed, except land and anything attached to the land. Classifications of property and various interests in property include:

■ *Classifications of Property*: All property that is not classified as real property is considered personal property. Personal property is made up of tangible and intangible property. Tangible property is property that can be moved, while intangible property cannot be physically possessed.

■ *Components of Ownership*: Ownership of personal property includes all rights related to the property. Possession of personal property includes only the right to control the property.

ACQUISITION OF PERSONAL PROPERTY BY INDIVIDUALS: There are several ways by which an individual can acquire personal property, including:

■ *Original Possession*: The first person to possess certain property, such as a wild animal, has original possession. Another example of this form of ownership is an original painting or other creation.

■ *Voluntary Transfers of Possession*: A voluntary transfer from an owner to another is one method of acquisition. Examples include transfers by purchase, gift, gift causa mortis, inheritance, and intestate succession. Three requirements for a valid gift are: 1) the donor intends to make a present gift; 2) the donor delivers the property to the donee; and 3) the donee accepts the gift. A gift causa mortis is a gift that is made while the donor is alive, but the gift is made in contemplation of immediate death. The requirements for a valid gift causa mortis are: 1) the donor intends to make a gift; 2) the gift is made in contemplation of death; and 3) the donor actually dies from the contemplated cause.

■ *Involuntary Transfers of Possession*: Personal property may be involuntarily transferred.

1) **Accession**: Accession occurs when a person adds value to property that the person does not own.

2) **Innocent trespasser**: Generally, title to the property remains with the original owner. However, an innocent trespasser may acquire title in the following situations: (a) due to work performed on the property, it has lost its original identity; (b) a great difference in value exists between the original property and the improved property; or (c) a completely new type of property has been created and the innocent trespasser added a major portion of the new property. If the original owner retains title to the property, the innocent trespasser can recover the value of the improvement. However, a willful trespasser cannot acquire title to the improved property.

3) **Confusion**: Confusion occurs when personal, fungible property of two or more individuals is mixed together and cannot be separated. If confusion occurs without any misconduct, the parties each receive an undivided interest. However, if misconduct is involved, different rules apply. If the new mixture cannot be divided, title passes to the innocent party, but if it can be divided, the wrongdoer is entitled to receive a portion of the new mixture.

4) **Lost, Mislaid, & Abandoned Property**: Lost property has been unintentionally lost by the true owner; the owner does not know where it is. Mislaid property is intentionally set somewhere by the owner, but the owner forgot to pick it up. Abandoned property is thrown away by its owner, with no intent to retain ownership. The person who finds property must determine if it is abandoned, rather than lost or mislaid. Courts consider three factors in deciding if an owner intended to give up possession: 1) location of the property, 2) value of the property, and 3) usefulness of the property.

5) **Property Lost at Sea and Salvage Rights**: Property lost at sea is subject to salvage, meaning compensation paid to persons who help save a ship or its cargo, in whole or in part, from impending danger, or recovered from actual loss, in cases of shipwreck recapture. Federal admiralty courts have authority to grant exclusive salvage rights and salvage awards to salvors who have the intention and the ability to save the property.

PROTECTION OF PERSONAL PROPERTY:

- *Conversion*: Conversion occurs when a person wrongfully takes or interferes with the property of another. The rightful owner may recover the property and sue for damages.
- *Escheat*: If the rightful owner of property cannot be found, the subject property escheats to the state.
- *Unclaimed Property Statutes*: Many states have replaced their escheat laws with unclaimed property statutes, which define when property is unclaimed and how it is to be disposed of.
- *Judicial Sale*: A judicial sale may take place in order to enforce a civil judgment. If a losing party does not pay a judgment ordered by a court, the prevailing party may execute upon the judgment and have the sheriff seize property of the losing party, which is then sold at a sheriff's sale.
- *Repossession of Property*: A secured party may repossess (retake) personal property if a debtor has defaulted on a secured obligation.

BAILMENTS OF PERSONAL PROPERTY: A bailment is a relationship that occurs when one person temporarily possesses personal property owned by another with the consent of the owner, and for a specific purpose. The person who holds the property is bailee, and the owner is the bailor.

- *Bailee's Duty of Care*: There are three bailment categories that determine the bailee's liability.
- *Classifications of Bailments*: The three types of bailments are:

  1) **A bailor benefit bailment**: This bailment solely benefits the bailor. The bailee is responsible for gross negligence in caring for the bailment property.

  2) **Mutual benefit bailment**: When both the bailor and bailee benefit, a mutual benefit bailment is established. In this situation, the bailee is liable for ordinary negligence.

  3) **Bailee benefit bailment**: Bailment benefits only the bailee. A bailee is liable for slight negligence.

- *Constructive Bailments*: Many states recognize constructive bailments. A constructive bailment arises even though there is no formal agreement between the property owner and the possessor of the property who lawfully came to possess it. A court may determine that the possessor should be treated as a constructive bailee in order to serve justice.
- *Limitations on a Bailee's Liability*: State laws place limits on a bailee's liability or, conversely, limit disclaimers of liability. Otherwise, the bailment contract may either increase or decrease liability, subject to any statutory limitations.
- *Termination of a Bailment*: A bailment terminates at the end of the period specified by the parties. If no ending point is discussed, the bailment relationship is terminable at will by either the bailor or the bailee. The bailment also terminates if the subject property is destroyed.
- *Bailee's Duty to Return the Property*: As a general rule, the bailee is required to return the bailment property to the bailor. Exceptions to this rule include: 1) the subject property is lost or stolen through no fault of the bailee; 2) the subject property is taken by legal process; 3) the property is claimed by someone with better legal title; or 4) the bailee takes a lien on the property.

STUDY HINTS FOR NRW CASE STUDIES

The following study hints may be helpful when resolving the NRW case studies.

NRW 42.1	➢ Since NRW its computer system, it had the exclusive right to use and protect it. ➢ Review the material dealing with conversion and Protection of Personal Property.
NRW 42.2	➢ Review the material on classifications of bailments, focusing on the duty of care of the bailee under bailment law.
NRW 42.3	➢ Review the material on contractual limitations of liability.

MATCHING EXERCISE

Select the term or concept that best matches a definition or statement set forth below. Each term or concept is the best match for only one definition or statement.

Terms and Concepts

a. Accession
b. Bailee
c. Bailment
d. Bailor

e. Confusion
f. Conversion
g. Escheat
h. Gift causa mortis

i. Judicial sale
j. Negotiable instruments
k. Possessory lien
l. Transfer tax

Definitions and Statements

_____ 1. Transferable documents used as credit instruments and as substitutes for money, including checks, drafts, promissory notes, and certificates of deposit.

_____ 2. Tax on the ability to transfer assets.

_____ 3. Security interest granted by law which allows a bailee to keep property if the bailor fails to pay for a bailment or for work performed on the property.

_____ 4. Owner of property that is the subject of a bailment.

_____ 5. Person who has possession of property under a bailment.

_____ 6. Wrongful taking or interference with the personal property of another.

_____ 7. Transfer of possession of personal property to another, with an understanding that the property shall be returned.

_____ 8. Gift made in expectation of immediate death.

_____ 9. Transfer of ownership of property to the government.

_____ 10. Improvement to the property of another.

_____ 11. Court-ordered sale of property.

_____ 12. Commingling of fungible property of two or more people .

COMPLETION EXERCISE

Fill in the blanks with the words that most accurately complete each statement.

1. A(n) _____ _____ _____ for value is a person who buys property in good faith, for a reasonable value, and without actual or constructive knowledge that there are problems with the transfer.

2. A valid transfer of a gift requires _____, _____, and _____.

3. In a bailor benefit bailment, the bailee is liable for only _____ _____ .

4. In a mutual benefit bailment, the bailee is liable for _____ _____.

5. In a bailee benefit bailment, the bailee is liable for _____ _____.

TRUE-FALSE EXERCISE

Write **T** if the statement is true, write **F** if the statement is false.

_____ 1. The law treats mislaid property the same as abandoned property.

_____ 2. A hunter kills a wild animal. The hunter has original possession of the animal.

_____ 3. A willful trespasser cannot acquire title to property by accession.

_____ 4. The finder of lost property is generally entitled to keep the property unless a statute requires that the property be given to the police.

_____ 5. Once property escheats to the state, the rightful owner cannot reclaim it.

_____ 6. A bailee generally forfeits a possessory lien by willingly returning the property to the bailor.

_____ 7. A bailment cannot be implied from the conduct of parties.

_____ 8. A valid gift requires that the donor presently intend to make the gift.

_____ 9. A bailment for the sole benefit of the bailor is created when a person gratuitously keeps and takes care of the property of another.

_____ 10. A bailee receives only possession of bailed goods; a bailee does not receive title to the goods.

APPLICATION OF CONCEPTS

MULTIPLE CHOICE QUESTIONS

_____ 1. Grandma, who was in good health, intended to make a present gift of her car to Mindy. Grandma wrote: "I give my Porsche to Mindy," and she gave Mindy the keys to the car, which was located 150 miles away. Prior to Mindy's taking possession of the car, Grandma died. Under these facts:
   a. Grandma did not make a valid inter vivos gift of the car to Mindy.
   b. Grandma made a valid inter vivos gift of the car to Mindy.
   c. Grandma made a valid gift causa mortis of the car to Mindy.
   d. Grandma only promised to make a gift, which promise was revoked when she died.

_____ 2. Dirk rented a tuxedo from Dapper Dan for $50 per night. This bailment is a:
   a. Bailment for the benefit of the bailor.
   b. Bailment for the benefit of the bailee.
   c. Mutual benefit bailment.
   d. Gratuitous bailment.

_____ 3. Select the correct answer.
a. Rosie rented a locker at the Airport and she put a bag in the locker. Rosie kept the locker key. In this case, the bag has been delivered and accepted by Airport, and Airport is a bailee.
b. Hill rents a boat to Dan. The boat is located at a lake 30 miles away. Hill gives Dan keys to the boat. Dan drives to the lake and takes possession of the boat. In this case, the boat has been delivered to and accepted by Dan, and Dan is a bailee.
c. Unknown to Lon, Jeff left a bike at Lon's house. In this case, the bike has been delivered to and accepted by Lon, and Lon is a bailee.
d. Ken parked a car in a self-service lot and Ken kept the keys. The parking lot is a bailee.

_____ 4. Roxie agreed to repair Tom's TV for $100. Pursuant to their contract, Tom delivered the TV to Roxie and Roxie properly repaired the TV. Under these facts:
a. If Tom refuses to pay the repair charge, Roxie has a lien on the TV and she can keep the TV until Tom pays the $100 charge.
b. Roxie is obligated to insure the TV while it is in her possession.
c. Roxie has a duty only to exercise slight care for the TV, and she will be liable for damage to the TV only if it results from her gross negligence.
d. Roxie is entitled to use the TV for her personal use.

SHORT ANSWER QUESTIONS

Answer the following questions, briefly explaining the reason for your answer.

1. Uncle Rich promised to give his niece, Cindy, $10,000 for her birthday. Cindy was so excited that she ran up $10,000 on her credit card. Outraged by Cindy's irresponsible behavior, Uncle Rich told Cindy that he would not give her anything. Can Cindy sue Uncle Rich for the money?

_____

_____

2. Mary brought her car to Fred's Garage for repairs. When Fred charged Mary $500 for the repairs, Mary thought it was too much and refused to pay. Fred told Mary that he would not give her the car until she paid. Did Fred act properly?

_____

_____

3. Ralph asked Judy to take his Ferrari to the garage for him. While driving to the garage, Judy could not help herself and drove the car at 100 mph when the posted speed limit was only 45 mph. Under state law, driving 30 miles above the speed limit is considered reckless (grossly negligent) driving. Judy wrecked the car. Is Judy liable to Ralph for the damage to his car?

_____

_____

4. Jethro was in the hospital and he believed he would die. He told Sally May, his girlfriend, that he wanted her to have his car when he died. Sally May immediately took possession of the car. Jethro recovered. However, two weeks after being released from the hospital, Jethro was struck by a hit and run driver and he died shortly afterwards. Who is entitled to the car - Sally May or Jethro's estate?

_____

_____

CASE PROBLEMS

Answer the following case problems, explaining your answers.

1. Acme Rentals rents equipment. Its lease contract states that it is not liable for any injuries or property loss that may be caused by its equipment. The contract also states that any person renting equipment is liable for any damage or loss to the equipment, regardless of the reason for the casualty or loss. Harry rented two cement mixers from Acme. One was stolen by a third party. The other mixer tipped over and fell on Harry's foot, breaking it. It tipped over because an Acme employee had negligently failed to replace a brace that had previously broken off. (a) What type of bailments are involved in this case? (b) Is Harry liable for the stolen mixer? (c) Is Acme liable for Harry's broken foot?

_____

_____

_____

_____

2. Jake wanted to go water skiing, but he did not have any skis. Jake's friend, Luis, lent Jake a pair of skis. While Jake was skiing, a defective foot support on one ski accidentally tore loose, causing Jake to fall and break his arm. Luis did not know that the foot support was defective. However, Luis did not inspect the skis before lending them to Jake. (a) What type of bailment is involved in this case? (b) Describe the duty that Luis owed to Jake. (c) Is Luis liable to Jake for Jake's injuries? (d) Is Jake liable to Luis for damage to the skis?

_____

_____

_____

_____

CHAPTER 43   Intellectual Property, Computers, and the Law

CHAPTER REVIEW

INTRODUCTION: Intellectual property is intangible property that is the product of human creativity.

COPYRIGHTS: Copyright law protects original works of authorship fixed in any tangible medium of expression that can be perceived, reproduced, or otherwise communicated, such as literary works, paintings, and films. Copyright law only protects the expression of ideas; not the ideas themselves.

- *Protection and Infringement*: A copyright entitles its owner to reproduce the work, prepare derivative works, distribute copies of the work, and perform and publicly display the work. Infringement of a copyright is shown by evidence that the defendant had access to the work and the defendant's work shows substantial similarities to the owner's work. "Fair use" is the most common defense to an infringement action, since it is permissible to use copyrighted work for certain limited purposes.
- *Remedies*: If infringement is proven, the court may order an injunction, the destruction of infringing items, and payment of damages.
- *International Dimensions*: Under the Berne Convention, each member nation must extend its laws to protect citizens of other members nations and works originally published in a member nation must be protected in all member states without having to comply with any additional formalities.
- *Computers*: The 1980 Computer Software Copyright Act allows computer programs to be copyrighted.

PATENTS: Patent law protects inventions, and gives inventors the exclusive right to their inventions. Patentable inventions include a process, machine, manufacture, composition of matter, and useful improvements thereof. To be patented, an invention must be 1) original, 2) useful, and 3) nonobvious. Utility patents last for 20 years and design patents last for 14 years. After expiration of a patent, others can use the previously patented invention in any way they wish.

- *Protection and Infringement*: There are three types of patent infringements: direct, indirect, and contributory. A direct infringement involves a person who makes, uses, or sells a patented invention. An indirect infringement involves inducing others to infringe. A contributory infringement occurs when a party sells a component of a patented invention knowing the component is specially made for use with the patented item.
- *Remedies*: If infringement is proven, the court may order an injunction and payment of damages.
- *International Dimensions*: Under the Paris Convention, like the Berne Convention, member nations must honor the patent laws of other member nations.
- *Computers*: The Supreme Court has held that some types of computer programs are patentable.

TRADEMARKS: Trademarks are used to identify goods, and trademark law prevents others from using the same or deceptively similar name to identify their goods.

- *Protection and Infringement*: A trademark can be any word, name, symbol, device, or a combination thereof that is used to identify and distinguish the services or goods of one party from those of another. A trademark can be protected only if it is distinctive, meaning that it is arbitrary, fanciful, or suggestive. Generic or descriptive marks or marks using people's surnames cannot be protected unless they have acquired a "secondary meaning." Trademarks are protected from uses that bear a "likelihood of confusion" for consumers. "Fair use" is a defense to a trademark infringement claim.

- *Remedies*: Remedies include injunction, return of profits, damages, and punitive damages.

- *International Dimensions*: Under the Paris Convention, as with patents, member nations must honor the trademark laws of other member nations.

TRADE SECRETS: A trade secret is: 1) secret business information that gives its owner a competitive advantage 2) because the information is not known to competitors and is difficult or costly to acquire.
- *Protection*: Factors considered when deciding whether material is a trade secret include: 1) extent to which the information is known outside the owner's business; 2) extent it is known by employees; 3) steps taken to guard the information's secrecy; 4) value of the information to the owner and competitors; 5) money expended in developing the information; and 6) difficulty of others acquiring the information.
- *Liability*: Liability for misappropriating trade secrets may be based on either a breach of contract theory and or wrongful acquisition theory.
- *Remedies*: If misappropriation is proven, the court may order an injunction and payment of damages.
- *Computers*: Trade secret law protects computer programs. Employers should keep software developments secret and ensure that employees sign noncompetition and confidentiality agreements.

UNFAIR COMPETITION: Some extreme forms of competition (and infringements) are considered unlawful under the common law and/or statutes. "Palming-off," false advertising, and product disparagement are considered unfair competition. Remedies generally include injunctions and damages. Unfair competition laws may protect particularly strong marks from being used by others for a noncompetitive use if this use may lessen (dilute) the value or distinctiveness of the mark over time, (e.g., using a strong product mark to identify sexually-explicit products or services).

THE SEMICONDUCTOR CHIP PROTECTION ACT OF 1984: This law prohibits "reverse engineering" that seeks to copy computer chips or their protected components.

STUDY HINTS FOR NRW CASE STUDIES

The following study hints may be helpful when resolving the NRW case studies.

NRW 43.1	➤ Review the material on copyrights and copyright infringement. ➤ . Also, consider the issue of unfair competition and antidilution.
NRW 43.2	➤ Review the law relating to trademarks, including generic marks and secondary meaning. ➤ Also review the material relating to unfair competition and palming off.
NRW 43.3	➤ Contrast the duration for utility patents versus the potentially unlimited for protection of trade secrets under unfair competition law.

REVIEW OF KEY TERMS AND CONCEPTS

MATCHING EXERCISE

Select the term or concept that best matches a definition or statement set forth below. Each term or concept is the best match for only one definition or statement.

Terms and Concepts

a. Contributory infringement
b. Copyright
c. Direct infringement
d. Fair use

e. Indirect infringement
f. Infringement
g. Misappropriation
h. Patent

i. Proprietary
j. Trademark
k. Trade secret
l. Unfair competition

Definitions and Statements

_____ 1. Protection for creative works, such as books, movies, and theatrical productions.

_____ 2. Unauthorized use of a patent, trademark, or copyright.

_____ 3. Protection for novel, useful, and nonobvious inventions.

_____ 4. Making, using, or selling a patented invention without the holder's permission.

_____ 5. Sale of a material component of a patented invention, knowing that the component was specially made or adapted for use with the invention.

_____ 6. Inducing others to infringe upon a patent.

_____ 7. Word or symbol that identifies the source of a particular product.

_____ 8. Confidential business information that gives a party a competitive advantage over others.

_____ 9. Unauthorized use or appropriation of a trade secret.

_____ 10. Private, exclusive ownership.

_____ 11. Wrongful activities including palming-off, false advertising, and product disparagement.

_____ 12. Limited, permissible use of copyrighted and trademarked material.

COMPLETION EXERCISE

Fill in the blanks with the words that most accurately complete each statement.

1. International uses of copyrighted material are protected by the
_____.

2. Utility patents last for _____ years and design patents last for
_____ years.

3. An _____ may be ordered by the court to stop an infringement.

4. Trademark holders are protected from uses of their material that would cause a _____
_____ _____ for consumers.

5. List four factors that courts consider in order to determine whether information is a trade secret:

a. _____.

b. _____.

c. _____.

d. _____.

TRUE-FALSE EXERCISE

Write **T** if the statement is true, write **F** if the statement is false.

_____ 1. Trademarks protect inventions, such as a new machine or tool.

_____ 2. Patents may be used to protect certain artificially created life forms.

_____ 3. Software may be protected by copyright law or unfair competition law.

_____ 4. A new cartoon cannot be copyrighted because it is not a serious literary work.

_____ 5. The U.S. Constitution gives the states the right to regulate copyrights.

_____ 6. Under the Paris Convention, member nations must honor the patent laws of other member nations.

_____ 7. Ideas may be copyrighted so long as they are original.

_____ 8. "Fair use" may be a defense to a trademark infringement claim.

_____ 9. There are no international treaties that protect copyrights. Therefore, a person in the United States is free to copy works created by others in foreign countries.

_____ 10. Trade secrets are protected for only 20 years.

APPLICATION OF CONCEPTS

MULTIPLE CHOICE QUESTIONS

_____ 1. Ken invented a new type of mathematical calculator that he called "Wiser Guyser." Under these facts, the name "Wiser Guyser":
   a. Can be protected by registration for a patent.
   b. Can be protected by registration for a copyright.
   c. Can be protected by registration for a trademark.
   d. Cannot be protected.

_____ 2. Carl invented a new eating instrument for people who like to eat fast: a five-pronged fork. (Normal forks have only four prongs). Under these facts, can Carl patent his new fork?
   a. Yes, it is novel.
   b. Yes, it is useful.
   c. Yes, it is both novel and useful.
   d. No, it is an obvious derivative of an existing product, the four-pronged fork.

_____ 3. Which of the following names can be registered for trademark protection?
    a. "Motor oil," the name of a product that is used to lubricate engines.
    b. "Hot sauce," the name for a spicy food additive.
    c. "DuraBond," the name for a new type of glue.
    d. "Southern food," the name for food from the southern part of the United States.

_____ 4. Benders, a bar and grill, has been in business for many years, and it has an excellent reputation. John wanted his restaurant to be a success, so he remodeled his restaurant so the storefront looked the same as the unique design of Benders' establishment and he erected a sign over his restaurant reading "Benters." In this case, John is liable for:
    a. Patent infringement.
    b. Copyright infringement.
    c. Theft.
    d. Unfair competition.

SHORT ANSWER QUESTIONS

Answer the following questions, briefly explaining the reason for your answer.

1. Bill purchased a copy of a copyrighted computer program for $350. Bill made a copy of the program and gave it to Kim. Has Bill violated the law?

_____

_____

2. Selma wrote a computer program and copyrighted it under U.S. copyright law. Selma allowed a German to review the program, but the German firm stated that they were not interested in the program. Unknown to Selma, the German firm duplicated the program and is selling it in Germany. Discuss Selma's legal rights.

_____

_____

3. For many years, Wowee Corp. has manufactured and sold high-quality toy slot cars known as "Wowee Toys." Wowee has registered this trademark. One year ago, Waui Enterprises, a travel agency, commenced business and started marketing cruise packages called "Waui Cruises." Has Waui Enterprises violated Wowee Corp.'s trademark?

_____

_____

4. Jesse created a fictional tale about the life of a squirrel who became king of the animal world. He did not write it down, but instead told it neighborhood children. His tale was so popular with little children that he then wrote it down. Could Jesse have copyrighted his original tale? Can Jesse copyright the written version of this tale?

_____

_____

CASE PROBLEMS

Answer the following case problems, explaining your answers.

1. Over a five-year period, Jackson Corp. spent considerable time and money to develop a private list of 200,000 area homeowners. This list tracks home values, year of construction, and last home-repair project. This list has proven invaluable for marketing its home-improvement services. (a) Can Jackson protect its exclusive right to this list? (b) What is the best way for Jackson to protect this list? (c) If a competitor stole this list from Jackson and used it in the competitor's business, what remedies would Jackson have?

_____

_____

_____

_____

2. In 1990, Hillary Thompson began selling enormous pieces of sour ball candy called "Thompson's Giant Sour Ball Candies." By the 2000s, Hillary's candies had become nationally known, and people thought only of her candy when they heard the words "Thompson's Giant Sour Ball Candies." (a) Was Hillary entitled to trademark protection for the name of her candy when she first began to sell it? (b) Was Hillary entitled to trademark protection for the name of her candy by the 2000s? (c) What would be the best way for Hillary to protect her trademark?

_____

_____

_____

_____

CHAPTER 44   Wills, Estates, and Trusts

CHAPTER REVIEW

THE TRANSFER OF AN ESTATE: Everyone has an estate, no matter how small. States govern the transfer of estates under probate codes, which may vary greatly from state to state.

WILLS: A will specifies who should inherit property, can appoint a personal representative, and can name a guardian for minor children.
- *Formal Wills*: Formal wills are written, signed by the testator, and witnessed by at least two people.
- *Holographic Wills*: Holographic wills are valid if written and signed in the testator's own handwriting.
- *Nuncupative Wills*: Nuncupative wills are oral, and can usually dispose of only personal property.
- *Matching Wills*: Mutual wills are separate wills with matching provisions. These are appropriate for a husband and wife. In joint wills, two people sign the same document.

REQUIREMENTS FOR A VALID WILL: To execute a will a person must have testamentary capacity. This requires that a person; 1) understand the nature of his or her assets; 2) know who his or her close relatives are; and 3) understand the purpose of a will.

TESTAMENTARY DISPOSITIONS AND RESTRICTIONS: Generally, a will may exclude family members; however, spouses have the right to a share of the estate. There are limits on giving to charity and the duration of trusts. A will can be ignored if it was signed under fraud, duress, or undue influence.

INTESTATE SUCCESSION: Intestacy statutes govern the distribution for people who have no will, have an invalid will, or whose will does not completely dispose of their property.

PROBATE AND ESTATE ADMINISTRATION: Probate determines the validity of a will and ensures that estates are properly administered. Personal representatives administer the estate and owe fiduciary duties to the beneficiaries. The representative must notify creditors, pay debts, pay any estate taxes, and distribute the remaining assets according to the will.

AVOIDING PROBATE: Advantages: May reduce time and costs, and provides privacy. Disadvantages: The estate will still pay taxes, there may be more paperwork, and creditors will not be discharged for failing to file a claim against the estate.

TRANSFER TAXES: The federal government taxes the transfer of property by an estate tax, gift tax, and generation-skipping transfer tax. States have gift and estate or inheritance taxes.

RETIREMENT PLANS: Pension plans have both income tax and transfer tax consequences. Employer plans may be defined-benefit or defined-contribution plans.

DURABLE POWERS OF ATTORNEY AND LIVING WILLS: A durable power of attorney appoints a person to make medical decisions in certain situations. A living will states a person's wishes concerning life-prolonging medical treatment.

TRUSTS DEFINED: A fiduciary relationship where specific property is transferred to the care of a trustee.

EXPRESS TRUSTS: A trust must have a creator, a trustee, and one or more beneficiaries.

- *Private Trusts*: Trusts created for an individual and having a limited duration.

- *Charitable Trusts*: Trusts where money is given to a charity tax-free.

- *Additional Types of Express Trusts*: Other trusts include accumulation (reinvests income), sprinkling (trustee determines which beneficiary receives income and how much), spendthrift (protects the beneficiary from imprudent spending), and discretionary (trustee has discretion to pay or not pay the beneficiaries).

ADVANTAGES OF TRUSTS: Trusts are flexible, and payments to the trust may be spread out over time.

DISADVANTAGES OF TRUSTS: If the trust is irrevocable, the creator cannot withdraw money for emergencies.

SELECTION OF TRUSTEES AND EXECUTORS: Corporate fiduciaries (trustees and executors) do not die, and generally have the expertise to serve in these capacities. However, corporate fiduciaries charge fees.

DUTIES OF TRUSTEES AND EXECUTORS: Trustees must preserve trust property and make it productive. As fiduciaries, trustees must act with the care, skill, and prudence of a businessperson managing his or her own property. An executor's duties are similar to those of a trustee. Both parties are fiduciaries of the beneficiaries. The executor files estate and inheritance tax returns, pays taxes that are due, and files accounts with the probate court.

IMPLIED TRUSTS: Implied trusts are created by operation of law or imposed by courts.

- *Resulting Trusts*: Arise when an owner fails to make a complete disposition of property or places title to property in the name of another without intending to make a gift.

- *Constructive Trusts*: An equitable remedy to redress a wrong and prevent unjust enrichment.

STUDY HINTS FOR NRW CASE STUDIES

The following study hints may be helpful when resolving the NRW case studies.

NRW 44.1	➢ Consider the advantages and disadvantages of a formal will. ➢ Also consider advantages and disadvantages of a trust.
NRW 44.2	➢ Review the section on " Durable Powers of Attorney and Living Wills."
NRW 44.3	➢ Ask yourself what the trust should accomplish. Should the trust reinvest income; should the trustee have discretion; should the children be protected from imprudent spending?

REVIEW OF KEY TERMS AND CONCEPTS

MATCHING EXERCISE

Select the term or concept that best matches a definition or statement set forth below. Each term or concept is the best match for only one definition or statement.

Terms and Concepts

a. Affidavit

b. Codicil

c. Community property

d. Decedent

e. Domicile

f. Honorary trust

g. Intestate share

h. Personal representative

I. Probate

j. Probate codes

k. Residuary clause

l. Testamentary capacity

m. Testator

n. Testatrix

o. Trust

Definitions and Statements

_____ 1. A clause that disposes of the remainder of an estate.

_____ 2. The procedure for verifying that a will is authentic and should be implemented.

_____ 3. Portion of the estate that a person is entitled to inherit if there is no valid will.

_____ 4. State statutes that deal with the estates of incompetents, people who have made wills, and people who have died.

_____ 5. An arrangement in which one person or business holds property and invests it for another.

_____ 6. A special form of joint ownership between husband and wife.

_____ 7. A man who makes a will.

_____ 8. A woman who makes a will.

_____ 9. Written statement made under oath.

_____ 10. A person who manages the financial affairs of the estate.

_____ 11. A person who has died.

_____ 12. An arrangement that does not meet trust requirements and thus is not enforceable as a trust, although it may be carried out voluntarily.

_____ 13. One's permanent legal residence.

_____ 14. Sufficient mental capability or sanity to execute a valid will.

_____ 15. A separate written document that modifies an existing will.

COMPLETION EXERCISE

Fill in the blanks with the words that most accurately complete each statement.

1. _____ are persons who actually inherit property from the decedent.

2. The _____-_____ doctrine permits a court to modify a trust in order to follow the creator's charitable wishes as closely as possible.

3. The legal document that specifies the recipients of a trust, their interests, and how the trust should be managed is called a _____ _____.

4. Lineal descendants, such as children and grandchildren, are called _____.

5. The legal document that specifies how a person feels about life-prolonging medical treatment if the person should become very ill with no hope of recovery is called a _____ _____.

TRUE-FALSE EXERCISE

Write **T** if the statement is true, write **F** if the statement is false.

_____ 1.   In most states, a will must leave assets to the testator's family members and other relatives.

_____ 2.   In most states, a formal will must be witnessed by two disinterested persons.

_____ 3.   Probate of a will is an optional procedure; a will is generally effective without probate.

_____ 4.   Property of a person who dies without a will is distributed according to intestate succession.

_____ 5.   A constructive trust arises by operation of law and serves to prevent unjust enrichment or redress a wrong.

_____ 6.   If a person is severely ill, a living will allows that person's property to be distributed before the person dies.

_____ 7.   In many states, a creditor forfeits the right to be paid if the creditor fails to file a claim with a decedent's probate estate within the time required by law.

_____ 8.   Courts generally will award intestate shares to pretermitted heirs on the grounds that the omission was a mistake.

_____ 9.   A decedent's debts must be paid by an estate prior to distributions to beneficiaries.

_____ 10. A personal representative must be a family member.

APPLICATION OF CONCEPTS

MULTIPLE CHOICE QUESTIONS

_____ 1.   Arthur used drugs heavily for years. Due to his drug use, Arthur suffered permanent mental impairment, and he could not recall to whom he was related or what he owned. Nonetheless, Arthur executed a properly signed and witnessed will. The will left everything to Joe, a recent acquaintance. Nothing was left to Arthur's daughter, about whom Arthur had forgotten. Under these facts:
   a.   The will is invalid because a testator cannot disinherit a child.
   b.   The will is invalid because Arthur did not have testamentary capacity.
   c.   The will is valid. A testator may disinherit a child, and a will is valid if it is properly signed and witnessed.
   d.   a and b.

_____ 2.   Niles is trustee of a trust. The trust beneficiaries are Niles's nieces. The trust has $100,000 cash. In most states, what would Niles be permitted to do as trustee?
   a.   Niles may invest the cash in U.S. Treasury bonds and corporate stocks.
   b.   Niles may make an interest-free loan of the trust's cash to his business.
   c.   Niles may delegate all of his duties under the trust to his wife.
   d.   Both a and c.

_____ 3. While single, Murray executed a will, leaving his estate to his parents. Several years later, Murray married Nancy. Two years later, Nancy gave birth to Murray's son. During that same year, Murray mistakenly tore his will in half, thinking it was waste paper. Under the laws of at least some states, which event may have revoked Murray's will (in whole or in part)?

    a. Murray's marriage to Nancy.

    b. The birth of Murray's son.

    c. Murray's tearing of the will.

    d. Both a and b.

_____ 4. Select the correct answer.

    a. Testator typed a will, signed it, but no one witnessed his signature. In most states, the will is a valid formal will.

    b. Testator wrote out a will in his own handwriting, signed it, but no one witnessed his signature. In most states, the will is a valid holographic will.

    c. Testator typed a will, signed it, and had two persons witness his signature. Under the will, both witnesses were to receive substantial amounts of money on Testator's death. In most states, the will is a valid formal will.

    d. Both a and c.

SHORT ANSWER QUESTIONS

Answer the following questions, briefly explaining the reason for your answer.

1. Roger is married to Paula. Their marriage has been on the rocks, and Roger decides not to leave anything to Paula in his will. If Roger dies while still married to Paula, can Paula claim anything against Roger's estate? (Assume Roger died in a common-law state.)

_____

_____

2. Ted's will states that his estate should be divided equally between his two children, Marcy and Leslie. Marcy and Leslie have since died. Marcy has left two children, and Leslie has left four. How will the estate be divided using per capita with representation?

_____

_____

3. Mike, a rich and successful writer, would like to leave money to his nephew, Mark. However, Mike is concerned that Mark is financially irresponsible. Advise Mike on how he should structure the gift to Mark.

_____

_____

4. Jake is rich and eccentric. He has $10 million that he would like to place in a trust to benefit all of his descendants forever. Can Jake create a trust that will last forever?

_____

_____

CASE PROBLEMS

Answer the following case problems, explaining your answers.

1. Abe died intestate, leaving an estate of $200,000. He is survived by a wife, three children, and a cousin. Assume Abe died in a state that follows the Uniform Probate Code procedure for intestate succession. How much will each of the following persons receive: (a) Abe's wife? (b) Abe's three children? (c) Abe's cousin?

_____

_____

_____

_____

2. Luis created a trust and named Mary as trustee. The trust deed does not specify whether it is revocable or irrevocable. While Mary served as trustee, she irresponsibly made speculative investments that caused the trust to lose money. (a) Under the law of *most* states, is the trust revocable or irrevocable? (b) Did Mary breach any duty? (c) What remedies are available for Mary's conduct?

_____

_____

_____

_____

STUDY GUIDE ANSWERS

CHAPTER 1 - INTRODUCTION TO LAW

MATCHING EXERCISE

1.	l	6. a	11. e
2.	h	7. d	12. c
3.	i	8. g	13. f
4.	k	9. m	14. o
5.	n	10. b	15. j

COMPLETION EXERCISE

1. Enforceability
2. preventive law
3. police power
4. order
5. Commutative justice, distributive justice

TRUE-FALSE EXERCISE

1. F	2. T	3. T	4. T	5. T
6. F	7. T	8. T	9. F	10. T

MULTIPLE CHOICE QUESTIONS

1. b	2. c	3. d	4. d

SHORT ANSWER QUESTIONS

1. Yes. Under the doctrine of *stare decisis*, lower courts are generally obligated to follow existing precedents.
2. The Jacksons can sue under the civil law. They should request an injunction.
3. Senator Adams' position represents the theory of natural law. Senator Bend's perspective reflects the sociological theory of law.
4. Lexington may search out an attorney by checking the state bar association directory of *Martindale-Hubbell*. Also talking to friends or business associates who have had similar problems may be helpful.

CASE PROBLEMS

1. (a) This law is an example of commutative justice - everyone is treated the same. (b) This law serves the needs to be reasonable, definite, and practical. (c) This law in not flexible.

2. (a) Attorney fee arrangements may be hourly (fee is based on an hourly rate); contingent fee (fee is equal to a percentage of what the attorney recovers); or a flat fee (a one-time fee). (b) An hourly fee would be appropriate. A flat-rate fee would be difficult to determine and a contingent fee would similarly tend to either over compensate or inadequately compensate the attorney.

CHAPTER 2 - BUSINESS ETHICS

MATCHING EXERCISE

1. k
2. i
3. c
4. f

5. g
6. j
7. e
8. h

9. l
10. d
11. a
12. b

COMPLETION EXERCISE

1. Ethics
2. Morals
3. veil of ignorance
4. amoral
5. different from

TRUE-FALSE EXERCISE

1. T
6. T

2. F
7. T

3. T
8. F

4. T
9. T

5. T
10. F

MULTIPLE CHOICE QUESTIONS

1. d
2. b
3. a
4. d

SHORT ANSWER QUESTIONS

1. *Caveat emptor*, "let the buyer beware."
2. Egoism. From a financial perspective, not recalling the jackhammer is perceived to be in the company's best financial interests.
3. Rule utilitarianism. Pal's wants to produce the most good for its universe, its employees. Complying with all laws is perceived to be the best way to do this.
4. The general manager is choosing to be loyal to his employer, which is generally considered to be moral conduct in our society. However, it is doubtful that this loyalty accomplishes a morally right consequence in this situation.

CASE PROBLEMS

1. (a) Gordon acted morally because he acted in accordance with his individual belief's regarding what is right and wrong. (b) However, Gordon's acted unethically, as measured by society's views regarding what is proper or improper conduct. (c) In any event, Gordon acted illegally; the legal system had declared it unlawful to sell cigarettes to minors and Gordon was legally bound to obey this rule.

2. (a) The companies in this case acted solely in a reactive manner; they undertook to change only after their legal problems arose. (b) Clearly, the companies could have taken a more proactive approach; curtailing their activities, conducting tests to discover or verify harm. (c) The companies acted unethically in this case. Society does not condone this type of behavior.

CHAPTER 3 - INTERNATIONAL LAW

MATCHING EXERCISE

1.	j	6.	b	11.	f
2.	a	7.	c	12.	l
3.	o	8.	n	13.	g
4.	d	9.	i	14.	h
5.	e	10.	m	15.	k

COMPLETION EXERCISE

1. Foreign Corrupt Practices Act
2. International Court of Justice
3. Dumping
4. UNCITRAL
5. Any three of the following: agent; distributor; franchise; foreign subsidiary.

TRUE-FALSE EXERCISE

1. F		2. T		3. F		4. T		5. F	
6. T		7. F		8. T		9. T		10. F	

MULTIPLE CHOICE QUESTIONS

1. c	2. d	3. b	4. b

SHORT ANSWER QUESTIONS

1. Gill should be concerned with the EU competition laws. Gill can obtain a negative clearance (exemption) from the EC Commission.
2. Two approaches are: a) cash in advance, and b) require a letter of credit as payment.
3. ArmorTech must obtain an appropriate export license from the U.S. government. Because of the product's military significance, its export may be limited or banned.
4. NAFTA, a trade agreement between the United States, Mexico, and Canada. The World Trade Organization that can issue binding regulation relating to the international trade of many countries.

CASE PROBLEMS

1. (a) Bill should study the laws and culture of Ruritania. For instance, his style of negotiations would be considered rude and offensive in Ruritania and many other countries. Also, the possibility of nationalization and political unrest should never be overlooked.

2. (a) No. U.S. antitrust laws do not generally apply to the foreign conduct of foreign companies.
(b) Yes. U.S. antitrust laws may be enforced against the Abuk companies in U.S. courts if their conduct violates U.S. law and their conduct has a substantial impact on U.S. domestic commerce.

CHAPTER 4 - THE AMERICAN LEGAL SYSTEM AND COURT JURISDICTION

MATCHING EXERCISE

1. o	6. c	11. a
2. m	7. g	12. j
3. h	8. d	13. b
4. l	9. e	14. n
5. k	10. i	15. f

COMPLETION EXERCISE

1. case, controversy
2. standing
3. jurisdiction
4. *in personam*
5. long-arm

TRUE-FALSE EXERCISE

1. F	2. T	3. F	4. T	5. F
6. F	7. F	8. F	9. F	10. T

MULTIPLE CHOICE QUESTIONS

1. b	2. c	3. c	4. c

SHORT ANSWER QUESTIONS

1. No. Unless authorized by statute for violation of a particular law, persons do not have standing to sue for violation of a law unless they establish that they have been personally harmed by the law's violation.
2. No. This is a political question, which the legislature, not the courts, must decide.
3. (a) Substantive law - it involves a question of the parties' legal rights and duties. (b) Procedural law - it involves how the lawsuit must be initiated.
4. It is an invalid *ex post facto* law to the extent that it seeks to retroactively criminalize past conduct. It is a valid exercise of the state's police power to the extent that it applies prospectively.

CASE PROBLEMS

1. (a) Yes. Both parties are "doing business" in Nebraska. They are conducting an on-going business, taking advantage of Nebraska law. (b) Yes. The plaintiff can use the Nebraska long-arm statute, if necessary, to serve process on TWC and Ramon outside of the state. They allegedly committed a tort in Nebraska, which is a generally sufficient ground for invoking the long-arm statute. Service on the defendants will give the Nebraska court *in personam* jurisdiction over the defendants.

2. Yes. Janet and Carson are residents of different states, establishing diversity jurisdiction. In addition, the lawsuit involves more than $75,000, the second element necessary invoking the jurisdiction of U.S. district courts based on diversity.

CHAPTER 5 - CONSTITUTIONAL REGULATION OF BUSINESS

MATCHING EXERCISE

1. o
2. g
3. h
4. l
5. j

6. m
7. a
8. k
9. n
10. d

11. e
12. i
13. b
14. f
15. c

COMPLETION EXERCISE

1. Administrative agencies
2. economic; social
3. just compensation
4. substantive; procedural
5. rational basis; compelling state interest; substantially important state interest

TRUE-FALSE EXERCISE

1. T
6. T

2. T
7. T

3. F
8. F

4. F
9. F

5. F
10. T

MULTIPLE CHOICE QUESTIONS

1. d

2. a

3. b

4. b

SHORT ANSWER QUESTIONS

1. Yes. The diner is serving to out-of-state customers and thus has an impact on the national economy.
2. No. The law is narrowly tailored to protect the government's substantially important goal of protecting people from unqualified lawyers.
3. Yes. The government has deprived the landowner of the property's present use.
4. Yes. This law is an unreasonable and irrational way of advancing a legitimate government interest.

CASE PROBLEMS

1. (a) Yes, because Amax does business in several states. (b) Yes. The commerce clause allows the federal government to regulate interstate activities. (c) Colorado may regulate Amax in those areas where it has concurrent power with the federal government. (d) Colorado may not pass laws that discriminate against Amax because it is an out-of-state company.

2. This is a government regulation that results in invidious discrimination. The Level 2 Test applies because the law implicates a suspect classification. This law does not pass this test because there are less burdensome ways of accomplishing this objective.

CHAPTER 6 – DISPUTE RESOLUTION

MATCHING EXERCISE

1.	j	7.	x	13.	o	19.	t
2.	f	8.	u	14.	i	20.	v
3.	w	9.	p	15.	s	21.	e
4.	b	10.	h	16.	d	22.	k
5.	n	11.	a	17.	r	23.	q
6.	l	12.	g	18.	c	24.	m

COMPLETION EXERCISE

1. mediator
2. Uniform Arbitration Act
3. facilitate; evaluate
4. Advisory arbitration
5. fast; relatively inexpensive; experts determine parties' rights.
6. Discovery
7. judgment
8. cross-examination
9. appeal
10. depositions, interrogatories, production of documents and things, physical or mental examination, request for admissions

TRUE-FALSE EXERCISE

1.	F	2.	F	3.	T	4.	T	5.	F
6.	F	7.	T	8.	T	9.	T	10.	F
11.	F	12.	F	13.	T	14.	F	15.	F
16.	F	17.	T	18.	T	19.	T	20.	T

MULTIPLE CHOICE QUESTIONS

1.	c		5.	b
2.	a		6.	d
3.	d		7.	c
4.	a		8.	a

SHORT ANSWER QUESTIONS

1. Hin should review the facts relating to the occurrence, writing down important points, including the names and addresses of witnesses etc. Also, he should bring with him any potentially relevant documents.

2. The fee agreement for the living will is a flat fee, meaning a fixed fee. The second fee is a contingent fee. In the first arrangement, the attorney will receive $120, and in the second the attorney will receive 40% of the amount, if any, that is awarded to Chad.

3. The jury will determine questions of fact, including whether there was a contract and whether the vegetables were tainted. The jury will also determine the amount of damages, if any.

4. The judgment of a trial court is not a final judgment. If the judgment is upheld on appeal, the doctrine of *res judicata* will bar the parties from again litigating the same claims.

5. Neuron and BioMed will jointly select an arbitrator. The arbitrator should be familiar with the law and arbitration, and also have an expertise in this area of science.

6. The mediator could use caucusing (meeting separately with each party) or shuttle mediation (going back and forth between the parties, carrying proposals and comments).

7. In a minitrial, a neutral party, such as a retired judge, is hired to hear the matter outside of court. Each side presents their side of the story, using experts if appropriate. Executives from each company attend the minitrial and, following its conclusion, the executives meet to try to resolve the matter.

8. In most states, Gina can sue her former landlord in small claims court.

CASE PROBLEMS

1. (a) Mediation would allow the parties to avoid litigation, saving both time and money. This approach would also allow the parties to potentially work out a compromise solution. (b) One possible solution would be to restrict the hours during which the grinder is used.

2. (a) The purpose of summary judgement is to resolve a lawsuit before trial when there are no genuine issues of material fact to be decided. (b) Summary judgment is not appropriate in this case because the issue of who ran the red light is an important, disputed fact. (c) Under the restated facts, summary judgment would be appropriate because there are no factual issues, only legal issues.

CHAPTER 7 - TORTS

MATCHING EXERCISE

1. f
2. k
3. b
4. a

5. h
6. e
7. d
8. l

9. g
10. c
11. j
12. i

COMPLETION EXERCISE

1. private (civil); public (criminal)
2. Intentional
3. material fact
4. false imprisonment
5. duty, breach, proximate (legal) causation, harm/injury

TRUE-FALSE EXERCISE

1. F
6. T

2. T
7. T

3. T
8. T

4. T
9. T

5. T
10. F

MULTIPLE CHOICE QUESTIONS

1. d
2. d
3. c
4. d

SHORT ANSWER QUESTIONS

1. Defamation (slander). Requirements include a false statement of fact, intentional communication to a third person, and harm to reputation.
2. No. Although Fran and Northern would have committed the tort of false imprisonment under the common law, states have statutes that shield them from liability in situations such as this.
3. Yes. Dan committed an unlawful, offensive touching of Jessie.
4. Yes. She has committed the tort of trade disparagement. She wrongfully injured the reputation of the Blue Bull Cafe.

CASE PROBLEMS

1. Will has committed fraud. Will intentionally misstated a material fact, intending for persons such as Lilly to rely upon his misstatements, and Lilly did reasonably rely on the untruths to her detriment.

2. (a) In this case, WDC owed three duties in particular to the homeowners: not to expose them to an unreasonable risk of harm (negligence); not to use its land in such a way that it would unreasonably interfere with the homeowners' right to enjoy their homes (nuisance); and not to come upon the property of the homeowners (or put into motion things that would come upon the homeowners' property (trespass). (b) WDC has liability under nuisance law. Its liability for negligence and trespass is likely, but not certain. Foreseeability and proximate causation are the most difficult issues for all of these torts.

CHAPTER 8 - CRIMES AND BUSINESS

MATCHING EXERCISE

1. h	6. k	11. a
2. d	7. g	12. b
3. o	8. f	13. i
4. n	9. j	14. l
5. m	10. c	15. e

COMPLETION EXERCISE

1. persons; property
2. act; mental state
3. RICO
4. probable cause
5. Duress; insanity; intoxication; justification

TRUE-FALSE EXERCISE

1. T	2. T	3. F	4. T	5. T
6. F	7. F	8. F	9. F	10. T

MULTIPLE CHOICE QUESTIONS

1. c	2. d	3. d	4. a

SHORT ANSWER QUESTIONS

1. Norma will be charged with arson. It must be established that Norma did a criminal act with the requisite mental state of intent.
2. Samuel committed burglary. It must be proven that he forcibly entered the building with the intent to steal.
3. Since the crime in question is a strict liability crime, all that must be proven is that Cal committed the prohibited act; a criminal mental state is not required. Cal is guilty.
4. Samuel committed criminal fraud (theft by deception). It must be proven that Samuel made a false statement of a material fact, knowing that it was false and with the intent that Roland rely upon it, and Roland did reasonably rely on the statement resulting in a financial loss.

CASE PROBLEMS

1. (a) The Acme supervisors are probably guilty of some form of manslaughter, such as involuntary or negligent manslaughter. (b) Acme would also be held criminally accountable for this crime since it was committed by its agents who were acting within the scope of their employment.

2. (a) Allen committed criminal fraud and also federal crimes such as mail fraud. Allen's conduct also RICO since his activity constitutes an enterprise that engaged in a pattern of racketeering. (b) Allen may be fined and/or imprisoned. (c) Mrs. Hinton can sue for rescission of the contract, restitution (return of her money), and treble (triple) damages under federal RICO law.

CHAPTER 9 - INTRODUCTION TO CONTRACT LAW AND CONTRACT THEORY

MATCHING EXERCISE

1. e
2. g
3. b

4. d
5. i
6. a

7. h
8. f
9. c

COMPLETION EXERCISE

1. legally enforceable
2. consideration
3. legal capacity
4. genuine assent
5. legal

TRUE-FALSE EXERCISE

1. T
6. F

2. F
7. T

3. T
8. T

4. T
9. T

5. F
10. T

MULTIPLE CHOICE QUESTIONS

1. d

2. b

3. d

4. b

SHORT ANSWER QUESTIONS

1. Yes. The parties have an implied contract.
2. A legally enforceable contract was never formed, only a social obligation arose.
3. Jason may rescind (terminate) the contract and recover his money (restitution). Alternatively, Jason may affirm the contract and sue for damages for the decreased value of the car.
4. No. A court would likely find that the contractual term in question is unenforceable because it violates public policy. (Also, under the UCC, such a term is presumably unconscionable).

CASE PROBLEMS

1. (a) This contract is a secured transaction (mortgage loan) that is governed by the common law of contracts. (b) This contract is a contract for the sale of goods and it is governed by UCC Article 2. (c) This is a service contract and it is governed by the common law of contracts.

2. (a) The parties did not enter into a contract. There was never a valid agreement (offer and acceptance) for painting the car. (b) Ken is legally obligated under quasi contract to pay for the reasonable value of the painting. He received a benefit and, under the facts of the case, he would be unjustly enriched if he did not pay for the work rendered.

CHAPTER 10 - CONTRACTUAL AGREEMENT: MUTUAL ASSENT

MATCHING EXERCISE

1.	k	6.	i	11.	m
2.	g	7.	o	12.	n
3.	d	8.	c	13.	l
4.	f	9.	e	14.	a
5.	b	10.	h	15.	j

COMPLETION EXERCISE

1. mutual assent
2. invitations to deal
3. offer, acceptance
4. counteroffer
5. revocation; counteroffer; rejection; lapse of time

TRUE-FALSE EXERCISE

1. F		2. T		3. T		4. F		5. T
6. T		7. F		8. T		9. T		10. T

MULTIPLE CHOICE QUESTIONS

1. b		2. d		3. c		4. b

SHORT ANSWER QUESTIONS

1. No. The circumstances indicate that Kelly was not serious about making an offer, so Kelly never made an offer that Lorenz could have accepted. Contractual intent is lacking in this case.

2. Yes. This offer was sufficiently definite and objectively indicated the required contractual intent.

3. Yes. Tricia's first offer was terminated by Jason's counteroffer, but Tricia accepted Jason's counteroffer, thereby forming a contract.

4. Yes. Unlike the common law "mirror image" rule, the UCC does not require that an acceptance be identical to the terms of the offer.

CASE PROBLEMS

1. (a) No. Sally's advertisement was an invitation to deal; advertisements are generally not offers. (b) Yes. Measured by the objective standard, Bryan clearly indicated an intent to be bound by the terms of his offer if it were accepted. Moreover, he never communicated to Sally that his acceptance was conditional. (c) Yes. Sally's acceptance formed a contract with Bryan.

2. (a) Bess must communicate her acceptance. (b) Fred's offer will lapse after a reasonable amount of time has passed. (c) Bess may communicate an acceptance in any reasonable commercial manner. (d) Under the mailbox rule, Bess' acceptance will be effective when she places it in the mail.

CHAPTER 11 – CONSIDERATION (THE BASIS OF THE BARGAIN)

MATCHING EXERCISE

1. k	6. n	11. m
2. o	7. b	12. e
3. h	8. c	13. g
4. j	9. l	14. a
5. i	10. f	15. d

COMPLETION EXERCISE

1. composition agreement
2. Moral consideration
3. unconscionable
4. preexisting duty
5. firm offer

TRUE-FALSE EXERCISE

1. T	2. T	3. F	4. T	5. F
6. F	7. T	8. F	9. T	10. F

MULTIPLE CHOICE QUESTIONS

1. c   2. d   3. b   4. a

SHORT ANSWER QUESTIONS

1. No. The services previously rendered by Randy as a voluntary undertaking falls into the category of past discrimination, which is not consideration to form a contract.

2. Yes. A party need not suffer a hardship to give consideration. Consideration simply requires a party to undertake a new legal obligation that they did not previously have.

3. No. Ina had a preexisting duty to paint and prep the house.

4. Yes. Linda may have entered into a bad bargain, but the bargain was not unconscionable. The law does not evaluate the adequacy of the considerations exchanged.

CASE PROBLEMS

1. (a) Ralph's promise to complete the existing project is merely a promise to perform a preexisting duty, which is not consideration. (b) Ralph's second promise obligates him to perform new work, which is consideration and renders the agreement a legally enforceable contract.

2. (a) No. In general, a person is not legally entitled to rely on another's promise. (b) CompuTech's promise is not legally enforceable under promissory estoppel since Ralph's reliance was not reasonable. (c) Ralph should have entered into a contract with CompuTech before quitting his job and moving to Wyoming.

CHAPTER 12 - CONTRACTUAL CAPACITY AND REALITY OF CONSENT

MATCHING EXERCISE

1. c
2. d
3. g
4. a
5. e

6. b
7. f
8. h

COMPLETION EXERCISE

1. Legal (contractual) capacity
2. testamentary devise
3. ambiguity
4. unilateral
5. bilateral

TRUE-FALSE EXERCISE

1. T	2. T	3. F	4. F	5. T
6. T	7. F	8. F	9. F	10. T

MULTIPLE CHOICE QUESTIONS

1. a   2. a   3. c   4. a

SHORT ANSWER QUESTIONS

1. No. Slick Larry never deprived Angela of her ability to exercise her free will. Being "pushy" is not duress.
2. No. This statute is only intended to raise revenue for the government and it is not designed to protect the public.
3. Yes. Alvin had a fiduciary relationship with Sandy. His conduct violated his duty of utmost loyalty, and his duty to make full disclosure to Sandy.
4. No. This was just a bad bargain. Earl was sophisticated in antique cars and simply made an error in judgment about the car's actual value.

CASE PROBLEMS

1. (a) Protective (regulatory). (b) This contract is void and unenforceable because it violated a licensing statute that was designed to protect the public. (c) Jim will be denied any recovery. In general, when an agreement is declared illegal and void, the court will deny any remedy.

2. (a) Yes, both parties were mistaken regarding the same material fact. (b) Dynamic must prove that the mistake was mutual, the mistake was factual in nature, and the matter was material, meaning an important consideration in deciding whether or not to contract.

CHAPTER 13 - LEGALITY OF SUBJECT MATTER AND PROPER FORM OF CONTRACTS

MATCHING EXERCISE

1.	m	8.	u	14.	v	20.	r
2.	p	9.	e	15.	z	21.	o
3.	y	10.	s	16.	c	22.	j
4.	x	11.	d	17.	w	23.	i
5.	q	12.	f	18.	t	24.	g
6.	a	13.	k	19.	b	25.	n
7.	h					26.	l

COMPLETION EXERCISE

1. *mala in se*
2. price-fixing agreement
3. usury
4. undue influence, fraud, duress, mistake, or lack of consideration
5. general usage
6. contracts to answer for the debt of another; contracts for interests in land; contracts not to be performed within one year; contracts made in consideration of marriage; contracts of executors and administrators of estates; contracts for the sale of goods for $500 or more

TRUE-FALSE EXERCISE

1. T	2.	F	3.	F	4.	F	5. T
6. F	7.	T	8.	T	9.	F	10. T

MULTIPLE CHOICE QUESTIONS

1.	a	4.	b
2.	a	5.	d
3.	d	6.	a

SHORT ANSWER QUESTIONS

1. No. This statute is only intended to raise revenue for the government and it is not designed to protect the public.

2. Yes. Ben had a fiduciary relationship with Dee. His conduct violated his duty of utmost loyalty, and his duty to make full disclosure to Dee.

3. No. It is possible that Steve may fully perform within one year because he may die during this time.

CHAPTER 13 - LEGALITY OF SUBJECT MATTER AND PROPER FORM OF CONTRACTS (CONTINUED)

4. No. TSRC's contractual obligation to employ Ivan was subject to a condition precedent that was not satisfied (Ivan did not pass the security check). Thus, TSRC's duty was discharged (terminated).

5. This contract is legally enforceable. Under the UCC, the writing requirement is satisfied if one merchant to a contract sends to the other merchant contracting party a sufficient written confirmation and the merchant receiving the confirmation does not object, in writing, within 10 days of receipt.

CASE PROBLEMS

1. (a) Protective (regulatory). (b) This contract is void and unenforceable because it violated a licensing statute that was designed to protect the public. (c) Jim will be denied any recovery. In general, when an agreement is declared illegal and void, the court will deny any remedy.

2. (a) Yes. This is a contract for the sale of land. (b) Yes. The paper states the material terms of the contract and it is signed by Jim, who is refusing to perform. (c) Since the paper satisfies the writing requirement under the Statute of Contracts, the oral agreement is legally enforceable.

3. (a) This is a totally integrated contract because it states the entire agreement of the parties. (b) Yes. Because the term "computer system" is ambiguous, Ralph may use parol evidence to explain the intended meaning of this term. (c) Ralph can present evidence of usage of trade and general usage.

CHAPTER 14 – CONTRACT INTERPRETATION AND THE RIGHTS OF THIRD PERSONS

MATCHING EXERCISE

1. k		5. e		9. f	
2. c		6. d		10. b	
3. l		7. h		11. j	
4. i		8. g		12. a	

COMPLETION EXERCISE

1. intent

2. first in time

3. waiver of defense

4. warranties

5. An assignment is forbidden when it may: (a) materially change the duty of the promisor, (b) materially impair the chance of return performance, or (c) materially increase the burden or risk to the other party.

6. fully-integrated

7. partially-integrated

8. general usage

TRUE-FALSE EXERCISE

1. F	2. F	3. F	4. T	5. F
6. T	7. T	8. T	9. T	10. F

MULTIPLE CHOICE QUESTIONS

1. a	2. b	3. a	4. d

SHORT ANSWER QUESTIONS

1. No. Last Bank knew about and accepted the assignment and, therefore, its rights are vested.

2. Yes, the assignment was valid. Nonetheless, FTC regulations allow Laurie to assert her defense against Third Bank because the transaction is a consumer credit transaction.

3. No. The assignment will materially increase the burden and risk for Mike and, therefore, Air Freight cannot assign its contractual rights without Mike's consent.

4.   Juan must pay Rosa $2,700. Yes. Rosa has only the same right to enforce the contract that Jasper has. Therefore, her right to be paid is subject to a $300 set-off, for the breach by Jasper.

5. The court can look at Al's and Pete's course of dealing, meaning their repeated, prior acts in carrying out the contract in question.

CASE PROBLEMS

1. (a) Harry's is a third-party beneficiary of the contract because it may receive a benefit from performance of the contract. However, Harry's is only an incidental beneficiary because neither the city nor Virgil's intended to directly benefit Harry's. (b) Because Harry's is only an incidental beneficiary, it cannot sue Virgil's to enforce its proper performance of the contract.

2. (a) This is a delegation. (b) JobFinders was entitled to delegate its typing duties because these are standardized duties that anyone can properly perform. (c) JobFinders, as delegator, remains liable to Trina for the improper performance. A delegation of duties does not generally terminate the delegator's legal obligation to make sure that the work is properly performed.

CHAPTER 15 - CONTRACTUAL DISCHARGE AND REMEDIES

MATCHING EXERCISE

1.	g	6.	i	11.	m
2.	k	7.	o	12.	d
3.	e	8.	l	13.	f
4.	n	9.	b	14.	c
5.	h	10.	a	15.	j

COMPLETION EXERCISE

1. Discharge
2. duty to mitigate
3. Consequential
4. Punitive
5. Specific performance

TRUE-FALSE EXERCISE

1. T	2. T	3. T	4. F	5. T
6. F	7. T	8. T	9. T	10. F

MULTIPLE CHOICE QUESTIONS

1. c	2. a	3. a	4. d

SHORT ANSWER QUESTIONS

1. No. It is not impossible to do the work, only Theo cannot do it. This type of personal inability does not establish the defense of impossibility. Theo must hire someone else to do the work.
2. Josh's must mitigate its damages, i.e., it must take reasonable steps to avoid/minimize its damages.
3. No. This contract is a personal-satisfaction contract. Moreover, it does involve Albert's personal taste and, therefore, he has the right to personally determine whether the work is satisfactory or not.
4. Craftsman committed a material breach of contract. Todd may recover $3,500, the amount necessary to put him in the same financial position he would have been in had Craftsman properly performed.

CASE PROBLEMS

1. (a) A contract may be discharged if an unforeseeable event makes it impossible for anyone to perform the contract. (b) A contract may be discharged when an unforeseeable event frustrates the essential purpose for the contract. (c) No. The fluctuation in prices for natural gas was foreseeable. This is a risk that Mark implicitly took on, and he cannot now escape from his contractual duties.

2. (a) Wainwright has substantially performed the contract, meaning, it completed its duties with a small, unintentional deviation. (b) Wainwright can enforce the contract. (c) The Johnsons must pay the contract price ($100,000) minus damages for Wainwright's nonmaterial breach ($500), that is, a total of $99,500.

CHAPTER 16 - FORMATION OF THE SALES CONTRACT: CONTRACTS FOR LEASING GOODS

MATCHING EXERCISE

1.	e	6.	m	11.	c
2.	f	7.	o	12.	i
3.	l	8.	h	13.	j
4.	a	9.	b	14.	d
5.	k	10.	n	15.	g

COMPLETION EXERCISE

1. good faith
2. reasonable time (not to exceed three months)
3. accommodation
4. usage of trade
5. Statute of Frauds

TRUE-FALSE EXERCISE

1. T		2. T		3. F		4. F		5. F
6. T		7. F		8. F		9. T		10. F

MULTIPLE CHOICE QUESTIONS

1. d   2. d   3. d   4. c

SHORT ANSWER QUESTIONS

1. UCC Article 2 governs this transaction because it is a contract for the sale of goods. Yes. As a general rule, an offeror can revoke an offer at anytime and for any reason prior to acceptance.
2. No. As an exception to the general rule stated above, a merchant who makes a firm offer cannot revoke it for the time stated, and consideration is not required to make this promise legally binding.
3. Yes. Although a sales contract for $500 or more is generally required to be evidenced by a writing to be enforceable, this rule does not apply if the goods are to be specially made, they cannot be readily resold, and the seller has substantially begun to make or acquire the goods.
4. Yes. Shawna sent Kim a written confirmation of their agreement and Kim did not object to the confirmation, in writing, within ten days.

CASE PROBLEMS

1. (a) Yes. (b) The parties entered into a valid requirements contract. (c) Since the sales contract has open terms, the UCC implies that the price shall be a reasonable price at time and place of delivery, quantity shall be the Town Market's reasonable requirements, and the good shall be delivered within a reasonable time (but in time for the festival) at Perrone's place of business.
2. (a) Yes. The acceptance appears to be definite and seasonable (timely). (b) No. Since John is a nonmerchant, the new term is treated merely as a proposal for him to consider. (c) If John had agreed to the new term, then it would be part of the contract.

CHAPTER 17 – TITLE AND RISK OF LOSS

MATCHING EXERCISE

1. g	6. o	11. f
2. h	7. l	12. i
3. m	8. k	13. e
4. j	9. b	14. d
5. n	10. a	15. c

COMPLETION EXERCISE

1. consignment
2. sale or return
3. voidable
4. sale on approval
5. EXW: seller fulfills its obligations when goods are made available to the buyer at the seller's premises.
   FCA: seller must hand over goods to a named carrier, cleared for export, at the named location.
   CFR: stands for cost and freight; seller must clear the goods for export and bears all risks until the goods pass over the ship's rail at the port of shipment.
   DES: seller must make the goods available to the buyer on board the ship, prior to clearing the goods for import, at the named port.

TRUE-FALSE EXERCISE

1. T	2. T	3. F	4. T	5. F
6. T	7. F	8. F	9. F	10. T

MULTIPLE CHOICE QUESTIONS

1. b	2. b	3. a	4. c

SHORT ANSWER QUESTIONS

1. Yes. This was an entrustment and Ted received good title.
2. Cindy. This was a shipment contract and, therefore, the risk of loss during transportation fell on Cindy.
3. No. This is a sale on approval transaction. The risk of loss never passed to Kathy because she never accepted the bike.
4. May 1. A buyer has an insurable interest in goods as soon as they are existing and identified.

CASE PROBLEMS

1. (a) No. As a generally rule, a buyer receives only the same title to goods as the seller possessed. In this case, Skweeky Kleen had no title (void title) to Jane's car and, therefore, it could pass nothing but a void title to Buyer. Jane may recover the car from Buyer.

2. When the buyer has properly rejected nonconforming goods, the buyer may treat the risk of loss, to the extent of any deficiency in insurance coverage, as resting from the beginning on the seller. Therefore, the seller would be liable for the uninsured portion of the loss, i.e., $2,000.

CHAPTER 18 – PERFORMANCE AND REMEDIES

MATCHING EXERCISE

1.	a	5.	h	9.	j
2.	e	6.	b	10.	l
3.	d	7.	f	11.	c
4.	i	8.	k	12.	g

COMPLETION EXERCISE

1. adequate assurance
2. four years
3. ten days
4. replevin
5. substantially impairs

TRUE-FALSE EXERCISE

1. F	2. T	3. T	4. T	5. T
6. T	7. F	8. T	9. F	10. F

MULTIPLE CHOICE QUESTIONS

1. c   2. c   3. b   4. d

SHORT ANSWER QUESTIONS

1. A&A should make a written demand for assurance from Royal Grocery. It may also choose to suspend its performance until an adequate assurance is provided.
2. Jake can revoke his acceptance of the ostriches and recover the amount paid. In addition, he would be entitled to sue the seller for any damages he suffered due to the seller's breach.
3. Jodi would be entitled to stop shipment of the figurines.
4. The parties' contractual obligations are discharged by operation of law (justification).

CASE PROBLEMS

1. Hotshot basically has two remedies in this case: replevin and damages. Because the goods are not available elsewhere and are essential to Hotshot's business, Hotshot may replevin them from Chile's. In addition, Hotshot is entitled to sue Chile's for any damages resulting from its breach.

2. (a) In order to protect her rights, Hilda should immediately give notice of breach of contract to Mistro. This notice should also identify all nonconformities. If she wishes to reject, she should do so, subject to Mistro's right to cure. (b) Mistro may cure by delivering a conforming piano within the original contract time or within an additional reasonable time. (c) If Mistro fails to cure, then Sally may reject the piano, cancel the contract, and sue Mistro for damages.

CHAPTER 19 - WARRANTIES AND PRODUCT LIABILITY

MATCHING EXERCISE

1. e
2. c
3. b

4. d
5. i
6. h

7. a
8. f
9. g

COMPLETION EXERCISE

1. *caveat emptor*
2. a basis of the bargain
3. warranty against infringement
4. AS IS
5. negligence; strict liability

TRUE-FALSE EXERCISE

1. T
6. F

2. F
7. T

3. F
8. F

4. T
9. F

5. T
10. T

MULTIPLE CHOICE QUESTIONS

1. d
2. c
3. d
4. b

SHORT ANSWER QUESTIONS

1. No. This is not a statement of fact that can be proven; it is sales puffing.
2. Brown Corp. is liable for breach of the warranty of merchantability. Its X-100 model is not fit for the ordinary purposes that mountain bikes are used, and it is also doubtful that it would be without objection in the trade as it is described.
3. Yes. Len has breached the implied warranty of fitness for a particular purpose. Len knew that Walt was contemplating a particular use for the rod and that Walt was relying on Len to furnish a suitable rod.
4. No. In this case Bobbie was relying on her own judgment, not Acme's judgment. Therefore, the warranty of fitness for a particular purpose did not arise.

CASE PROBLEMS

1. (a) In general, MicroView can disclaim all implied warranties. Disclaimers made in accordance with Article 2 are not unconscionable. (b) MicroView cannot disclaim the warranty of merchantability by including an inconspicuous disclaimer in its contracts. To exclude this warranty, a disclaimer must be conspicuous and mention "merchantability." (c) The statement "AS IS" would exclude the warranties of merchantability and fitness for a particular purpose.

2. The outcome of this case would be somewhat uncertain. All elements for strict liability are present, except the requirement that the goods be unreasonably dangerous is problematic in this case. In many states, the question is whether the automobile would meet the reasonable expectations of the consumer.

CHAPTER 20 - INTRODUCTION TO NEGOTIABLES:
UCC ARTICLE 3 AND ARTICLE 7

MATCHING EXERCISE

1. j	5. a	9. h
2. d	6. l	10. i
3. g	7. c	11. f
4. k	8. b	12. e

COMPLETION EXERCISE

1. maker; payee
2. check
3. document of title
4. bill of lading
5. drafts, checks, promissory notes, certificates of deposit

TRUE-FALSE EXERCISE

1. F	2. T	3. T	4. T	5. T
6. F	7. T	8. T	9. F	10. T

MULTIPLE CHOICE QUESTIONS

1. b	2. d	3. c	4. c

SHORT ANSWER QUESTIONS

1. This instrument is a draft, also known as a trade acceptance or sales draft. Jerry has no obligation to pay it prior to acceptance. After he accepts it, he will have primary liability to pay.
2. The bank has no duty to pay Roger prior to its acceptance of the check. If Burton has sufficient funds in his account to pay, then the bank owes Burton a duty to pay based on the parties' depositary contract.
3. Ajax has the right to receive the goods in accordance with the terms of the document of title.
4. Pay by check. If the check is payable to the order of the creditor, then Kendall will be protected from liability if the check is lost or stolen in route.

CASE PROBLEMS

1. (a) Smithson issued a check. When issued, the check was order paper. (b) As the drawee of the check, the Old Yorker Bank has no legal obligation to Molly to pay the check prior to acceptance. After acceptance, the bank has primary liability to pay.

2. (a) The document is a bill of lading. (b) It reflects the ownership rights to the goods being shipped and a contract between Transatlantic Truckers and Connecticut Crabbers. (c) Transatlantic is liable for the loss.

CHAPTER 21 - NEGOTIABILITY

MATCHING EXERCISE

1. i
2. g
3. c

4. h
5. b
6. d

7. a
8. f
9. e

COMPLETION EXERCISE

1. nonnegotiable
2. maker; drawer
3. money
4. four corner
5. typed

TRUE-FALSE EXERCISE

1. F
6. T

2. T
7. T

3. T
8. T

4. F
9. F

5. F
10. F

MULTIPLE CHOICE QUESTIONS

1. c
2. c
3. d
4. b

SHORT ANSWER QUESTIONS

1. No. The obligation is not unconditional; it is conditioned upon the occurrence of an event that is not certain to occur.
2. Yes. It meets all six requirements for a negotiable instrument.
3. No. It is not payable for a sum certain. The amount of principal cannot be determined from the face of the paper.
4. Yes. Checks are negotiable and their negotiability cannot be taken away by writing on them that they are nonnegotiable.

CASE PROBLEMS

1. (a) To be negotiable, an instrument must be: 1) written; 2) signed by the drawer or maker; 3) state an unconditional promise to or order to pay; 4) a fixed sum of money; 5) payable on demand or at a definite time; and 6) payable to bearer or to the order of a party. (b) This instrument fulfills all six requirements when issued and, therefore, it is negotiable.

2. (a) No. The sum to be paid is not for a certain amount, and the obligation to pay is conditioned upon completion of the project. (b) Even though the note is nonnegotiable, it still establishes a contractual obligation to pay. (c) Yes. Since it is a nonnegotiable instrument, subsequent transferees who take the note cannot be a HDC and, therefore, they take the note subject to all defenses, both personal and real.

CHAPTER 22 - NEGOTIATION AND HOLDERS IN DUE COURSE/HOLDERS BY DUE NEGOTIATION

MATCHING EXERCISE

1. d	5. j	9. f
2. g	6. e	10. k
3. i	7. b	11. h
4. a	8. l	12. c

COMPLETION EXERCISE

1. bearer
2. holder
3. Good faith
4. blank indorsement
5. authorized delivery by the holder; proper indorsement by the holder

TRUE-FALSE EXERCISE

1. F	2. F	3. T	4. T	5. F
6. F	7. T	8. T	9. T	10. F

MULTIPLE CHOICE QUESTIONS

1. c	2. d	3. a	4. b

SHORT ANSWER QUESTIONS

1. No. Bob had notice that the document had possibly been altered.
2. Yes. Last Bank is a HDC and, therefore, it takes the check subject only to real defenses. Dana's defense of intoxication is only a personal defense and, therefore, it cannot be used to avoid liability.
3. No. The contractual defense of infancy (minority) is a real defense. Marie may raise this defense and avoid her liability to pay the note.
4. Yes. The defense of illegality is a real defense in this case and, therefore, Bob may raise this defense in order to avoid his liability to pay the check.

CASE PROBLEMS

1. (a) Special indorsement. (b) Blank indorsement. (c) Qualified indorsement. (d) Restrictive indorsement.

2. (a) Yes. The instrument is negotiable, and Julia was a holder who took the note by negotiation for value, in good faith, and without notice of any defect or defenses. (b) Jacob's defense of fraud in the inducement is a personal defense. (c) Jacob must pay the note to Julia because he has primary liability to pay it (as maker) and he cannot assert his defense against Julia because she is a HDC.

CHAPTER 23 – NEGOTIABLES: LIABILITY AND DISCHARGE

MATCHING EXERCISE

1. d
2. h
3. e

4. i
5. c
6. f

7. b
8. g
9. a

COMPLETION EXERCISE

1. maker
2. acceptance
3. midnight deadline
4. warranty liability
5. payment; tender of payment; cancellation and renunciation; impairment

TRUE-FALSE EXERCISE

1. T
6. T

2. F
7. T

3. T
8. T

4. T
9. F

5. F
10. F

MULTIPLE CHOICE QUESTIONS

1. a

2. b

3. c

4. d

SHORT ANSWER QUESTIONS

1. Pat has secondary liability as drawer of the check. Ken's Groceries has secondary liability as an indorser.
2. Yes. Peoria Bank accepted the check, thus incurring primary liability to pay whether or not Wally has sufficient money in his account to cover the check.
3. Shirley has secondary liability as the drawer of the check. John does not have any signature liability to pay because notice of dishonor was not given to him in a timely fashion.
4. No. A person does not have signature (contractual) liability to pay an instrument unless the person or an authorized agent signs it. Here, the forgery is a real defense that can be raised avoiding any claimed liability.

CASE PROBLEMS

1. James must pay the amount of the checks to Check-Rite. Under the "imposter rule," when a person is deceived into issuing an instrument to an imposter who pretends to be an intended payee and the imposter forges the payee's indorsement, then the issuer must pay anyone who, in good faith, subsequently pays or takes the instrument, in this case Check-Rite. Michelle still has a contractual right under its lease to demand James to pay her the rent for the two months in question.

2. (a) Mike is a primary party, and Patsy is a secondary party. (b) Mike's obligation is not subject to any conditions, whereas Patsy's liability is subject to proper presentment, dishonor, and notice of dishonor. (c) Mike must pay the note. Since presentment was not made in a timely fashion, she has no secondary liability to pay.

CHAPTER 24 - BANK-CUSTOMER RELATIONS/ELECTRONIC FUNDS TRANSFERS

MATCHING EXERCISE

1. e
2. f
3. b

4. g
5. d
6. h

7. c
8. i
9. a

COMPLETION EXERCISE

1. Article 4A
2. unauthorized signature
3. contract; agent; and debtor (also acceptable: agent, debtor, creditor)
4. due care
5. damages due to arrest; damages due to prosecution; other consequential damages that can be proven

TRUE-FALSE EXERCISE

1. F
6. T

2. F
7. F

3. F
8. F

4. T
9. F

5. T
10. F

MULTIPLE CHOICE QUESTIONS

1. d

2. c

3. d

4. a

SHORT ANSWER QUESTIONS

1. No. A bank may honor a check up to ten days after a customer's death; here, Susan presented Charlie's check 18 days after his death and the bank may not honor it.

2. Yes. Stop-payment orders are effective only for six months, so Maria's stop-payment order had expired in October. Although this check was stale, a bank may honor a stale check if it chooses.

3. No. A bank must be given a reasonable time to process a stop-payment order. Because Louis cashed the check before Sandy gave the bank the stop-payment order, the bank had no time to act.

4. No. The bank properly dishonored the check.

CASE PROBLEMS

1. If the bank can show that Jennifer acted negligently when she gave Travis important responsibilities without checking his background, Jennifer could have contributed to the unauthorized signature. If the bank is successful, Jennifer could be liable for the loss.

2. (a) Jeff has 30 days in which to examine his statement and report any errors. (b) Jeff gave timely notice because he reported the error in one week. (c) Last Bank may properly charge Jeff's account for $100.

CHAPTER 25 - SECURED TRANSACTIONS: ATTACHMENT AND PERFECTION

MATCHING EXERCISE

1. f
2. k
3. d
4. a

5. h
6. j
7. l
8. i

9. b
10. e
11. g
12. c

COMPLETION EXERCISE

1. Perfection
2. termination statement
3. automatic perfection
4. possession
5. possession by secured creditor; filing of financing statement; automatic perfection; Perfection by control of the collateral

TRUE-FALSE EXERCISE

1. F
6. F

2. T
7. T

3. F
8. T

4. T
9. T

5. T
10. F

MULTIPLE CHOICE QUESTIONS

1. b

2. d

3. c

4. a

SHORT ANSWER QUESTIONS

1. Yes. Vanessa has a perfected interest in the identifiable cash proceeds.
2. Farm products. Carter's should file the financing statement in the county where the farm is located.
3. Yes. The copier lease is a disguised sale, with the seller retaining a security interest.
4. Acme RV should file financing statements in all of the states where the leasing outlets are located and/or take such other steps as may be required by those jurisdictions to perfect the security interest.

CASE PROBLEMS

1. (a) The stove is equipment. (b) Yes. A security interest in equipment may be perfected by filing a financing statement centrally, which is typically with the secretary of state or comparable government office. (c) Perfection is important because it will help Alice ensure priority to the collateral over most subsequent secured parties who may claim an interest in the collateral.

2. (a) The note is an instrument. (b) Yes. There was an oral security agreement, value was given, the debtor has an interest in the note, and the secured party has possession of the note. (c) Yes. Possession of the instrument by the secured party perfects the interest. (d) June 1 until August 1.

CHAPTER 26 - SECURED TRANSACTIONS: PRIORITIES AND ENFORCEMENT

MATCHING EXERCISE

1.	n	7.	g	13.	l
2.	h	8.	c	14.	m
3.	f	9.	a	15.	q
4.	e	10.	o	16.	k
5.	i	11.	j	17.	p
6.	b	12.	d	18.	r

COMPLETION EXERCISE

1. collateral
2. file (perfect)
3. attach
4. twenty days
5. Priority
6. security agreement
7. breach of the peace
8. deficiency judgment
9. twenty-one
10. commercially reasonable

TRUE-FALSE EXERCISE

1.	F	6.	F	11.	F	16.	F
2.	T	7.	F	12.	T	17.	T
3.	T	8.	T	13.	F	18.	F
4.	F	9.	F	14.	T	19.	F
5.	F	10.	T	15.	F	20.	T

MULTIPLE CHOICE QUESTIONS

1.	d	5.	d
2.	b	6.	b
3.	d	7.	d
4.	a	8.	d

SHORT ANSWER QUESTIONS

1. The security interest secures both debts.

2. Tom's perfected security interest wins over Fran's unperfected security interest even though Fran's interest was the first one to attach.

CHAPTER 26 - SECURED TRANSACTIONS: PRIORITIES AND ENFORCEMENT
(CONTINUED)

3. Acme wins. The first to perfect generally wins.

4. First Catch. The buyer in the ordinary course exception applies in this case.

5. A secured creditor can use self-help to repossess collateral only if it can be done without committing a breach of the peace. Wheels violated this limit and is liable for damages.

6. No, Iris can waive her right to sale only after default occurs.

7. Sheldon may redeem prior to a sale of the collateral by paying $4,460, the amount of the outstanding debt plus costs of repossession and sale.

8. Thorsen's may be liable to Ricco because it commingled the bracelets in violation of the UCC. The bracelets were not fungible and Thorsen's had a duty to keep them separate and identifiable.

CASE PROBLEMS

1. (a) Logic must notify Hi-Tek unless Hi-Tek has waived its notice of sale. (b) Junior secured creditor must notify Logic that they claim an interest in the collateral. (c) Logic may choose either a private or public sale, so long as each is conducted in a commercially reasonable manner. (d) If a public sale is conducted, Logic is free to bid on the patent at such sale.

2. (a) The sales price is commercially reasonable. A&A took all reasonable steps possible to obtain the best price. The fact that it sold for less than its market value does not automatically make the sale commercially unreasonable. (b) Proceeds of the sale are first applied to the cost of the repossession and sale, second applied to payment of the balance of the secured debt owed to A&A.

3. (a) Merchant's has a perfected floating lien. (b) Trish has a perfected PMSI. (c) Merchant's wins. The perfected PMSI exception does not apply in this case because Trish did not perfect the PMSI prior to the debtor receiving the inventory collateral, as required by the Code.

CHAPTER 27 - OTHER CREDIT TRANSACTIONS

MATCHING EXERCISE

1. b	4. a	7. i
2. f	5. c	8. d
3. g	6. h	9. e

COMPLETION EXERCISE

1. Equal Credit Opportunity Act
2. Fair Credit Billing Act
3. bank cards; travel and entertainment cards; store or merchant cards.
4. Real Estate Settlement Procedures Act
5. unsecured credit; installment loans; mortgage loans; credit cards.

TRUE-FALSE EXERCISE

1. F	2. T	3. T	4. F	5. F
6. F	7. T	8. F	9. T	10. F

MULTIPLE CHOICE QUESTIONS

1. b	2. b	3. a	4. d

SHORT ANSWER QUESTIONS

1. The Truth in Lending Act is primarily intended to regulate and mandate disclosure by lender to credit applicants regarding the actual cost of the credit.
2. The interest charged by Ace is usurious, i.e., it exceeds the lawful rate of interest. Depending on the state, Ace may suffer a variety of penalties, such as forfeiture of the excess interest charged or the entire amount of interest.
3. Equal Credit Opportunity Act. Regent is entitled to consider Sandy's recent bankruptcy, but its discrimination against her based on her national origin was unlawful and a violation of the ECOA.
4. Sherry is liable for both charges made by Tricia.

CASE PROBLEMS

1. (a) This is a secured transaction because payment of the unpaid purchase price is secured by collateral. (b) This is an installment contract because it is a fixed debt with fixed periodic payments. (c) Among others, TILA and the Fair Debt Collection Act may apply to this transaction.

2. Manley is legally entitled to assert his defense of fraud against Carl even though Carl is a holder in due course. Because this is a consumer credit transaction, the FTC Holder in Due Course Rule allows Manley, a consumer, to assert any defenses that he might have had against Preston, such as fraud, against anyone who may take his promissory note, such as Car.

CHAPTER 28 - BANKRUPTCY

MATCHING EXERCISE

1. k
2. f
3. b
4. a

5. j
6. g
7. d
8. i

9. c
10. e
11. l
12. h

COMPLETION EXERCISE

1. unconstitutional
2. Article III
3. liquidation
4. three
5. $1 million
6. wage earner's
7. debtor in possession
8. court
9. binding
10. (a) is in the best interest of the creditors

    (b) is feasible

    (c) pays at least as much as liquidation

    (d) is fair to all creditors

TRUE-FALSE EXERCISE

1. T
2. T
3. F
4. F
5. T
6. T
7. F
8. T

9. F
10. T
11. T
12. F
13. F
14. F
15. F

MULTIPLE CHOICE QUESTIONS

1. c
2. d
3. b
4. d

CHAPTER 28 – BANKRUPTCY (CONTINUED)

SHORT ANSWER QUESTIONS

1. The life insurance policy, personal clothing, and the old car will likely be allowed as exemptions which Santos may keep for a "fresh start."

2. George is incorrect; the security interest in the boat was given for new value (Foster's $500 loan to Al.)

3. The creditor may seek to have the discharge revoked during the one-year period following the discharge because of Gordon's fraudulent behavior in transferring the money.

4. The agreement is valid and enforceable if filed with and approved by the court.

CASE PROBLEMS

1. Sara's creditors will have $6500 because the expenses of the proceeding are paid first. Sara will be permitted to keep her personal clothing and a specified amount of equity in her house under federal or most state exemption laws. If Sara wishes to keep the car, she can enter into a reaffirmation agreement with the dealer to continue the payments. The income taxes from the previous year may not be discharged.

2. The company may not repossess the fax machine after the bankruptcy is filed because that would violate the automatic stay; the company may retain its security interest. The lease payments will be partially allowed. Office Products will receive a pro rata portion with other general unsecured creditors after payment of expenses and taxes.

3. (a) No, they may not repossess, but they retain their security interest. (b) The court may approve the plan notwithstanding the objections of some creditors. (c) A plan may be confirmed even if some claims are not paid in full. (d) Conversion to Chapter 7 is usually granted only for wrongful acts by the debtor-in-possession.

CHAPTER 29 – AGENCY: CREATION AND TERMINATION

MATCHING EXERCISE

1. c
2. f
3. d

4. e
5. i
6. g

7. a
8. b
9. h

COMPLETION EXERCISE

1. general agent
2. consensual
3. gratuitous agency
4. duty of loyalty
5. agreement of the parties; notice by either party in an agency at will; fulfillment of purpose; revocation, renunciation, operation of law.

TRUE-FALSE EXERCISE

1. T   2. T   3. F   4. T   5. T
6. F   7. T   8. T   9. T   10. T

MULTIPLE CHOICE QUESTIONS

1. c   2. c   3. d   4. b

SHORT ANSWER QUESTIONS

1. Mary is a general agent. She handles many transactions over a long period of time on behalf of Juan.
2. Norton is an independent contractor. Although Acme would not normally be liable for Norton's torts, it would be in this case since he was retained to engage in an ultrahazardous activity on Acme's behalf.
3. The parties have a gratuitous, principal-agent relationship. Ron may serve as an agent even though he is a minor, and Jodi would be bound by a contract made on her behalf by Ron.
4. The agency will end in two years, as agreed. However, the parties can, by mutual agreement, agree to extend the agency for a further period of time.

CASE PROBLEMS

1. (a)The partners are agents of the partnership. (b) The partners are fiduciaries of the partnership, meaning they must act with loyalty and good faith in all partnership dealings. (c) Ratou clearly violated his fiduciary duty to the partnership. He was obligated to negotiate the best price he could obtain for the partnership, he should not have taken secret profits, and he should have disclosed his conflict of interest.

2. (a) Motorworks must bear the loss resulting from Joe's improper behavior. At the time Kathy paid Joe, he still had implied authority to accept her payment. When Joe purchased the tires from the supplier, he had apparent authority to do so, obligating Motorworks on the purchase contract. (b) Motorworks should have dismissed Joe on the spot to avoid problems like it has with Kathy, and it should have given actual and constructive to all others that Joe was no longer its agent.

CHAPTER 30 - AGENCY: LIABILITY FOR CONTRACTS

MATCHING EXERCISE

1. g
2. d
3. b

4. c
5. e
6. h

7. a
8. i
9. f

COMPLETION EXERCISE

1. Authority by estoppel
2. disclosed
3. undisclosed
4. time; geographical area
5. principal exists and is competent; agent is the agent for the principal; agent is authorized to enter into this type of contract on behalf of the principal

TRUE-FALSE EXERCISE

1. F	2. F	3. T	4. F	5. T
6. T	7. F	8. F	9. F	10. F

MULTIPLE CHOICE QUESTIONS

1. b   2. d   3. c   4. d

SHORT ANSWER QUESTIONS

1. The parties to the contract are Adams Co. And Tri-State Groceries. These same parties are liable to perform the contract. Ali has no liability on the contract.
2. Originally, Nolan had no authority to purchase the extra inventory. However, Ryan ratified the contract. Therefore, Ryan, not Nolan, is liable on the contract.
3. Elizabeth had implied authority to hire Rachel. Her authority is implied from her position. Yes, the store could have limited or even done away with Elizabeth's implied authority.
4. Yes. Roger had emergency authority to hire Jenni's LocustBusters.

CASE PROBLEMS

1. (a) Alton had no authority to purchase the ties on behalf of Preston's. (b) Because Alton had no authority to make the contract, no one is liable on the contract. (c) Alton is liable to All-Tied-Up for breach of warranty of authority. He is liable for any profits that All-Tied-Up would have made.

2. (a) Phyllis is a partially disclosed principal. (b) The patent holder must elect whether to hold Phyllis or Jenkins liable on the contract. (c) Phyllis can hold the third party liable on the contract since the third party knew there was a principal involved.

CHAPTER 31 - AGENCY: LIABILITY FOR TORTS AND CRIMES

MATCHING EXERCISE

1. g
2. f
3. i

4. c
5. h
6. b

7. d
8. a
9. e

COMPLETION EXERCISE

1. *respondeat superior*
2. vicarious
3. time, place
4. indemnification
5. Workers' compensation

TRUE-FALSE EXERCISE

1. F	2. T	3. T	4. F	5. T
6. T	7. T	8. F	9. T	10. F

MULTIPLE CHOICE QUESTIONS

1. b   2. c   3. d   4. a

SHORT ANSWER QUESTIONS

1. Rose is personally liable for her own tort. Orlando is vicariously liable for Rose's tort because it occurred within the course and scope of her employment duties.
2. Jessica is liable for her own negligence. Under the facts, Reliable is not vicariously liable for Jessica's negligence because it did not occur within the scope of her employment. When the accident occurred, Jessica was acting only with the intent to benefit herself, not Reliable.
3. Under the facts stated, it would appear that Mann Warehouse would be vicariously liable for Orville's tort. Mann had the right to control Orville's conduct, making Orville a servant, albeit a temporary one.
4. Bobby is liable for his own tort. Under the doctrine *respondeat superior*, Tony's is also liable since Bobby was acting within the course and scope of his duties. The deviation in terms of time and distance was small, and it was foreseeable. Thus, most courts would hold Tony liable despite this minor detour.

CASE PROBLEMS

1. (a) The relationship between Carol and Humboldt is that of employer-independent contractor.
(b) Under the general rule, Carol is not liable for the tort of an independent contractor, here Humboldt.
(c) On the other hand, Humboldt is liable to Roger under the doctrine of *respondeat superior*.

2. (a) Sandra's employer is not vicariously liable to Nora. The time and place where the accident occurred and Sandra's activities (personal lunch and nap) do not fall within the course or scope of employment. (b) If Sandra had also been running an errand for her employer at the time of the accident, most courts would impose vicarious liability on the employer.

CHAPTER 32 - FORMATION OF A BUSINESS

MATCHING EXERCISE

1.	f	5.	k	9.	a
2.	j	6.	g	10.	i
3.	e	7.	l	11.	b
4.	c	8.	d	12.	h

COMPLETION EXERCISE

1. *de jure*
2. certificate of incorporation
3. Promoters
4. *ultra vires*
5. insulation from unlimited personal liability; centralization of management; continuity of existence; free transferability of shares

TRUE-FALSE EXERCISE

1. T		2.	T	3. T		4. T		5. T	
6. F		7.	T	8. T		9. F		10. F	

MULTIPLE CHOICE QUESTIONS

1. c	2. c	3. c	4. d

SHORT ANSWER QUESTIONS

1. Doing business as a partnership, a limited partnership, or a limited liability company will effectively prevent investors from selling their interests to others without Harry's and Larry's consent. Also, in a corporation, the parties could restrict the transfer of investors' stock by an appropriate agreement.
2. Yes. This was neither a novation nor a release, merely an assumption by the corporation. Sean remains liable on the contract with the seller.
3. No. limited partners who advise general partners are not considered to be involved in management.
4. Probably not. There is insufficient evidence to indicate an intent that the truck is partnership property. Title remains in Lee's name and partners often use their own property when doing partnership business.

CASE PROBLEMS

1. (a) The corporation would be allowed to do what is reasonably necessary to conduct its business and, in many states, it can do anything that natural persons can do. (b) Yes. (c) Yes.

2. (a) Partnership: advantage - flow through taxation; disadvantage - all owners have equal control and unlimited personal liability. (b) Limited partnership: advantage - flow through taxation and, as general partners, control of business; disadvantage - as general partners, unlimited personal liability.
(c) Corporation: advantage - as majority shareholders, effectively control business and limited liability; disadvantage - losses taxed to corporation (unless make Subchapter S election).

CHAPTER 33 - OPERATION OF A BUSINESS ORGANIZATION

MATCHING EXERCISE

1. b	5. j	9. f
2. k	6. g	10. a
3. e	7. i	11. d
4. c	8. l	12. h

COMPLETION EXERCISE

1. joint; several
2. subscription agreement
3. cumulative preferred
4. notice to shareholders; quorum requirement; time and place for meetings
5. current net profits (retained earnings); (unrestricted) earned surplus

TRUE-FALSE EXERCISE

1. T	2. T	3. F	4. T	5. T
6. T	7. T	8. F	9. T	10. F

MULTIPLE CHOICE QUESTIONS

1. d	2. b	3. b	4. c

SHORT ANSWER QUESTIONS

1. Yes. A partnership agreement can provide for the payment of salaries to partners and it may specify how profits are to be divided.
2. Earl and Antonio may vote since they are common stockholders. As majority common stockholder, Earl has the ability to determine whether the proposal passes or not.
3. Yes. Although Ed violated the shareholder agreement and may be liable to the other shareholders, Hank was unaware of this fact and may enforce the agreement. The result would have been different had the restriction been conspicuously stated on the stock certificates.
4. Yes. Shareholders generally have a right to inspect corporate books for proper purposes. Determining the value of one's shares is a proper purpose.

CASE PROBLEMS

1. (a) The partnership is liable on the contract since Glen had authority to make it. (b) No. A dissolution does not eliminate partners' liability for partnership obligations. (c) Tim and Glen both have unlimited personal liability to the seller of the inventory if the partnership fails to pay this debt. (d) Yes. A partner who pays more than his or her share of a partnership obligation is entitled to indemnification (contribution) from the other partners for their portion of the debt that was paid.

2. Pat is liable to the corporation (and in some states to the corporation's creditors) for: (a) watered stock - $50,000 and (b) illegal dividend - $5,000.

CHAPTER 34 - BUSINESS TERMINATIONS AND OTHER EXTRAORDINARY EVENTS

MATCHING EXERCISE

1.	i	5.	f	9.	b
2.	g	6.	l	10.	d
3.	k	7.	c	11.	h
4.	e	8.	a	12.	j

COMPLETION EXERCISE

1. consolidation
2. short-form merger
3. voluntary or involuntary
4. unlawful for business to continue; a partner dies; a partner or the partnership becomes bankrupt
5. economies of scale; enhanced knowledge; diversification

TRUE-FALSE EXERCISE

1. F	2. T	3. F	4. T	5. F
6. T	7. T	8. T	9. T	10. T

MULTIPLE CHOICE QUESTIONS

1. d	2. b	3. b	4. b

SHORT ANSWER QUESTIONS

1. First, Bob can vote against the merger. If the merger is properly authorized, then Bob has the right, as a dissenting shareholder, to exercise his appraisal rights and have the corporation purchase his stock.
2. The court has the discretion to decide whether to grant the request for dissolution or not. Although insanity of a partner is grounds for requesting dissolution, dissolution is not automatic. In this situation, the court will likely grant the request if the insane partner's interest cannot be adequately protected.
3. A form of stock acquisition. The legal effect of this transaction is a sale of Lightning Corp. to Blinder Corp., i.e., a modified form of de facto merger.
4. First, Jim and Diane receive $17,000 and $12,000 respectively. Next, the partners each receive repayment of their contributions. Finally, the remaining $11,000 is shared equally by the three partners.

CASE PROBLEMS

1. Under the UPA: (a) They may continue the partnership business, if Clay's estate agrees. Otherwise, they must wind up. (b) The surviving partners are entitled to wind up the partnership. (c) Assets are distributed in the following order: Roscoe - $20,000; Tess - $10,000; the partners are repaid their capital contributions; the remaining $30,000 is split three ways among the partners and estate (same manner profits are shared).

2. (a) Knowledge: MicroChem has a process that MacroChem wants. Also, MacroChem has more experience and better access to capital. (b) The directors of each company must adopt a plan of merger; two-thirds of the outstanding shares of each corporation must approve. (c) MicroChem will cease to exist; MacroChem will survive, owning the firms' combined assets and taking on the firms' combined debts.

CHAPTER 35 - FRANCHISING

MATCHING EXERCISE

1. h	5. f	9. c
2. l	6. e	10. d
3. j	7. b	11. k
4. g	8. a	12. i

COMPLETION EXERCISE

1. termination, quality control
2. franchisee's investment capital; goodwill; assured distribution network; larger asset base
3. can start a business with limited capital; goodwill; franchisor's business expertise; assured supply
4. Forum shopping
5. notice

TRUE-FALSE EXERCISE

1. T	2. F	3. T	4. F	5. F
6. T	7. T	8. F	9. F	10. F

MULTIPLE CHOICE QUESTIONS

1. a	2. d	3. a	4. d

SHORT ANSWER QUESTIONS

1. Yes. According to some courts, failing to provide a suitable location may be a breach of contract.
2. Yes, because a person can start a franchise with limited capital and can benefit from the franchisor's business expertise.
3. No. Durman does not have enough goodwill and name recognition to make a good franchisor.
4. No. This would probably violate the antitrust laws.

CASE PROBLEMS

1. Yes. The parties' conduct conformed to the statutory definition of a franchisee - - Davis trained Graham, provided him with sales material, and allowed him to use D&D's logo (at least there was implied permission to use the logo because the sales material contained the logo), and in return Graham paid Davis a fee.

2. (a) Yes. Failing to meet reasonable quotas is adequate grounds to terminate a franchise. (b) Nevus should provide notice, generally around 90 days.

CHAPTER 36 - SECURITIES REGULATION

MATCHING EXERCISE

1.	i	6.	h	11.	g
2.	e	7.	f	12.	b
3.	n	8.	k	13.	l
4.	m	9.	o	14.	c
5.	j	10.	d	15.	a

COMPLETION EXERCISE

1. Securities Act of 1933
2. Securities Exchange Act of 1934
3. red herring
4. tombstone advertisements
5. short-swing profit

TRUE-FALSE EXERCISE

1. F	2. F	3. F	4. T	5. T
6. T	7. T	8. T	9. T	10. T

MULTIPLE CHOICE QUESTIONS

1. c
2. d
3. d
4. a

SHORT ANSWER QUESTIONS

1. Yes. The offering is less than $5 million and is made only to accredited investors.
2. No. "Grease payments" to low-level officials are allowed.
3. This is a short-swing profit and Margaret must pay the $10,000 to the corporation.
4. Yes. While the Supreme Court has yet to rule directly on the validity of the misappropriation theory, the SEC and lower federal courts would hold Randolph liable for misappropriating this information.

CASE PROBLEMS

1. (a) The Securities Exchange Act of 1934. (b) Tom must show that the Midas board of directors made a misleading statement or omitted a material fact that made the statement misleading. (c) Yes. The board's statement was more than misleading; it was untrue.

2. (a) Yes. Advertisements during the waiting period are limited to tombstone advertisements.
(b) CryoTech may begin to sell offered shares in the post effective period.

CHAPTER 37 - ANTITRUST LAW

MATCHING EXERCISE

1.	h	5.	i	9.	e
2.	l	6.	a	10.	k
3.	g	7.	d	11.	j
4.	f	8.	b	12.	c

COMPLETION EXERCISE

1. Price discrimination
2. treble damages
3. Monopoly power
4. Palming off
5. per se; rule of reason

TRUE-FALSE EXERCISE

1. F	2. T	3. F	4. F	5. F
6. F	7. T	8. T	9. F	10. F

MULTIPLE CHOICE QUESTIONS

1. c   2. a   3. a   4. d

SHORT ANSWER QUESTIONS

1. No. LubeTech's market position has been "thrust upon it" because it produces a quality product.
2. No. Charging a lower price is permissible if a product is obsolete.
3. Yes. This is a horizontal market division, a per se violation of § 1 of the Sherman Act.
4. No. Under the "failing company" doctrine, this merger will be permitted because it will keep Big Muscle from going out of business.

CASE PROBLEMS

1. (a) The relevant market is winter coats. (b) LeatherTech has not violated § 1. It controls less than 70 percent of the relevant market, i.e., winter coats.

2. (a) This is a tying arrangement. (b) Under the facts stated, CompuTron has not violated § 3 of the Clayton Act. (c) Although CompuTron is selling its products pursuant to a tying arrangement, it can defend its action because no competitor produces a disk that is compatible with the MiDSU and its disks are necessary to protect the MiDSU from harm.

CHAPTER 38 - CONSUMER PROTECTION

MATCHING EXERCISE

1. j
2. a
3. d
4. h

5. g
6. c
7. i

8. b
9. f
10. e

COMPLETION EXERCISE

1. Consumer Credit Protection Act
2. actual damages; statutory damages; attorney's fees
3. Regulation B
4. clear, conspicuous
5. Consumer Product Safety Commission

TRUE-FALSE EXERCISE

1. F   2. F   3. F   4. T   5. T
6. F   7. F   8. F   9. T   10. F

MULTIPLE CHOICE QUESTIONS

1. c   2. a   3. b   4. d

SHORT ANSWER QUESTIONS

1. Terence may not discriminate against Karen on the basis of marital status or future marital plans.
2. The CPSC may require a study of the injuries, issue warnings, require a recall, and ban future sales.
3. She may require the credit agency to include her statement regarding the information in the file.
4. Yes. Moore, a debt collector, violated the Fair Debt Collection Practices Act by telephoning Zach before 8 a.m.

CASE PROBLEMS

1. Maurice may choose to rescind or cancel his contract based on the Truth in Lending Act. This law applies because Maurice used his home as collateral. Maurice has a 3-day cooling off period in which to decide to cancel, although the power of rescission potentially lasts for three years from the consummation of the transaction or the sale of his property, whichever occurs first.

2. The agency is regulated by the Fair Debt Collection Practices Act. The agency may not contact third persons regarding payment of the debt. Civil damages, costs, attorney's fees and criminal penalties may be imposed.

CHAPTER 39 - ENVIRONMENTAL PROTECTION

MATCHING EXERCISE

1. j
2. a
3. d
4. h

5. g
6. c
7. k
8. b

9. f
10. l
11. e
12. i

COMPLETION EXERCISE

1. Executive Order
2. maximum contaminant levels
3. civil; criminal
4. major
5. waste (sometimes referred to as "solid waste")

TRUE-FALSE EXERCISE

1. T
6. F

2. F
7. F

3. T
8. T

4. T
9. T

5. T
10. T

MULTIPLE CHOICE QUESTIONS

1. a

2. d

3. a

4. c

SHORT ANSWER QUESTIONS

1. CERCLA. Under the facts, both Donald and the prior owner may be held liable.
2. Cows, Inc.'s discharges through pipes violate the CWA; the run-off does not.
3. Yes. Fred has standing because he has personally suffered a special damage that is greater than that suffered by the general public.
4. RCRA applies in this case since the conduct involves the transportation and disposal of wastes. Both Foster, the employee, and Acme, Foster's employer, are liable for violating the law.

CASE PROBLEMS

1. (a) Yes. The proposed project involves a major federal action. The action involves a potentially significant impact on the environment and the Forest Service indirectly has control over the project.
(b) Yes, an EIS must be prepared to determine the environmental impact of the proposed ski resort.
(c) The EIS must, among other things, evaluate the potential impact on the forest, water, and wildlife. It must also consider alternatives to the project.

2. (a) The Endangered Species Act applies in this case. (b) Among other things, Tony must assure that his project does not harm, wound, or kill any of the protected black-footed ferrets, or harm any significant habitats that may in turn harm or kill members of the species.

CHAPTER 40 - LABOR AND FAIR EMPLOYMENT PRACTICES

MATCHING EXERCISE

1. f
2. i
3. d

4. g
5. e
6. a

7. h
8. c
9. b

COMPLETION EXERCISE

1. Picketing
2. collective bargaining
3. race; national origin; religion; color; sex (gender)
4. Occupational Safety and Health Act
5. Americans with Disabilities Act (of 1990)

TRUE-FALSE EXERCISE

1. T
6. F

2. T
7. F

3. F
8. F

4. T
9. T

5. T
10. T

MULTIPLE CHOICE QUESTIONS

1. b

2. a

3. a

4. c

SHORT ANSWER QUESTIONS

1. Yes. The fact that Dr. Payne's patients prefer a female receptionist does not justify discriminating against Bill on the basis of his gender.
2. No. The top secret security clearance is a BFOQ and, therefore, Julio may be denied employment even
if this requirement may have a disparate impact on some ethnic minorities.
3. Yes. The requirement that firefighters be able to lift the weight in question constitutes a disparate impact violation of Title VII. Further, it is not a BFOQ because it is not necessary for employees to carry out the normal, essential functions of their job.
4. No. Religious educational institutions may make religion a BFOQ.

CASE PROBLEMS

1. Yes. Joe's actions constitute sexual harassment, a violation of Title VII. His conduct may constitute an "abusive work environment," although the further findings would be needed to fully establish this violation. However, his proposal for protecting her job is clearly a "quid pro quo" violation. The school may be liable for his conduct since he is, in effect, a supervisor in the school's employ.

2. (a) Jasper's refusal to hire Kim because of her accent would violate Title VII - it is discrimination based on her national origin. (b) The refusal to hire Kim because she is 50 is a clear violation of the Age Discrimination in Employment Act. (c) The refusal based on Kim's hearing difficulty violates the Americans with Disabilities Act. Jasper has a duty to reasonably accommodate this disability.

CHAPTER 41 - REAL PROPERTY AND JOINT OWNERSHIP

MATCHING EXERCISE

1. d
2. g
3. h
4. i

5. f
6. a
7. k
8. c

9. l
10. j
11. e
12. b

COMPLETION EXERCISE

1. Real property
2. warranty of habitability
3. warranty deed
4. adverse possession
5. Foreclosure; default

TRUE-FALSE EXERCISE

| 1. T | 2. T | 3. T | 4. F | 5. F |
| 6. T | 7. F | 8. F | 9. T | 10. F |

MULTIPLE CHOICE QUESTIONS

1. a   2. b   3. c   4. d

SHORT ANSWER QUESTIONS

1. Yes. A landlord has a duty to disclose latent defects.
2. Yes. This is an easement by implication.
3. No. Murray's lease for a fixed term required him to move out after three years; by staying, he became a tenant at sufferance.
4. No. A quit-claim deed only transfers what the grantor owned.

CASE PROBLEMS

1. (a) This was an express easement. (b) No, Karen is not properly using the easement. This is an excessive use that will extinguish the easement.

2. (a) Tenancy for a fixed term. (b) Yes; it is common for leases to require notice before termination (c) Steve can use the doctrine of constructive eviction to get out of his lease. (d) No.

CHAPTER 42 - PERSONAL PROPERTY AND BAILMENTS

MATCHING EXERCISE

1. j	5. b	9. g
2. l	6. f	10. a
3. k	7. c	11. i
4. d	8. h	12. e

COMPLETION EXERCISE

1. bona fide purchaser
2. intent; delivery; acceptance
3. gross negligence
4. ordinary negligence
5. slight negligence

TRUE-FALSE EXERCISE

1. F	2. T	3. T	4. T	5. F
6. T	7. F	8. T	9. T	10. T

MULTIPLE CHOICE QUESTIONS

1. b   2. c   3. b   4. a

SHORT ANSWER QUESTIONS

1. No. A promise to make a gift is generally not enforceable.
2. Yes, this was a valid possessory lien.
3. Yes. This was a bailor benefit bailment, making Judy liable for gross negligence. Driving at 100 mph (55 mph above the speed limit) is gross negligence.
4. Jethro's estate. There was no valid gift made to Sally May. Present intent was lacking for a valid inter vivos gift and Jethro did not die as expected, negating any gift causa mortis argument.

CASE PROBLEMS

1. (a) The bailments are mutual benefit bailments. (b) Harry is liable for the stolen mixer because he contractually agreed to take on this risk. (c) Acme is liable to Harry for his broken foot. Acme is liable for injuries resulting from its ordinary negligence.

2. (a) This is a bailee benefit bailment. (b) Luis owed Jake only a limited duty and would be liable only for gross negligence. (c) Luis' failure to inspect the skis is not gross negligence and, therefore, he is not liable to Jake. (d) Jake, on the other hand, owes a duty of great care. Nonetheless, there is no evidence that he was negligent at all. Thus, he is not liable to Luis for damage to the ski.

CHAPTER 43 - INTELLECTUAL PROPERTY, COMPUTERS, AND THE LAW

MATCHING EXERCISE

1.	b	5.	a	9.	g
2.	f	6.	e	10.	i
3.	h	7.	j	11.	1
4.	c	8.	k	12.	d

COMPLETION EXERCISE

1. Berne convention
2. twenty years; fourteen years
3. injunction
4. likelihood of confusion
5. extent that information is known outside of the business; extent that information is known by employees; measurers taken to guard the information's secrecy; value of the information to the owner and competitors; money spent in developing the information and the difficulty that others may have in producing the same information.

TRUE-FALSE EXERCISE

1.	F	4.	F	7.	F	10.	F
2.	T	5.	F	8.	T		
3.	T	6.	T	9.	F		

MULTIPLE CHOICE QUESTIONS

1.	c	3.	c	
2.	d	4.	d	

SHORT ANSWER QUESTIONS

1. Yes.
2. Since Selma copyrighted her program under U.S. law, she is entitled under the Berne Convention to protection from infringement in Germany. Thus, she can sue the German firm for infringement.
3. No. Although the names sound the same or substantially similar, there is little likelihood that consumers will be confused regarding who is furnishing the cruise packages.
4. Jesse could not copyright his original, unwritten tale - at that point it was, in essence, merely an idea. Once Jesse transcribed the tale, then he could copyright it.

CASE PROBLEMS

1. (a) Yes. This list is an original, creative work that is entitled to protection. (b) Jackson could protect it by copyrighting it or it could rely upon common law protection for it as a trade secret. The best way is the latter, because then this information will not be publicly disclosed and there is no limit on how long it may be protected. (c) Injunction, damages, destruction of the infringing material.
2. (a) Initially, Hillary was not entitled to trademark protection because the name was merely descriptive. (b) By the 1990s, the name had acquired a secondary meaning and was entitled to protection. (c) The best way to protect her trademark would be to register it with the federal government.

CHAPTER 44 - WILLS, ESTATES, AND TRUSTS

MATCHING EXERCISE

1. k
2. i
3. g
4. j
5. o

6. c
7. m
8. n
9. a
10. h

11. d
12. f
13. e
14. l
15. b

COMPLETION EXERCISE

1. Heirs
2. cy pres
3. trust deed
4. issue
5. living will

TRUE-FALSE EXERCISE

1. F   2. T   3. F   4. T   5. T
6. F   7. T   8. T   9. T   10. F

MULTIPLE CHOICE QUESTIONS

1. b   2. a   3. d   4. b

SHORT ANSWER QUESTIONS

1. Yes. Paula may claim her elective share (or forced share), which allows a disinherited spouse to elect to take a portion of the estate.
2. Each child will receive one-sixth of the estate.
3. Mike should create a spendthrift trust for Mark.
4. No. Under the Rule Against Perpetuities, trusts cannot last forever.

CASE PROBLEMS

1. (a) Abe's wife will receive the first $50,000 plus one-half of the remaining estate or $75,000. (b) The children will receive the remainder of the estate distributed equally, which would be $25,000 each. (c) Abe's cousin will receive nothing because Abe's wife and children have first claim to the estate.

2. (a) Most states presume that a trust is irrevocable. (b) A trustee must manage the trust as a reasonably prudent businessperson would manage his or her own business. Mary breached her fiduciary duty to safeguard the principal and make prudent investments. (c) Mary will be personally liable for the loss to the trust.